BUSINESS
STRATEGIES
IN
TRANSITION
ECONOMIES

INTERNATIONAL BUSINESS SERIES

SPONSORED BY
The Pacific Asian Management Institute, University of Hawaii

This series of books focuses on today's increasingly important phenomena: international business. Sponsored by the University of Hawaii's Pacific Asian Management Institute (PAMI), one of the key centers in the world for developing international business expertise, the series is devoted to international business, with an emphasis on the Asia-Pacific Region. Books in the series will help faculty, students, and business professionals acquire the knowledge and communication skills necessary for working in an ever-changing, international business environment.

Books in this series:

CHINA 2000: Emerging Business Issues
edited by Lane Kelley and Yadong Luo

CHINESE BUSINESS NEGOTIATING STYLE
by Tony Fang

BUSINESS STRATEGIES IN TRANSITION ECONOMIES
by Michael W. Peng

BUSINESS STRATEGIES IN TRANSITION ECONOMIES

MICHAEL W. PENG

Sage Publications, Inc.
International Educational and Professional Publisher
Thousand Oaks ▪ London ▪ New Delhi

For information:

Sage Publications, Inc.
2455 Teller Road
Thousand Oaks, California 91320
E-mail: order@sagepub.com

Sage Publications Ltd.
6 Bonhill Street
London EC2A 4PU
United Kingdom

Sage Publications India Pvt. Ltd.
M-32 Market
Greater Kailash I
New Delhi 110 048 India

HD 30.28 .P355 2000

Printed in the United States of America

Library of Congress Cataloging-in-Publication Data

Peng, Michael W., 1968-
    Business strategies in transition economies / by Michael W. Peng.
    p. cm. — (Sage international business series)

    Includes bibliographical references (p.) and index.
    ISBN 0-7619-1600-8 (cloth: perm. paper)
    ISBN 0-7619-1601-6 (pbk.: perm. paper)
    1. Business planning. 2. Strategic planning. I. Title. II.
Series.
    HD30.28 .P355 2000
    658.4′012—dc21   99-6593

00 01 02 03 10 9 8 7 6 5 4 3 2 1

Acquiring Editor: Harry Briggs
Editorial Assistant: MaryAnn Vail
Production Editor: Diana E. Axelsen
Editorial Assistant: Karen Wiley
Typesetter/Designer: Danielle Dillahunt

Contents

ACRONYMS AND ABBREVIATIONS

CEE   Central and Eastern Europe

GDP/GNP   Gross domestic product/gross national product

IMF   International Monetary Fund

IPO   Initial public offering

MNE   Multinational enterprise

NIS   Newly independent states (of the former Soviet Union)

OECD   Organisation of Economic Co-operation
           and Development

R&D   Research and development

SOE   State-owned enterprise

FOREWORD

The greater part of the huge Eurasian landmass consists of countries that are endeavoring to discard their socialist past. The success of this transition has fundamental economic and political consequences for all of us. The nations of the former Soviet bloc, China and Indochina, collectively form the world's largest potential market, which has a long way to grow before it reaches maturity. The transition from socialism that these countries are making, mostly with considerable social hardship, also provides a key test for the superiority of an alternative governance system based on a market economy and political democracy. The stakes are high.

As Mike Peng clearly demonstrates in this penetrating and far-reaching book, the success of economic transition depends vitally upon the quality of the strategies adopted by local and international firms operating in the countries concerned. Previously, attention has focused on the challenge of building new social institutions in the transition economies. This is understandable given the need to establish postsocialist civil frameworks, which was felt to be particularly urgent in Central and Eastern Europe. It has now become timely to focus on the development of business strategies appropriate to achieving high performance within the newly evolved frameworks. For, as this book makes eminently clear, the economic success of the transition economies depends vitally on the ability of firms to choose business strategies that suit the situation of each country, and, indeed, contribute to its further evolution.

The author's basic proposition—that successful strategies for firm growth have to be formulated in the light of institutional imperatives and constraints—is one that applies to all economies. The difference is that with transition economies we are entering new institutional territory that is still being constructed. It may take many years for them to shake off the legacy of their socialist past, if in fact they ever do entirely. We cannot assume that their transition path is necessarily leading to the same economic and social models as already exist in other countries. Despite certain homogenizing effects of globalization, capitalism and market economy take many forms around the world, which are shaped by a complex of factors including inherited social institutions, national resource endowments, and the actions of firms themselves. The transformational path taken by the transition economies is therefore not predetermined. Rather, it is emerging through strategic choices made by governments and firms.

The role firms play deserves more attention and that is why this is an especially relevant and timely book. As well as having to respond to the institutional environments enacted by transition economy governments, multinational corporations have their own highly significant part to play in assisting the development of competencies in these economies, including ways of conducting business efficiently. As Mike Peng says, new competitive rules and history chapters are being written as different firms respond to new challenges. He emphasizes that it is the resourcefulness of international and local firms, often in alliance with each other, in adjusting to the challenges presented by these evolving situations that particularly counts toward success. The most important contribution of this book lies in its detailed and informed analysis of the strategic choices open to firms in transition economies, which rightly eschews the easy assumption that existing tried-and-tested strategic approaches taken out of context can offer a quick fix.

Up to now, strategy research has failed to give due weight to the importance of transition economies. As Mike Peng observes in his concluding chapter, this leaves us with a disturbing paradox. While many Western MNEs have decided to concentrate disproportionately more resources to focus on these markets of tomorrow, the strategy field as a whole, despite efforts by some individual scholars, seems to have paid disproportionately less attention to these economies whereby millions of people and thousands of firms are collectively searching for competitive solutions to their problems. It is actually quite alarming that there were only four articles relating to transition economies between 1980 and 1998 in the preeminent international journal devoted to strategic management. The gap between research and practice in this area that Mike Peng seeks to close is an enormous one.

This book, however, does much more than just close a gap. In my view, it puts the whole study of transition economies onto a new basis through its integration of interdisciplinary sources, its comprehensive coverage, and its analytical insight. Much of this insight derives from a cumulative body of longitudinal research that the author has conducted during the 1990s with several collaborators. This research has combined qualitative and quantitative components. Mike Peng has realized what many other scholars have failed to do, that a complex process of strategic and institutional evolution such as we are seeing in the transition economies has to be informed by a qualitative appreciation of the rationales and processes involved within specific transitional contexts. If we are to offer relevant policy guidelines for governments, intermediate institutions, and firms, we have to understand what has led to the outcomes measured by economic and financial statistics. This book succeeds in opening up this understanding by carefully and systematically examining the rationales and contexts of business strategies adopted by different types of firm within the transition economies.

I have learned a great deal from reading this book and can recommend it without reservation. It is the first book to comprehensively summarize and extend cutting-edge strategy research with a focus on transition economies. It provides a readable and refreshing overview for seasoned scholars and executives working in this field, as well as valuable insights for newcomers. The book combines theoretical rigor with up-to-date evidence on a highly relevant topic. Mike Peng is already one of the world's leading strategy and management scholars working on transition and emerging economies, and this book adds significantly to his standing.

—John Child
Guinness Professor of Management Studies,
University of Cambridge
Distinguished Visiting Professor of Management,
University of Hong Kong

INTRODUCTION

This book began because of my interest in what are probably the most dynamic and fast-changing transitions of the world, which involve nearly one-third of the human race on a huge landmass ranging from Shanghai to St. Petersberg. Business strategies were hardly relevant in former socialist countries in East Asia, Central and Eastern Europe, and the newly independent states of the former Soviet Union 15 or 20 years ago. However, strategic management of business organizations has become increasingly important as competition intensifies throughout transition economies. Driven by a deep curiosity about "what is going on there?" this book probes into the workings of business strategies in these economies, and provides students, scholars, and managers with a better understanding of fundamental issues in strategy confronted by domestic and foreign firms competing in these newly opened markets.

This book could have been my doctoral dissertation. When I was selecting a focus for my dissertation in the early 1990s, this topic was on top of my list. However, my advisors suggested that I work on a different topic. "Business strategies in transition economies" would be too risky for a doctoral student, since such a topic was like a beast too wild to be captured, let alone tamed. As social scientists, we have been trained to employ a number of "cages" (theories and tools) to capture "beasts" (phenomena of interests). For rapidly evolving phenomena, we simply do not have suitable "cages" with which we can explore the beast in-depth. While I took their advice and pursued a different project for my dissertation (which resulted in my first book), I was also encouraged to explore this topic "on the side." And this is what I have been doing over the past decade. In the end, my work "on the side" has generated a lot more published articles than my dissertation research. The academic and professional market for ideas has clearly spoken for itself: The demand for knowledge and information about business strategies in transition economies is strong. However, individual articles generally push only a single point of view and do not provide an overall integrative framework. Therefore, it is a great pleasure to be able to summarize and integrate my research on business strategies in transition economies, as well as work done by other scholars around the world, in this book, which can be regarded as my "unborn" dissertation.

Whether companies can successfully employ competitive strategies will, to a large degree, determine the success or failure of the transitions toward market economies in these countries. As a result, this phenomenon has attracted a large number of practitioners and policymakers from Beijing to Budapest and numerous scholars and foreign advisers from Bonn to Boston. As a body of literature develops, it is useful to take inventory of what has been done, and identify new directions and challenges for the future. However, to the best of my knowledge, there has been no publication that provides a comprehensive, state-of-the-art overview of this rapidly expanding literature.

Attempting to fill such an important gap in the literature, this book distinguishes itself in three aspects: comparative, interdisciplinary, and relevant. It is relentlessly *comparative* in that it draws on common experience of firms and managers from not just one or two countries, but a broad range of transition economies. It covers both state-owned and non-state-owned enterprises, large and small firms, and domestic and foreign companies. It is *interdisciplinary* because it not only taps into findings from strategy studies, but also research in related management fields such as international business, organization theory, entrepreneurship, human resources, and marketing, as well as social science disciplines such as economics, sociology, and political science. Scholarly work in area studies such as Sinology and (post-)Sovietology has also been consulted extensively. Finally, it is *relevant* by focusing on firm-level issues confronting top executives who act as strategists for their organizations. A number of "Strategy in Action" inserts are used to illustrate how real managers deal with challenges. In contrast, most existing research is country- or region-specific with little cross-fertilization of insights from different transition economies such as China and Eastern Europe. A large number of publications are disciplinary driven without serious efforts to communicate across disciplinary boundaries. Another pitfall of the existing literature is that too many publications concentrate on state-level policies such as liberalization and privatization, and leave firm-level strategies unexplored. Fundamentally, it is business strategies crafted and implemented at the firm level that will make or break these transitions, thus calling for attention on firm-level strategies. As a social scientist housed in a business school, I take it upon myself to maintain a broad perspective, to build interdisciplinary bridges, and to strike a balance between theory and practice, rigor and relevance. These endeavors eventually culminate in the present book.

To be sure, the chapters that follow are just the entering wedges into the complex, dynamic, and largely unknown territory of strategies and competition in transition economies, and certainly not the final words on them. Companies' experiments and our learning about them are not likely to stop soon. One thing is for sure: Business strategies will become more important in differentiating the winners from the losers and mere survivors in these increasingly competitive economies in the new millennium, thus necessitating attention from students, scholars, and practitioners around the world.

Acknowledgments

This book is a reflection of my personal and professional journey embarked on since 1989. I began working on this research when I was a graduate student at the University of Washington in Seattle. Over the years, I have continued to work on it as a faculty member, first at the University of Hawaii, then at the Chinese University of Hong Kong, and, more recently, at The Ohio State University. At Washington, I thank Howard Becker, John Butler, Charles Hill, Anne Ilinitch (now at North Carolina), Richard Moxon, and Richard Peterson for taking me under their wings. At Hawaii, I enjoyed working with Dana Alden, Elaine Bailey, D. Bhawuk, Richard Brislin, Hong-Mei Chen, Bob Doktor, Eric Harwit, Laurence Jacobs, Lane Kelley, Yadong Luo, Oded Shenkar, Alvin So, Nick Synodinos, Glenn Taylor, and Nancy Wong. At the Chinese University, I thank Dean K. H. Lee and department chairman H. F. Lau for helping create a setting within which this kind of work was possible. I appreciate the collegiality of my colleagues, Kevin Au, C. F. Chan, Irene Chow, John Fukuda, Chuck Ingene, C. M. Lau, Ji Li, Thamis Lo, Yuan Lu, Shige Makino, K. C. Mun, Kent Neupert, Gongming Qian, Leo Sin, Raymond So, David Thomas, Denis Wang, Ryh-Song Yeh, Kitty Young, and Julie Yu. At Ohio State, I thank Dean Joseph Alutto, department chairman David Greenberger, and my new (and old) colleagues, Jay Barney, Venkat Bendapudi, Kate Conner, Jeff Ford, Jerry Greenberg, Rob Heneman, Steve Hills, Andrew Karolyi, Jay Kim, Howard Klein, Michael Leiblein, Roy Lewicki, Steve Mangum, Arnon Reichers, Cheryl Ryan, Oded Shenkar, Alice Stewart, and John Wanous, for their interest in having me.

Over the years, I have been fortunate to work with an interdisciplinary group of coauthors and coinvestigators on three continents. In North America, these include Oded Shenkar (Ohio State and Tel-Aviv), Yadong Luo, Eric Harwit, and Young-Jin Choi (all at Hawaii), Justin Tan (Cal State San Marcos), Anne Ilinitch (North Carolina), and Chao Chen and Patrick Saparito (both at Rutgers). In Asia, my collaborators are Kevin Au, Yuan Lu, and Denis Wang (all at CUHK), Howard Davies and Peter Walters (both at HKPolyU), Orlan Lee (HKUST), and Li Sun (Guoxin Securities). In Europe, I have teamed up with Trevor Buck (Leicester) and Igor Filatotchev (London). My research assistants at CUHK (Forrest Chan, Mandy Chan, Kenix Chow, and Gordon Law) and Ohio State (Heli Wang) were also very helpful, and I want to thank them for their assistance.

Among many people who made a contribution to this book, I especially want to thank John Child (Cambridge and HKU), not only for his pathbreaking work on managing in transition economies, which inspired a lot of my own research, but also for his time and efforts in writing a foreword for this book. I also appreciate the encouraging endorsements written by Jay Barney (Ohio State), Paul

Beamish (Western Ontario), and Oded Shenkar (Ohio State and Tel-Aviv), who read the entire manuscript after it was completed. In addition, several colleagues gave generously of their time to read different chapters as they were finished. These scholars are Trevor Buck (Leicester), Orlan Lee (HKUST), Shaomin Li (CityUHK), Yuan Lu, Kent Neupert, and Johnson Cao (all at CUHK), and Richard Moxon (Washington). Among them, Trevor and Yuan have been especially responsive, often providing their insights on a very short notice. I greatly appreciate such a spirit of scholarship, and, of course, I am responsible for all remaining errors.

In addition, many other colleagues have also contributed to my work by challenging and critiquing my ideas. Among them are Ming-Jer Chen (Pennsylvania), Roger Chen (San Francisco), Tailan Chi (Wisconsin-Milwaukee), Larry Farh (HKUST), Mike Geringer (Cal Poly), Don Hambrick and Kathy Harrigan (Columbia), Mike Hitt (Texas A&M), Bob Hoskisson (Oklahoma), Anne Huff (Colorado), Andrew Inkpen (Thunderbird), Ben Kedia (Memphis), Mingfang Li (Cal State Northridge), Hai Lin Lan (South China University of Technology), Majorie Lyles (Indiana), Kwok Leung and Shige Makino (CUHK), Ivan Manev (Maine), Klaus Meyer (Copenhagen), Mark Mizruchi (Michigan), M. K. Nyaw (Lingnan), Sam Park (Rutgers), Barbara Parker (Seattle), Sheila Puffer (Northeastern), Ming Jie Rui (Fudan), Steve Tallman (Utah), Mary Teagarden (Thunderbird), David Tse (HKU), Steve White (CUHK), Mike Wright (Nottingham), Katherine Xin (HKUST), and Aimin Yan (Boston U).

My ideas in this book were not born overnight. Instead, they have been presented at numerous conferences, seminars, and classrooms, and consequently sharpened as a result of such interaction with a wide range of audiences. In North America, I was invited to give seminars on this topic at Columbia (1997), Hawaii (1996-97), Japan-America Institute of Management Sciences in Honolulu (1997), Memphis (1999), North Carolina (1997), Ohio State (1997), Thunderbird (1997), and Western Ontario (1997), as well as annual meetings of the Academy of Management (1997 in Boston, 1998 in San Diego, and 1999 in Chicago) and Academy of International Business (1993 in Hawaii, 1994 in Boston, and 1996 in Banff). In Asia, I presented my work at the Chinese University of Hong Kong (1997), Foreign Trade University in Hanoi (1997), Fudan University in Shanghai (1998),

Hong Kong Polytechnic University (1996 and 1997), Hong Kong University of Science and Technology (1998), Lingnan College in Hong Kong (1996), Municipal Industrial Bureau of Beijing (1996), Shanghai Institute of Business Administration (1996), Shanghai Jiao Tong University (1996), and University of Hong Kong (1996 and 1998), as well as the AIB annual meetings in Seoul (1995) and the Asia Academy of Management inaugural conference in Hong Kong (1998). In Europe, my research was presented at the AIB annual meetings in Vienna (1998), Leicester Business School (1999), and Copenhagen Business School (1999). Moreover, my undergraduate, MBA, EMBA, and executive students at Washington, Hawaii, CUHK, and Ohio State have provided useful feedback and stimulating discussions for me to clarify my thoughts.

In addition, most of the ideas in this book have also been published in (or accepted by) leading scholarly journals, including *Academy of Management Journal, Academy of Management Review, Journal of International Business Studies, Journal of Management Studies, Organization Studies, Journal of Business Research,* and *Management International Review.* While I often struggle in the review process, in retrospect, I must thank all the editors and anonymous reviewers for forcing me to sharpen my ideas and propelling me to reach a higher level of scholarly excellence.

Mary Gander and Mary Rieder of Minnesota State University in Winona also deserve to be thanked, since it was their interest in China's transition economy that sparked my initial interest in this area. I also appreciate the support I received from Carlis Anderson, Roger Carlson, Joseph Foegen, Guile Schmidt, Michael Steiner, Douglas Sweetland, and Pat Tolmie during my studies there.

Outside the academic community, I thank hundreds of owners, managers, and officials who have participated in my interviews and surveys. Among them, Patrece Banks (Pacific Tide International) deserves to be singled out as a great friend and supporter. In addition, Donald Lu (United Holding), Connie Pang (A. T. Kearny), George Russell (Frank Russell Company), and Jack Zhou (Shanghai Industrial) have been especially helpful over the years in giving me their time and insights to help me carry out this work. At Sage, I thank Marquita Flemming and Harry Briggs (acquisitions editors), Diana Axelsen (production editor), Kris Bergstad (copy editor), and Jennifer Morgan missions editor), and Danielle Dillahunt (typesetter) for turning this manuscript into a book. I also thank Richard Brislin and Lane Kelley (series editors), who are my former colleagues at Hawaii, for their confidence in my work.

The financial requirements to carry out this type of work are enormous. I have been fortunate to be supported by three Centers for International Business Education and Research (CIBERs) funded by the U.S. Department of Education, first at Washington (1992-95), then at Hawaii (1995-97), and most recently at Ohio State (1998-99). Other organizations that supported my work include the Doctoral Program Office at the University of Washington (1991-95); President Chiang Ching-kuo Education Foundation in San Francisco (1993); Edna Benson Foundation in Seattle (1994); University Research Council at the University of Hawaii (1996-97); Department of Business Studies at the Hong Kong Polytechnic University (1997); a Dean's Discretion Grant, two Direct Allocation Grants, and a Student Campus Work Scheme Grant from Shaw College, all at the Chinese University of Hong Kong (1997-98); and a Competitive Earmarked Research Grant from the Hong Kong Research Grants Council (1998-99). While I thank all of them for supporting my work throughout these years, I want to especially express my gratitude to the Chinese University, where the writing of this book was started and finished during a good part of 1998. The University not only tolerated my presence while I was concentrating on the book, but also provided extraordinarily generous financial support that a visiting faculty member normally would not be able to expect elsewhere.

It is not an accident that this book focuses on transitions. My life in the past decade is full of transitions; I have lived in six different cities (Shanghai; Winona, Minnesota; Seattle; Honolulu; Hong Kong; and Columbus) with *four* trans-Pacific moves! When I started my research career, my wife, Agnes, was a published poet and novelist. As we move to different cities, she has become a financial analyst, picking up an MBA on the way. Despite all these changes, her love, passion, and support for me have remained unchanged. Agnes has not only endured the hardship of working on this seemingly never-ending project, but has also been a first reader of every word in this book and has offered sage advice on how to improve along the way. One of her noticeable changes is that she has now become increasingly demanding in terms of the quality of my writings. Attempting to satisfy the appetite of such a roll-up-the-sleeves-and-get-it-done kind of practitioner has constantly reminded me of the real world, where relevance, succinctness, and fun count. A great deal of thanks also go to my parents, who have always believed in my ability and encouraged me to set ambitious goals. This book represents an answer to their call for excellence. I also thank Aunt Zhikang, whose support and encouragement have greatly influenced who I am now. Finally, I thank my late grandfather, who passed away before I was born, but whose early studies in the 1920s-30s have provided much needed guiding light for my own journey. To all of you, my thanks and my love.

Mike W. Peng
Columbus, Ohio

To Agnes,
poet, novelist, and financial analyst

1 BUSINESS STRATEGIES: AN OVERVIEW

Know yourself, know your opponents; encounter a hundred battles, win a hundred victories.

—Sun Tzu (approximately 500 B.C.)

Strategy is about competing and winning. This book investigates business strategies employed by domestic and foreign firms in formerly socialist countries that are currently undergoing transitions, namely, those in East Asia (i.e., China, Mongolia, and Vietnam), Central and Eastern Europe (e.g., the Czech Republic, Hungary, and Poland), and the newly independent states of the former Soviet Union (e.g., Latvia, Russia, and Ukraine). Strategy and competition were hardly relevant in these countries during the heyday of socialism, since the state used to make important decisions and issue orders and quotas for managers to fulfill. Business strategies are becoming increasingly important during the transition, however, thus necessitating attention from students, scholars, and practitioners of strategic management.

Since the terrain for competing in these transition economies is new and the events are rapidly unfolding, there is a great deal of rumbling and soul-searching. While some firms are winning in the new competition, many are losing. What is going on there? What determines these firms' success or failure? How to improve the odds of success? These are the underlying questions that motivate the writing of this book, which addresses fundamental issues in business strategies confronted by managers at domestic and foreign firms competing in these countries. This book differentiates itself from a large number of works on transition economies by (a) adopting a firm-level, strategic management perspective and (b) focusing on the common patterns of strategic responses across a broad range of transition economies. In comparison, most publications on economic transitions concentrate on state-level policies, such as reform, liberalization, and privatization, and most are country- or region-specific works with little cross-fertilization of insights from different transition economies such as China and Eastern Europe. In this chapter, I will first introduce the basic concept of strategy, followed by an overview of the major issues that we will explore throughout the book.

WHAT IS STRATEGY?

Strategy as a term has very strong military roots, dating back to the work of Sun Tzu, a Chinese strategist, written in approximately 500 B.C. The application of the principles of military strategies to business competition is a more recent phenomenon. Since the 1960s, in response to the rise of strategic planning in large Western corporations, scholars have become more and more interested in "strategic management" (Andrews, 1971; Ansoff, 1965; Chandler, 1962; Schendel & Hofer, 1979). As a result, a large number of definitions of *strategy* have been attempted (Porter, 1980, 1996). Consider how a leading scholar, Alfred Chandler (1962), defined strategy: "the determination of the basic long-term goals and objectives of an enterprise, and the adoption of courses of action and the allocation of resources necessary for carrying out these goals" (p. 13). This definition, emphasizing the rational aspects of strategy embodied in explicit, formal planning as in the military, was challenged by Henry Mintzberg and his colleagues (Mintzberg & McHugh, 1985; Mintzberg & Waters, 1985), who suggested that strategy is a pattern in a stream of actions or decisions. Mintzberg (1989) further noted that a strategy is more than a plan, it can be a ploy, a pattern, a position, or a perspective. He argued that in addition to the *intended* strategies that Chandler and others emphasized, there can be *emergent* strategies that are not the result of conscientious, "top-down" planning, but are the outcome of a stream of smaller decisions from the "bottom up." As we will see, these insights are very helpful for understanding business strategies in transition economies, where formal, intended strategies are rare, and informal, emergent strategies are numerous.

Since most practitioners and researchers in strategic management are interested in the relationship between the actions taken by a firm and its performance (Summer et al., 1990), we will follow Hill and Jones (1998) to adopt an operational definition of *strategy* throughout the book: "*Strategy* is a pattern of decisions and actions that enables an organization to improve or maintain its performance" (p. 3).

Graphically (Figure 1.1), a strategy entails an organization's assessment of its own strengths (S) and weaknesses (W) at point A, its desired performance levels at point B, and the opportunities (O) and threats (T) in the environment that may facilitate or hinder the attainment of its goal to reach point B. This kind of assessment, called a SWOT analysis, resonates very well with Sun Tzu's teachings on the importance of knowing "yourself" and "your environment." After such an assessment, the decisions and actions that connect points A and B become the organization's strategy, or more specifically, its intended strategy. However, given so many uncertainties in the environment, not all intended strategies may realize themselves, and some may become unrealized strategies. On the other hand, other unintended decisions and actions may become emergent strategies with a thrust toward point B. Overall, this definition of strategy enables us to build on the strengths of earlier definitions given by Chandler and Mintzberg by acknowledging the existence of both intended and emergent strategies. According to this operational definition, a "good" strategy is one that "neutralizes threats and exploits opportunities while capitalizing on strengths and avoiding or fixing weaknesses" (Barney, 1997, p. 27). "Strategic management" thus is the "process through which strategies are chosen and implemented" (Barney, 1997, p. 27).

In summary, strategy is not a rule book, a blueprint, or a set of programmed instructions. Rather, it is the unifying theme that

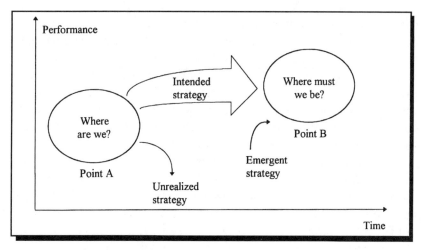

Figure 1.1. The Essence of Strategy

gives coherence and direction to various decisions made by an organization and its top leaders, to which we now turn.

STRATEGIES AND STRATEGISTS

Just as military strategies and generals have to be studied simultaneously, an understanding of business strategies would be incomplete without an appreciation of the role that top managers play as strategists (Child, 1972, 1997). Since the directions and operations of an organization typically are a reflection of its top managers, their personal choices and preferences, based on their own culture, background, and experience, may affect how strategies are crafted and implemented (Hambrick & Mason, 1984). In the case of business strategies in transition economies, managers who have accumulated most of their experience in the socialist era employ strategies that are dramatically different from those chosen by managers who are less influenced by the previous regime. Older managers tend to be more risk-averse and to employ more defensive strategies. Younger managers, on the other hand, are more entrepreneurial and more willing to take risk. Likewise, when foreign firms enter these countries to compete, their managers, often out of habit, attempt to use familiar recipes in these new settings. Therefore, although this book focuses on business strategies, it is also about strategists who maneuver and compete in transition economies.

FUNDAMENTAL ISSUES IN STRATEGY

Since strategic management is such a vast subject area, and business strategies in transition economies encompass such a huge territory, which has hardly been explored, it is enticing to attempt to cover every branch of this topic. In contrast, we will focus our attention only on *fundamental* issues, which act to define a field and to orient the attention of students, scholars, and managers in a certain direction. Specifically, we will attempt to answer five fundamental questions in strategy, drawn from the work of Rumelt, Schendel, and Teece (1994, p. 564), in the context of transition economies:

1. Why do firms differ?
2. How do firms behave?
3. How are strategy outcomes affected by strategy processes?
4. What determines the scope of the firm?[1]
5. What determines the international success and failure of firms?

Note that the perspective taken in these questions—and throughout the book—is that of the business firm interested in using competitive strategies to navigate the waters of economic transitions. This firm-level perspective should not be confused with national- or state-level "strategies" such as reform and privatization discussed in numerous other works such as the World Bank (1996). I will touch upon these public policy issues only as background, not as a focus of the book. A second important point to bear in mind is that these questions will be approached from the standpoint of top managers acting as strategists for their firms. Just as these five questions differentiate the field of strategic management from other disciplines (Rumelt et al., 1994), these two perspectives distinguish this book from other studies focusing on public policy issues or human resources, marketing, and/or operations standpoints.

In every modern economy, firms, just like individuals, differ. The first question, "Why do firms differ?", thus seems obvious and hardly generates debate (Carroll, 1993; Nelson, 1991). However, since much of our knowledge about "the firm" is from research on stylized firms in the West, "the firm" in transition economies exhibits a number of striking differences with which we are unfamiliar, such as a lack of complete discretion to acquire and allocate resources and little knowledge and experience to compete in a competitive, market-based economy. These features highlight "an important facet of diversity among organizations operating in different environments" (Peng & Heath, 1996, p. 492). Therefore, answering this question in transition economies helps us probe into the roots of the *nature* of the firm, which has puzzled scholars since the publication of Coase's seminal article in 1937.

Since strategy is about the choice of direction for the firm, answering the second question, "How do firms behave?", will enable us to understand the uniqueness of business strategies in transition economies. The dominant assumption in traditional strategy research is that the firm behaves like a rational individual interested in goal attainment. However, this assumption may not be borne out in reality, since the rationality of individuals such as managers is often constrained by their own preferences and biases as well as by environmental forces (Cyert & March, 1963; Williamson, 1985). Sometimes, firms led by managers in transition economies behave in a way that does not appear "rational," such as seeking breaking even instead of profit maximization as their goals and hoarding numerous slack resources to the point of inefficiency. As reforms deepen, some leading firms start to employ more competitive strategies aiming to improve performance. Many other firms simply follow without knowing the benefits of doing so (Powell & DiMaggio, 1991; Scott, 1995). Knowing why these strategic choices are made and why firms behave in certain ways can shed considerable light on business strategies in these countries.

In most modern organizations, strategy is not the choice of a single individual, but is the result of organizational processes and procedures. The answer to the third question, "How are strategy outcomes affected by strategy processes?", helps us appreciate the internal workings of organizations in transition economies. The socialist firm differs from its capitalist counterpart in a number of respects, such as the involvement of the state and the party, the concern for equity as opposed to efficiency, and the propensity to engage in personalized exchange relationships. Understanding these organizational dynamics enables us to understand why certain strategic choices are made over others in these countries.

The fourth question, "What determines the scope of the firm?", focuses on the growth of the firm (Peng & Heath, 1996). Traditionally, this question was irrelevant under central planning. The scope of the firm was not determined by managers, but by planners in the government. Managers had neither interest nor incentive to pursue the growth of the firm. During "sink-or-swim" transitions in which the state has become increasingly reluctant to bail out money-losing firms, many managers have found that they have very little choice but to join the new competition: Otherwise, their firms may end up "sinking" (Peng, 1997a). To many firms, to compete means to grow—but how to grow, in what modes, in what industries, and in which regions (countries)? These decisions ultimately boil down to the scope of the firm. While research on the scope of the firm in the West is far from reaching a consensus among managers and researchers (Hoskisson & Hitt, 1994; Dess, Gupta, Hennart, & Hill, 1995; Rumelt, 1974), work on firm growth in transition economies focusing on what determines the scope of the firm is even more rudimentary (Khanna & Palepu, 1997). Therefore, answering this question helps generate insights on the dynamics underlying the new competition in transition economies.

Finally, "What determines the international success or failure of firms?" While the first four questions pertain mostly to the unique attributes of indigenous firms in transition economies, the last question explores how foreign firms compete in these countries. Although some firms from these transition economies have internationalized, such as the Chinese "red chip"[2] conglomerates active in Hong Kong (Au, Peng, & Wang, in press) and the Russian aerospace and arms manufacturers (Elenkov, 1995), for our purposes, international competition means competing in these newly opened markets, which have become the new battleground for multinationals. Interestingly, firms from different countries exhibit different strategic choices, with different outcomes (Estrin & Meyer, 1998; Stross, 1990). Some invest earlier in search of first-mover advantages, and others choose to wait and see

(Luo & Peng, 1998, 1999). Some enter these countries primarily via joint ventures, and others prefer wholly owned subsidiaries. Therefore, answering this question helps us understand how global competition has been extended to these transition economies.

In sum, these five questions represent some of the most fundamental "puzzles" in strategic management. While other questions could be raised, they "all relate in one way or another to the five developed here" (Rumelt et al., 1994, p. 570). Therefore, answering these five *strategic* questions embedded in the context of transition economies will be the primary focus of this book.

BUSINESS STRATEGIES . . . IN WHERE?

Transition Economies and Emerging Economies

Before proceeding, it will be important to clarify the geographic focus of this book. I treat "transition economies" in East Asia, Central and Eastern Europe (CEE), and the newly independent states (NIS) of the former Soviet Union as a group, and explore common patterns of organizational evolution and business strategies in these countries. Since almost every country in the world can legitimately claim that its economy is undergoing some form of transition, using the label "transition economies" here may be contestable. I suggest that "transition" is always a matter of degree, and that the degree of changes in the 30 countries on the Eurasian landmass (see Table 1.1 for a full list) is unprecedented in recent history, thus justifying the term *transition economies* here (Aldcroft & Morewood, 1995; Cook & Nixson, 1995; World Bank, 1996). In my earlier work, I used a longer term: "planned economies in transition" (Peng, 1994; Peng & Heath, 1996). Other writers employed terms such as "socialist economies in transition" (Campbell, 1991), "post-communist economies" (Kornai, 1995), and "postcommunist and reforming communist states" (Milor, 1994). In the past, this group of countries had a few relatively agreed-upon labels such as "centrally planned economies," "socialist countries," and "communist states." Their rapid transitions since the 1980s have made it difficult to label them collectively. Throughout the book, I will

TABLE 1.1 Transition Economies and Emerging Economies

	Transition Economies	*Emerging Economies*[a]
Africa	—	South Africa
Asia	China, Mongolia, Vietnam	China, Hong Kong, India, Indonesia, Malaysia, the Philippines, Singapore, South Korea, Taiwan, Thailand
Central and Eastern Europe (CEE)	Albania, Bosnia-Herzegovina, Bulgaria, Croatia, the Czech Republic, Hungary, Macedonia, Poland, Romania, Slovak Republic, Slovenia, Yugoslavia (Serbia)	The Czech Republic, Hungary, Poland
Latin America	—	Argentina, Brazil, Chile, Colombia, Mexico, Venezuela
Middle East	—	Israel, Turkey
Newly Independent States (NIS) of the former Soviet Union	Armenia, Azerbaijan, Belarus, Estonia, Georgia, Kazakhstan, Kirghiz Republic, Latvia, Lithuania, Moldova, Russia, Tajikistan, Turkmenistan, Ukraine, Uzbekistan	Russia
Southern Europe	—	Greece, Portugal
Total	30	25

NOTE: a. The list of emerging economies comes from the *Economist* ("Emerging-Market Indicators," 1998, p. 94).

use the term *transition economies* to refer to these countries, not only because of its compositional simplicity, but because of its emphasis on changes and transitions. Chapter 2 will contain a more detailed discussion of the dynamics of these transitions.

In this sense, "transition economies" are not necessarily the same as "emerging economies," which is another loosely defined term. Shown in Table 1.1, a recent issue of *The Economist* (see "Emerging Market Indicators," 1998, p. 94) listed 25 countries as "emerging economies," including 10 in Asia (China, Hong Kong, India, Indonesia, Malaysia, the Philippines, Singapore, South Korea, Taiwan, and Thailand); 6 in Latin America (Argentina, Brazil, Chile, Colombia, Mexico, and Venezuela); 2 in the Middle East (Israel and Turkey); 1 in Africa (South Africa); 2 in nonsocialist Europe (Greece and Portugal);

and 4 in the former Soviet bloc (the Czech Republic, Hungary, Poland, and Russia). We will cover only five of them in this book, namely, China and the four countries in the former Soviet bloc. Another example is a recent call for papers on "Enterprise Strategies in Emerging Economies" in the *Academy of Management Journal* (1998). It listed 10 big emerging economies (in alphabetical order): Argentina; the Association of Southeast Asian Nations (ASEAN, including Brunei, Indonesia, Malaysia, Singapore, Thailand, the Philippines, and Vietnam); Brazil; Greater China (including mainland China, Hong Kong, and Taiwan); India; Mexico; Poland; South Africa; South Korea; and Turkey. Among this group of "emerging economies," this book will cover only mainland China, Poland, and Vietnam.

A Focus on Transition Economies

Following authoritative publications such as Kornai (1992, 1995) and the World Bank (1996), this chosen focus on transition economies moving away from state socialism reflects a fundamental belief that, despite wide country-specific variations, there is a *common logic* underlying the transitions in these countries, which in turn results in *similar patterns* of strategic responses to such environmental turbulence (Chapter 3 expands this point in more detail). The task, therefore, is to use multinational triangulation to generalize from the emergence of strategic management in these countries, based on the experience of practitioners over there, the advice from officials and advisors guiding the process, and the findings of scholars around the world (Peng & Peterson, 1994). On the other hand, the book does not overgeneralize. It recognizes that the strategies and strategists it examines come from countries with diverse histories, cultures, and geography, as well as different social, political, and economic development. In fact, it explores the links among these factors that stimulate or prevent certain business strategies from being formulated and implemented during the transition.

ORGANIZATION OF THE BOOK

There are eight chapters in the book. Following this chapter, Chapter 2 provides a brief overview of the economies in transition that will be covered. Chapter 3 spells out a conceptual framework, called an institutional perspective, that focuses on the dynamic interaction among institutions, organizations, and strategic choices in these countries. Concentrating on domestic firms, Chapters 4, 5, and 6 discusses the strategies of state-owned enterprises, reformed and privatized firms, and private entrepreneurial start-ups, respectively. Chapter 7 highlights strategies employed by foreign firms competing in these countries. Finally, discussions, implications, and conclusions are drawn in Chapter 8. The five fundamental questions will be explored throughout the chapters and summarized in the last one.

NOTES

1. The original question was, "What are the functions of the headquarters unit in a multi-business firm?" (Rumelt, Schendel, & Teece, 1994, p. 564). I have paraphrased this question to make it more parsimonious (see Rumelt et al., 1994, p. 44).

2. Red chips are mainland-China-based companies that list their shares on the Hong Kong stock exchange. In 1993, there were 21 red chips listed in Hong Kong. By the end of 1997, the number had increased to 75, representing 15% of the capitalization of all listed firms in Hong Kong (including 36 China-affiliated corporations and 39 China corporations, or the so-called H-shares). In 1997 alone, red chips raised 60% of new capital through initial public offerings in Hong Kong (see Au, Peng, & Wang, in press, De Trenck, 1998, and Peng, Au, & Wang, 1999, for details).

2 Economies in Transition

It is impossible to cross a chasm in two leaps.

—Vaclav Havel

We have to touch the stones when crossing the river.

—Deng Xiaoping

Toward the end of the 20th century, fundamental transitions swept through a huge landmass from the former boundaries separating East and West Germany to China's southern border with Hong Kong. By the time this book reaches its readers, it will have been 10 years since the fall of the Berlin Wall and more than 20 years since the beginning of the economic reforms in China. What is going on in these countries? What has prompted them to give up classical state socialism, which they took pains to construct decades earlier, and move toward market economies? As a historical excursion, this chapter will survey the evolution of socialism in these countries and highlight the characteristics of their transitions, which will form the background for our analysis of business strategies in these economies throughout the rest of the book.

SOCIALIST COUNTRIES
IN TRANSITION

Table 2.1 lists the 12 countries that this book considers as transition economies as of 1989. Despite significant differences in individual attributes, these 12 countries were all members of "a broader, clearly identifiable class of social-political-economic system" that was called the *socialist* system for an extended period of time (Kornai, 1992, p. 5). A sustained period of Communist Party rule and interest in classical state socialism in these countries distinguishes them from other countries that may also consider themselves as "socialist," such as the Scandinavian countries that for decades have had social democratic governments.

Since the early 1990s, these 12 countries have evolved into a group of 30 countries due to the reunification of Germany and the breakup of the former Czechoslovakia, the former Soviet Union, and the former Yugoslavia (Table 2.2). Following the World Bank (1996), this book covers the transitions going on in these 30 countries grouped as Central and Eastern Europe (CEE), the newly independent states (NIS) of the former Soviet Union, and East Asia (China, Mongolia, and Vietnam). Further grouping of these countries into subgroups such as Visegrad, Baltic, Transcaucasus, and Central Asia is also noted in Table 2.2.

This book does not set out to provide a comprehensive and detailed analysis of any particular country in this group. There are a great many differences in their approaches to transitions, some peaceful (Czechoslovakia) while others violent (Romania); some through "shock therapy" (Poland and Russia) and others through a "gradualist" approach (China and Vietnam). The emphasis here is to downplay the individual differences and to focus on common patterns of business strategies that have emerged across a broad range of these countries. In order to achieve this goal, it is necessary to back off from the most detailed accounts of present-day events and to concentrate on more fundamental problems and mechanisms in these economies.

Although the classical system of state socialism has been phased out in almost all of these countries, it is important to understand how it worked. The very nature of the transitions toward market economies is that each of these countries is still saturated with remnants of the

TABLE 2.1   Socialist Countries and Their Reforms and Transitions

Country	Year of Communist Takeover	Key Dates in Reforms and Transitions	Political Events Connected With the Key Dates
1. Soviet Union	1917	1953-1964	Excesses of Stalinism denounced
		1985	Gorbachev came to power
		1991	The Soviet Union was dissolved
2. Mongolia	1921	1990	Communist government stepped down
3. Albania	1944	1990	Multiparty system established
4. Yugoslavia	1945	1949	Broke away from the orthodox Soviet bloc
		1990	First multiparty elections in certain republics
		1991	The former Yugoslavia broken up
5. Bulgaria	1947	1989	Communist government stepped down
6. Czechoslovakia	1948	1968	"Prague Spring" crushed by Soviet military
		1989	"Velvet Revolution"
		1993	The former Czechoslovakia split in two
7. Hungary	1948	1956	Reform program crushed by Soviet military
		1968	New Economic Mechanisms launched
		1989	Multiparty system declared
8. Poland	1948	1981	Solidarity trade union crushed by martial law
		1989	Noncommunist government formed
9. Romania	1948	1989	Communist government removed by military
10. China	1949	1978	Economic reforms launched
		1989	Pro-democracy movement crushed by military
11. East Germany	1949	1989	Berlin Wall fell
		1990	Reunited with West Germany
12. Vietnam	1954	1987	Economic reforms launched

TABLE 2.2   Basic Economic Indicators of the Thirty Transition Economies[a]

Country	Population: 1994 (million)	GNP per capita: 1995 (US$)	GNP per capita: 1995 PPP (US$)	Annual GNP growth (%) 1981- 1989	Annual GNP growth (%) 1990- 1995
Central and Eastern Europe (12)					
Albania	3.2	670	—	1.7	-3.8
Bosnia-Herzegovina (Y)*	4.7	—	—	—	—
Bulgaria	8.4	1,330	4,480	4.9	-4.7
Croatia (Y)*	4.8	3,250	—	—	-5.5**
The Czech Republic (V)	10.3	3,870	9,770	1.8	-2.5
Hungary (V)	10.3	4,120	6,410	1.8	-2.1
Macedonia (Y)*	2.1	820	—	—	-8.8**
Poland (V)	38.5	2,790	5,400	2.6	0.1
Romania	22.7	1,480	4,360	1.0	-3.6
Slovak Republic (V)	5.3	2,950	3,610	2.7	-2.6
Slovenia (Y)	2.0	8,200	—	—	1.0**
Yugoslavia (Serbia) (Y)*	—	—	—	—	—
Newly Independent States (15)					
Armenia (T)*	3.7	730	2,260	3.5	-12.2
Azerbaijan (T)*	7.5	480	1,460	2.9	-18.3
Belarus	10.4	2,070	4,220	5.0	-9.5
Estonia (B)	1.5	2,860	4,220	0.2	-7.9
Georgia (T)*	5.4	440	1,470	1.2	-23.3
Kazakhstan (C)	16.8	1,330	3,010	2.0	-12.3
Kirghiz Republic (C)	4.5	700	1,800	4.0	-9.5
Latvia (B)	2.5	2,270	3,370	3.7	-9.7
Lithuania (B)	3.7	1,900	4,120	1.8	-11.2
Moldova	4.4	870	—	—	-12.3
Russia	148.4	2,240	4,480	3.0	-8.1
Tajikistan (C)*	5.8	360	—	3.3	-15.6
Turkmenistan (C)	4.4	—	—	4.0	—
Ukraine	51.9	1,630	2,400	—	-12.0
Uzbekistan (C)	22.4	970	2,370	3.4	-3.1
East Asia (3)					
China	1,190.9	620	2,920	11.1	10.2
Mongolia	2.4	310	1,950	5.7	-1.9
Vietnam	72.0	240	—	4.4	7.6

SOURCES: Adapted from the World Bank (1996, pp. 171-172; 1997b, pp. 214-215).
NOTE: a. Subgroups include the Baltics (B), Central Asia (C), Transcaucasia (T), Visegrad (V), and republics of the former Yugoslavia (Y). Missing data are indicated by "—" Countries severely affected by regional tensions are indicated by "*," 1991-1995 average is indicated by "**," and "PPP" stands for purchasing power parity.

state socialist system (Campbell, 1991). As a result, we cannot appreciate the scale and scope of the current problems without an understanding of the old system, to which we next turn.

PLANNING AND CONTROL UNDER STATE SOCIALISM

The state socialist system covered approximately one third of the world's population at one time. It not only included the 12 original countries listed in Table 2.1, but also a diverse range of other countries such as Angola, Cambodia, Congo, Cuba, Laos, and North Korea. While numerous other attributes, such as communist ideology and party rule, are also important, we will highlight only certain characteristics that are important for the development of strategic management during the transitional era, namely, the practice of central planning and bureaucratic control.

Central Planning

As opposed to "market" economies, a most fundamental feature of state socialism is the use of central planning, thus giving rise to such terms as the "centrally planned economy." "The planning system in the latter fulfills most functions that the market does in the former" (Peng, 1994, p. 231). The intellectual forerunners of the socialist system saw planning as one of socialism's great advantages when compared with capitalism. Specifically, Marx, Engels, Lenin, and their followers argued that in a capitalist economy the anarchy (or the "invisible hand," according to Adam Smith) of the market and the fluctuations in supply and demand led to boom-bust cycles of overproduction, unemployment, and recession. They believed that these problems could be overcome by central planning, which would do away with mass unemployment. Central planning could avoid crises of overproduction, recession, and the incalculable losses they involve. The moment in history that seemed to support this argument was when the West was suffering from the devastating consequences of the Great Depression in the 1930s, such as production cutbacks and millions of unemployed. At the same time, the first 5-year plan was

TABLE 2.3   The Share of the Public Sector in Gross Domestic Product[a]

Country	Year	Share of the Public Sector (%)
Socialist countries at the outset of their reforms and transitions		
China	1978	78
Czechoslovakia	1988	99
East Germany	1988	96
Hungary	1988	93
Poland	1988	81
Soviet Union	1985	95
Vietnam	1987	71
Yugoslavia	1987	86
Capitalist countries as a comparison group		
Austria	1979	15
France	1983	17
Great Britain	1981	11
Italy	1982	14
Turkey	1985	11
United States	1983	1
West Germany	1982	11

SOURCES: *China:* State Statistical Bureau (1997, p. 411). *Soviet Union:* Buck and Cole (1987, p. 35). *All other socialist countries:* Kornai (1992, p. 72). *France and Great Britain:* Aharoni (1986, p. 18). *All other capitalist countries:* Malanovic (1989, p. 15).
NOTE: a. Given the existence of substantial informal, "gray" activities not captured by official statistics, the percentages should be viewed only as official estimates of the extent to which the public sector has contributed to GDP.

accomplished in the Soviet Union with flying colors (Kornai, 1992). As an alternative to market-based capitalism, the central planning system that originated in the Soviet Union and later spread to China and Eastern Europe could be regarded as an organizational innovation that was diffused to many countries (Peng, 1994; Skocpol, 1976).

Bureaucratic Control

In most countries that adopted the central planning system, the plan was prepared by the most powerful bureaucratic agency, the national planning office. A fundamental feature of this system is its use of bureaucratic control to undertake economic transactions and achieve coordination among economic players, as opposed to using the market to facilitate these activities (Ericson, 1991). Moreover, most of the firms are state-owned enterprises (SOEs), which occupy the "commanding heights" of the socialist economy.[1] Table 2.3 indicates the extent to which the state sector contributed to various socialist economies. For SOEs, the central planning bureaucracy asserts itself in a large number of activities:

1. *Establishment of a firm.* In a capitalist economy, the question of "entry" is decided by entrepreneurs and owners. Under state socialism, the "entry" decision for SOEs is made by the planning bureaucracy (Kornai, 1992).

2. *Liquidation of a firm.* In a capitalist economy, "exit" may be forced by competition: A firm has to declare bankruptcy and/or merge with others when it becomes insolvent. In a state socialist economy, it is the bureaucrats who decide whether to subsidize, liquidate, break up, or merge SOEs (Granick, 1990).

3. *Management of production.* The firm's setup and managers selected by the bureaucracy are instructed to perform what the annual production plan dictates them to do. As a result, the scale and scope of the SOE are firmly controlled by the planning bureaucrats (Granick, 1975).

4. *Allocation and distribution of products and materials.* For a great many products, the bureaucracy assigns the user to a certain producer and lays down how much of a particular product the producer is obliged to provide and the user to receive. Through such planning and coordination, the bureaucracy substantially takes the place of the market (Richman, 1965, 1969).

5. *Decisions on pricing, investment, technology, and foreign trade.* The power to make these decisions rests in the hands of the bureaucrats. SOE managers, as a result, act mainly as order takers of the bureaucracy (Beissinger, 1988; Child, 1994; Lu, 1996).

6. *Appointment, promotion, and dismissal of managers.* The selection of SOE managers is entirely in the hands of the bureaucracy (Berliner, 1988; Granick, 1962).

7. *Allocation and management of labor.* Workers in a socialist firm are assigned by the bureaucracy and are paid according to some centralized compensation scheme determined by the same bureaucracy. They are entitled to virtually lifetime employment, and managers have little discretion to discipline workers (Tung, 1982; Walder, 1989).

In sum, the principal objective of socialist firms is to meet physical production targets set by central planners. Firms do not emphasize profits, quality, variety, or customer service, still less inno-vation. Managers, most of them production engineers and political officers, are judged in terms of output rather than client satisfaction. Financial performance is irrelevant. Despite all these problems, which are now well known, the state socialist system, as an alternative to market capitalism, did work for a time, at least initially—albeit with extraordinary human and environmental costs. Plans were fulfilled by and large, if not precisely, according to state priority. Thus, defense and military contracts were especially likely to be accomplished. With such a system, these countries rapidly industrialized, with increasing output and the provision of basic education, health care, housing, and jobs to most of the population. During the 1950s and 1960s, the economic gap between planned and market economies appeared to be narrowing. Over time, however, fundamental problems began to sur-face, which will be dealt with next.

STATE SOCIALISM: A GRAND FAILURE

Shattered Dreams

State socialism was built on a belief unquestioned by its archi-tects and their lieutenants: that socialism is superior to capitalism. The main assumption behind this belief was that socialism could develop the economy more efficiently and productively by eliminating the inefficiencies of capitalism, such as overcapacity, unemployment, and recession (Thompson & Vidmer, 1983). The end result, naturally, was that socialist countries would eventually attain higher standards of living than their capitalist counterparts. In 1958, Soviet leader Nikita Khrushchev publicly announced, during his tour of the United States, that the Soviet Union would soon "bury" America in economic competition. He further asserted that by the early 1970s "the USSR will take the first place in the world" in economic output and that this "will secure our people the highest living standards in the world" (Brzezinski, 1989, p. 35). Not to be outdone, China's leader Mao Zedong coined the term "Great Leap Forward" to describe his ambi-tious campaign launched in the late 1950s, which, according to his calculations, would enable China to surpass Great Britain in GDP in 15 years and the United States in 30 years (Zhao, 1997).

However, the subsequent evolution of state socialism has completely rejected such a Messianic belief. Led by the Communist Party, the state socialist system had the capacity to make huge policy errors that could devastate an entire economy. Most of the severe famines of the 20th century occurred in socialist countries (Nolan, 1995). The ongoing one in North Korea is only a recent example. During the Soviet collectivization campaign in the 1920s and 1930s, famine caused as many as seven million deaths. Mao's Great Leap Forward in the early 1960s resulted in a disastrous famine that cost as many as 30 million lives (Nolan, 1995, p. 15). Despite their impressive military, defense, and heavy industries, virtually all socialist countries, regardless of their culture, history, and geography, suffered from persistent shortages, especially in consumer goods and foodstuffs. Such shortages led to the term "economics of shortage," coined by Kornai (1980).

As a result, people in these countries had a lower standard of living not only compared with the West but also with the newly industrialized countries. By the 1980s, socialist countries—with roughly one third of the world's population—accounted for only 10% of global exports[2] and a mere 3% of technological innovations. By 1983, there was one car for every 1.8 Americans, 2.5 West Germans, 2.8 Italians, or 4.4 Japanese, but one car for every 5.8 Czechs, 10.8 Poles, or 14.2 Soviets.[3] It is startling to note that under apartheid in South Africa, even blacks owned more cars per capita than did citizens of the Soviet Union (Brzezinski, 1989, pp. 237-238).

By 1970, Soviet per capita GNP reached 45% of the U.S. level ($5,123 vs. $11,413 in 1983 dollars). The Soviet economy climbed to more than half the size of that of the United States and continued to grow faster, threatening to close the gap. Yet since the 1970s, Soviet growth lost momentum, and its investment generated nearly zero returns (World Bank, 1996). As a result, by 1985 its per capita GNP dropped to 44% of the U.S. level ($6,863 vs. $15,511 in 1983 dollars; Brzezinski, 1989, p. 259). Much worse, the country that believed itself destined to become the world's premier economic power fell behind not only the United States but also Japan (Buck & Cole, 1987). Between 1960 and 1985, with a population less than half of that of the Soviet Union, Japan caught up in GNP after trailing by more than a 3-to-1 ratio at the outset. During the same period, Japanese per capita GNP experienced a 373% growth (from $2,508 in 1960 to $11,864 in 1985, in 1983 dollars), while the Soviet growth during these 25 years was 94% (Brzezinski, 1989, p. 259).

Although it may be difficult to compare the standard of living of the West with some countries that joined the socialist camp from a very low level of economic development (e.g., Vietnam), the spectacular economic success of West Germany, South Korea, Taiwan, and Hong Kong certainly made their socialist cousins in East Germany, North Korea, and China, respectively, pale by comparison. At the time of reunification, East Germany had a quarter of West Germany's population but produced a mere tenth of its gross domestic product (World Bank, 1996, p. 10). By the 1980s, labor productivity in South Korea was ten times higher than in North Korea (Kornai, 1992, p. 385). The Chinese cotton-yarn industry experienced a startling 21% *decline* in total factor productivity between 1936 and 1986 (Cheung, Archibald, & Faig, 1993, p. 23). In contrast, Taiwan and Hong Kong experienced sustained strong growth during the postwar decades, securing themselves as the acknowledged "economic tigers" in East Asia (Hamilton & Biggart, 1988; Seagrave, 1995). By the 1980s, the tiny island state of Singapore alone exported more machinery to industrialized countries than did all of Eastern Europe combined. Without a doubt, classical state socialism is a "grand failure" (Brzezinksi, 1989).

Coordination and Incentive Problems

What has gone wrong? While there are numerous political and social problems that underlie state socialism, fundamental economic, managerial, and organizational problems lie in two areas: coordination and incentive. The *coordination problem* stems from the intrinsic inefficiency of using central planning and bureaucratic control to coordinate economic activities. Specifically, state socialism suffers from the overconcentration of managerial responsibilities in the hands of the government bureaucracy, which attempts to coordinate gigantic, national economies (Ericson, 1991). Each country in this group could be regarded as a "Centrally Planned Economy, Inc.," with the planning office acting as corporate headquarters and industrial ministries and

SOEs as divisions as typically found in large Western corporations (Peng, 1996). The Soviets themselves termed their economy a "single national economic complex" (Spulber, 1991). More lucid terms, such as the "USSR, Inc." and "China, Inc.," have often been used in the media (Macleod, 1988).

By the late 1980s, according to the estimation of a Soviet economist, a fully balanced, checked, and detailed national plan for the next year would not be ready, even with the help of supercomputers, for 30,000 years (Maltsev, 1990)! The reality is that bureaucrats in the planning office simply do not have enough information to substitute for that supplied by prices in a market economy. As a result, plans are often subject to revisions and adjustments, which create further confusion and inconsistency (Naughton, 1994). In the end, there may be no real plan, just a series of improvisations and a host of informal economic transactions beyond the reach of the central plan.

Together with the coordination problem, there is a huge *incentive problem* throughout these countries. State socialism regards private ownership as a "sin" of capitalism that led to the greed of private owners—that is, capitalists—who "exploit" workers. A natural remedy, therefore, would be to convert property from private to public hands embodied in SOEs. Because the socialist state has multiple, conflicting objectives, such as developing the economy, creating wealth, and maintaining full employment and social services, it has inadequate resources to monitor what is going on in thousands of SOEs (Naughton, 1994). Lacking reliable information about the true capability of SOEs, planners depend heavily upon the firms' performance during the previous year. Therefore, SOE managers have little incentive to maximize output and profits, since overfulfillment will result in upward adjustment of the target for the next year (Granick, 1990). As a result, managers typically bargain with the state for a performance target as low as possible, and hoard as much slack as possible in order to ensure plan fulfillment (Peng & Heath, 1996; Tan & Peng, 1998b). In addition, failure to perform does not create a threat to SOE managers; instead, for political reasons, the state typically subsidizes money-losing SOEs, thus creating "soft budget constraints" that further reduce managers' incentive to improve efficiency (Kornai, 1980). It is not surprising that the idea of employing competitive business strategies was very alien to SOE managers, who had neither pressure nor incentive to perform well, other than mere plan fulfillment, during the classical socialist era.

Although SOEs in theory are the "property of the whole people," in practice there is no individual, family, or small group of partners to whom one can point as owners. As a result, "state property belongs to all and to none" (Kornai, 1992, p. 75). The lack of powerful incentive based on property ownership led to a loss of incentive not only among managers, but also among rank-and-file employees. Despite the official ideology calling for the need to instill "a sense of ownership" and for employees to work "like proprietors," it was practically impossible for a truly proprietary motivation to develop (Jensen & Meckling, 1976).[4] Since extra work did not translate into extra pay and other rewards, employees had little incentive to improve the quality and efficiency of their work (Tung, 1981; Walder, 1989). In contrast, given the generally low pay and poor living standards, the degrading situation can be summarized by a widely circulated saying among people in socialist countries: "They pretend to pay us, and we pretend to work."

The Debate on Socialism: Theory and Evidence

While the problems associated with state socialism manifested themselves throughout the 1970s and 1980s, it is important to note a theoretical debate on socialism that took place *before* its widespread adoption. Spearheaded by Ludwig von Mises (1935), the antisocialism school suggested that socialism, in the absence of private property and market mechanism, would be incapable of using bureaucratic control to reach market-equilibrium prices to balance supply and demand. The prosocialism school, represented by Oscar Lange (1936-1937), took issue with this view, arguing that, in theory, the central planning office is able to set market-clearing equilibrium prices and does so, in fact, by stimulating the market mechanism. Specifically, when it sees excess demand it raises prices, and when it detects excess supply it reduces them. Therefore, according to Lange, state socialism is capable of balancing supply and demand.

The sharpest repudiation of socialism came from Friedrich Hayek (1945). He argued that the fundamental problem for socialism is not whether it can set equilibrium prices, but the incentives to obtain and speedily apply the necessarily dispersed information scattered in many different places of an economy. In this respect, the market, competition, and private firms led by managers and entrepreneurs are far superior to central planning. Decision making at a lower level by managers and entrepreneurs trying to fill the gaps in demand with competitive business strategies is simply more efficient than bureaucrats who try to coordinate everything on a gigantic scale. Moreover, these private-firm managers and entrepreneurs would have stronger incentives than SOE managers and bureaucrats. Looking back after 50 years and with a mountain of evidence from the global failure of socialism, it is remarkable to note that Hayek, who could reason only conceptually at the time of his writing, was right on every point in the debate.

Summarizing the theoretical arguments and empirical evidence of the "socialist debate," Nobel laureate Milton Friedman (1990) wrote in a letter addressed to China's leader Zhao Ziyang, who hosted his visit to China in 1988:

> No country that has relied on detailed central planning has been able to achieve a high level of prosperity for the masses of its people. On the other hand, every country that has achieved a high level of prosperity for the masses of its people has relied primarily on *free private markets* to coordinate economic activities. (p. 124; original emphasis)

In brief, during the past quarter century, the monumental failure of socialism became more striking in light of massive increases in global trade, private investment, and economic growth in many nonsocialist countries. Consequently, reforms and transitions became inevitable.

REFORMS AND TRANSITIONS AT A GLANCE

Triggering Events

The failures and problems of state socialism led to the accumulation of economic difficulties, public dissatisfaction, and loss of confidence in those in power. During the era of state socialism, incremental reforms appeared in most of these countries, such as Hungary's experiments between 1953 and 1956 and in 1968, Czechoslovakia's reforms in 1968, and "revisionist" initiatives introduced by Khrushchev in the 1950s and by Brezhnev in the 1960s and 1970s in the former Soviet Union (Adam, 1989). However, strong inertia, embodied in the deep structures of the classical socialist ideology, prevented any significant changes until recently when major transitions were initiated (Brus & Laski, 1989). A former communist leader, President Boris Yeltsin of the new Russia, summarized the frustration with state socialism and incremental reforms in 1991:

> I think that the experiment which was conducted on our soil was a tragedy for our people and it was too bad that it happened on our territory. It would have been better if the experiment had been conducted in some small country . . . so as to make it clear that it was a utopian idea, although a beautiful one. (cited in Williamson, 1993, p. 104)

Only deep crises could trigger major reforms and transitions (Blanchard et al., 1991). In China, the Cultural Revolution (1966-1976) led by Mao and his fundamentalist associates, the "Gang of Four," resulted in an economy totally ruined and confidence in state socialism nearly destroyed by the late 1970s. In 1978, China embarked on economic reforms aimed at moving away from state socialism and lifting its one billion people from poverty to modernity (Shirk, 1993). A similar crisis occurred throughout CEE and the Soviet Union by the mid-1980s, triggered by Soviet leader Mikhail Gorbachev's *glasnost* (openness) and *perestroika* (restructuring) campaigns (Gorbachev, 1987). Ironically, these two campaigns designed to *partially reform* state socialism resulted in people's increasing awareness of the excesses of the system and *total rejection* of socialism (Czarniawska, 1986; Shelton, 1989). In 1989, with an unexpected suddenness, the Berlin Wall fell and the Iron Curtain melted down (see Table 2.1). Then, by 1991, the Soviet Union, the bastion of world socialism, ceased to exist and was replaced by 15 new countries. Virtually overnight, people in CEE and the NIS voted communist governments out of office and shifted their political and economic orientations toward a market economy (Chirot, 1991).

Two Paths

Two distinct paths of reforms and transitions have emerged in the past two decades. Led by Poland in 1990 and adopted by most CEE and NIS countries, the first is to launch a rapid, all-out program, undertaking as many reforms as possible in the shortest possible time. This approach aims to replace central planning with the rudiments of a market economy in a single burst of reforms called a "big bang" (Adams & Brock, 1993; Lipton & Sachs, 1990; Sachs, 1993). The rationale of this approach is well captured by President Vaclav Havel of the Czech Republic: "it is impossible to cross a chasm in two leaps" (World Bank, 1996, p. 9). Experience in CEE and the NIS shows that some changes can indeed happen overnight—central planning can be abolished, markets liberalized, and restrictions on private ownership lifted—all with the stroke of a pen. However, many other reforms are inherently slow. Privatization typically takes longer than expected, and changing the governance of former SOEs takes even longer. Developing market-supporting institutions, such as legal, regulatory, and financial systems, takes years and even decades.

China and, later, Vietnam have employed a second approach, characterized by incremental, partial reforms deepening over time. Summarized by Chinese leader Deng Xiaoping's phrase, "touching the stones to cross the river," this "gradualist" approach started with localized experiments, first through decollectivization of agriculture and moved on to open doors to foreign investment, liberalize prices, and phase out central planning (Jefferson & Rawski, 1994; Perkins, 1994). These steps were first taken at the margins and then more extensively (Naughton, 1994). Instead of undertaking massive privatization of SOEs, the state allowed for other forms of ownership, such as "collective" firms owned by local governments, foreign-invested firms, and private firms, to emerge and flourish. The share of output produced by these non-SOE firms rose sharply, reducing SOEs' share from 78% of China's total industrial output in 1978 to 28% in 1996

(State Statistical Bureau, 1997, p. 411). Meanwhile, the role of central planning and bureaucratic control was substantially reduced.

Different Outcomes

Given these two different paths from plan to market, what have the progress and outcomes been so far in terms of economic growth and market liberalization? In economic growth, China and, to a lesser extent, Vietnam outdistanced the rest of the pack by a wide margin (Lardy, 1994; Nolan, 1995; Overholt, 1993). Shown in Table 2.2, average annual GDP growth in China was 11.1% during the 1981-1989 period, and 10.2% during 1990 to 1995. Vietnam achieved annual GDP growth of 4.4% and 7.6%, respectively, during these two periods. In comparison, the 10 countries in CEE experienced, on average, 3.3% annual *decline* from 1990 to 1995, which was their first period of transition. The best-performing country in this group, Slovenia, barely achieved 1% GDP growth during the period. Even worse, none of the NIS countries had any growth during the 1990 to 1995 period; on average they experienced 11.8% annual GDP *decline*, with the "best" case being Uzbekistan, which had 3.1% average annual decline (World Bank, 1996, pp. 171-172).

In terms of market liberalization, by the mid-1990s, many countries in CEE and the NIS were essentially market economies, with open trade, currency convertibility, and liberal policies toward business entry and exit. Among them, seven countries in the so-called Group 1 identified by the World Bank (1996, p. 14), namely, Croatia, the Czech Republic, Hungary, Macedonia, Poland, the Slovak Republic, and Slovenia, made the most far-reaching progress in their departure from state socialism.[5] A few other CEE and NIS countries still retained extensive price controls and state trading monopolies. With more extensive controls on SOEs, the East Asian countries were less liberalized than many CEE and NIS countries (Davies, 1995; Li, He, & Yau, 1998). However, rapidly liberalizing markets and prices also came with very high prices in inflation throughout CEE and the NIS. Shown in Table 2.4, except in Hungary, where most prices had been liberalized before 1990, all CEE and NIS countries suffered from a burst of very high inflation between 1990 and 1995. The worst record was held by Georgia in 1994, which had a staggering 18,000% annual inflation (World Bank,

TABLE 2.4 Average Annual Inflation Rates (%) in Transition Economies, 1990-1995

Country	1990	1991	1992	1993	1994	1995
Central and Eastern Europe						
Albania	0.0	35.5	225.9	85.0	28.0	8.0
Bulgaria	22.0	333.5	82.0	72.8	89.0	62.0
Croatia	135.6	249.5	938.2	1,516.0	98.0	4.1
The Czech Republic	10.8	56.7	11.1	20.8	10.2	9.1
Hungary	29.0	34.2	22.9	22.5	19.0	28.2
Macedonia	120.5	229.7	1,925.2	248.0	65.0	50.0
Poland	586.0	70.3	43.0	35.3	32.2	27.8
Romania	5.1	174.5	210.9	256.0	131.0	32.3
The Slovak Republic	10.8	61.2	10.1	23.0	14.0	9.9
Slovenia	549.7	117.1	201.0	32.0	19.8	12.6
Newly Independent States						
Armenia	10.3	100.0	825.0	3,732.0	5,458.0	175.0
Azerbaijan	7.8	105.6	616.0	833.0	1,500.0	412.0
Belarus	4.5	83.5	969.0	1,188.0	2,200.0	800.0
Estonia	23.1	210.6	1,069.0	89.0	48.0	29.0
Georgia	3.3	78.5	913.0	3,126.0	18,000.0	160.0
Kazakhstan	4.2	91.0	1,610.0	89.0	48.0	29.0
Kirghiz Republic	3.0	85.0	854.6	1,208.7	280.0	45.0
Latvia	10.5	124.4	951.2	109.0	36.0	25.0
Lithuania	8.4	224.7	1,020.3	390.2	72.0	35.0
Moldova	4.2	98.0	1,276.0	789.0	327.0	30.0
Russia	5.6	92.7	1,353.0	896.0	303.0	190.0
Tajikistan	4.0	111.6	1,157.0	2,195.0	452.0	635.0
Turkmenistan	4.6	102.5	492.9	3,102.0	2,400.0	1,800.0
Ukraine	4.0	91.2	1,210.0	4,735.0	842.0	375.0
Uzbekistan	3.1	82.2	645.0	534.0	746.0	315.0
East Asia						
China	1.6	3.0	5.4	13.0	21.7	17.0
Mongolia	0.0	208.6	321.0	183.0	145.0	75.0
Vietnam	67.5	67.6	17.5	5.2	8.0	17.0

SOURCE: Adapted from the World Bank (1996, p. 174).

1996, p. 174). Although China and Vietnam also oscillated between boom and bust in growth and inflation, the magnitudes were relatively small compared with those in other transition economies.

In short, virtually all socialist countries initiated reforms and transitions in the past two decades. However, their chosen paths seemed to have been diametrically opposed, with dramatically different outcomes.

THE MARKET TRANSITION DEBATE

Why has China been able to reform in a partial, phased manner and still grow rapidly, whereas even Group 1 countries in CEE and the NIS have suffered huge declines in output and mounting inflation? These different outcomes in reforms and transitions have led to a vigorous market transition debate among scholars around the world, policymakers in transition economies from Beijing to Budapest, and foreign advisors from Bonn to Boston (Brada, 1993; Hoen, 1996; Naughton, 1995; Peck & Richardson, 1992; Szelenyi & Kostello, 1996; Williamson, 1995).

Big-bang advocates argued that life in the "economic emergency room" necessitates shock therapy in areas such as price liberalization and mass privatization (Lipton & Sachs, 1990; Sachs, 1993). Like a jump start for a dead car, this approach can at least trigger more gradual reforms (Grosfeld, 1995). Termed the "valley of tears" (Figure 2.1), this dramatic economic decline in countries treated with shock therapy has been attributed to the Schumpeterian "creative destruction" of old, moribund industries (Holzmann, Gacs, & Winckler, 1995). For example, "there is simply no reason why the economies of the Soviet Union should produce 80 percent more steel than the United States, as the Soviet Union was doing in the late 1980s" (Sachs, 1994, p. 508). Since some of the lost output consisted of goods no longer wanted, such as weaponry, "decline" in such output is not necessarily bad. In addition, official statistics may overstate the output decline in these economies. They largely fail to include output from informal and private sectors, whose growth provides a substantial cushion in some countries against the decline in the state sector (World Bank, 1996). For example, one study of private firms in Russia found that as much as 90% (!) of business activities of this sector were unreported (Sharma & Merrell, 1997). Moreover, the pain of the big bang may finally be over, at least for some countries that have had sustained and consistent reform

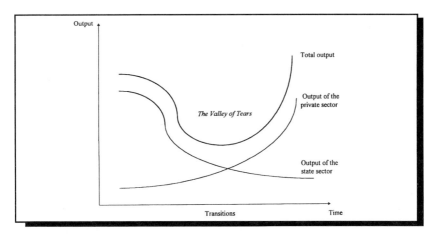

Figure 2.1. The "Valley of Tears" Due to Output Decline During the Transition

efforts (Lavigne, 1996; Layard & Parker, 1996). Shown in Figure 2.2, by 1995, while labor productivity continued to drop in Russia and Ukraine, it started to rebound in Bulgaria, Croatia, the Czech Republic, and Romania. More encouragingly, labor productivity was a third *higher* than prereform levels in Poland and Hungary (World Bank, 1996, pp. 18-20). Finally, it is important to note that the big-bang school has a clear political motivation for using rapid liberalization and privatization to dismantle the socialist state in CEE and the NIS as quickly and irreversibly as possible (Brada, 1995; Sachs, 1993).

On the other hand, the "gradualist" school was appalled by the profound social and economic costs of undergoing shock therapy (Chen, Jefferson, & Singh, 1992; Jowitt, 1991; Murrell & Wang, 1993; Overholt, 1993). Some scholars argued that what happened to CEE and the NIS might be "shock without therapy." Taking a more evolutionary approach (Nelson & Winter, 1982), these writers emphasized the Chinese experience of gradually "growing out of the plan," as opposed to literally "dropping the plan" (Naughton, 1994; Poznanski, 1995). With the outbreak of armed conflict in countries such as the former Yugoslavia and parts of the NIS, they suggested that dislocation, trauma, and uncertainty associated with the big bang can open the floodgates of disorder and chaos. Writing about the Russian transition, Islam (1993) reported that "most Russians feel that they are

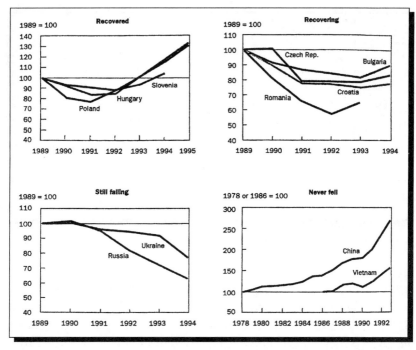

Figure 2.2. Industrial Labor Productivity in Selected Transition Economies
SOURCE: Adapted from the World Bank (1996, p. 20).

going from the zoo to the jungle" (p. 66). Basically, these authors argued that despite its socialist past, the state should not become weak or even vanish now; instead, it should remain strong in order to foster an orderly, phased transition toward a market economy by developing market-supporting institutions (Amsden, Kochanowicz, & Taylor, 1994; Fischer & Gelb, 1991). In the absence of market-supporting institutions such as a property-rights-based legal, regulatory, and financial framework, big-bang style privatization would only lead to chaos.

A third group of writers asked: How big is a "big bang" (Brada, 1993)? In the case of China, the 1978 decision to embark on reforms can be regarded as a big bang. Harding (1987), for example, called these reforms China's second *revolution*, which, almost by definition, qualifies as a big bang. Before 1989, China was widely regarded as the most radical reforming socialist country. Only since 1989 has it lost such a

TABLE 2.5 Russia and China: Two Very Different Countries				
	Russia		China	
Indicators	1990	1994	1978	1994
Sectoral employment structure (%)				
Industry	42	38	15	18
Agriculture	13	15	71	58
Services	45	47	14	25
Total	100	100	100	100
Employment in the state sector (%)	90	44	19	18
GDP per capita (US$)				
From *World Bank Atlas*	4,110	2,650	404	530
At purchasing power parity (PPP)	6,440	4,610	1,000	2,510

SOURCE: Adapted from the World Bank (1996, p. 21).

distinction. For countries in CEE and the NIS, "dramatic first steps may be necessary but will hardly suffice to succeed" (van Brabant, 1995, p. 179). Since the transition process always involves a combination of major steps and incremental changes (Peng, 1994), the big bang versus gradualism debate seems to be fundamentally flawed. The debate, according to van Brabant (1995), may simply have become "a waste of energy" and "a pointless exercise in semantics" (p. 179).

One way to understand the differences in reform policies and transition outcomes is to adopt an evolutionary or "path-dependent" perspective, recognizing that these countries are bounded by their initial conditions at the outset of reforms (Nelson & Winter, 1982; Poznanski, 1995). Comparing Russia and China illustrates this perspective (Naughton, 1995; Nolan, 1995). Shown in Table 2.5, when their transitions began, Russia had an economy far more developed than China's, with per capita income more than six times higher ($6,440 in Russia in 1990 vs. $1,000 in China in 1978, using 1983 U.S. dollars at purchasing power parity; World Bank, 1996, p. 21). More than 90% of the Russian workforce was employed in the state sector. The big bang unleashed in 1992 enormously shocked the economy. Shifting large numbers of people into new, nonstate firms and into formerly depressed sectors such as services required deep structural adjustment and painful retrenchment of the state sector. SOE employees and managers, on the other hand, demanded that the state continue to provide subsidies and keep firms afloat. The pain was intensified by the legacy of decades of central planning that had resulted in extreme regional specialization, with many one-company towns leading to few local employment alternatives. Decision making was highly centralized and controlled by the bureaucrats in Moscow. In such an economy, there simply was not a whole lot of room to reform and grow incrementally.

At the outset of its reforms, China had a largely agricultural economy, with 71% of employment in that sector. Poor infrastructure and an emphasis on local self-sufficiency led to a low level of regional specialization and large numbers of small and medium-sized "collective" firms owned by local governments (Byrd & Lin, 1989; Walder, 1995). The economy was far less centrally planned and administered than the Soviet economy (Huang, 1996). As a first major step, liberalizing agriculture through decollectivization led to immediate payoffs, largely because of improved incentives on the part of farmers (Choe, 1996). As a result, agriculture experienced on average 10% annual growth between 1981 and 1984, which allowed for the reallocation of surplus agricultural labor to new rural collective firms. These firms created 100 million new jobs between 1978 and 1994, and greatly stimulated competition and growth. Since SOEs in China had generally lackluster performance, and nearly half of them were in the red at the outset of the 1990s (Peng, 1997a), much of China's growth has been fueled by the growth of the collective firms, which contributed more than 40% of the total industrial output by 1996 (State Statistical Bureau, 1997, p. 411). In sum, compared with Russia's industrial economy, China started its reforms largely as an agrarian economy with a far greater scope for reallocating labor to collective industries, which resulted in rapid industrialization and, hence, growth.

As this comparison illustrates, differences in initial conditions and structural characteristics can explain a great deal of the divergence of transition policies and outcomes across countries. Given the path-dependent nature of different countries' development, reform policies must recognize the differences in initial conditions; they cannot simply be transplanted between dramatically different countries such as Russia and China (Winiecki, 1995; Wu & Reynolds, 1988). In the final analysis, reform policy choices also boil down to leaders' political will in terms of how far they are willing to break away from state socialism. Radical reformers interested in getting completely rid of the yoke of socialism, whether the classical or "reformed" version, would naturally be more likely to choose the big bang, whereas hesitant leaders interested in "reforming" state socialism would be unlikely to entertain the big-bang approach. In the end, given the differences in initial conditions and political will, the market transition debate in search of a "best" way has remained largely inconclusive.

A STRATEGIC MANAGEMENT PERSPECTIVE

A New Perspective

Given the *firm-level* emphasis of this book focusing on business strategies, I do not intend to participate from any particular side in the market transition debate, which is mostly concerned with *state-level* strategies and policies. However, a new strategic management perspective can help us understand the essence of this debate and allow us to bypass its current deadlock.

On the basis of the difference drawn between intended and emergent strategies discussed in Chapter 1, we can suggest that the big-bang approach stems from a belief in the top-down, *intended strategies* crafted by determined reformers such as Havel and Yeltsin, who had a clear vision of what they intended to achieve. Their goals are a complete break from state socialism and a whole-hearted embrace of free-market principles and democratic values. The gradualist approach, on the other hand, reflects *emergent strategies* employed by cautious leaders such as Deng and Gorbachev, who knew the general direction but were unable to articulate clearly an overall vision. As a result, emergent strategies have to entail a stronger willingness to allow local experiments to emerge from the "bottom up,"[6] to entertain a higher degree of ambiguity, and to tolerate a stronger propensity to move back and forth (Fischer & Gelb, 1991).

Recent authors in strategic management unanimously acknowledged the existence and merits of *both* intended and emergent strategies (Barney, 1997; Besanko, Dranove, & Shanley, 1996; Grant, 1991; Hill & Jones, 1998; Hitt, Ireland, & Hoskisson, 1997; Mintzberg, 1989). Even in countries such as Poland and Russia, which have adopted an intended big-bang approach such as a centralized program for rapid privatization, emergent strategies such as "spontaneous" privatization (i.e., managers and employees take SOE assets into their own hands in the absence of official sanction) have been widespread. On the other hand, countries such as China and Vietnam have also featured a number of intended top-down strategies that complement grassroots, emergent reform activities. Taken together, there is always a combination of both intended and emergent strategies. Janos Kornai (1995), from Hungary, the best-known East European economist and a strong advocate of a more direct approach in transitions, in his book titled *Highways and Byways*, highlighted exactly the same point:

> Let us assume that the destination is now clear, at least for the ruling parties and government in some particular country or other. Even then, there is still no map of any kind showing the route taken by the road that leads to it. Only from the height [altitude] of a spaceship can the "first road" appear to be a single vast route. From the height [altitude] of a helicopter it can clearly be seen that it consists of numerous greater or lesser main roads and side roads, zigzagging paths, ascents and precipitous slopes. . . . Every highway and byway leads to capitalism eventually, of course, but precisely what kind do they lead to, how fast, at the cost of how many sacrifices, and with whom as the winners and whom as the losers? Each fork in the road poses a choice problem. So although most people accept and endorse the "main direction," there are innumerable dilemmas ahead. . . . Socialist transition, while representing a clear choice of the main road ahead . . . , nevertheless leaves the decisions on numerous subsequent problems still open. (pp. x-xi)

Echoing these insights on the coexistence of intended and emergent reform strategies, we suggest that, given the current deadlock of the market transition debate, more attention be directed toward more concrete and substantive areas of inquiry. Specifically, instead of focusing on state-level policies and strategies during the transition, a better focus will be a *firm-centered* perspective, concentrating on competitive strategies employed by domestic and foreign firms in transition economies. This book is dedicated to such a task.

Advantages of the New Perspective

Compared with the state-centered approach, there are three principal advantages associated with this firm-centered perspective. First, a firm-centered approach concentrates on the *dependent variable* of state-level policies, which is how to stimulate the growth of competitive firms that in turn will drive the growth of the economy (Culpan & Kumar, 1995). Since all reform policies, whether through a big bang, gradualism, or a combination of both, aim at improving the performance of the economy, adequate attention to how individual firms strategically respond to these environmental changes is important and so far has been largely underexplored in the literature on market transitions (Peng, 1994, 1997a; Peng & Heath, 1996).

Second, in all transition economies, the state has become weak, compared with the heyday of state socialism (Amsden et al., 1994). Although the state is still influential, continued reliance on a state-centered approach may ignore a vast array of social, economic, and organizational dynamics that accompany the transition process (Nee & Matthews, 1996; Stark, 1992, 1996). Even before the transition, many individuals and organizations took on a life of their own, with little interference from the state (Allmendinger & Hackman, 1996; Nee & Stark, 1989; Shlapentokh, 1989). During the transitional era, how these economic players react and respond to a weakened state and environmental turbulence deserves more attention.

Finally, a firm-centered approach connects state-level policies such as liberalization and privatization with individual-level managerial decisions such as restructuring and networking, thus creating a critical macro-micro link that is often missing in social science research (Peng, Buck, & Filatotchev, 1999). A strategic management perspective focusing on strategies and strategists allows for such an integration (Peng & Luo, 1998, 1999).

In sum, as a part of the expansion of strategy frameworks (Marcus, Goodman, & Grazman, 1995), a strategic management perspective is adopted throughout the book. Compared with much of the market transition debate concentrating on state-level policies and strategies, this firm-level focus has a number of unique advantages and insights rarely seen in the literature.

CONCLUSIONS

For students, scholars, and practitioners of strategic management, it is important to understand the nature of classical state socialism, its failures and problems, the current transitions and their outcomes, as well as the debate surrounding these issues. The experience of Frank Russell Company, contemplating how to invest in these economies (Strategy in Action 2.1), can serve as a case in point here. Drawn from the historical excursion in this chapter, this background provides the critical environment in which opportunities and threats arise to confront strategic managers of the firm. It is in such an environment that business strategies are formulated and implemented in transition economies.

Strategy in Action 2.1

Frank Russell Company Eyes Transition Economies

Headquartered in Tacoma, Washington, Frank Russell Company is a large pension fund consulting and management company that employs 1,000 associates and maintains offices in London, New York, Sydney, Tokyo, Toronto, and Zurich. At the outset of the 1990s, it served more than 200 corporate clients in 16 countries with combined assets of more than $400 billion. A pioneer in the professionalization of pension fund management in the United States and abroad, the company focused on three areas: institutional consulting, investment management, and data services. The direction for future growth that Chairman George Russell envisioned was to bring pension fund investors to what he called the "unknown markets" in China, CEE, and the NIS. Toward that end, in 1990 George Russell organized a strategic alliance called the Russell 20-20 Group, consisting of 20 money management firms and 20 major pension funds, most of which were clients of Frank Russell Company, such as ARCO, AT&T, Boeing, BP America, Caterpillar, General Electric, General Motors, IBM, and Xerox. Collectively, the Group represented $500 billion in assets. The mission of the Russell 20-20 Group was to organize and take advantage of its collective resources in search of investment opportunities in these transition economies. In 1992 and 1993, members of the Russell 20-20 Group formed a delegation to visit China, Czechoslovakia, and Poland.

Compared with other forms of investment, pension fund investments are among the most conservative, because pensions are the lifeblood of a company's retirees. The Employee Retirement Income Security Act (ERISA) required that any investment by pension plans be made in a prudent manner and only after a maximum level of "due diligence" (verification conducted to ensure that all risks have been considered and the chance of losing the investment is minimal) has been carried out. The conservative criteria for pension investment in any country, therefore, would include (a) a stable monetary system; (b) free market pricing of goods, services, and foreign exchange; (c) predominantly private ownership of property; (d) existence of relatively independent and incorrupt fiduciary, bureaucracy, and police forces; and (e) the rule of law. In the early 1990s, however, none of the transition economies met these criteria. "We can wait for these criteria to appear," argued George Russell, "but if we do, the exceptionally high returns in these markets will have been earned by other investors." After much deliberation, a more realistic set of investment criteria was agreed upon by the Russell 20-20 Group, including (a) the presence of a Western partner; (b) a sound monetary system; (c) privatization in play and found acceptable; (d) acceptable tax rates; and (e) reasonable free trade policies. As a result, the first-ever major investment to CEE from the U.S. pension pool was made by seven members of the Russell 20-20 Group, which invested $50 million in the newly created Polish Private Equity Fund to assist private enterprises in Poland. George Russell hoped that as transition economies become more "normal," his company would eventually have an office in Beijing, one in Moscow, and another one in Warsaw, Prague, or Budapest.

SOURCES: Author's own interviews and company documents.

NOTES

1. The "commanding heights" metaphor was coined by Lenin and cited by Kornai (1992, p. 71). SOEs also exist in a large number of nonsocialist countries; however, they usually do not occupy such "commanding heights" in the economy. As a result, they will not be dealt with in detail here. Interested readers can consult Aharoni (1986), Hafsi, Kiggundu, and Jorgensen (1987), Kole and Mullherin (1997), Lioukas, Bourantas, and Papadakis (1993), Mazzolini, (1980), Ramamurti (1987), and Zif (1981).

2. This figure excludes exports among members of the Council for Mutual Economic Assistance (CMEA), which was a common market of socialist countries set up in 1949 and dissolved in 1991. Its members in 1990 were Bulgaria, Cuba, Czechoslovakia, East Germany, Hungary, Mongolia, Poland, Romania, the Soviet Union, and Vietnam.

3. The statistics for car ownership in China were more embarrassing. In 1980, there was one car for every 25,000 people. In 1984, the ratio dropped to one car for every 11,000 people. By 1997, there was one car for every 286 people (Eric Harwit, personal communication, April 1998, updating his work in Harwit, 1995).

4. In the language of agency theory, owners are principals and employees are agents. Although principals have to rely on agents to achieve certain tasks, principals and agents have a fundamental conflict of interest (Jensen & Meckling, 1976). To ask managers and employees to act "like proprietors" is basically asking agents to act like principals, which is doomed to failure. These issues will be explored in more depth in Chapters 4 and 5.

5. The World Bank in its *World Development Report* (1996, pp. 13-14) divided CEE countries, the NIS, and Mongolia into four groups. In addition to Group 1, there were Group 2 (Albania, Bulgaria, Estonia, Latvia, Lithuania, Mongolia, and Romania), Group 3 (Armenia, Georgia, Kazakstan, Kyrgyz, Moldova, and Russia), and Group 4 (Azerbaijan, Belarus, Tajikistan, Turkmenistan, Ukraine, and Uzbekistan), in descending order of market liberalization in the period from 1989 to 1995.

6. A well-known example of local decisions and experiments leading to an emergent reform strategy was the practice of small-scale decollectivization of agricultural communes in Sichuan province of China with the blessing of governor Zhao Ziyang in the late 1970s. When agricultural performance improved substantially in that province, Deng Xiaoping and other national leaders took notice, and adopted and diffused this practice throughout the rest of the country, launching the first major wave of post-Mao reforms (Zhao, 1997).

3 Institutions, Organizations, and Strategic Choices

Both what organizations come into existence and how they evolve are fundamentally influenced by the institutional framework. In turn, they influence how the institutional framework evolves.

—*Douglass C. North (1990, p. 5)*

Much of our knowledge about business strategies comes from research on Western firms. According to a competition-based view originating in industrial economics, a firm is usually portrayed as a profit maximizer that competes with others in the industry, erects entry barriers, and bargains hard with suppliers and buyers (Porter, 1980). Another perspective, called the resource-based view, suggests that a firm can be considered as a collection of technological, financial, and organizational resources (Penrose, 1959). Business strategies, thus, entail acquiring and deploying these resources in a way that is value-adding, unique, and difficult for competitors to imitate (Barney, 1991). Recently, such competition- and resource-based views on strategy have been challenged by scholars who argue that, in addition to focusing on competition and managing its resources, a firm also needs to take into account broader influences from such sources as the state, society, and culture when crafting and implementing its strategies (Oliver, 1997; Powell & DiMaggio, 1991). These influences are broadly considered as institutional frameworks.

Since no firm can be immune to the institutional frameworks in which it is embedded (Granovetter, 1985), this view can certainly be applied to firms in the West. Moreover, it may have even stronger validity for firms in transition economies, which are more susceptible to institutional influences and institutional changes (Child, 1994; Grancelli, 1995; Li, 1996; Lu, 1996; Peng & Heath, 1996; Shenkar & von Glinow, 1994; Tsoukas, 1994). Therefore, this chapter first introduces an institutional perspective on business strategy.[1] In the second part of this chapter, we will use an example of growth strategies of the firm to illustrate how this institutional perspective helps shed light on business strategies in transition economies.

INSTITUTIONS AND ORGANIZATIONS

According to Douglass North (1990), the 1993 Nobel laureate in economics, *institutions* are "the rules of the game in a society or, more formally, are the humanly devised constraints that shape human interaction" (p. 3). Examples include laws, regulations, cultures, and norms. As a result, institutions assert themselves in the political, social, and economic aspects of a society (DiMaggio & Powell, 1983; Scott, 1995). Institutions are important because they provide a structure for everyday life by defining and limiting the set of choices of individuals and organizations. Consequently, an *institutional framework* is defined by Davis and North (1971) as: "the set of fundamental political, social, and legal ground rules that establishes the basis for production, exchange, and distribution" (p. 6). This framework is made up of both formal and informal constraints around individual and organizational behavior (North, 1990). *Formal constraints* include political rules, judicial decisions, and economic contracts. *Informal constraints*, on the other hand, include socially sanctioned codes of conduct and norms of behavior, which are embedded in culture and ideology. North (1990) suggested that in situations where formal constraints fail, informal constraints will come into play to reduce uncertainty and provide constancy to individuals and organizations.

Institutional frameworks interact with both individuals and organizations. They influence individuals' decision making by signaling which choices are acceptable and determining which norms and behaviors are socialized in a given society (Powell & DiMaggio, 1991). Institutional frameworks also affect the actions of organizations by constraining which actions are acceptable and supportable within the framework (Aldrich & Fiol, 1994). In a nutshell, institutions help reduce uncertainty for individuals and organizations as they interact with each other.

Why is it so important to reduce uncertainty? Two underlying reasons emerge. First, there can be many sources of uncertainty that can be potentially devastating. Political changes may render long-range planning by individuals and companies obsolete; failure to perform transactions as spelled out in contracts may result in economic losses. Second, when confronting uncertainty, individuals prefer to have better control over their lives, and organizations such as business firms prefer to minimize surprises in their transactions with other parties (Pfeffer & Salancik, 1978). Economic transactions can be costly, complex, and difficult, thus leading to the term *transaction costs.* Oliver Williamson (1985), a guru on transaction cost theory, used a metaphor to define transaction costs:[2]

> In mechanical systems we look for frictions: Do the gears mesh, are the parts lubricated, is there needless slippage or other loss of energy? The economic counterpart of friction is transaction cost: Do the parties to exchange operate harmoniously, or are there frequent misunderstandings and conflicts that lead to delays, breakdowns, and other malfunctions? (pp. 1-2)

Just as all physical interfaces involve friction forces, all economic transactions entail costs. An important source of these costs is *opportunism,* defined as "self-interest seeking with guile" (Williamson, 1996, p. 378). Examples include misleading, cheating, and confusing other parties in a transaction, which may create a great deal of uncertainty, anxiety, and surprise (Chen, Peng, & Saparito, 1999). Since transaction costs are nontrivial, economic organizations will try to employ strategies that minimize these costs (Williamson, 1975, 1985). Attempting to reduce these transaction costs, institutional frameworks serve to facilitate certainty-enhancing strategies by spelling out *the rules of the game* so that deviations (e.g., contract disputes) can be mitigated with relative ease (e.g., via arbitration or courts in the case of contract disputes). In other words, institutional frameworks can provide important strategic planning assumptions for firms contemplating their moves in the "game" of economic competition (Murtha & Lenway, 1994). Without these frameworks, transaction costs may become prohibitively high, to the extent that certain transactions simply would not take place (North, 1990).

Interactions between institutions and organizations that reduce transaction costs shape economic activity. As a result, any analysis of firm behavior, such as strategy, "must take into account the nature of institutional framework" (Peng & Heath, 1996, p. 500).

AN INSTITUTIONAL PERSPECTIVE ON BUSINESS STRATEGY

Strategies are about choices, which are made by strategists. Therefore, an analysis of business strategies needs to "recognize the exercise of choice by organizational decision makers" (Child, 1972, p. 10). Given the influence of institutional frameworks on firm behavior, any strategic choice that firms make is inherently affected by the formal and informal constraints of a given institutional framework (North, 1990; Oliver, 1991, 1997). Viewed with this perspective, much of the strategy literature, which largely focuses on Western firms, does not discuss the specific relationship between strategic choices and institutional frameworks. To be sure, the influence of the "environment" has been featured in the literature since the 1970s (Aldrich, 1979; Hannan & Freeman, 1989; Lawrence & Lorsch, 1969; Pfeffer & Salancik, 1978). However, what has dominated this research is a "task environment" view that focuses on economic variables such as market demand and technological change. Until recently, scholars have rarely looked beyond the task environment to explore the interaction among institutions, organizations, and strategic choices (Scott, 1995). In-

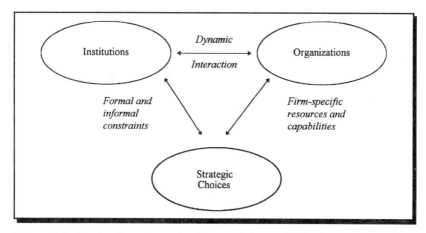

Figure 3.1. Institutions, Organizations, and Strategic Choices

stead, a market-based institutional framework has been taken for granted by most writers.

Such neglect is unfortunate, because strategic choices are selected within, and constrained by, institutional frameworks. It is precisely such institutional frameworks that have prompted Western firms to choose certain strategies and constrained them from choosing others (Hillman & Keim, 1995). "Today," wrote John Child (1997, p. 54), one of the most influential writers on strategic choice, "we are much more conscious of" the importance of the relationships between organizations and institutions. An institutional perspective on business strategy, therefore, focuses on the dynamic interaction between institutions and organizations, and considers strategic choices as the outcome of such an interaction (Figure 3.1). Specifically, strategic choices are not only driven by firm-specific resources and capabilities that traditional strategy research emphasizes (Barney, 1991; Porter, 1980), but are also a reflection of the formal and informal constraints of a particular institutional framework that decision makers confront (North, 1990; Oliver, 1997; Scott, 1995).

By the 1990s, more and more scholars had come to realize that institutions matter (Powell & DiMaggio, 1991; Scott, 1995; Williamson, 1996). While taking institutions seriously is only a first step, working out the analytic logic of their influence is the second, and explicating the underlying mechanisms comes next (Williamson, 1995, p. 193). As a result, scholars have become increasingly interested in exploring "how they [institutions] matter, under what circumstances, to what extent, and in what ways" (Powell, 1996, p. 297). This book can be considered as a part of this broad intellectual movement in search of a better understanding of the relationship among institutions, organizations, and strategic choices.

Given that "economic (and political) models are specific to particular constellations of institutional constraints that vary radically . . . in different economies" (North, 1990, p. 110), seeking universal "laws" that have validity in all countries is probably doomed to failure (Cheng, 1994; Numagami, 1998; Rosenzweig, 1994). I have a more modest goal here, namely, attempting to probe into the workings of business strategies in a given context, transition economies. Therefore, I turn to the institutional frameworks in these countries in the next section.

INSTITUTIONAL FRAMEWORKS IN TRANSITION ECONOMIES

Given the multidimensional nature of institutional frameworks, a complete description is beyond the scope of this discussion. I will focus only on those formal and informal constraints before and during the transition that have a bearing on business strategies in these economies (see Table 3.1 for an overview).

Formal Constraints Before and During the Transitions

As described in Chapter 2, the most fundamental features of planned economies before the transitions were the use of central economic planning and bureaucratic control. These two areas constituted the primary formal constraints that managers had to confront. Given the overwhelming effect on firm behavior asserted by the planning regime, managers had neither the need nor the incentive to "strategize" in order to compete (Kornai, 1992). Indeed, the notion of "competitive strategies" was very alien to them.

TABLE 3.1 Institutional Frameworks in Transition Economies: Primary Formal and Informal Constraints

	Before the Transition	*During the Transition*
Formal constraints	Central planning regime	Lack of credible legal framework
	Bureaucratic control	Lack of stable political structure
		Lack of strategic factor markets
Informal constraints	Networks and personalized exchanges	Networks and personalized exchanges

During the transition, fundamental changes in the institutional framework have occurred in these countries, which, in turn, have directly affected business strategies. The most notable change in formal constraints has been the gradual dismantling of the central planing regime, which has been replaced by more market transactions. In other words, formal constraints from the planning regime have been weakened. At the same time, however, the necessary formal constraints of a market-based economy, especially a well-defined property-rights-based legal framework, have also been lacking (Clarke, 1991; Kirby, 1995; Litwack, 1991). *Property rights* are "the rights individuals appropriate over their own labor and the goods and services they possess" (North, 1990, p. 33). As a prerequisite for markets to function smoothly and to reduce transaction costs, a property-rights-based legal framework enforced by the state brings the costs of transacting through markets under control (North, 1990). According to the World Bank (1985), "a decentralized market economy cannot function properly without a comprehensive system of commercial laws" (p. 10), because the lack of such a legal framework would lead to high transaction costs (Boisot & Child, 1988; "The Pirates of Prague," 1996).

In the past, planned economies were ruled by power relations and bureaucratic controls. The state policed firms through its bureaucratic controls to curb opportunism and allocate resources, albeit inefficiently. With plenty of bureaucratic regulations, there was little need for formal laws to define exchange relationships among economic actors. During the transition, as the state gradually relinquishes its role in policing economic exchanges, SOEs are granted more and more autonomy, and the government increasingly tolerates more private firms outside the state sector. Increased exchanges among autonomous economic units call for an adequate legal framework that enforces property rights. The establishment of such a formal framework takes a long time, however, and transition economies all lack the capacity to build a legal infrastructure rapidly. Worse yet, given the weakened capacity of the state, even if some laws come into effect, whether they will be vigorously enforced is another matter (Amsden, Kochanowicz, & Taylor, 1994; Davies, 1995; World Bank, 1997b). According to Peter Murrell (1996), an influential scholar on transition economies:

> The quality of laws is quite low, in many cases lacking internal consistency and completeness. Moreover, these laws are often a facade without foundation. Missing are the appropriately structured agencies, effective courts, the customary practice of enforcing private rights, the professionals, the scholarly and judicial opinion, and the web of ancillary institutions that give substance to written law. In the large majority of [transitional] countries, especially in the former USSR, it will take a generation, or more, for the legal system to buttress capitalism in a manner imagined by the drafters of the many new laws. Although these laws are beginning to affect behavior, they are presently of no more than marginal significance. (p. 34)

The lack of such a legal framework has resulted in a sharp rise in opportunistic behavior, such as managers and employees taking SOE assets into their own hands through "spontaneous" privatization at the expense of the public, and officials seeking rents in the form of bribery when performing their normal tasks. Put another way, "an economy transitioning toward market-based measures without an adequate legal framework is a place for opportunism, and transaction costs are bound to be high" (Peng & Heath, 1996, p. 503).

In addition, the lack of legal framework is also accompanied by the lack of political certainty in these countries. Such a lack of credible, irreversible commitment to market institutions leads to a great deal of ups and downs similar to a roller-coaster ride (McCarthy, Puffer, & Simmonds, 1993). In China, where the Communist Party still holds power, the reform process has been characterized by years of political liberalization and then reaction, the most notable case being the setback in June 1989. Such fluctuations in the political arena have generated a lot of uncertainty for the business community, which generally prefers the opposite (Murtha & Lenway, 1994). For example, Chinese managers reported in a survey that among eight environmental factors that have an impact on firm performance, they perceived the state regulatory regime to be the most influential, most complex, and least predictable (Tan & Litschert, 1994). As a result, they often have to maintain a "disproportionately greater contact" with government officials in order to reduce such uncertainty (Child, 1994, p. 154). Managers whose access to government officials is limited may be surprised by what the government does. For instance, in April 1998, without public discussion or consultation, the Chinese government suddenly announced a ban on direct marketing activities, despite nearly $200 million invested by American firms such as Amway, Avon, and Mary Kay, and an estimated involvement of 20 million Chinese agents ("Ultimatum for the Avon Lady," 1998).

The same is true in CEE and the NIS (see Table 3.2), where 68% and 79%, respectively, of the surveyed executives expressed dissatisfaction with unpredictable changes in laws and policies, the highest among 3,600 firms in 69 countries surveyed in 1996 (World Bank, 1997b, p. 35). With so much uncertainty, it is not surprising that managers in CEE and the NIS have to devote a large portion of their time to negotiating with the government. The same survey conducted by the World Bank (1997b, p. 43) found that 31% and 52% of firms in CEE and the NIS, respectively, have to devote more than 15% of managers' time to negotiating with officials. In comparison, only 10% of the firms in high-income OECD countries have to spend more than 15% of managers' time to deal with the government. Similar to the findings of Tan and Litschert (1994) in China, Elenkov (1997) reported that the political and regulatory sector commands the highest level of attention among managers in Bulgaria. Overall, it is safe to conclude that the political structure in transition economies is not conducive to reducing uncertainty, thus further increasing transaction cost problems for firms attempting to navigate such turbulent waters.

TABLE 3.2 Dealing With Formal Institutional Constraints:
A Global Comparison

	Percentage of Respondents Dissatisfied With Unpredictable Changes in Laws and Policies	Percentage of Firms Devoting More Than 15% of Managers' Time to Negotiating With the Government
Central and Eastern Europe	68	31
Newly Independent States (former Soviet Union)	79	52
High-income OECD[a]	33	10
Latin America and Caribbean	60	38
Middle East and North Africa	49	38
Sub-Sahara Africa	60	37
South and Southeast Asia	28	25

SOURCE: Adapted from the World Bank (1997b, pp. 35, 43) based on a global survey of more than 3,600 firms in 69 countries conducted in 1996.
NOTE: a. Organization for Economic Co-operation and Development.

Relatedly, the lack of an adequate legal framework and the lack of a stable political structure have resulted in the underdevelopment of "strategic factor markets," such as financial markets that would ensure the proper transfer of ownership (Barney, 1986). Because "price-making [strategic factor] markets require well-defined and enforced property rights" (North, 1981, p. 42), such strategic factor markets are one of the most important preconditions for both the successful sale of state assets and the independent development of private firms (Rapaczynski, 1996). Without the development of these markets, the route of economic transitions is bound to be treacherous (Frye, 1997; Gordon & Rittenberg, 1995; Kumar, 1997; Meszaros, 1993; Xia, Lin, & Grub, 1992).

In sum, while the primary formal constraints in socialist economies consisted of central planning and bureaucratic control, changing formal constraints in these economies have had three mutually reinforcing characteristics: (a) lack of a credible, property-rights-based legal framework, (b) lack of a stable political structure, and (c) lack of strategic factor markets. Overall, these formal constraints are characterized by extreme volatility and unpredictability, which, as will be shown later, have a strong bearing on business strategies in transition economies.

Informal Constraints Before and During the Transitions

North (1990) noted that "although formal rules may change overnight as the result of political and judicial decisions, informal constraints embodied in customs, traditions, and codes of conduct are much more impervious to deliberate policies" (p. 6). As discussed earlier, during the transition, while previous formal constraints (i.e., the planning regime and bureaucratic control) have been weakened, the formal constraints for a market-based economy (i.e., legal framework, political stability, and strategic factor markets) have also been lacking. As a result, "informal constraints rise to play a *larger* role in regulating economic exchanges in these countries during the transition, and have considerable influence over both the behavior of individual managers and their firms, as well as the generation of new formal constraints" (Peng & Heath, 1996, p. 504).

The main informal constraints come from the network contacts that were extensively used to coordinate economic activity before the transition (Peng, 1994). For example, "virtually every Soviet enterprise has an employee who works as an 'expeditor' (*tolkach* [Russian]), whose primary responsibility is to establish long-run personal relationships with other organizations for the purpose of procuring needed supplies, particularly in emergency circumstances" (Litwack, 1991, p. 88). Not surprisingly, these "expediters" tend to be great vodka drinkers! Vertical relationships between superiors and subordinates and those between planners and enterprise managers also tended to be highly personal and to involve extensive bargaining (Child, 1994; Lu, 1996; Rona-Tas, 1994). Many managers commonly gave large gifts to superiors in the ministries and party apparatus (Berliner, 1988; Grossman, 1977; Shlapentokh, 1989). These gifts are generally not bribes in the sense of being a direct exchange for specific goods and services at one moment in time; rather they are an investment in a long-term personal relationship (Peng & Luo, 1999; Xin & Pearce, 1996).

Of course, these networks predated the transitions in recent decades (Berliner, 1988; Carroll, Goodstein, & Gyenes, 1988; Nee & Stark, 1989). During the transition, preexisting networks of affiliation are activated, and network ties become much more important as informal constraints to reinforce previous ties (Johnson, 1997; Sedaitis, 1998). The propensity for using networks and personalized exchanges certainly depends on the cultural embeddedness of such practices (Granovetter, 1985; Hofstede, 1991). One might argue that, in China, such practices may be more widespread because of that country's Confucian tradition of collectivism (Earley, 1993; Tsui & Farh, 1997). However, the notion of collectivism is not limited to China. Collectivism has also been empirically found among workers in the former Yugoslavia, the only Eastern European country in Hofstede's (1980) global survey. These Yugoslav employees were found to exhibit a high level of collectivism, similar to that in two Chinese societies, Hong Kong and Taiwan. Anecdotal evidence in CEE and the NIS suggested that the level of collectivism in these countries may be higher than that in the more individualistic West (Davis, 1996; Puffer, 1992, 1994; Whitley, Henderson, Czaban, & Lengyel, 1996). For example, Gennday Zyuganov (1996), a presidential candidate in Russia, wrote that "Russians associate the word 'communist' with traditional concepts of community that are deeply rooted in Russian Orthodoxy and the national mentality" (p. 36).

In addition to such *cultural* influences on the propensity to use network contacts to get things done, *institutional* imperatives of a Soviet-type economy moving toward a more market-driven society, especially the lack of a legal infrastructure discussed earlier, may also necessitate the widespread activation of, and extensive reliance on, personalized, network-based exchanges (Peng, 1997a). In the absence of formal market-supporting institutions, many managers find it necessary to take into their own hands such matters as seeking information, obtaining finance, interpreting regulations, and enforcing contracts (Khanna & Palepu, 1997). In other words, although arising from different cultures, "the notions of *blat* (connections) and *mir* (collective) in Russia are perhaps as important as *guanxi* (connections) in China" (Peng & Heath, 1996, p. 505).

In brief, a great deal of network-based, personalized exchanges can be found in these economies both before and during the transitions. Reducing uncertainties in economic exchanges during an extremely volatile period, they constitute an important part of the informal constraints that shape the emerging institutional frameworks. These *informal* constraints become more important during the transition because they offer some constancy and predictability in times of fundamental changes in the *formal* institutional frameworks.

Summary

In this section, the institutional frameworks in transition economies have been described, with a focus on formal and informal constraints. In addition, I have argued that, whereas formal constraints have changed from the central planning regime and bureaucratic controls to more market-based measures, the transition process has been volatile and uncertain, without an adequate legal framework, a stable political structure, and functioning strategic factor markets. On the other hand, informal constraints characterized by network-based personalized exchanges have continued to have a bearing on firm behavior—perhaps even more so during such times of flux. How these institutional frameworks interact with organizations to generate strategic choices during the transition will be dealt with in the next section.

STRATEGIC CHOICES FOR FIRM GROWTH: AN EXAMPLE

Business strategies can take many different forms. In this section, a particular set of strategies is highlighted as examples, namely, those centered on the growth of the firm. These strategies in transition economies, I believe, can best illustrate the institutional perspective that is focused on in this chapter (see Peng, 1994, 1997a, in press-a; Peng & Heath, 1996).

Three Strategic Choices for Firm Growth

How to lead the growth of the firm is a classical problem confronting organizational strategists (Penrose, 1959). Firm growth

TABLE 3.3 Strategic Choices for the Growth of the Firm

Strategic Choice	Mode of Organizing	Institutional Prerequisite
Generic expansion	Hierarchy (internal organization)	Capable managers
Mergers and acquisitions	Market	Functioning strategic markets
Interorganizational networks	Hybrid (neither hierarchy nor market)	Trust and mutual understanding
		Resource complementarity

SOURCES: Adapted from Peng (1997a, p. 388) and Peng and Heath (1996, p. 499).

can be measured in multiple ways, such as expansion of organizational size measured by assets and employment; increase in sales and profits; as well as generation of new activities and lines of products and services (Chandler, 1962; Greiner, 1972; Starbuck, 1965). An underlying reason behind the growth of the firm is that the firm, headed by its top managers, is motivated to grow (Penrose, 1959). Therefore, an understanding of the growth of the firm must start with the strategic choices made by top managers (Child, 1972, 1997). These strategies typically are (a) generic expansion, (b) mergers and acquisitions, and/or (c) developing network relationships (Table 3.3).

Given the resource-based perspective, which portrays the firm as a bundle of resources such as physical, financial, and organizational resources, firm growth can be viewed as an attempt by top managers to utilize fully the firm's resources (Penrose, 1959). At any given time there may be some idle resources, such as excess production capacity, uncommitted cash flows, and underemployed staff. The firm grows into new areas where the excess capacity in currently underutilized resources can be better utilized (Yip, 1982). The internally generated nature of such growth is thus called *generic expansion*. Apparently, there is a limit to such growth, since no firm is able to generate internally driven expansion indefinitely. The principal constraint on growth is the availability of capable, experienced managers to spearhead the expansion (Penrose, 1959).

A second growth strategy focuses on *mergers and acquisitions* (Haspeslagh & Jemison, 1991). The rationale is that as the firm grows larger, it will have more complex relationships with its suppliers, buyers, and other transaction parties. These complicated exchange relationships may cause transaction problems, such as contract disputes, thus leading to high transaction costs. As a result, it pays to acquire other firms in order to bring some of these relationships under control—hence the term "internalization" (Williamson, 1975, 1985). Yet for acquisitions to take place successfully, there must be efficient strategic factor markets, such as financial markets, so that firm ownership and associated property rights can be transferred smoothly (Jensen & Ruback, 1983). According to the transaction cost perspective, while a generic expansion strategy corresponds with the mode of "hierarchy" (or internal organization), acquisitions take place through the mode of "market" (Williamson, 1975, 1985).

A third strategy for growth centers on developing interorganizational relationships, or *networks*, with other firms (Powell, 1990). It reflects the focal firm's inability to possess all the necessary resources to undertake generic expansion alone or to acquire other firms. Rather, it represents the firm's efforts to gain access to complementary resources in other firms based on trust and mutual understanding between them (Jarillo, 1988, 1989). Overall, this interorganizational perspective focuses on a network-based, hybrid strategy of growth, which is "neither market nor hierarchy" (Hennart, 1993; Powell, 1990; Williamson, 1991).

In summary, firms typically choose one of these three strategies when they grow. How firms in transition economies achieve their growth will be dealt with in the next section.

Firm Growth in Transition Economies

Despite the ups and downs of the environment, some firms in transition economies have achieved stunning growth in recent years. According to the latest statistics published by *Business Week* ("Global 1000 and Top 200 Emerging Market Companies," 1998, pp. 81-84), Gazprom of Russia and China Telecom of China have become the first and third largest companies, measured by market capitalization ($32.9 billion and $20.7 billion, respectively), in emerging economies, which not only include all the transition economies covered in this book, but also countries such as Brazil, Mexico, South Korea, and Taiwan

TABLE 3.4 Ten Largest Companies (Measured by Capitalization) in Developed, Emerging, and Transition Economies (1998)		
Developed Economies (Nationality/ Capitalization*)	Emerging Economies (Nationality/ Capitalization*	Transition Economies (Nationality/ Capitalization*)
1. General Electric (USA $271.64)	1. Gozprom (Russia $32.91)	1. Gozprom (Russia $32.91)
2. Microsoft (USA $208.98)	2. Telebras (Brazil $32.76)	2. China Telecom (China $20.68)
3. Shell (Neth./UK $195.64)	3. China Telecom (China $20.68)	3. Unified Energy (Russia $7.59)
4. Coca-Cola (USA $193.53)	4. Telemex (Mexico $20.00)	4. Lukoil Holding (Russia $7.29)
5. Exxon (USA $172.50)	5. Eletrobras (Brazil $18.10)	5. Matav (Hungary $5.91)
6. Merck (USA $139.85)	6. Petrobras (Brazil $17.87)	6. SPT Telecom (Czech Rep. $4.14)
7. Pfizer (USA $133.03)	7. Taiwan Semiconductor (Taiwan $14.60)	7. Surgutneftegaz (Russia $2.73)
8. NTT (Japan $130.91)	8. Hellenic Telecom (Greece $13.33)	8. Yukos Holding (Russia $2.68)
9. Wal-Mart (USA $123.47)	9. Cathay Life Insurance (Taiwan $12.75)	9. Rostelekom (Russia $2.04)
10. Intel (USA $121.16)	10. Telesp (Brazil $12.26)	10. Mosenergo (Russia $1.73)

SOURCE: Adapted from "Global 1000 and Top 200 Emerging Market Companies," 1998.
*Market value in billions of U.S. dollars as of May 29, 1998.

(Table 3.4). These rankings would place Gazprom and China Telecom as the 115th and 197th largest firms, respectively, in the 1998 global ranking of companies in developed countries ("Global 1000," 1998).[3]

While not every company can grow to become a Gazprom or a China Telecom, it is evident that a lot of firms in transition economies have achieved strong growth. How, then, do they do it? More specifically: (a) Do firms in these economies have excess resources? (b) Do they grow through generic expansion or acquisitions? (c) Do they grow by developing interorganizational relationships? Drawing on recent research, we will systematically look for answers to these questions below.[4]

Excess Resources. A firm may not want to grow unless it possesses excess resources that are not fully utilized (Penrose, 1959). Despite the differences in firm size and ownership, firms usually have certain types of excess, slack resources. Specifically, SOEs, which tend to be larger, often have relatively strong technological capabilities, idle production capacity, and excess human resources—in other words, underutilized *tangible resources.* They are, however, weak on *intangible resources,* such as entrepreneurial drive and managerial talents. One intangible resource that SOEs do have in relative abundance is political support from the government, which hands out subsidies, credit guarantees, tax and loan write-offs, as well as grants a favorable hearing of their problems. We may call such an intangible resource an important "political resource" (Boddewyn & Brewer, 1994) or "institutional capital" (Oliver, 1997).

On the other hand, smaller private and collective enterprises are typically starved for tangible resources in areas such as finance, personnel, and production scale. However, their entrepreneurial drive, willingness to take risk, and market orientation more than compensate for their lack of tangible resources. As a result, they are eager to apply these intangible resources in new areas where they can generate stronger growth. Moreover, as they gradually grow larger and stronger and gain legitimacy, their size and scale grow, too, approaching those of the SOEs in some industries. Nevertheless, there is one crucial resource that private and collective firms cannot match with SOEs, namely, political support from the government.

In summary, although SOEs tend to have excess physical resources as well as an abundance of political support, private and collective firms usually possess strong intangible resources in search of better opportunities, but lack the level of political support that SOEs receive.

Generic Expansion or Acquisitions. Having established that there are certain excess, slack resources that can be utilized more productively in various types of firms, we move on to see whether they can grow by either generic expansion or acquisitions, the two traditional growth strategies. Each strategy has its institutional preconditions (see Table 3.3). A prerequisite for generic expansion is a staff of capable managers to help steer the growth process (Penrose, 1959). For firms in transition economies, the current lack of a large number of managers familiar with the workings of a market-based economy is one of the major challenges (Puffer, 1992, 1994; Sharma, 1993; Warner, 1992). In the case of *privatized* firms in Russia, while many former SOE managers are "muddling through" (McCarthy & Puffer, 1995, p. 67), replacing them with younger and better educated managers— who are presumably more adaptive and less influenced by the old way of SOE management—still does not necessarily lead to performance improvement (Peng, Buck, & Filatotchev, 1999). These findings, therefore, cast doubt on the capabilities of these "new" managers.

In the case of acquisitions, the firm not only needs to have excess resources and capable managers, but also has to operate in financial markets supported by a property-rights-based legal framework (Jensen & Ruback, 1983). Otherwise, no genuine acquisition can take place, except when the government orders financially healthy SOEs to take over failing ones ("The Next Hot Spot for M&A: Shanghai," 1995; Peng, 1997a). Despite the establishment of financial markets in such cities as Budapest, Prague, Moscow, Shanghai, and Warsaw since the early 1990s, the regulations tend to be "overlapping, repetitive, clumsy, ill-organized, and poorly-drafted" (Lau & Johnstone, 1995, p. 130; see also Frye, 1997). As a result, by and large, a strategy of mergers and acquisitions is not likely to be viable, at least initially. More recently, with the maturing of strategic factor markets and the emergence of a fledgling legal framework throughout transition economies, mergers and acquisitions have been reported (Capener, 1996; Johnson, 1997; Peng, Luo, & Sun, 1999). However, the government is still extensively involved, and genuine mergers and acquisitions, according to the acquiring firms' strategic objectives, are not likely to take place on a large scale soon.

Developing Networks Through Boundary Blurring. Having largely been denied the routes of growth via generic expansion or acquisitions, many firms in transition economies have taken an alternative route, namely, forming enterprise groups, joint ventures, industry associations, and other forms of interfirm networks. These networks serve as *strategic alliances* for the firms involved, allowing them to pool resources, share technology, and invest in each other. Essentially, these are loosely structured networks blurring firm boundaries on the basis of trust and mutual understanding (Peng & Heath, 1996).

In business jargon, networking means knowing the "right people" and making connections to accomplish individual and organizational goals (Granovetter, 1973, 1985; Powell & Smith-Doerr, 1994). In the recent academic literature, networking is defined as an individual's attempt to mobilize personal contact in order to profit from entrepreneurial opportunities (Burt, 1992, 1997) and/or a firm's effort to cooperate with others in order to obtain and sustain competitive advantages (Jones, Hesterly, & Borgatti, 1997; Powell, 1990). A networking strategy allows firms to overcome the problem of not having enough resources to accommodate growth, by gaining access to complementary assets that are not directly acquired or owned (Jarillo, 1988, 1989). Essentially, *interpersonal* relationships cultivated among top managers are translated into *interorganizational* networks among the firms they lead (Peng, 1997a; Peng & Luo, 1999).

Why do different types of firms converge on such a network-based strategy for growth? For larger SOEs seeking growth, networking with smaller private and collective firms enables the SOEs to lease out certain excess capacity to the more entrepreneurial firms, but avoid the politically sensitive task of ownership transfer (see Strategy in Action 3.1 for an example). For smaller firms, teaming with larger SOEs not only leads to access to a larger asset base, but also results in sharing some of the political support that SOEs have as long as SOEs remain as the nominal "heads" of these networks (see Strategy in Action 3.2 for an illustration). Note that these networking strategies are not limited to domestic firms within a given country. The rise of joint ventures between domestic and foreign firms is also an important facet of a network-based strategy at work, because joint ventures are a specific form of strategic alliance (Peng & Heath, 1996, pp. 518-519). Local firms are interested in the technology, capital, and management expertise that foreign firms bring, all of which are typically not available domestically (Hooley, Cox, Shipley, & Fahy, 1996; Lyles & Salk, 1996; Shenkar & Li, in press). Foreign firms, on the other hand, lack the critical resources to succeed in these new markets, such as knowledge about the host country, contacts with the government, and an ability to handle the local workforce (Inkpen & Beamish, 1997). As a result, joint ventures allow both sides to tap into each other's complementary resources while achieving joint growth (Kogut, 1988; Luo, 1997; Yan & Gray, 1994). In sum, a variety of firms in transition economies, both domestic and foreign, have chosen to achieve growth through strategies that center on developing interorganizational relationships and networks with various partner firms.

Strategy in Action 3.1

The Growth of China Energy

China Energy is one of China's largest industrial conglomerates, with power and energy development as its core business. Incorporated in 1982, it is a state-owned enterprise controlled by the Ministry of Energy. In order to grow, it has organized the China Energy Group, taking advantage of its close relationships with the central government and profits generated by its lucrative energy-related operations. In addition, the Group has also entered a number of other industries such as petrochemistry, railroad construction, forest products, real-estate development, financial services, and foreign trade. Such diversification moves used to take the China Energy Group into constant collisions with other central ministries and local bureaus that had nominal control over nonenergy businesses that China Energy sought to enter, until it was given special status in the central economic plan in 1992 to allow it to bypass some of the bureaucratic headaches. At that time, only 15 enterprise groups in China had received this prized special status that gave them a freer hand in pursuing a growth strategy.

During a series of interviews conducted over a 7-year period (1989-1996), China Energy managers suggested that the firm's generic expansion attempts were unsuccessful because it lacked expertise in nonenergy-related industries. Its acquisition attempts were equally disappointing; it was not able to acquire certain target firms that it wanted to add to its portfolio. Instead, it experienced several mandatory "acquisitions" of other ailing SOEs under directives from the Ministry of Energy, because China Energy was considered to be well run and profitable. As a result, China Energy's efforts concentrated on cultivating an enterprise group in which it played the leading role as the "dragon's head." Member firms collaborated extensively under its leadership without formally changing ownership structures and affiliation relationships.

SOURCE: From Peng, M. W. (1997a), "Firm Growth in Transitional Economies: Three Longitudinal Cases From China, 1989-96. *Organization Studies, 18*(3), pp. 385-413. Copyright 1997 by de Gruyter. Adapted with permission.

Strategy in Action 3.2

The Growth of Lucky Transportation

Lucky Transportation was established in 1992 by three entrepreneurs in Shanghai, China. A private firm in disguise, it chose to register as a collective enterprise out of fear of policy changes and state exploitation. Its operations centered on providing trucking services to the construction industry in the new Pudong area of Shanghai. Its entry into the market was well timed, since Shanghai's recent construction boom called for more trucking services. Compared with employees at SOEs, managers and workers at Lucky Transportation were more motivated, better educated, and better paid, which resulted in a higher level of productivity. After losing money for the first year, it became profitable in the second year, reaching a 50% profit margin in 1993, and a 61% profit margin in 1995.

However, its growth was full of frustrations. As the "new kid on the block," it encountered an enormous amount of difficulty in getting contracts, especially from state-owned construction companies. Because it could raise only a limited amount of funds from private owners, its options for generic expansion were quite limited. Furthermore, acquisitions remained problematic for such a young firm. Therefore, when I first visited it in 1993, its owners were concentrating their efforts on joining an enterprise group headed by a state-owned construction firm. It was accepted by the group in 1994. When I revisited in 1996, it was not only operating its highly efficient truck fleet to meet the construction needs of the group, but was also leasing the fleet and personnel of a state-owned trucking company, which was also a part of the group. The state-owned trucking company had not been profitable before. Lucky Transportation, in addition to achieving its own growth, helped its state-owned counterpart grow by providing contract management services.

SOURCE: From Peng, M. W. (1997a), "Firm Growth in Transitional Economies: Three Longitudinal Cases From China, 1989-96. *Organization Studies, 18*(3), pp. 385-413. Copyright 1997 by de Gruyter. Adapted with permission.

In a volatile and uncertain environment, managers have to scan the environment by processing a large amount of information (Elenkov, 1997). Networks reduce transaction costs and stabilize economic activities by having members engage in "reciprocal, preferential, and mutually supportive action" (Peng & Heath, 1996, p. 514). During transitions, when governments often issue confusing and conflicting announcements (e.g., during the Russian coups in 1991 and 1993), there is little reason to take any announcement too seriously. Therefore, information passed through networks from reliable sources becomes far more trustworthy. In other words, information passed through networks is richer and more useful (Daft & Lengel, 1986), thus allowing network members to make better informed decisions. Such information passed through the networks can be especially helpful in selecting the right partner with whom to network (Eisenhardt & Schoonhoven, 1996; Gulati, 1995, 1998; Parkhe, 1993). In other words, networks constructed by managers who have known each other and established a basic level of trust and mutual understanding will result in a lower likelihood of cheating, undercutting, and other opportunistic behavior, thus saving on *transaction costs* (Williamson, 1985, 1991, 1996).

These networks not only involve firm managers, but also many government bureaucrats, officials, and cadres (Nee, 1992; Rona-Tas, 1994; Walder, 1995). Despite the political changes throughout CEE and the NIS, only the top echelon of the state hierarchy has been replaced, and most middle- and lower-level bureaucrats have retained their positions in the government (Parish & Michelson, 1996). In the case of China, while Beijing has decentralized some of its power, the continuity of the government has been largely preserved (Huang, 1996). Moreover, decentralization has only made many local officials more powerful (Peng, 1996, in press-b). As a result, throughout transition economies, officials at various levels of the government still have considerable power to approve projects, allocate resources, and arrange financing and distribution. The upshot is that they occupy a privileged, central location in the complex web of relations that firms have to manage during the transition (Child, 1994; Lu, 1996; Peng, 1997a).

Specifically, these bureaucrats can use their personal networks within the government to gain access to valuable business information, credit, subsidies, and approvals. The rising levels of patronage and corruption in these countries suggest that many actors recognize these advantages. In China, Peng and Luo (1998, 1999) found that managers' connections with officials are *more* important than those with managers at other firms. Even when these officials join the business sector, they may still be able to command substantial advantage due to their valuable, unique, and hard-to-imitate contacts with their former colleagues in the government, which, again, can be regarded as "political resources" (Boddewyn & Brewer, 1994) or "institutional capital" (Oliver, 1997). In Hungary, Rona-Tas (1994, pp. 58-60) reported that between 1989 and 1991, while the general population experienced a 59% income increase, ex-cadres-turned-entrepreneurs more than doubled their income. In comparison, entrepreneurs with no political background increased their income by 73% (see Table 6.4 in Chapter 6). Overall, the scale and scope of involvement in these networks by current and former government officials are nontrivial (see Chapter 6 for details).

Nevertheless, a network-based strategy for firm growth is not without problems. The first problem is the lack of codification of information, routines, and capabilities. This concern stems from an information-processing perspective that views the firm as an organization that constantly receives, processes, and manipulates information (Casson, 1997; Cyert & March, 1963; Galbraith, 1973). Historically, the typical firm in planned economies is a single-plant enterprise that is often called "ABC Factory." Coordinating the activities of an enterprise network with several members, which may span several regions (sometimes several newly independent countries, as in the case of the NIS; see Filatotchev, Buck, & Wright, 1992), requires a *geometric expansion*[5] of the firm's information-processing capacity (Hill & Hoskisson, 1987; Jones & Hill, 1988). Many firms simply lack this capacity (see Table 3.4 for an example of how large some of them have become). Moreover, in an uncertain time, managers' extensive networking activities, often with dubious components like gift giving and bribery, make them reluctant to keep written records for the organization (Boisot & Liang, 1992). We may suggest that much of the network-related information possessed by these managers is of a nonroutine, "soft" nature, which is hard to codify and quantify (Peng, Luo, Shenkar, & Harwit, 1997). As a result, delegation can be prohibitively expensive, and the departure of key managers may directly affect certain firms' capabilities and performance (Tsang, 1998). In the long run, excessive reliance on such uncodified, "soft" information may hinder the firm's ability to undertake generic expansion, which requires a staff of capable managers willing and able to train new recruits.

A second problem is organizational. In many firms, the information-processing problem is further compounded by the lack of a formal organizational basis for these enterprise networks (also called groups, associations, and alliances, among other terms). They often "do not operate as unified groups" (Johnson, 1997, p. 341). Decision making in these networks tends to be case by case, with extensive negotiations and bargaining among members (Peng, 1997a; Peng & Tan, 1998; Wu, 1990). The loosely structured nature of these networks is based on trust, reputation, and mutual understanding, which can be broadly considered as *social capital* (Coleman, 1988; Fombrun, 1996; Fukuyama, 1996; Granovetter, 1985). Trust and reputation, unfortunately, can be easily exploited if there are divergent economic interests, especially when the enforcement regime is weak (Hill, 1990; Miles & Snow, 1992; Peng & Shenkar, 1997; Zucker, 1986). As a result, there is a recent movement throughout different transition economies to establish large, fully incorporated enterprises and business groups with a unified command structure and a number of subsidiaries, as opposed to loosely connected network members. Examples include the push for a "modern enterprise system" in China (Peng, 1997a) and for "financial industrial groups" in Russia (Johnson, 1997; Prokop, 1995; also see Chapter 4 for details).

Consequently, these activities declare the need for a strategy of mergers and acquisitions to achieve growth. Such a need, in turn, has fueled the urgency to strengthen the formal institutional constraints, namely, to establish an adequate legal framework to allow for such market-based transactions (Frye, 1997). In other words, the failure of *formal* institutional frameworks has led to the reliance on *informal* constraints, which results in a network-based strategy. Furthermore, the problems of such a strategy call for strengthening *formal* institutional frameworks (Parish & Michelson, 1996), and therefore the interaction between institutions and organizations comes full circle. Specifically, it evolves precisely in a manner described by North (1990, p. 5) in that strategic choices made by organizations are influenced by the institutional framework, and "in turn, they influence how the institutional framework evolves."

Summary and Discussion

This section has used the example of the growth of the firm to illustrate the dynamic interaction between institutions and organizations that results in the selection of certain strategic choices. Specifically, given the inherent institutional constraints as the "rules of the game" in transition economies (see Table 3.1), many firms have to avoid growth strategies typically adopted by Western firms, such as generic expansion and acquisitions. Instead, they are more likely to settle on a network-based strategy of growth, which is a hybrid, a *compromise* between their desire to achieve generic expansion and their inability to achieve full-scale acquisitions.

To be sure, we are not suggesting that a network-based strategy is the only way to achieve firm growth in transition economies; recent work has found that mergers and acquisitions are increasingly being used (Blasi, Kroumova, & Kruse, 1997; Capener, 1996; Johnson, 1997; Peng, Luo, & Sun, 1999). As is true of any economy, a multiplicity of growth strategies in these economies can be found, including generic expansion, acquisitions, and networks. What has been consistently reported in a large number of studies from different transition economies is that, at least during the 1980s and early to mid-1990s, developing interorganizational networks appears to be a *predominant* strategic choice, which should not be confused with being the *only* choice.

There are numerous explanations that can be used to interpret these findings. I will highlight the economic, cultural, and institutional perspectives. An *economic* perspective suggests that networks and alliances foster economies of scale and scope through resource sharing (Contractor & Lorange, 1988). They facilitate organizational learning through the exchange and diffusion of production technology and organizational capabilities (Kogut, 1988). According to this perspective, the emergence of network-based strategies in transition economies can be viewed as part of the larger, global movement in which more and more firms, including many in the West, have chosen to grow not by generic expansion or acquisitions but by networks and alliances (Davidow & Malone, 1992; Dunning, 1995; Gulati, 1998; Nohria & Eccles, 1992; Snow, Miles, & Coleman, 1992)

A second perspective focuses on the *cultural* specificity of these practices. In light of the Chinese propensity to build interpersonal ties and rely on connections (*guanxi*) to get things done (Hwang, 1987; Kao, 1993; Redding, 1990; Seagrave, 1995) and the widely reported networking practices in other Asian firms in countries such as Japan, Korea, and Taiwan (Au, Peng, & Wang, in press; Hamilton & Biggart, 1988; Yeung, 1997; Weidenbaum & Hughes, 1996), it may not be surprising to find that Chinese managers opt to use a network-based strategy to achieve firm growth. These findings are consistent with the view that strategic choices are inherently affected by the national culture in which the firm is embedded (Hofstede, 1991; Schneider, 1989). What *is* surprising is the similar findings of a network-based strategy in countries such as Bulgaria (Davis, 1996), the Czech Republic (Soulsby & Clark, 1995), Hungary (Rona-Tas, 1994; Stark, 1996; Whitley et al., 1996), and Russia (Buck, Filatotchev, & Wright, 1998; Burawoy & Krotov, 1992; Davis, Patterson, & Grazin, 1996; Johnson, 1997; Krueger, 1995; Puffer, 1994; Sedaitis, 1998). Note that in these countries there is little influence of the Chinese or Asian culture. Nevertheless, the emergence of a network-based strategy, which "blurs" existing organizational boundaries and creates "recombinant property" (Stark, 1996), has been widely reported. For example, field work at 10 large Hungarian firms found that the networking behavior of these firms appears to be more "relational" and similar to "Asian" practices, than "Anglo-Saxon-style" arm's-length transactions (Whitley et al., 1996, p. 409). In other words, despite the lack of cultural affinity between these Eastern European firms and their Chinese counterparts, their boundary-blurring behavior is remarkably similar. What is going on here? Apparently a "culturalist" explanation, while insightful, is not enough to explain these convergent findings from a variety of countries and firms. It is here that an institutional perspective can help reconcile the findings.

Recall the focus of the *institutional* perspective on the interaction between institutions and organizations (North, 1990). This perspective suggests that it is precisely the failure of formal institutional preconditions, such as a legal framework, a stable political structure, and strategic factor markets, that results in firms' inability to rely on generic expansion, acquisitions, or a combination of these. On the other hand, it is the persistence of informal constraints, mostly embodied in managers' interpersonal networks, that facilitates a network-based strategic choice for growth. In essence, micro, interpersonal networks that managers develop with each other and with officials are being translated into macro, interorganizational networks that allow for the growth of the firm, resulting in a dynamic *micro-macro* link (Peng & Luo, 1998, 1999).

Although the institutional perspective on strategy represents a new development in the field of strategy, it is entirely consistent with the classic SWOT view discussed in Chapter 1. Understanding a firm's internal resource conditions can be considered a part of the assessment of its strengths (S) and weaknesses (W). Contemplating strategic choices in conjunction with formal and informal constraints of institutional frameworks is, in essence, a search for opportunities (O) and a determination to minimize threats (T) in the environment. The contribution of the institutional perspective is an expansion of the notion of the "environment," which includes broader influences than were typically considered by traditional strategy writers.

Finally, it is important to note the link between the institutional perspective and the five fundamental questions in strategy highlighted in Chapter 1. As discussed throughout this chapter, why firms differ (Question 1), how firms behave (Question 2), how strategy processes affect strategy choices (Question 3), and what determines the scope of the firm (Question 4) are all strongly influenced by the formal and informal institutional frameworks in which the firm is embedded. Although we have not explicitly discussed Question 5 here, namely, what determines the international performance of the firm, work by Michael Porter (1990), one of the most influential thinkers in strategy, has comprehensively demonstrated the link between a country's institutional frameworks and the international competitiveness of its firms. This point will be borne out in Chapter 7, when we discuss the strategies of foreign firms in transition economies.

CONCLUSIONS

This chapter has argued and demonstrated that an understanding of business strategies in transition economies has to look beyond the competition- and resource-based views that characterize much of the strategy literature in the West. Given that firms in these countries are deeply embedded in their institutional frameworks and are profoundly influenced by the changes in these frameworks, an institutional perspective will be necessary. Specifically, this perspective focuses on the dynamic interaction between institutions and organizations, and considers strategic choices as the outcome of this interaction. Using strategies for the growth of the firm as an example, I have drawn on recent research to illustrate how this interaction takes place and leads to certain strategic choices. With this example as a backdrop, in the next four chapters I will systematically explore the strategies of state-owned enterprises, privatized firms, private start-ups, as well as foreign companies in these countries in more depth.

NOTES

1. This chapter draws heavily on my previous work published in Peng (1994), Peng (1997a), and Peng and Heath (1996), as well as a forthcoming article (Peng, in press-a).

2. The formal definition of *transaction costs* is "the *ex ante* costs of drafting, negotiating, and safeguarding an agreement and, more especially, the *ex post* costs of maladaptation and adjustment that arise when contract execution is misaligned as a result of gaps, errors, omissions, and unanticipated disturbances; the costs of running the economic system" (Williamson, 1996, p. 379).

3. These rankings were based on market capitalization as of May 29, 1998. At that time, the 115th and 197th largest firms in developed economies were Astra of Sweden and Canon of Japan, respectively ("Global 1000," 1998, p. 50).

4. This section draws heavily on the findings of a series of studies that my colleagues on three continents and I did on the growth of the firm in transition economies (Peng, 1994, 1997a, 1997b, 1999, in press-a, in press-b; Peng, Buck, & Filatotchev, 1999; Peng & Heath, 1996; Peng & Luo, 1998, 1999; Peng, Luo, Shenkar, & Harwit, 1997; Peng, Luo, & Sun, 1999; Peng & Tan, 1998; Tan & Peng, 1998a, 1998b, 1999).

5. A geometric expansion is a *nonlinear* increase. A linear increase takes the following form: If $X = Y$, then $X + 1 = Y + 1$ (one unit of increase in X will result in one unit of increase in Y). A geometric expansion has the following nonlinear property: If $X = Y$, then $X + 1 = Y + n$ where $n > 1$ (one unit of increase in X will lead to more than one unit of increase in Y).

4 Strategies of State-Owned Enterprises

> The economic problem of society is mainly one of rapid adaptation in the particular circumstances of time and place.
>
> —*Friedrich Hayek (1945, p. 524)*

State-owned enterprises (SOEs) used to dominate the economic landscape of every socialist country. During the transition, despite the wishful thinking of some policymakers, advisors, and scholars, SOEs have not been totally dumped into "the dustbin of history." For better and worse, many of them have continued to play an important—albeit somewhat reduced and different—role in transition economies. In light of Hayek's (1945) teaching quoted above, SOEs' fundamental challenge lies in whether they can rapidly adapt to a changing environment. In this chapter, I focus on their strategies during the transition. A stylized SOE probably represents "the largest amount of variance" in many dimensions when compared and contrasted with the typical

Western firm with which we are familiar, thus enabling a full illustration of the diversity among organizations operating within different institutional frameworks (Peng & Heath, 1996, p. 516).

As an organizational form, the SOE has a unique nature that is distinguished by state ownership. This chapter first provides an overview of the nature of the SOE, which is followed by an exploration of the rationale behind different strategies chosen by the SOE during the transition.

THE NATURE OF THE FIRM

The nature of the firm has puzzled observers ever since Ronald Coase first asked a seminal question, "Why do firms exist?" in 1937, which eventually led him to win the Nobel Prize in Economics in 1992. Logically, this question is the foundation of the five fundamental questions in strategy that we endeavor to answer in the context of transition economies. Therefore, it will be useful to highlight the evolution of answers to this question in order to understand the nature of the SOE. Most research on the nature of the firm can be organized according to the following four schools of thought: (a) neoclassical, (b) contractual, (c) property rights, and (d) resource-based.

The Firm as a Profit Maximizer

Known as the *neoclassical theory*, the perspective of the firm as a profit maximizer has been developed over the past hundred years or so and has become the original "theory of the firm" in economics. It views the firm as a production function that maximizes its profits by responding to the supply and demand of its products in the marketplace. Despite its simplicity and elegance, this theory has long been criticized for its failure to account for the empirical reality that many firms do not appear to maximize their profits (Cyert & March, 1963; March & Simon, 1958). Nor does it explain how production is organized within the firm. Not knowing what, exactly, is going on inside the firm, the firm thus becomes a "black box" in which input is transformed into output (Nelson & Winter, 1982). Later development in the literature has tackled these problems.

The Firm as a Nexus of Contracts

Instead of viewing the firm as a profit-maximizing black box, scholars who share a "contractual" view of the firm have suggested a more *microanalytic* approach by focusing on transaction as the "basic unit of analysis" (Williamson, 1985, p. 18). According to this perspective, the firm is an organizer of transactions both inside and outside its boundaries. Transactions with outside parties are the well-known *market* transactions. The contributions of this new perspective are the attention given to internal transactions within an organizational *hierarchy*, leading to a famous term: "market versus hierarchy" (Williamson, 1975). These insights suggest (a) that markets and hierarchies are alternative means of organizing transactions; (b) that transactions undertaken via markets may have high costs due to uncertainty, opportunism, and other contractual problems; and (c) that firms arise because, under some circumstances, they are more efficient at solving transaction cost problems than market transactions are (Cheung, 1969, 1983; Coase, 1937; Williamson, 1975, 1985, 1996). Consequently, this perspective has been called *transaction cost theory*.

Another group of scholars focused on a particular set of transactions, namely, those between principals such as owners and agents and such as managers and employees (Alchian & Demsetz, 1972; Jensen & Meckling, 1976). Because the agent may not completely share the principal's goals and because the agent tends to have better information about the details of the tasks, the agent may have both the motivation and the opportunity to behave in a way that maximizes his or her own utility at the expense of the principal's (Berle & Means, 1932; Marris, 1964). As a result, this new perspective, often called *agency theory*, introduces conflict of interest into the firm. Primary remedies are (a) better incentive for the agent and (b) better monitoring by the principal. Overall, transaction cost and agency theorists have proposed a new "contractual" way to view the firm, which can be regarded as a *nexus of contracts* (Cheung, 1983).

The Firm as a Set of Property Rights

As the "rights individuals appropriate over their own labor and the goods and services they possess" (North, 1990, p. 33), property rights have attracted considerable scholarly attention, leading to an influential *property rights school* (Alchian, 1965; Alchian & Demsetz, 1972; Barzel, 1989; Demsetz, 1983; Grossman & Hart, 1986). Similar to the contractual view of the firm, the property rights school regards the firm as a more complex entity than a mere profit maximizer. In a nutshell, this literature suggests that ownership matters. Ownership rights can take three forms: (a) rights to income generated from the property; (b) rights to control and use the property; and (c) rights to transfer or sell the property (Furubotn & Pejovich, 1974, p. 4). As an embodiment of the property rights of the owners, a firm can be viewed as a place where the owners achieve their goals of asset utilization.

The Firm as a Collection of Resources and Capabilities

While the three previous perspectives arise out of the work of economists, the last and most recent perspective on the nature of the firm, often called the *resource-based view* of the firm, has been advocated by strategy and organizational scholars since the 1980s (Conner, 1991; Wernerfelt, 1984). This view traces its intellectual roots to the work of Penrose (1959), which considers a firm as a collection of various technological, financial, and organizational resources (see Chapter 3). Over time, some resources are developed into capabilities that enable the firm to attain competitive advantage (Barney, 1991, 1997; Nelson & Winter, 1982; Teece, Pisano, & Shuen, 1997).[1]

Considering a firm to be much more than a static profit maximizer, the resource-based view shares the frustration of both the contractual and property rights schools discussed above vis-à-vis the traditional neoclassical theory of the firm (Conner, 1991). On the other hand, resource-based scholars challenge the contractual and property rights views for their overemphasis on the *negative* aspects of the firm, such as the focus on curbing opportunism, solving agency problems, and getting property rights "right" (Conner & Prahalad, 1996; Ghoshal & Moran, 1996; Kogut & Zander, 1992). Instead, the resource-based view concentrates on the *positive* aspects of the firm, notably, the dynamic creation, acquisition, and deployment of resources and capabilities that are value-adding, unique, and hard to imitate by competitors (Barney, 1991).

Summary

Our understanding of the nature of the firm has evolved from it being a profit maximizer, to being a nexus of contracts, to a set of property rights, and, more recently, to a collection of resources and capabilities. Each of these theories has made significant contributions. On the other hand, these theories are based almost exclusively on the experience of the Western firm, and, consequently, often pay little attention to the wider institutional influences discussed in Chapter 3. Whether they have a bearing on the nature of the socialist SOE will be explored next.

THE NATURE OF THE SOCIALIST STATE-OWNED ENTERPRISE[2]

Although a simple distinction is often made: capitalism is associated with private ownership and socialism with public ownership—hence the term *"state-owned* enterprise," SOEs are not an organizational form found exclusively in socialist countries (Aharoni, 1986; Zif, 1981). In light of the four theories on the nature of the firm discussed above, we can argue that the socialist SOE fundamentally is an expression of property rights and that architects of the socialist SOE single-mindedly believed and practiced this perspective to such an extent that they ignored other viable schools of thought on the nature of the firm. Further, we may suggest that efforts to reform SOEs throughout transition economies reflect a new understanding that appreciates the contributions of more contemporary theories of the nature of the firm.

The Socialist SOE as a Set of Property Rights

Architects of socialism such as Lenin, Stalin, and Mao were devoted students of Karl Marx. In this regard, Marx might be regarded as the forerunner of the modern property rights theory of the firm, which emerged about 100 years *after* Marx (1867/1967) first published his treatise, *Capital*, in 1867. Marx and his followers regarded private ownership as a "sin" of capitalism that contributed to the greed of private owners, that is, capitalists, who "exploited" workers. A natural remedy, therefore, was to convert private property to public. The end result became the socialist SOE, which would represent a different set of property rights.

As noted earlier, "property rights" encompass a comprehensive set of rights of the owner. Their complexity necessitates a breakdown into three smaller and analytically more manageable sets (Furubotn & Pejovich, 1974, p. 4):

1. *Rights to income generated from the property.* According to official ideology, the SOE is the property of "the whole of the people." In practice, the nominal owner of the SOE is the state, represented by the national government. The government, therefore, has full rights to income generated by the SOE. Such income flows into the central budget of the state. No distinction is made between what is described under capitalist economies as corporate "taxes" paid to the state and what qualifies as "profits" of the firm (Kornai, 1992, p. 73).

2. *Rights to control and use the property.* Who has these rights in socialist countries depends on who controls the state budget and who sets all the economic parameters (e.g., prices, wages) that affect the operations of the SOE. The answer to these two questions is the same: The bureaucracy. As noted in Chapter 2, the state bureaucracy under classical socialism literally determines the establishment, scope, pricing, management, labor, and liquidation of the firm, as well as taking care of profits, losses, and financing (Granick, 1975, 1990).

3. *Rights to transfer or sell the property.* These rights, again, strictly belong to the state bureaucracy. While transferring one SOE from the jurisdiction of one government agency to another is frequent in socialist economies (Huang, 1996; Peng, 1996), the right to sell the SOE is hardly relevant since, under state socialism, these rights cannot be exercised by anyone, not even the "state" as the nominal owner. Official ideology dictates that the SOE cannot be sold, leased out, given away, or inherited. Otherwise, it may become a "dangerous" capitalist firm forbidden by classical socialism (Ireland & Stewart, 1995).

Overall, public ownership, embodied in the SOE, has been widely regarded as one of the most important criteria of state socialism. The SOE, therefore, not only serves the economic function of organizing production, but also serves as a political vehicle for achieving socialism. Political motivations for such thinking aside, we can argue, *from the standpoint of the theory of the firm*, that architects of classical socialism and their lieutenants were strong believers and committed practitioners of the property rights theory of the firm—albeit from a entirely different tradition and a totally opposite direction.

The motto of the property rights school is to "get property rights right." The vast array of the political, economic, and organizational practices associated with the SOE in socialist economies before the transition can be summed up by this motto: They were all trying to "get property rights right." In particular, it was believed that public ownership is a panacea, and that once a firm becomes an SOE, its employees would become its owners and would work for themselves instead of for the exploitative capitalist owner. Improvement in productivity, efficiency, and overall economic performance would naturally follow (Boisot, 1996). Unfortunately, as reviewed in Chapter 2, these practices seemed to have gotten the property rights all *wrong*, resulting in many SOEs becoming "permanently failing" organizations (Meyer & Zucker, 1989) and, consequently, the whole regime a "grand failure" (Brzezinski, 1989).

Can the Socialist SOE Be a Profit Maximizer?

In theory, the socialist SOE can be a profit maximizer, at least according to Oscar Lange (1936-1937), who argued for exactly this point in the "socialist debate" before World War II. In practice, however, the socialist SOE has been found to be anything but a profit maximizer (Granick, 1990; Kornai, 1992). As is shown in Table 4.1, while the "normal" private firm in a competitive market economy has a primary interest in increasing (if not purely maximizing) profit, the SOE under state socialism tends to be interested in fulfilling the plan quota and thus winning recognition from its administrative superiors. The differences in the objectives assert a decisive influence on the behavior of the firm.

In terms of market entry and exit, a competitive firm is surrounded by existing rivals and potential entrants (Porter, 1980). This sense of threat of competition is absent from the life of a socialist SOE,

TABLE 4.1 The Socialist SOE Versus the "Normal" Private Firm

Main Features	State-Owned Enterprise Under State Socialism	"Normal" Private Firm in a Competitive Market Economy
Primary interest	Increasing output for recognition from superior organizations for plan fulfillment	Increasing (if not purely maximizing) profits for competitive advantage
Entry and exit	Bureaucracy decides all entries and exits	Market determines all entries and exits
Financing	From the state	From private sources
Budget constraint	Soft	Hard
Product demand	Firm sure of demand, which is determined by the bureaucracy	Firm unsure of demand, which fluctuates according to the market
Product supply	Fixed in quantity and product mix	Flexible in quantity and product mix
	Little incentive to improve quality	Interested in product improvement
Price responsiveness	Weak. Prices are usually arbitrarily set by the bureaucracy	Strong. Prices are set by the firm in response to demand

whose entry and exit are determined by the very "visible hands" of the bureaucracy. A fundamental reason that the private firm constantly faces competitive threat is that it has a *hard budget constraint*. If it makes continuous losses, it will become bankrupt. In contrast, the "death" of the SOE, like its birth, is in the hands of the bureaucracy. If the bureaucracy thinks that an SOE is worth supporting, it can provide financial support regardless of the SOE's performance. Given that the SOE is usually regarded as an ideological bastion embodying a number of political values, such as public ownership, full employment, and socialist achievement, it is not surprising that the firm typically has a *soft budget constraint* allowing it to dip into the state coffers (Kornai, 1980). As a result, the SOE, which has seemingly indefinite budgetary resources, faces little threat of failure—unless its budget is being hardened.

In terms of product demand, the private firm is never sure of the market fluctuation. However, it has a very strong interest in swift and flexible adaptation of its supply to the changing demand. If it notices certain unsatisfied demand, it will attempt to seize the opportunity by adjusting its output or changing its selling prices. After all, the private firm "lives off the market." On the other hand, the socialist SOE, as well as its bureaucratic superiors, has no such motivation. The demand for the firm's product is certain, at least within the cycle of a (1-, 2-, or 5-year) plan. Therefore, the SOE has little incentive to adjust production level and/or price level to adapt to changing needs. In brief, the socialist SOE may be regarded as an *output maximizer;* it is miles away from being a profit maximizer.

During the transition, the socialist legacy has become a strong inertial force. Years of socialization under the old system have made managers reluctant to accept profit maximization as the most important goal driving their decisions. For example, an influential Russian Economic Barometer survey in 1994 (Aukutsionek, 1997, p. 158) found that only 31% of the Russian CEOs regarded "maximizing profit" as their most important business objective (see Table 4.2). In comparison, 51% and 36% of the respondents regarded "maximizing output" and "maintaining workforce," respectively, as their foremost goal. Also shown in Table 4.2, in a similar study conducted by the authoritative Chinese Managers Survey System (1997, p. 126) in 1997, 60% of surveyed SOE managers in China reported that they viewed "maximizing profit" as the most important objective of the firm, behind "improving employees' income" (74%) and "vitalizing the firm" (66%). In contrast, Chinese managers at private, joint stock, foreign joint venture, and wholly foreign-owned firms unanimously rated "maximizing profit" as their most fundamental business objective (Table 4.2). It is important to note that these surveys took place in 1994 and 1997 in Russia and China, respectively, years *after* the transitions started. Given that most Russian firms had already been privatized at that time (Blasi, Kroumova, & Kruse, 1997), most of the respondents would have been CEOs of privatized companies. Nevertheless, their SOE mentality is still evident. We can infer that if such a survey had taken place earlier, the percentage of SOE respondents viewing "maximizing profit" as the most important goal would have been much smaller.

During the transition, maximizing the output, maintaining the workforce, and improving employees' income unite the interests of

TABLE 4.2 Top Three Objectives of the Firm in Russia (1994) and China (1997)

Percentage of CEOs who answered: "Which of the following is the most important objective of your firm?" (Multiple answers allowed)	Russia (500 firms) All firms	China (3,154 firms)[a]					
		SOE	COE	POE	JSC	FJV	WFOE
1. Maximizing profits	31	60	60	53	72	67	71
2. Maintaining workforce	36	—	—	—	—	—	—
3. Maintaining output	51	—	—	—	—	—	—
4. Improving employees' income	—	74	73	53	58	57	47
5. Vitalizing the firm	—	66	62	40	61	61	65

SOURCES: Adapted from Aukutsionek (1997, p. 158) and Chinese Managers Survey System (1997, p. 126).
NOTE: a. SOE: State-owned enterprise; COE: Collectively owned enterprise; POE: Privately owned enterprise; JSC: Joint stock company; FJV: Foreign joint venture; WFOE: Wholly foreign-owned enterprise.

SOE management, the workforce, and the state, which is in fear of massive unemployment (Shleifer & Vishny, 1994). As a result, reducing unprofitable output to maximize profit remains a low priority as long as there is a soft budget constraint. Transforming the SOE's objective from output to profit maximizing can be expressed in the following model:

$$(4.1) \qquad Q = (1-n)\, Q_1 + n\, Q_2$$

where Q is the total volume of output during the transition, Q_1 the output in the output-driven planned economy, Q_2 the output in the profit-driven market economy, and n the degree of transition (ranging from the initial state $n = 0$, no transition, to the final state $n = 1$, complete transition). Further, initially,

$$(4.2) \qquad Q_2 < Q_1$$

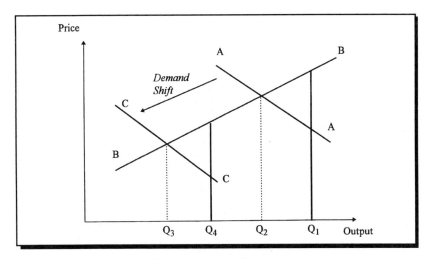

Figure 4.1. Can the Socialist SOE Be a Profit Maximizer?

This can be shown graphically in Figure 4.1. A profit-maximizing firm will produce Q_2, determined by the supply (BB) and demand (AA) curves. An output-maximizing SOE, on the other hand, will produce Q_1, which includes a large part of unprofitable output and is therefore larger than Q_2. A typical SOE, at the start of the transition, was producing Q_1, and it seemed that after a change in its objective its output would fall to the market-determined intersection of supply and demand at Q_2. However, as the result of the decline in the demand for its products, the point of intersection itself shifted and now corresponds to Q_3 (for simplicity we assume a fall in demand from AA to CC with a fixed cost curve). Instead of reducing output to Q_3, the SOE, however, may have reduced output to Q_4, still with some unprofitable production. Output therefore still remains too high, and there is room for further reduction, from Q_4 to Q_3, if the firm is truly interested in profit maximization.

In sum, the behavior of the SOE under state socialism is not consistent with the goal of profit maximization suggested by neoclassical theory. As a result, the SOE has experienced a great deal of difficulty attempting to maximize profits during the transition.

Can the Socialist SOE Be a Nexus of Contracts?

The "exploitative" contractual relations between owners and employees in a capitalist firm were harshly criticized by Marx (1867/1967) and his followers. What has later become evident is that the socialist SOE is still a nexus of contracts, albeit a different set of contracts that are spelled out less clearly and less efficiently than their capitalist counterparts (Boisot, 1996; Pearce, 1991). Although employees were politically proclaimed to be the new owners, they had neither full rights to income generated from the SOE, nor rights to control the property, much less the rights to transfer or sell their "own" property. The state bureaucracy became the de facto owner possessing all these important rights. As a result, SOE employees, including managers, ended up being agents working for the state and its representatives in the bureaucracy. Therefore, the conflicts of interest between principals and agents discussed by agency theory became highly relevant. While managers might want to maximize their own power, prestige, and income, employees might be more interested in free housing, entertainment, medical care, and schooling rather than profit maximization or, for that matter, socialist achievement (Boisot & Child, 1988). In addition, these agents faced little threat of being dismissed by their principals (Pearce, 1991; Tung, 1981, 1982; Walder, 1989). Called the "iron rice bowl" by the Chinese, lifetime employment was the norm, leaving little incentive for employees to work hard and improve performance (Frese, Kring, Soose, & Zempel, 1996; Shenkar & Ronen, 1987).

Upon discovering these *incentive* problems, it was customary to invoke ideology calling for the need to instill "a sense of ownership" and for employees to work "like proprietors." However, as long as there were inherent conflicts of interest between the principals and agents, it was practically impossible for a truly proprietary motivation to develop (Jensen & Meckling, 1976). The failure to employ *spiritual* incentives typically led to *material* incentives such as bonuses to give SOE employees a measure of interest in raising profits. However, it was normally a loose and weak interest. Since the egalitarian ideology was interested in suppressing the widening of income gaps, the scale of the incentive schemes employed was typically insignificant, and bonuses were usually distributed equally.

In addition to having incentive problems, the socialist SOE also suffers from a number of *monitoring* problems. Because the central bureaucracy needs to oversee too many SOEs, it does not have enough resources to monitor every SOE. Decentralization efforts to delegate the jurisdiction of the SOE to lower-level governments only partially solves this information overload problem, since local authorities also have little time, resources, and interest to focus on individual SOEs (Peng, 1996). Because the planners have imperfect information about the capabilities of the SOE, a plan—in other words, a "contract" between the principals in the government and the agents who run the SOE—often has to be imprecise and be subject to bargaining and revision. SOE managers, not surprisingly, often ask for more resources than they can effectively utilize, resulting in an "investment hunger" as well as a great deal of organizational slack (Kornai, 1992; Tan & Peng, 1998b). Moreover, failure to perform poses little danger to SOE managers, who tend to be protected by a soft budget constraint. Finally, other political and social functions of the government further distract it from vigorously monitoring the efforts of the SOE.

In brief, the socialist SOE is a nexus of contracts, despite the official denunciation of "capitalistic" contractual relationships between owners and employees. A large part of the SOE's problems stems from a failure to properly delineate the contractual responsibilities and rights of owners, managers, and employees, thus leading to enormous agency problems.

Can the Socialist SOE
Be a Collection of Resources?

The socialist SOE has long been considered a collection of *production* resources. In fact, it was the acquisition and possession of these resources that largely fueled the socialist revolution throughout the early part of the 20th century. However, worldwide practices seem to indicate that the socialist SOE is merely such a set of production resources, no more, no less. This is at odds with the *resource-based* view of the firm, which suggests that in addition to possessing productive resources, a firm also encompasses technological, financial, and organizational resources (Penrose, 1959). During the heyday of social-ism, the SOE mostly concerned itself with (largely manufacturing) production. Technological research and development was usually un-dertaken by specialized research institutes outside the boundaries of the firm (Afanassieva & Couderc, 1998; White, 1998). Financial resources mainly came from the state, and the firm did not need to raise its own financing. The planning, organization, and coordination of production, again, were not in the hands of the firm, but in the hands of the bureaucracy that oversaw the command economy. More-over, the SOE also relied on outside entities such as the Communist Party and the labor bureau to provide cadres, managers, labor recruits, and a host of other human resources (Child, 1994).

Such a narrow view of the firm as a set of production resources has led some Western observers to proclaim that there are no real "firms" in socialist economies. If anything, the socialist economy as a whole resembles to a certain degree a large corporation, which not only incorporates production resources, but also technological, financial, and organizational capabilities (Lawrence & Vlachoutsicos, 1990; Peng, 1996). As a result, the notion of "USSR, Inc.," or "China, Inc.," has often been voiced (Macleod, 1988). The SOE, in essence, resembles a branch plant with limited decision-making capacity within a large Western corporation. During the transition, it is apparent that the firm needs to take on other roles, such as developing technology, raising financing, and strengthening organizational capability, if it intends to survive and compete in an increasingly market-driven economy. As a result, reforms to expand the *scope* of the firm, which are embodied in competitive strategies, become inevitable.

Summary

As is evident from its name, the socialist SOE is in essence a set of property rights concentrated in public ownership. Such a single-minded, "property rights" view of the firm has resulted in a failure to understand the nature of the SOE from other important theories of the firm. Specifically, emphasis on the nature of public ownership has prevented the SOE from being a profit maximizer, resulted in a failure to specify contractual rights associated with the firm, and led to inadequate development of the firm's important resources in areas such as technological, financial, and organizational capabilities. Viewed from such a perspective, business strategies adopted by SOEs during the transition can be regarded as attempts to take on different properties inspired by contemporary theories of the firm.

STRATEGIES OF STATE-OWNED ENTERPRISES

The Need for Strategies

The notion of competitive strategy was alien to many SOE managers, who were used to living off the soft budget constraint provided by the state (Henley & Nyaw, 1986). However, the transition from a planned economy to a market-based economy "changes fundamental managerial assumptions, criteria, and decision making, and represents a genuine transformation of the business" (Tan & Litschert, 1994, p. 3). The time has come when SOEs may have to strategize in order to survive (Oliver, 1991; Peng & Heath, 1996). Recall the fundamental changes in the formal institutional constraints embodied in the central planning regime and bureaucratic control described in Chapter 3. Gradually, the state relinquishes its role of administering central economic plans and assuming financial responsibilities of SOEs. Instead, SOEs are granted more and more autonomy as well as financial independence to compete in the transition economy (Child, 1994).

Many SOEs find themselves being pulled from the "commanding heights" of the economy into a sink-or-swim situation in the emerging ocean of competition. Although most of them are newcomers to the game of competition, they are nevertheless under stress to learn how to play—fast. First, the loosened institutional environment has introduced numerous private, cooperative, and collective firms that are more dynamic and entrepreneurial than SOEs (see Chapter 6). Second, a great number of foreign firms, including many powerful multinational enterprises from the West, have penetrated their markets and created tremendous pressure for local firms (see Chapter 7). Finally, a large number of former SOEs have been converted, reformed, or transformed into privatized, joint stock companies that fight with their ex-colleagues for market shares (see Chapter 5). Taken together,

TABLE 4.3 Strategies of the SOE During the Transition: Theory and Practice

Theory of the Firm	SOE Practice
Property rights theory: The firm as a set of property rights	Ask for more government support to safeguard the "state-owned" nature of the firm, which embodies the socialist property rights theory in favor of public ownership
Neoclassical theory: The firm as a profit maximizer	Maximize profits because of government mandate, opportunities in new markets, and/or the sheer necessity for retrenchment
Transaction cost and agency theories: The firm as a nexus of contracts	Strengthen contracts within the firm by requiring managers to be accountable through contracts, demanding security deposit, and/or, in some cases, auctioning off the SOE
Resource-based theory: The firm as a collection of resources and capabilities	Develop resources and capabilities through establishing interorganizational relationships with domestic and foreign firms in the form of strategic alliances, joint ventures, enterprise networks, industry associations, and/or business groups

these challenges have created a new environment in which the typical SOE can no longer afford to be passive but has to join the competition.

Despite the vast array of business strategies employed by SOEs during the transition, we can draw on the four major theories of the firm to group them into four respective categories (Table 4.3). While a large number of SOEs have continued to rely on the time-honored method of asking for more government support, many others have risen to the occasion by undertaking strategies that better reflect the teachings of different theories (Gordon & Li, 1991; Kostera, 1995). We will start with the most traditional strategy, followed by progressively more competitive strategies.

Strategy I: Asking for More Government Support

An Emergent Strategy. This strategy is no different from that used by SOE managers before the transition. Therefore, this no-brainer approach is not really a strategy by design, but by default. The other way to understand it is that it represents an "emergent" strategy during the transition (Mintzberg, 1989). As shown in Chapter 3, old habits die hard, even during times of radical change. Most SOE managers are used to lobbying the government. Equipped with their "political resources" (Boddewyn & Brewer, 1994) and "institutional capital" (Oliver, 1997), these managers are skilled at cultivating relationships with their bureaucratic superiors and taking advantage of socialist principles in favor of providing their firms with a soft budget constraint. As a result, their first reaction when facing financial difficulties is usually to ask for more support from the government in the form of direct subsidies, low-cost loans, tax holidays, and other preferential treatment (Chen & Faure, 1995). In addition to such financial support, the government can also help the declining firms by asking, coercing, or, in some cases, ordering more profitable SOEs to "acquire" the weak ones (Peng, 1997a). Further, a sympathetic government can raise entry barriers against non-SOE firms through delays (or rejections) in project approval, and make life difficult for such firms already in operation by changing the rules of the game in favor of SOEs. Moreover, unprofitable SOEs threaten the state with massive unemployment should they go under. For many employees, as well as their families, the SOE is not only their place to work, but also their place to eat, play, attend school, watch movies, and go to hospital—in short, their place to live (Shenkar, 1996). Therefore, massive layoffs due to SOE failure will not only create enormous unemployment and chaos, but also lead to a breakdown of the social fabric.

Scale and Scope of Government Support. How hard SOEs try to obtain continued government support and how successful these efforts are depend on the credibility of the government's commitment to reform. In Poland, where the first "shock therapy" was launched, subsidies to SOEs shrank rapidly, from more than 16% of GDP in 1986 to 5% in 1992 (World Bank, 1996, p. 45). Given such a commitment to irreversible transitions, Polish managers interviewed in 1990 had little doubt that if they failed to make their firms competitive, the firms would close, regardless of how loud they cried—and indeed many Polish SOEs that existed in 1989 had disappeared by the mid-1990s (Pinto, Belka, & Krajewski, 1993). Russian reforms, although extensive, were neither as coherent nor as credible. While total federal subsidies to SOEs fell from 32% of GDP in 1992 to about 6% in 1994, local government subsidies to enterprises have actually *increased* (World Bank, 1996, p. 45). As a result, managers have a strong incentive to maneuver among different levels of government, trying to maximize the subsidies, tax exemptions, and other benefits that they can obtain (Child & Lu, 1996a, 1996b; Lu & Heard, 1995).

Despite the often-heard rhetoric, the overall resolve to "bite the bullet," so to speak, to transform SOEs, is probably the weakest in China, where the communist government still tries to safeguard public ownership as a foundation of its socialist ideology. At the outset of the 1990s, officially about 45% of SOEs were making losses, although anecdotal evidence put the percentage a lot higher (Peng, 1997a, p. 390; see also Chinese Academy of Social Sciences, Project Team, 1997). By the mid-1990s, SOEs employed more than 100 million people, more than 70% of China's industrial workers ("Wake-Up Call for China's State Sector," 1996, p. 63). The government throughout the 1980s and until the late 1990s pledged that "every attempt will be made to help these [state-owned] firms get out of their current financial plight" (quoted in Peng, 1997a, p. 396). As a result, by the mid-1990s, SOEs soaked up 75% of government investment and 70% of bank credit (World Bank, 1996, p. 46). Despite this high level of support, their performance as a whole has been dismal. The contribution of SOEs to total industrial output declined from 78% in 1978 to 48% in 1992 (State Statistical Bureau, 1993, p. 409). While the declining *output share* of the SOE sector may be an encouraging sign for private sector development, the *profit share* of the SOEs is more alarming: By 1996, SOEs contributed less than 1% of China's industrial profits ("Wake-Up Call," 1996, p. 63).[3] Net losses in the SOE sector reportedly eclipsed the entire equity of China's banks, making the entire banking system technically bankrupt and, thus, debt write-off impossible. In short, some SOE managers have been too successful in dipping into the state coffers. In the end, the government may end up having very little that it can offer to support the large number of SOEs in need.

In sum, from a theory-of-the-firm point of view, continuously asking for more government support reflects certain SOE managers' and government officials' belief in the socialist *property rights theory,* which places a strong value on the "state-owned" nature of the firm.

However, such a belief originated from a bankrupt ideology that has become increasingly out of fashion in light of new theories of the firm that guide practices. These theories are detailed in the following sections.

Strategy II: Maximizing Profits

Emergence of a Profit Orientation. For many SOEs not in "strategic" industries (e.g., defense, telecommunications, and airlines), which the state is more willing to support, the chance of obtaining more support from an increasingly reluctant government is becoming more remote. As a result, they have been pushed to follow *neoclassical theory* to do what a firm should be doing, namely, maximizing profits. At least two factors contribute to the emergence of the profit orientation of SOEs. First, even for those still under the planning regime, the target in output has been gradually replaced by a new government mandate in profits (Ramamurti, 1987). Instead of using output as the performance criterion, the government has shown an increasing interest in using profits to gauge SOEs' performance (Walder, 1995). For example, Lu (1996, p. 161) reported that among the six Chinese SOEs he tracked longitudinally since 1985, three had an output target and three a profit target in 1985. By 1993, all of them sought profits as their primary target.

Second, SOEs historically have been laden with a large amount of organizational slack, such as underutilized capacity, underemployed staff, and discretionary funds not channeled into productive areas (Peng & Heath, 1996). The Chinese Academy of Social Sciences Project Team (1997, p. 132) estimated that, nationwide, SOEs' efficiency would not be affected if one third of their employees were let go. My own interviews with top managers at one of the largest SOEs in China revealed that the firm was laden to the same extent with excess human resources (Peng, 1997a, p. 395). Since both the government and SOE managers are afraid of the social costs of massive layoffs and the lack of strategic factor markets to sell off or lease some of these resources (see Chapter 3), many SOEs are desperate to deploy these excess resources in new areas in order to improve profitability (Guthrie, 1997). As a result, venturing into new areas, such as real estate, trading, hotels, and a host of other service industries unrelated to their traditional manufacturing base, has been widely practiced (Lan, 1998;

Stark, 1996). *Diversification*, especially into areas and industries unrelated to the firm's traditional "center of gravity" in manufacturing, calls for a new set of skills and capabilities that SOEs often do not possess, and such a strategy often backfires in the long run (Hoskisson & Hitt, 1994; Rumelt, 1974). In the short run, however, many SOEs are interested in these practices simply as a "lifeboat" strategy (Guthrie, 1997, p. 1261).

Retrenchment. For numerous other SOEs that have neither the excess resources nor the vision and determination to seek growth in new areas, the only way out is *retrenchment* (Bruton & Rubanik, 1997). While many SOEs in China are protected by a socialist government still interested in preserving public ownership—albeit a declining interest—and by the growth of the economy offering opportunities to venture into other industries, their counterparts in CEE and the NIS, which have to confront shock therapy, are not so lucky. These firms encounter a new government no longer embracing the principle of public ownership, and a declining economy in which demand for the products SOEs traditionally make has all but disappeared (Ernst, Alexeev, & Marer, 1996; Estrin, Brada, Gelb, & Singh, 1996; Estrin, Gelb, & Singh, 1995). As a result, many SOEs in CEE and the NIS have to cut costs, reduce assets, lay off employees, as well as a host of other retrenchment measures directed toward survival (Barker & Mone, 1994; DeWitt, 1998). In contrast to the growth of the firm highlighted in Chapter 3, many SOEs are interested in the *shrinking* of the firm through downsizing and downscoping[4] (Buck, Filatotchev, & Wright, 1998; Wright, Hoskisson, Filatotchev, & Buck, 1998). Shedding such peripheral assets as educational and medical facilities usually comes first, followed by reductions in pension payments. Before workers are officially laid off, they are typically on the payroll for a long time; whether they actually get paid is another matter. As experience in the West has shown (Pearce & Robbins, 1994), retrenchment is typically slow and painful. In addition, SOE managers in transition economies are also influenced by their socialization under classical socialism, which has become "constraints on capitalism" (Holt, Ralston, & Terpstra, 1994). When implementing retrenchment measures, a lot of them are uncomfortable with making tough, unpopular decisions and simply procrastinate, attempting to "muddle through" the process (McCarthy & Puffer, 1995).

Overall, whether by government mandate, by opportunities in new markets, or by the sheer necessity of retrenchment, profit orientation has been gradually established at many SOEs, which is consistent with the teachings of the neoclassical theory of the firm. The upshot is that, graphically, the firm will increasingly make decisions according to supply and demand and produce at Q_2 or Q_3 in Figure 4.1. The case of the turnaround of the Szczecin Shipyard in Poland suggests that, although painful and challenging, such a process is possible (Strategy in Action 4.1).

Strategy in Action 4.1

The Turnaround of the Szczecin Shipyard in Poland

Shipbuilding has a long and distinguished history in Poland. The Szczecin Shipyard is one of Poland's three largest shipyards. It is capable of manufacturing a broad range of ships, ranging from frigates for the navy to container ships. Before the 1990s, it sold primarily to Eastern bloc countries. As a large SOE, it had numerous peripheral assets, including an apartment complex, three technical schools, a medical center, an entertainment center, and two company-owned resorts. However, the collapse of the Soviet Union resulted in cancellation, on short notice and without compensation, of eight ships already under construction. Soviet insolvency pushed the firm from a debt level of nearly zero in 1990 to a total of approximately $190 million by 1991. Moreover, the new government, having committed itself to a radical shock therapy policy, was no longer willing to automatically bail out the firm as before. Not surprisingly, the SOE was soon engulfed in a deep financial crisis.

Headed by a new management team installed in 1991, the shipyard embarked on its turnaround in three ways. First, to maximize profits, the new management focused on curtailing cash flow into peripheral activities. The company-owned resorts and entertainment center were sold. The apartment complex, technical schools, and the medical center were given away to the city for free.

Second, a new product strategy was chosen to more efficiently utilize the shipyard's capacity. Management found that container ships had both substantial demand and price premiums in the world marketplace. Moreover, it was found that the shipyard's technical strengths lay in 12,500-ton medium-sized container ships. As a result, virtually all of the shipyard's capacity was moved to container ships by early 1993, resulting in shortened product-cycle times. Between 1991 and 1993, turnaround time for a single ship was reduced from 3 years to 11 months, a world-class standard.

Finally, given the disappearance of orders from the now defunct Soviet Union, courting Western buyers became a must. Two leading German firms placed a small order in 1990. By 1992, they took delivery of the ships 6 months earlier than they could have in Germany, and also realized 20% to 30% cost savings. Because these two reputable firms were opinion leaders among German shippers, their orders were quickly followed by a large number of orders from other German and Western companies.

By any measure, the turnaround of the shipyard was remarkable. It not only shortened its product cycle, but also substantially raised productivity: Output per worker improved from 20 corrected gross tons (CGT) per year to 28.5. More impressive was the SOE's success in international competition. Its share in the worldwide 12,500-ton container ship market rose from an insignificant presence in 1990 to a remarkable 40% by 1993, and the shipyard became the world's dominant producer of vessels in this category. All these changes took place when the firm was still an SOE; it was privatized in 1993.

SOURCE: Adapted from Johnson, Kotchen, and Loveman, 1995.

Strategy III: Strengthening Contracts

Emergence of Contracts. A fundamental failure of the socialist SOE is the lack of clear specification of the contractual rights and responsibilities of managers and employees (Boisot, 1996). As noted in Chapter 2, the end result becomes widespread agency problems summed up by the saying, "They pretend to pay us, and we pretend to work." A large part of SOE reforms, therefore, focus on strengthening various contracts within the firm, thus following the teachings of the *contractual view of the firm* (Cheung, 1983). The objective is to (a) provide better incentives to the agent, who may be more willing to perform; and (b) implement better monitoring mechanisms for the principal to deter agency problems. While numerous contractual relationships involving nonmanagerial employees are being introduced to SOEs (Bellman, Estrin, & Lehmann, 1995; Child, 1994), I will focus on management contracts here, because of their relevance to business strategies.

How to properly *select, motivate,* and *monitor* managers has not only been a thorny issue for SOEs everywhere (Aharoni, 1981, 1986), but also a universal problem for all companies around the world that are not directly managed by owners (Berle & Means, 1932; Marris, 1964). Virtually all management contracts cannot foresee all possible contingencies, and, as a result, have to be incomplete (Williamson, 1975). Such incompleteness, in turn, enables managers to find many excuses for their lack of performance, such as policy change, demand shift, technological shock, and plain bad luck, except their own incompetence (Roll, 1986). Despite the inherent pitfalls in management contracts, attempting to specify them at SOEs in transition economies is still much better than not having these contracts at all.

Management Contracts and Auctions. With a longer history of transition, SOEs in China, as well as their principals in the government, have accumulated more experience in this respect. Specifically, a "management responsibility system" has been implemented at many SOEs since the 1980s (Child, 1994). This system requires that SOE managers sign multiyear contracts (usually 3 to 5 years) that commit them to meet a number of specified performance indicators. These indicators typically include output goals, cost reduction, and, most important, profit targets (Groves, Hong, McMillan, & Naughton, 1995). To prevent managers from undertaking excessive on-the-job consumption, many contracts also specify minimum levels of reinvestment in the enterprise. Whereas managers in the West often have a stake in the firm in the form of stock holdings and options, SOE managers also have a stake in the welfare of the firm since their pay, especially bonuses, is typically linked to firm performance.

These practices represent a fundamental departure from classical socialism, whereby managers as well as other employees were supposed to be the "owners" of the SOE. Die-hard communists and socialists put up a strong fight against this encroachment of "capitalistic" practices. Not surprisingly, not every SOE manager is willing to sign such a contract. How, then, to select managers who will be willingly disciplined by these contractual obligations? A more radical solution is to use competitive auctions to select managers. This practice "is quite revealing of the extent to which market ideas have penetrated the Chinese state-owned enterprise system" (Groves et al., 1995, p. 878). After all, an auction is an extreme *market* method to determine the value of the property through an instant, competitive bidding process (McAfee & McMillan, 1987). It is used only when there is great uncertainty about the value of the goods, such as a painting by Picasso or a dress worn by Princess Diana. In a fully functioning managerial labor market, information about potential managers comes from their previous track records. In a transition economy, information about managers' past performance is either unreliable or nonexistent. Auctions thus become an alternative source of information revealing managerial capabilities.

Managerial auctions are typically set up by local governments, which control most SOEs in China. The auction usually specifies that a specified amount of SOE profits be submitted to local authorities and that the residual profits be at the managers' discretion, subject to satisfying other performance measures (e.g., output, cost reduction, and reinvestment). The winning CEO is usually required to put up a security deposit, which can be forfeited if the firm fails to perform as promised. By local standards, the deposit is substantial. Groves and colleagues (1995, p. 879) reported a mean of 8,500 yuan in 1989, which was nearly *four times* the average annual managerial salary at SOEs (2,177 yuan). Moreover, some managers did indeed lose some or all of their security deposit due to poor performance. According to agency theory (Jensen & Meckling, 1976), the security deposit represents *bonding costs* that *signal* to the principals the intention of the agents, in the absence of concrete information about the agents' past performance, present capabilities, and future potential. In other words, these devices minimize the transaction costs between the principals and agents (Williamson, 1975, 1985).

Since no ownership equity is transferred from the government to managers, the auctions are in essence a competitive *leasing* process. Why would managers be interested in such a process? Because the auction process allows for better opportunities to attain power, prestige, and income, compared with the stagnant system in the old SOE where only political loyalty and seniority count. Why are local governments interested in auctioning off the SOEs? As principals, they have become sick and tired of continuously feeding the SOEs with little hope of turnaround under the classical system. Because of the soft budget constraint, former SOE managers run the firm with little risk to themselves. By making new managers de facto owners of the *residual claim* (i.e., the income generated from the operations after satisfying multiple performance dimensions), the principals not only provide a stronger set of incentives to agents, but also shift risk (i.e., through a security deposit) to agents (Grossman & Hart, 1986). In essence, the budget constraint of the auctioned SOE is being *hardened*, forcing it to maximize profits (see the previous section). As a result, principals are able to assert better disciplinary influence over managers by making the managers accountable for their own performance (Walder, 1995).

The auctions and contracts not only allow the principals to better *select* and *motivate* managers, but also result in better *monitoring* of managerial efforts by the local authorities. First, although "state ownership" and "central control" are often found to be associated with the SOE, as reforms deepen, the jurisdiction of the SOE has increasingly been transferred to lower-level governments through decentralization (Granick, 1990; Walder, 1995). With a limited amount of resources, lower-level governments are more likely to have hard budget constraints than a centrally administered system. Thus, local governments have a strong incentive to monitor and discipline the SOE. Second, compared with the central bureaucracy, which has to oversee thousands of SOEs, local authorities need to monitor a much smaller number of SOEs under their jurisdiction. As a result, they are able to do a better job because of the more manageable information-processing demands (Byrd & Lin, 1989; Nee, 1992). Finally, through auctions and contracts, local authorities can put poorly performing firms on a "shorter leash," by requiring a shorter contractual period, more frequent performance reviews, and a larger security deposit from managers who bid for these firms (Groves et al., 1995, p. 881). Managers could be—and have been—fired for poor performance.

Management Turnover. Despite the conventional view of relatively rigid management structure at SOEs, some SOE managers, especially those who have gone through the auctions and contracts in China, are hired, fired, and paid increasingly well during the transition. Agency theory suggests that if CEOs, as agents, stay on the job too long, they are likely to accumulate more power, which allows them to assert influence independent of the principals—in short, a hotbed of severe agency problems can arise (Hill & Phan, 1991; Jensen, 1987). To the extent that CEO tenure can be regarded as a measure of potential agency problems, Groves and colleagues (1995, pp. 879-880) found very surprising results: While the average American and Japanese CEO had an average tenure of 7.1 and 7.7 years, respectively, the average tenure of CEOs at Chinese SOEs during the 1980s was 5.5 years. In other words, Chinese SOEs during the transition experienced *more* top management turnover than their capitalist counterparts. Apparently, due to contracts and auctions, Chinese SOE managers change jobs sufficiently frequently to allow for the emergence of a functioning "managerial labor market." As different teams of managers bid for the rights to manage the auctioned SOE, this market starts to resemble some elements of the "market for corporate control" in the West. Moreover, while these contracts and auctions were pioneered by SOEs in China, CEE and the NIS have increasingly adopted these practices in order to combat accountability problems of the socialist SOE (Ernst et al., 1996; Estrin et al., 1995; Estrin et al., 1996).

In a nutshell, with numerous and frequent management and other kinds of contracts, the socialist SOE has gradually become the *nexus of contracts* portrayed by the contractual view of the firm. While these practices are not a panacea to solve the SOE's wide-ranging accountability problems, they represent a major organizational innovation before full-fledged privatization takes place (see Chapter 5). The end result of these contracts and auctions is that they allow for capable new blood to enter the SOE's management ranks, managers who may be more interested in leading the firm to compete in the new environment, as opposed to dipping into the state coffers as before.

Strategy IV: Developing Resources and Capabilities

A Capability Gap. Given that the classical socialist SOE encompasses only production resources and a host of peripheral functions such as running housing units, schools, and hospitals, an urgent task during the transition, as implied by the *resource-based view of the firm*, is to develop other important business resources and capabilities in such crucial areas as technology, finances, and organization. However, such firm growth in transition economies faces enormous challenges in that few firms are as capable (and lucky) as the Szczecin Shipyard in Poland (see Strategy in Action 4.1) to have enough abilities to develop these multidimensional resources all by themselves (Peng & Heath, 1996). Most SOEs are handicapped by both a lack of capital and a lack of strategic factor markets, nor can most SOEs hope to acquire these necessary resources through mergers and acquisitions (Peng, 1997a). As a result, they usually rely on developing interorganizational networks by tapping into the complementary resources at partner firms (see Chapter 3).

From Informal Collaboration . . . For SOEs, developing these resources usually starts with limited, informal cooperation, such as the joint marketing cooperation between the manufacturers of MiG and Sukhoi fighters in Russia (see Strategy in Action 4.2). Informal cooperation may gradually lead to more formal joint ventures and strategic alliances, like the thousands of such entities established between foreign and domestic firms in every transition economy (Beamish, 1993). The extensive international collaboration of major Russian aerospace SOEs (Table 4.4) can serve as a case in point here (Elenkov, 1995). Typically strong in a few areas, such as basic research and low-cost manufacturing, and handicapped in others, such as marketing, these Russian aerospace SOEs have used a number of collaborative forms such as comarketing, coproduction, joint R&D,

cross-licensing, and joint ventures with a host of foreign partners in order to develop their own resources.

Strategy in Action 4.2

MiG and Sukhoi Join Hands

Throughout the Cold War, thousands of MiG fighters made by the Mikoyan Moscow Aircraft Production Organization (MAPO) were synonymous with "bogeys" widely recognized by air force pilots in the free world. During the transition, the state-owned MAPO ran into great difficulty because the Russian government cut back its orders (no orders for new aircraft between 1992 and 1998) and, with the dissolution of the Warsaw Pact, CEE air forces started to import fighters from the West. In new export markets, MAPO found that its previously popular MiG aircraft were not as successful as those made by the state-owned Aviation Military Industrial Group Sukhoi, MAPO's traditional rival in Russia. While Sukhoi aircraft had not been as famous as MiGs, Sukhoi scored big hits in the 1990s by securing sizable contracts from China, India, and Vietnam, including more than 150 Su-27s as direct exports and 300 under licensed production. More impressive, the Indonesian and South Korean air forces, traditionally exclusive markets for U.S. fighters, expressed a strong interest in Sukhoi fighters (but eventually had to cancel negotiations due to the Asian financial crisis since 1997). MAPO, in comparison, sold only approximately 70 to 80 MiG-29s to India and Malaysia in the 1990s. As a result, MAPO found that it had little choice but to cooperate with Sukhoi. To be sure, initial cooperation was limited, involving only a joint marketing strategy and a sharing of some avionics. However, in light of the merger between Boeing and McDonnell Douglass, the top two aircraft makers in the United States, further and more in-depth cooperation between the traditional rivals MAPO and Sukhoi became more important in their strategic deliberations.

SOURCE: From "Russia's Aircraft Rivals Set to Become Partners," 1998.

Over time, however, many inexperienced SOEs often find that joint ventures with foreign firms do not necessarily upgrade the SOEs'

TABLE 4.4 Developing Resources and Capabilities Through International Collaboration: The Case of Russian Aerospace SOEs

Russian Firms	Comarketing	Coproduction	Joint R&D	Cross-Licensing	Joint Ventures
Energia Khrunichew		Rockwell (U.S.)			Lockheed (U.S.) Kayser (Germany)
Illyushin	Pratt & Whitney (U.S.)	Collins (U.S.) GM Allison (U.S.)	Digital (U.S.)	GE (USA) SNECMA (France)	
Mikoyan (MAPO)		SNECMA (France)	Daewoo (Korea) Hughes (UK)	Dassault (France)	
Tupolev		Aerospatiale (France)	DASA (Germany)		
Sukhoi			Gulfstream (U.S.)		

SOURCE: Adapted from Elenkov (1995, p. 72)

capabilities, though they often help foreign firms penetrate domestic markets (Inkpen & Beamish, 1997). Given that joint ventures are inherently a race to learn from each other (Hamel, 1991), many SOEs are doomed to failure in the long run due to their limited learning and absorptive capacity on the one hand (von Glinow & Teagarden, 1988), and foreign firms' reluctance to transfer technology and management know-how to potential competitors on the other hand (Shenkar & Li, in press).

. . . *to Formal Business Groups.* Alarmed by massive losses of domestic markets to foreign companies (see Chapter 7), many SOE managers, as well as their allies in the government, have realized that individual SOEs stand little chance of defending their markets against the onslaught of multinational giants from abroad (Yin, 1993). Further, even though SOEs that are joint venture partners may be kept afloat in the short run, they are unlikely to acquire and develop competitive resources from foreign partners in the long run. Therefore, only by establishing large-scale business groups among domestic firms do the SOEs stand a chance of survival and prosperity. As a result, the movement to organize large-scale business groups (called "financial-industrial groups" in Russia and "enterprise groups" in China) began in earnest in the 1990s.

While loosely connected enterprise networks and industry associations mushroomed throughout transition economies in the 1980s (Burawoy & Krotov, 1992; Peng, 1997a), the new business groups in the 1990s, mostly led and formed by large, powerful SOEs (and also including domestic non-SOEs), represent a new breed. They have sought to create a unified command structure through cross-share holdings, board interlocks, and tight cooperation among member firms. Preliminary evidence suggests that interlocking directors sitting on member firms' boards help member firms in these groups improve financial performance (Keister, in press). Moreover, these groups usually have the blessing of the government, which, out of nationalistic (if not ideological) concerns, does not wish to see domestic markets totally occupied by foreign firms (Freinkman, 1995; Johnson, 1997; Prokop, 1995). Inspired by the development of state-led business groups in Asia, especially the Korean *chaebol*, these large business groups in transition economies aim to become national champions in their respective industries ("The Bigger, the Better," 1998). Given the massive number of SOE problems discussed earlier, the government has realized that due to its limited and weakened capacity, there is little hope to support all SOEs. What is possible, according to a recent Chinese policy, is to "grasp the big and release the small" ("Can China Reform Its Economy?" 1997). In other words, the government is willing to let a large number of small and medium-sized SOEs be privatized, acquired, or go bankrupt, but it is interested in supporting a limited number of large SOEs through the development of consolidated business groups.

While the dust has hardly settled on these new developments, what is interesting—and perhaps alarming in light of the wide-ranging failure of the Korean *chaebol* since 1997—is that as far as these large business groups are concerned, government intervention has *increased* in recent years (Lan, 1998). A new breed of bureaucrats no longer play a passive role in managing and monitoring the SOEs; instead, they become more assertive, often citing the necessity to protect and

enhance state assets. For many SOEs that have had a taste of autonomy and independence during the transition, the revival of state
intervention may not be welcome (Peng, 1997a). In such cases, the
bureaucrats do not hesitate to change the "rules" of the game in order
to threaten the resisting firms, such as delisting from the stock market,
denying access to low-cost state loans, and blacklisting them for any
future state support (Lan, 1998). Not surprisingly, in the end it is often
the bureaucrats who prevail. As the establishment of the two large oil
industry groups in China shows (Strategy in Action 4.3), the effect of
these activities, in the name of developing SOE resources and capabilities, may severely dampen competition in these new markets in
the long run.

Strategy in Action 4.3

Slick Maneuvers of Two Large Oil-Industry Groups in China

China's oil industry has attracted significant investment interest
among such multinational oil companies as Amoco, Arco, Caltex, and
Exxon of the United States; Total of France; British Petroleum; and Saudi
Aramco. By 1996, foreign oil companies had spent an estimated $200
million in staff time, feasibility studies, and hosting of Chinese delegations. Despite great hopes for a share of China's growing domestic
market, foreign companies were greatly disappointed by the reorganization of two large oil-industry groups in July 1998.

Alarmed by foreign dominance in China's automobile and electronics industries, the central government seemed determined to prevent the crucial oil industry from following the same path. The government realized that, given its relatively small size, the typical Chinese
SOE in this industry stood little chance competing against gigantic
Western multinationals, and that forming large business groups was a
"must" in order to create the needed scale and scope. With the blessing
of the government, two large SOE groups, China National Petroleum
Corporation (CNPC) and China Petroleum Group (Sinopec), which had
previously competed in most provinces, agreed to collaborate in a
fashion that resembled a classic monopoly collusion. Specifically, they

agreed to carve up the domestic market into two regions by swapping some assets with each other. CNPC was given the north and west, and Sinopec the south and east. Each of these groups included a set of companies that covered the entire vertical integration chain of the oil industry, ranging from oil exploration to refineries, transportation, and retail service stations. The reorganized CNPC group had 19 member companies, including the Daqing oilfield. The new Sinopec included 12 companies, including the Shengli oilfield. The two groups intended to reduce competition with each other by withdrawing from each other's territory, and to become dominant within their own turf by employing their muscle to shut out potential foreign entrants. While each of these groups maintained a few peripheral joint ventures with foreign firms, the doors to joint venture refineries, the category in which international oil companies showed greatest interest and that had the most lucrative prospects for China's domestic market, were largely closed. Experts estimated that it would take at least a decade before the doors to foreign competition would be really open in this industry.

SOURCES: Fesharaki & Wu, 1996; "Slick Maneuvers," 1998.

Overall, developing resources and capabilities constitutes one of the most important SOE strategies during the transition. Whether through informal collaboration or more formal cooperation culminating in large business groups, numerous SOEs have strengthened resources in areas where they are traditionally weak, such as technology, marketing, and financing (Ernst et al., 1996; Jefferson & Rawski, 1994; Rawski, 1994). To the extent that a firm's name embodies its resource repertoire, the evolution of the typical title of the SOE during the transition is illuminating. Traditionally, as a single plant, the SOE is usually an "ABC Factory." As it grows, it is increasingly called "XYZ Company." More recently, becoming a group (or a member of it) indicates resourcefulness, power, and prestige. As a result, the number of firms sporting the word *Group* in their title has been on the rise.

Summary and Discussion

Theories and Practices. Drawing from four major theories on the nature of the firm, I have argued and demonstrated that various strategies adopted by SOEs during the transition can be regarded as a desire to follow the teachings of these theories. While asking for more government support does not really constitute a well-crafted strategy, it reflects the continued belief in the property rights view of the firm, at least its socialist version. Maximizing profits is clearly in line with the neoclassical theory of the firm. Strengthening contracts within the firm, especially through auctioning the enterprise and signing contracts with managers, moves the SOE one step closer to the realities of the firm as a "nexus of contracts" portrayed by the contractual view of the firm. Finally, developing resources and capabilities, through a number of cooperative activities, highlights a strong interest to acquire and sustain competitive advantage suggested by the resource-based view of the firm.

It is important to note that while strategies in these four areas are analytically distinct according to different theories, they can also occur simultaneously. In other words, an SOE can cry for more government help, maximize profits, strengthen contracts, and develop resources and capabilities *at the same time.* This is hardly surprising, since the four major theories, while portraying the firm from different angles, overlap considerably (Conner, 1991). What is interesting is that these theories, originally developed to analyze the capitalistic firm, do not have much relevance to the SOE under state socialism (except the applicability of the property rights school from a totally *opposite* direction!) (Shenkar & von Glinow, 1994). More recently, these theories appear to be significantly insightful as the socialist SOE employs a number of strategies to transform itself out of its former self during the transition. In other words, as the SOE becomes a more "normal" firm, these theories emerge to be more useful. Although most SOE managers, government officials, and foreign advisors may not be clearly aware of the influence of these theories, an explicit understanding of these theories may not only help them to make sense of their actions, but can also be beneficial to open up their horizons as they contemplate the next strategic move. In this case, theories do seem to be able to guide practices.

Problems and Prospects. While consistent with different influential theories, the strategies adopted by SOEs are not without problems. For many SOEs, asking for more help from the government merely lengthens the death process, and the government's unwillingness to allow many SOEs to go bankrupt only adds time bombs to the economy in the long run. While maximizing profits through retrenchment is important, using diversification as a "lifeboat" strategy (Guthrie, 1997), without knowing much about the limits of such a strategy, can easily backfire. Firms in transition economies will be better off if they pay more attention to the international experience of failed diversification and take advantage of the cumulative findings by Western scholars (Dess, Gupta, Hennart, & Hill, 1995; Hoskisson & Hitt, 1994; Rumelt, 1974). Although management contracts and SOE auctions represent a "great leap forward" in strengthening contracts within the firm, the socialist SOE, without privatization, suffers from a permanent failure to draw a line separating administrative and managerial responsibilities. Without a property-rights-based legal and regulatory framework (see Chapter 3), SOE managers are afraid of uncertain policy changes when their contract expires. As a result, during their contract period, they tend to engage in excessive short-run maximizing behavior, such as dispersing large sums of bonuses to themselves and employees, at the expense of the long-run interests of the firm (Boisot & Child, 1988; Cheung & Xing, 1994). In terms of developing resources and capabilities, while cooperation to access complementary assets based on firms' own strategic choices is necessary, forming large business groups with increasing government intervention casts a dark shadow over the development of these groups.

Under state socialism, SOEs occupy the "commanding heights" of the economy, crowding out all other organizational forms (if any). In a diversified market economy, SOEs are but one organizational "species" competing with other species, such as private, joint venture, and wholly foreign-owned firms (Tan & Peng, 1998a). Although there is no question that most SOEs have become more competitive compared with what they were 10 or 20 years ago, the quest for a sustainable market niche in the economy (Hannan & Freeman, 1989) ultimately boils down to how strong they are *relative to* other competing organizational forms. While some notable exceptions do exist (see Strategy in Action 4.1), most SOEs, no matter how reformed they become, are not as proactive, dynamic, and entrepreneurial as their non-SOE competitors. Instead, SOEs tend to be relatively passive Defenders,[5] witnessing their previously protected markets being gradually chipped away by other, aggressive firms (Tan & Litschert, 1994). Compared with other organizational forms, SOEs have increasingly been associated with stagnation, low prestige, and low pay. Although SOE reforms, especially the auctions and contracts, have nurtured a new generation of capable managers, many managers have left SOEs, created their own start-ups, and/or joined private, joint venture, or wholly foreign-owned companies in search of better pay, promotion, and other opportunities. Many managers and employees who stay at the SOEs are those with few alternative employment options elsewhere. Therefore, the departure of capable managers from SOEs does not bode well for these firms. Finally, many firms have chosen to maintain their "SOE" status on the books for political benefits, and have in effect become privatized through leasing and auctioning (see Chapter 6). Some firms carry the interesting title of being "state-owned, private-operated" enterprises, significantly blurring the traditional boundaries separating SOEs from non-SOEs. Overall, the long-run viability of the SOE, relative to that of other competitive organizational forms in transition economies, is highly questionable.

In light of the massive scale of SOE failure and the global wave of privatization everywhere, the decision to privatize the vast majority of SOEs was made throughout CEE and the NIS in the early 1990s. Belatedly and halfheartedly, by the mid-1990s the Chinese government realized that entirely supporting its SOE sector was no longer a viable option, and that privatization was inevitable.

Governments in transition economies have increasingly reached the consensus not to keep these dinosaurs alive at all cost. However, society pays a heavy price when SOEs richly endowed with historical investment and human talents self-destruct. The goal is not to embalm dinosaurs though subsidies, protectionism, and preferential treatment—as socialist governments often do—but to ensure that large companies do not become dinosaurs in the first place. It appears that private firms, driven by an instinct to maintain competitiveness, may have a better chance of survival than SOEs in the long run. How to privatize SOEs will be explored in the next chapter.

▨ CONCLUSIONS

From a time when there was little need for competitive strategies, SOEs in transition economies have come a long way to exhibit a number of strategic behaviors that better reflect the teachings of the different theories of the firm. To answer the five fundamental questions in strategy posed in Chapter 1, I have shown that firms differ (Question 1) because of differences in institutional frameworks (see also Chapter 3). Operating in a different environment, the classical SOE under state socialism bears little resemblance to the "normal" firm described by various theories. As the institutional frameworks in transition economies take on some (but not all) of the elements of market economies, the SOE's strategies increasingly reflect what theories suggest the firm should be doing. Similarly, how firms behave (Question 2) can be traced to the different constraints under which they operate. SOEs with soft budget constraints have little incentive to maximize profits, strengthen contracts, and develop resources. Once hard budget constraints are imposed, their behavior has gradually to become consistent with what different theories of the firm posit.

Question 3 asks how strategy outcomes are affected by strategy processes. As discussed in Chapter 3, the selection of various strategic choices is the product of the interaction between institutions and organizations. To the extent that the institutional framework still allows for soft budget constraints, SOE managers are likely to continue to hope to be able to dip into state coffers. On the other hand, when the institutional environment becomes more competitive and SOEs face a sink-or-swim situation, they will usually struggle to learn how to swim as fast as they can. The scope of the firm (Question 4) is determined by what a firm is expected to do. The SOE under state socialism is merely a production unit performing a function similar to that of a branch plant in a large corporation in the West. Therefore, it is not expected to undertake R&D, marketing, financing, and multi-unit coordination. Instead, it has other functions, such as maintaining full employment and providing social welfare. During the transition, the SOE is expected to compete, thus calling for the development of a number of new resources and capabilities. With some exceptions such as the Russian aircraft and arms manufacturers (Elenkov, 1995) and Chinese red chip conglomerates active in Hong Kong (Au, Peng, & Wang, in press; "A Chinese Banquet of Red Chip Stocks," 1997; de Trenck, 1998), the last question, What determines the international success and failure of firms? has only limited applicability to most SOEs in transition economies. This chapter, therefore, does not focus on this question. Chapter 7, on the strategies of foreign firms, will concentrate on this question.

In conclusion, theories of the firm can greatly help us answer some fundamental questions in strategy about the SOE. For students, scholars, and practitioners, this chapter suggests that these theories not only can shed light on what firms did in the past, but can also be beneficial to guide what firms should be doing as they continue their transition in the future.

NOTES

1. Although some authors tried to make a distinction between "resources," "capabilities," and another closely related term, "core competencies" (Teece et al., 1997), "it is likely that they will become badly blurred in practice" (Barney, 1997, p. 144). Moreover, it seems that a debate about the terminology will not be of much value to practitioners. Therefore, following Barney (1997), as well as my first book (Peng, 1998), the terms *resources* and *capabilities* are used interchangeably and often in a parallel sense throughout this book.

2. Strictly speaking, the features of the "socialist SOE" portrayed in this section belong to the SOE "under state socialism" as described in Chapter 2. For compositional simplicity, we will use the term "socialist SOE" throughout the chapter. While the focus here is on SOEs in socialist and transition economies, it is important to note that, for several decades, SOEs have existed in many other parts of the world, such as Canada (Sexty, 1980), France (Hafsi & Koenig, 1988), Greece (Lioukas, Bourantas, & Papadakis, 1993), India (Khandwalla, 1992; Ramamurti, 1987), Italy (Mazzolini, 1980), and the United States (Kole & Mullherin, 1997).

3. The Chinese Academy of Social Sciences Project Team (1997, pp. 132-133) reported that during 1994 the 34,000 SOEs in China operated 16,783 schools and 3,619 medical facilities. The expenditures to operate these educational and medical facilities, together with those to provide housing and pension benefits to SOE employees and families, were about 10% *higher* than the total profits of these firms. Non-SOE firms, on the other hand, typically do not have to shoulder these burdens.

4. *Downscoping* is a term coined by Hoskisson and Hitt (1994). It refers to a firm's efforts to reduce the scope of its business from covering a number of industries and market segments to a smaller set that is more manageable.

5. Being a Defender is a major type of strategy in a typology proposed by Miles and Snow (1978). Other strategies in this typology include Prospector, Analyzer, and Reactor. Defenders are typically firms with a narrow product market, a stable customer group, and an established organizational structure managed by relatively old executives. Using a sample of firms in China, Tan and Litschert (1994) reported that SOEs tend to take on a Defender strategy. In a follow-up study, Tan and Peng (1998a) found that in transition economies, while SOEs follow a Defender strategy, private firms and foreign joint ventures are more likely to be Prospectors and Analyzers, respectively. See Chapter 8 for more details.

5 Strategies of Privatized and Reformed Firms

The owner of a business, when contemplating any change, is led by his own interest to weigh the whole gain that it would probably bring to the business, against the whole loss. But the private interest of the salaried manager, or official, often draws him in another direction: the path of least resistance, of greatest comfort and least risk to himself.

—Alfred Marshall (1920)

Chapter 4 suggests that no matter how "reformed" SOEs have become, most of them continue to suffer from a host of governance and performance problems. As a result, privatizing these enterprises has become central to the transition process. It contributes to the transformation of an entire economic system from one in which politicians, planners, and bureaucrats make most resource allocation decisions to one in which private firm managers begin to assume that role.

Although state ownership is being phased out across different transition economies, the term *privatization*, which implies a rejection of public ownership, has not been universally accepted. In China and Vietnam, where the Communist Party is still in power, euphemisms such as "reform," "corporatization," and "equitization" have been used to refer to the process.[1] Even for many officially "privatized" firms in CEE and the NIS, the state still maintains substantial influence. As a result, in this chapter no conceptual distinction is made between "privatized" and "reformed" companies. Instead, we are interested in three more substantive questions: (a) What kind of private firms can former SOEs become? (b) What are the different paths of privatization? (c) What are the strategic responses of these firms that are privatized and/or reformed?[2]

TYPES OF PRIVATE FIRMS

Many people believe that once an SOE is privatized, it will automatically become a "private" firm and behave accordingly. Such a view, however, proves to be naive, since there are a range of private ownership configurations that a non-SOE can take, such as (a) employee control, (b) manager control, (c) owner control, and (d) investor control, each with different strategic implications. Each of them will be highlighted below (see Table 5.1 for a summary).

The Employee-Controlled Firm

As an "unconventional" capitalist firm, the employee-controlled firm is controlled by *nonmanagerial* employees, who usually hold a majority of the shares (Ben-Ner, 1988). Only a relatively small number of firms (e.g., agricultural cooperatives) are organized as employee-controlled firms at their inception. Most employee-controlled firms are the result of an employee *buyout,* which typically occurs when the firm is urgently in need of capital. By taking equity, employees essentially transform themselves from agents to principals. Since principals are less likely to shirk, the employee-controlled firm, according to agency theory, should have more motivated employee-owners, less need for monitoring, and, therefore, better performance.

On the other hand, the employee-controlled firm tends to have difficulties in decision making (Bonin, Jones, & Putterman, 1993; Hansmann, 1990). Specifically, it is very costly for employees to be

TABLE 5.1 Types of Private Firms: Benefits and Problems		
Type of Firms	*Benefits*	*Problems*
Employee-controlled	• Reduced agency problems	• Inefficient decision making
		• Work well only when firm size is small and employees are homogeneous in skills and interest
Manager-controlled	• Reduced agency problems	• Possibility of management entrenchment
	• Short-term boost in performance	• Long-term competitiveness may be sacrificed
Owner-controlled	• Simple structure	• Small scale
	• Reduced agency problems	• Inability to raise large sums of capital
Investor-controlled	• Able to raise large sums of capital and attain large scale and scope	• Complex and bureaucratic
	• Professional managers	• Separation of ownership and control, which may be breeding ground for agency problems
	• A number of corporate governance mechanisms to protect shareholder interest	• Limited effectiveness of corporate governance mechanisms

directly involved in the firm's decision-making process. These problems arise because employees have different skills and interests in the governance of the firm. While some employee-owners may be more interested in reinvesting profits in the firm for long-term benefits, many others are interested in short-term consumption by paying themselves above-the-market wages. The firm, as a result, has problems in capital accumulation. The greater these differences, the greater the costs of reaching agreement, and the greater the dangers of either failing to agree at all, or of making economically inefficient compromises. As a result, employee ownership would operate best in situations where employees are relatively homogeneous and where the firm is small. Conversely, problems are especially likely to be severe when employees represent diverse skills and interests and when firm size is large.

In sum, the employee-controlled firm, like any other organizational form, has both benefits and costs. It seems that, on balance, the benefits of reduced agency problems may be outweighed by the costs of inefficient decision making when the firm size is large.

The Manager-Controlled Firm

The manager-controlled firm is an enterprise whose shares are mostly owned by a group of senior managers. Since the early part of the 20th century, most large corporations in the West have been run by professional managers but owned by a different group of shareholders (Berle & Means, 1932). As agents, managers without equity involvement may have little incentive to maximize shareholder wealth. Instead, managers may maximize their own utilities, such as power, money, prestige, and job security, at the expense of shareholders' interests (Jensen & Meckling, 1976; Marris, 1964). A remedy is to transform managers from agents to principals by allowing them to take equity stakes in the firm in order to provide more incentives to motivate managers (Demsetz & Lehn, 1985).

Similar to employee-controlled firms, few firms are organized as manager-controlled firms when they are founded. Most manager-controlled firms are the result of a management *buyout*, whereby a group of managers use personal savings and take on debt to buy firms' stock (Fox & Marcus, 1992). Once having become principals, managers are naturally more motivated to work harder. Moreover, debt further compels managers to improve firm performance (Jensen, 1987). In the West, manager-controlled firms typically experience some performance improvement, especially during the immediate aftermath of a buyout (Phan & Hill, 1995). The long-term impact of such a transformation, however, is unclear. Some studies found that since managers are eager to service the personal debt, they tend to be more interested in short-term profit maximization at the expense of the firm's long-term competitiveness, especially in the area of research and development (Long & Ravenscraft, 1993; Reich, 1989).

What, then, is the *optimum* level of management ownership? Research in the West has suggested that the optimum level of management ownership appears to be between 5% and 10%, beyond which firm performance actually deteriorates (Morck, Shleifer, & Vishny,

1988). It appears that a high level of management ownership increases managerial power, presents managers with little risk of being removed by shareholders, and is likely to result in management entrenchment (Finkelstein, 1992; Finkelstein & Hambrick, 1996). Furthermore, managers with high equity ownership are typically very rich, particularly in the case of large public corporations in the West. As a result, they may have little interest in further maximization of the market value of their firms relative to their interest in the pursuit and consumption of various "perks" (Jensen, 1993).

In sum, management ownership helps solve agency problems on the part of managers. However, management control is not a panacea. Too much management control of the firm may result in short-term profit maximization and management retrenchment, which do not bode well for the firm's long-term interests.

The Owner-Controlled Firm

The owner-controlled firm is the classical, simple "private" firm owned and run by a single owner (or a single family of owners) with no separation between ownership and control. While owner-controlled firms usually have a simple structure and are less prone to having agency problems, they tend to be small and to have a severe handicap, namely, limited sources of financing. No matter how wealthy the owner and his or her (sometimes extended) family are, there is a limit to how much capital this family group can raise. If the owner-controlled firm survives long enough, it will sooner or later confront a critical point at which its desire to keep the firm in family hands will have to be compromised by its need for more capital, which in turn will introduce outside investors and influence into the firm (Fukuyama, 1996). Over time, the owner-controlled firm may evolve into an investor-controlled firm (which we turn to next) as the proportion of outside capital overshadows the contributions provided by the owners.

The Investor-Controlled Firm

With few exceptions, one being the Ford Motor Company,[3] most of the large corporations in the West today are investor-controlled firms. These firms are able to raise large sums of capital externally and, as a result, are more likely to attain the scale and scope necessary to survive and prosper in the increasingly competitive economy (Chandler, 1990). While the original owner family may still wish to retain the control rights after the initial introduction of outside investors, it has to confront the growing difficulty of finding competent managers to head the firm (Penrose, 1959). Over time, the size of the firm may reach such an extent that no family can generate enough sons, daughters, in-laws, and other relatives who are both capable *and* interested in running the business. At this point, introducing professional managers not related to the owner family becomes a necessity (Fukuyama, 1996; Peng, 1999). Professional managers bring to the firm much-needed expertise on the one hand, but also present a thorny issue of the separation of ownership and control on the other hand. First noted by Berle and Means (1932) nearly 70 years ago, the mechanisms of how to govern the complex, investor-controlled corporation, namely, *corporate governance,* have attracted significant attention (Hart, 1995; Jensen, 1993).

In the West, there are a number of governance mechanisms that investors can employ. These mechanisms can be grouped as voice-based and exit-based. *Voice-based* mechanisms refer to shareholders' willingness to work with existing management by "voicing" their concerns. *Exit-based* measures, in contrast, indicate that shareholders no longer have patience with incumbent managers and are willing to "exit." There are three primary voice-based measures. First, investors elect their representatives to form boards of directors to safeguard their interests (Fama & Jensen, 1983; Mizruchi, 1983). Second, managers' pay can be linked to stock market performance of the firm (Bruce & Buck, 1997). Third, the managerial labor market serves to reward managers who maximize shareholder wealth and penalize those who do not (Jensen, 1987).

However, each of these voice-based mechanisms has its limitations. Directors on the board are often nominated by top managers, who tend to nominate their own friends, colleagues, and associates. These directors, in turn, may not be able or willing to challenge the decisions of top managers (Coffee, 1991; Dalton, Daily, Ellstrand, & Johnson, 1998). Linking pay to stock market performance is also problematic, since the fluctuation of companies' share prices is influenced by a wide range of factors, many of which are beyond managers' control (Zahra & Pearce, 1989). Moreover, total executive compensation in the West not only includes salaries, but also bonuses and stock options. Once all components of compensation are taken into account, there is very little sensitivity in the link between pay and performance (Jensen & Murphy, 1990; Kaplan, 1994). Unlike the product market, the managerial labor market suffers from a lack of transparency and causality in that managers can always attribute their poor performance to external factors beyond their control (e.g., changes in regulatory policies). As a result, rewarding winners and disciplining losers in such a highly imperfect market is a daunting task. In a nutshell, under some circumstances, shareholders' "voice" may be too weak to have much impact.

When these voice-based governance mechanisms fail, a number of exit-based mechanisms, such as mergers, acquisitions, takeovers, and proxy fights, can be employed, leading to a *market for corporate control* (Jensen & Ruback, 1983). As the most hostile governance mechanisms, these strategies are often used as an external governance of last resort, utilized only when internal control mechanisms have failed (Jensen, 1993). Specifically, the market for corporate control disciplines managers by replacing poorly performing incumbent managers with a new team of managers. Taken together, the first three voice-based mechanisms aim at fine-tuning the firm, while the exit-based market for corporate control enables the "wholesale" removal of deeply entrenched managers (Jensen, 1993).

As a radical approach, the market for corporate control has its own limitations. First, it is very costly to wage such financial battles (Jensen & Ruback, 1983). Second, these fights, takeovers, and restructuring typically result in a profound sense of conflict, stress, and alienation among managers and employees, which in turn leads to abnormally high turnover among acquired firms (Buono & Bowditch, 1989). Finally, a large number of mergers and acquisitions seem to be driven by sheer overconfidence (Haspeslagh & Jemison, 1991; Roll, 1986), and the long-term performance of postmerger firms is not particularly impressive (Ravenscraft & Scherer, 1987).

Overall, there are multiple governance mechanisms in investor-controlled firms. Together, they lead to reasonably effective, though far from perfect, corporate governance in the West.[4] These mechanisms will be increasingly important in transition economies as firms are being privatized.

Summary

It is important to understand what types of private firms former SOEs become. Among the four "ideal" types of private firms, the owner-controlled firm is the simplest and the investor-controlled firm the most complex. In comparison, employee- and manager-controlled firms occupy a middle range in terms of structure and governance.

PATHS OF PRIVATIZATION

Privatization in transition economies takes place in an environment characterized by a relative lack of legal, regulatory, and financial institutions (DeCastro & Uhlenbruck, 1997; Earle, Frydman, & Rapaczynski, 1993; Fogel, 1995). Legislation has to be enacted that, for the first time, introduces Western-style property rights, financial reporting requirements, and securities and bankruptcy laws. These new "rules of the game" individually and in combination result in a set of formal constraints in an emerging institutional framework (see Chapter 3). Overall, privatization legislation and policies are concerned with three objectives: (a) the *speed* of privatization, (b) the political and economic *acceptability* of the process, and (c) the impact on firm *performance* (Wright, Filatotchev, & Buck, 1997). There are some inherent trade-offs among them. For example, rapid privatization often necessitates disposal of SOE assets at minimal prices and involves governance mechanisms that yield few gains in efficiency. As a result, there is a need to balance these three objectives (Glaeser & Scheinkman, 1996; Katz & Owen, 1995; Laban & Wolf, 1993; Ramamurti, 1992; Rapacki, 1995). As will be seen below, differing paths of privatization are usually the result of different emphases on these objectives.

Privatizing Through Employee and Management Buyouts

A Two-Phase Model of Privatization. Most Western advisors have recommended that SOEs be transformed into investor-controlled firms with strong governance mechanisms (e.g., Sachs, 1993). Many reform-

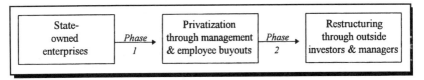

Figure 5.1. A Two-Phase Model of Privatization and Restructuring of Former SOEs

ers in CEE and the NIS have attempted to follow this advice; however, their efforts have been frustrated in many ways (Blasi, Kroumova, & Kruse, 1997; Boycko, Shleifer, & Vishny, 1995, 1996; Buck, Filatotchev, & Wright, 1998; Estrin, 1994; Frydman, Rapaczynski, & Earle, 1993). A prerequisite for investor-controlled firms is simply the availability of outside investors. Unfortunately, throughout the region, domestic investors had little capital in the early 1990s, when CEE and the NIS were going through shock therapy (see Chapter 2). Foreign investors, despite their financial abundance, hesitated to provide a large sum of capital in an uncertain environment. As a result, due to the lack of outside investors, the initial privatization usually results in substantial insider control of the firm through employee and management buyouts (Earle & Estrin, 1996; Wright, Filatotchev, Buck, & Robbie, 1993; Wright, Hoskisson, Filatotchev, & Buck, 1998). Therefore, the process of restructuring former SOEs through privatization has typically taken the two steps depicted in Figure 5.1, first through employee and management buyouts and then through possible outside investors and managers, as opposed to a single burst of becoming investor-controlled firms overnight.

Management and Employee Buyouts. The initial wave of privatization actually took place *before* privatization laws and policies were enacted. Since the mid-1980s, numerous SOEs were leased to managers, employees, and employees' collectives in order to improve SOE performance (Peng, 1994, pp. 240-242; see also Chapter 4). Throughout transition economies, as the general political environment became more favorable to privatization but before such legislation was enacted, many employees and managers took advantage of the chaotic and ambiguous situation by seizing SOE assets. While such "spontaneous" privatization was fast and rampant, the acceptability of these "lawless" practices to the media, the public, and the government was low. Although SOE assets, in theory, belong to all citizens, it seems that some insiders, in particular managers, have unfairly enriched themselves at the expense of rank-and-file employees and the wider society. Shown in Strategy in Action 5.1, managers' stripping of the assets of Apisz in Hungary serves as a case in point as to why such unregulated, "spontaneous" privatization has received a lot of criticism (Wright et al., 1993).

Strategy in Action 5.1

Spontaneous Privatization at Apisz in Hungary

Apisz was a state-owned wholesaler and retailer of stationery, toys, and fancy goods, and was widely regarded as one of the most successful companies in Hungary. At the beginning of 1989, the company's senior management took advantage of the chaotic situation and "spontaneously" bought out the firm *before* privatization legislation was enacted. The management changed the firm's Articles of Association and made the change in ownership irreversible. Then Apisz's management considered that it, rather than the government, had the right to sell the firm. Top managers estimated that the firm was worth at least HUF 1 billion,[a] the level at which they started negotiations with potential buyers. By mid-1990, when privatization negotiations were largely completed, involved parties were willing to buy the firm at HUF 2 billion. The second buyout was to be funded by Citibank with involvement from the Berger group, a dominant supplier to Apisz. It was proposed initially that employees would own 36%, Citibank 36%, Berger 15%, and others 13%, and that managers as sellers would receive most of the proceeds. Because of widespread concern over this process, the Supreme Court of Hungary considered the legality of the transaction. Although the Supreme Court stated that the registration of the new firm was unlawful, it could not invalidate it in the absence of privatization legislation. Nevertheless, issues raised by the case, particularly concerns about managers who enriched themselves from transactions in which their authority to sell assets was dubious, and perceptions that foreigners were benefiting from the sale of state-owned assets at undervalued prices, were instrumental in the enactment of privatization legislation to better regulate the process.

SOURCE: Wright, Filatotchev, Buck, & Robbie (1993, p. 31).
NOTE: a. The exchange rates at that time were: US$1 = HUF59.1 (1989 average) and HUF63.2 (1990 average).

In the early 1990s, governments throughout CEE and the NIS quickly enacted formal legislation and regulations, thus launching the official process of privatization. Politically, these policies were motivated by a desire to phase out SOEs as soon as possible; determined reformers wanted to make the process as irreversible as possible. As a result, speed in the privatization process was paramount. To avoid political backlash, acceptability was also an important criterion. At that time, privatization through employee and manager buyouts was typically the only feasible path. There were usually four reasons behind such a policy choice. First, because there were few alternative sources of privatization, employee and manager buyouts appeared to be the fastest route to privatization, which served the political purpose of quickly phasing out SOEs (Boycko et al., 1996; Filatotchev, Hoskisson, Buck, & Wright, 1996). Second, given the turmoil and uncertainty unleashed by the wide-ranging transitions in shock therapy, reformers felt that it was necessary to buy insider support for privatization by allowing and encouraging insiders to take equity, on the argument that even insider-dominated privatization is better than state ownership (Blasi et al., 1997). Third, according to agency theory, insiders, who are now owners, should be more interested in restructuring because they can benefit from higher profits (Phan & Hill, 1995). Finally, given that many SOEs had already been "spontaneously" privatized (see Strategy in Action 5.1), taking them back from the new owners in the absence of another group of private owners would be practically difficult and politically explosive (Blasi et al., 1997).

In practice, formal privatization typically took three routes: (a) voucher buyouts, (b) subsidized loans, and (c) direct purchases. In the early 1990s, most citizens in CEE and the NIS had negligible savings, especially in the face of hyperinflation (see Chapter 2). In order to facilitate participation by the wider population, governments in countries such as the Czech Republic and Russia typically issued vouchers to all adults, who could then exchange them for enterprise stock (Estrin, 1994; OECD, 1996). To encourage buyouts, subsidized loans are often provided by the state on favorable terms. In Hungary and Poland, for example, buyers have to pay at least 10% and 20%, respectively, of the purchase price, using their own resources, and the rest can be financed at a relatively low interest rate to be repaid in 5 to 15 years (Wright et al., 1993, p. 41).

While direct purchases needed buyers to spend hard-earned personal savings, voucher buyouts in essence were a "giveaway" requiring little sacrifice and risk on the part of the voucher bearer. Subsidized loans occupy the middle range of sacrifice and risk. In general, the more buyers endure personal sacrifice and the more risk they take on, the more likely the postprivatization firm will exhibit value-maximizing behavior. Given a large number of voucher buyouts involving little sacrifice and risk, the question of whether the privatized firm will engage in much-needed restructuring looms large on the horizon (Filatotchev, Wright, & Buck, 1992, 1995).

Although many SOEs were auctioned openly, the rules were generally stacked in favor of insiders, who could buy out their own firms at a deep *discount,* have *preemptive* rights to the equity before other investors could make a bid, or both. In Hungary, for example, the rules for share subscriptions often weighted ownership toward managers and long-time employees through a system of points reflecting tenure on the job, position, and salary (Wright et al., 1997, p. 217). Insiders also obtained considerable assistance from the state to carry out privatization (Earle & Estrin, 1996). Among the 435 firms that participated in the first round of privatization in Hungary (Table 5.2), 58% and 31% of the privatization capital for employee- and manager-controlled firms, respectively, was provided by the state as loans. In contrast, domestic outside investors were able to obtain only 28% of capital as loans from the state, and foreign investors received no such credit. Table 5.2 also gives information on the relationship between the price paid for privatization and the "nominal value" of the enterprises. Although the nominal value of the SOEs in a transition economy was highly uncertain, it was taken seriously by officials anxious to avoid accusations of "giving away the country" to foreigners and former communist cadres (the *nomenklatura*). The ratio between

TABLE 5.2 Organizational Diversity After the First Round of Privatization in Hungary, 1994

Ownership Types[a]	SOE	ECE	MCE	DCE	FCE	Total Sample
Sample	5	67	120	226	14	435
Inside owners	4%	89%	88%	7%	5%	14%
Outside owners	16%	4%	4%	84%	90%	49%
Domestic investors	16%	4%	4%	84%	6%	46%
Foreign investors	0	0	0	0	84%	3%
Other	5%	0	0	0	0	1%
State ownership	75%	8%	7%	8%	4%	8%
Size (number employed)	315	231	156	255	330	231
State loans/price	—	58%	31%	28%	0	33%
Price/nominal value (discount)	—	76%	76%	88%	87%	83%

SOURCE: Adapted from Earle and Estrin (1996, p. 42), based on data compiled by the State Property Agency.
NOTE: a. SOE: State-owned enterprise; ECE: Employee-controlled enterprise; MCE: Manager-controlled enterprise; DCE: Domestic outside investor-controlled enterprise; FCE: Foreign investor-controlled enterprise. The sample is nonrandom. It includes all the firms that participated in the first round of "self-privatization."

price paid and the value of the firm thus becomes an indicator of the *preference* shown by officials toward different kinds of new owners. It seems that all new owners received some discount off the nominal value (the average was 17%), but insiders received the largest discount (24%). Outsiders, both domestic and foreign, received a discount of 12% to 13%.

The end result was that the majority of former SOEs became employee- and manager-controlled firms (Table 5.3). In Romania and Russia, for example, employee and management buyouts after the first wave of privatization accounted for approximately 98% and 90%, respectively, of all privatization cases. In these firms, a substantial percentage of the shares was controlled by employees and managers, ranging from 51% in Poland to 95% in Romania (Earle & Estrin, 1996, p. 29).

The country that granted by far the fewest concessions to insiders was the Czech Republic (Ernst, Alexeev, & Marer, 1996; Takla, 1994).

TABLE 5.3   Employee and Management Ownership After the First Wave of Privatization in CEE and the NIS

Country (sample)	Companies With Employee and Management Control	Percentage of Privatization Cases	Average Percentage of Shares Held by Employees and Managers
Czech Republic (first wave of voucher privatization)	3	1	4.4
Hungary (self-privatization)	187	43	42.0
Poland (private liquidation)	1,478	75	50.8
Romania (all large privatization)	600	98	95.0
Russia (all large privatization)	6,300	90	65.0

SOURCE: Adapted from Earle and Estrin (1996, p. 29).

No special discounts or preemptive rights were made available to employees, managers, or, in fact, any group, with the exception of preferring Czech citizens over foreigners. As a result, in only 1% of the *large* privatization cases did employees and managers acquire majority control. On average, the shares of a large privatized firm held by employees and managers were only 4.4% (Table 5.3). On the other hand, in *small* firm privatizations, employees and managers were still able to purchase an estimated nearly half of the shops and service establishments sold in open auctions (Earle & Estrin, 1996, p. 39).

While employee- and manager-controlled firms had their own weaknesses alluded to earlier, on balance, initial privatization through employee and management buyouts was widely regarded as "a great success" (Boycko, Shleifer, & Vishny, 1993, p. 180). For example, in Russia, 19,000 SOEs were privatized in the short span of 2 years (1992-1994), the largest privatization program in scale and scope in history (Blasi et al., 1997; Boycko et al., 1993, 1996). In comparison, worldwide, fewer than 1,000 firms were privatized between 1980 and 1987 (Peng & Heath, 1996, p. 504). Overall, firms were being privatized at a breathtaking pace, and the population approved of privatization and actively participated in the process. Poland, for instance, closed its Ministry of Privatization in September 1996, citing the completion of its job. Privatization does a lot more than just reshuffle assets. Most fundamentally, it puts an end to central planning as a way to organize economic activities and hence represents a decisive step toward capitalism wherein firms have real owners whose rights become increasingly clear.

Privatizing Through Outside Investment

Restructuring: Paths and Problems. After the initial euphoria about the fall of communism and the rise of private enterprise, it soon became apparent, on one hand, that smaller privatized firms, as well as new private start-ups, exhibit a great deal of entrepreneurship throughout transition economies (Barberis, Boycko, Shleifer, & Tsukanova, 1996), and, on the other hand, that most large privatized firms controlled by insiders have engaged in little restructuring (Ash & Hare, 1994). The dynamism of smaller firms will be discussed in the next chapter. This section focuses on the critical task of stimulating restructuring at large privatized firms through outside investment.

There are usually three potential paths of restructuring: (a) changing product mix, (b) reducing capacity and employment, and/or (c) reorganizing structure. Because each of these paths has different implications for various groups of employees, each group is likely to block particular paths that will threaten its position. As noted earlier, widely dispersed employee ownership, in combination with a large firm size, increases the costs and reduces the speed of reaching efficient decisions, and is not conducive to restructuring (McDonald, 1993). Put bluntly, Boycko and colleagues (1996, p. 317) argued that employee control may simply be "bad for restructuring."

Given the paralysis at many employee-controlled firms, many managers believe that concentrating ownership in the hands of "experts"—that is, themselves—will be better. Shown in Table 5.4 (column 5), Russian CEOs *wished* that the optimal level of management ownership were 44%, which was twice as much as the highest level of shares that they actually controlled (at 22% in 1994) (Blasi et al., 1997, p. 193). As a result, managers use a number of tactics to increase their control of the firm, such as buying shares from employees, restricting

TABLE 5.4   Evolution of Ownership Structure in Privatized Russian Firms, 1993-1996: A Survey of Surveys

Survey Time (sample)	(1) 1993 (142 firms)	(2) 1994 (139 firms)	(3) 1995 (314 firms)	(4) 1996 (357 firms)	5) What Do CEOs Want?
Insiders (%)	65	66	59	58	69
Managers (%)	9	22	12	18	44
Employees (%)	56	44	47	40	25
Outsiders (%)	22	22	31	33	24
Large investors (%)	—	16	23	27	—
Small investors (%)	—	6	8	6	—
State (%)	13	12	10	9	7

SOURCES: (1) Blasi and Shleifer (1996, p. 80); (2) Buck, Filatotchev, and Wright (1998, p. 93); (3) Peng, Buck, and Filatotchev (1999, p. 36); (4) and (5) Blasi, Kroumova, and Kruse (1997, p. 193).

employees' rights to sell their shares to outsiders, and sometimes illegally changing corporate charters from "one share one vote" to "one shareholder one vote" (Blasi et al., 1997). Also shown in Table 5.4 (first four columns), in Russia, between 1993 and 1996, managers as a group increased their equity position from less than 10% to nearly 20%, and employees' shareholding decreased from nearly 60% to 40%.

Although some managers may be interested in restructuring, they typically lack the necessary skills and capabilities (Puffer, 1992, 1994). Majority control by managers, "while far superior to state ownership, gives managers too much control relative to what is needed to speed up efficient restructuring" (Shleifer & Vasiliev, 1996, p. 77). What has happened is extensive entrenchment of former SOE managers unqualified for their new roles and delays in corporate restructuring. These agency problems, found extensively in the West, are *magnified* in transition economies, which lack other effective governance mechanisms, such as competitive product markets, efficient managerial labor markets, and transparent capital markets, whereby different teams of investors and managers can contest for corporate control (Hanson, 1997). In the absence of other forms of governance, managers and employees may form a coalition of entrenched interests that resist reform (Filatotchev et al., 1996; McCarthy & Puffer, 1995). In sum, although employee control of large, former SOEs may be inefficient, management control does not appear to facilitate much-needed restructuring either.

Second Phase of Privatization. Influenced by an agency theory proposition that "the presence of large outside investors is conducive to efficiency" (Boycko et al., 1996, p. 318; Fama & Jensen, 1983), most governments in CEE and the NIS launched a second phase of the privatization program in the mid-1990s in order to attract more outside investors, introduce stronger governance, and restructure former SOEs. In Russia, for example, in order to lure more outside investors, the government in 1994 set a new limit of 10% share ownership for insiders, rather than the 51% cap allowed during the first phase (McCarthy & Puffer, 1995, p. 59).[5] In Hungary, a new policy in 1993 set a cap of 50% of the shares plus one share as the maximum level of equity that incumbents can obtain in a buyout (Wright et al., 1997, p. 223). Throughout CEE and the NIS there is evidence that the initially dispersed ownership held by employees becomes more concentrated over time, mainly in the hands of managers as well as outside investors (see Table 5.4 for the case of Russia, 1993-1996).

Three underlying factors contribute to this evolution of ownership structure. First, employee-owners may be tempted to sell their shares. Given their widely dispersed ownership within a firm, it is difficult to exercise meaningful control in the face of managerial dominance. Moreover, the employee-owners are more interested in diversifying their holdings in order to protect themselves from their own firm's bankruptcy risk, which could result in a total loss of their capital. In addition, in a hyperinflationary environment, the basic need of making ends meet creates incentives for employee-owners to sell their shares for cash. Thus, over time, employee ownership may be slowly eroded as individual employees find ways of selling their shares.[6]

Second, managers, however reluctantly, may find that they have very few alternatives other than accommodating some outside investors. By the mid-1990s, most managers had generally exhausted their own financial resources. Their firms are typically in desperate shape, trying to "swim" instead of "sinking" in the new competition (Peng & Heath, 1996). As a "blood transfusion," outside capital that would help the firm stay afloat is tempting, and, thus, some accommodation of outside investors will be necessary.

Lastly, the increasing willingness and sophistication of outside investors who participate in the second phase of privatization also result in more outside involvement. Other than managers, there are a number of outside investors to whom employee-owners can sell their shares, including (a) rich individuals, (b) institutional investors, and (c) domestic and foreign companies. Since few outside investors would risk providing capital to firms that are completely controlled by insiders, outsiders typically insist on certain control rights through their representatives on the board. As a result, how they deal with incumbents illustrates an example of the dynamic interaction of institutions and organizations discussed extensively in Chapter 3. Rich individuals who invest in a given firm (so-called informal venture capitalists, or business angels) are typically friendly to the management, and their role is difficult to discern at this point because of the lack of disclosure of their involvement. As a result, we focus here on the role of the other two groups of more influential and visible outside investors.

Institutional Investors. This group includes investment funds, pension funds, and venture capital funds. While they have emerged as the movers and shakers of the world of high finance in the West in the past few decades, their involvement in transition economies began only in the 1990s. Two groups of distinctive strategic approaches have been identified (Wright et al., 1997, pp. 226-227). The first, "restructuring," group comes closest to the typical approach employed by institutional investors in the West. Specifically, these funds are interested in relying on voice-oriented corporate governance, by exerting pressure to restructure, which may ultimately include the ejection of insiders from positions of control. In practice, however, ejecting insiders may be difficult unless funds can persuade a majority of employee-owners to remove incumbent management. Nevertheless, these institutional investors have become increasingly active. In Russia, for example, approximately 10% of the CEOs were removed at the *first* shareholder meeting by coalitions of institutional investors and employees (Shleifer & Vasiliev, 1996, p. 74). It is not surprising at all that incumbent managers would go the extra mile to prevent employees from selling their shares to these outside investors.

The second group of institutional investors, the exit-oriented "traders," attempt to identify enterprises whose shares are underpriced and trade them for a profit. While these investors assert some pressure on managers, a high level of trading indicates a lack of commitment of funds to a long-term, hands-on relationship with a newly privatized company. Given the general undervaluation of privatized firms, windfall gains can be generated simply by selling the stakes acquired at privatization ("Russia's State Sell-Off," 1994). It is also questionable whether these funds have adequate monitoring skills to deal with the vast number of privatized firms.

In the long run, institutional investors are likely to emerge as a major force in corporate governance in transition economies. At present, however, there is still little evidence of their impact, mostly because of their "newness" in this environment.

Domestic and Foreign Companies. In transition economies, the involvement of other domestic companies in privatized firms is viewed qualitatively differently from that of foreign companies. Recall Chapter 3, in which I discussed the extensive networks of domestic firms based on their managers' informal personal relationships.[7] Throughout transition economies, there is a movement toward establishing more formal interfirm networks connected by cross-share holdings, interlocking directorates, and parent-subsidiary relationships. Examples of these new networks include the "financial-industrial groups" in Russia (Freinkman, 1995; Johnson, 1997; Prokop, 1995) and the "enterprise groups" in China (Peng, 1997a; Wu, 1990). Investment by domestic companies is usually an extension of these efforts toward establishing more formal linkages. Typically, firms that have had previous cooperative relationships pool resources (Sedaitis, 1998). Because of this mutual trust, the investing firm (or the so-called white knight) is not likely to be resisted by incumbents at the receiving firm. At the same time, however, deep restructuring of the receiving firm cannot be expected.

The equity involvement of foreign firms is an entirely different ball game. Although, as noted earlier, acquisition of controlling interests by domestic institutional investors is not embraced enthusiastically, such acquisition is viewed more and more acceptable than acquisition by foreign firms (Gurkov & Asselbergs, 1995). Because foreign companies are likely to introduce massive restructuring and major shifts in product mixes to meet Western requirements (see Strategy in Action 7.4 in Chapter 7 for an example), employee-controlled firms are naturally unwilling to accept foreign investors whom they perceive may want to initiate plant closures and massive layoffs. Managers, similarly, are afraid of being restructured out of their jobs and are therefore unwilling to cede control. Facing such sentiments, foreign firms may also be reluctant to become involved unless they can obtain majority control.

Adding to this complexity is the role of the government, which is in fear of being criticized as "giving the country away" on the one hand, and is interested in foreign capital, technology, and expertise on the other hand (Brouthers & Bamossy, 1997). As a result, joint ventures between domestic and foreign firms are typically preferred, and outright foreign equity control is not widespread (Beamish, 1993; Peng, in press-b). In Russia, for instance, foreign companies controlled approximately only 1.6% of total equity by the mid-1990s, thus necessarily limiting their "voice" (Blasi et al., 1997, p. 193). Overall, political processes tend to compromise the nominal independence of outside directors. Given the generally unfriendly and even hostile attitude toward foreign equity control, foreign companies, even when they are represented on the board, often do not vigorously challenge incumbent managers for fear of political reaction (Shleifer & Vasiliev, 1996).

A more feasible way for foreign companies to establish equity control is first to enter as joint venture partners without necessarily majority control, then to develop mutual trust with local partners, followed by increases in the equity level and eventual buyout of domestic firms (see Chapter 7). Through such a sequential approach, foreign firms can gradually build up their credentials as responsible "domestic" players exhibiting a long-term commitment to the local economy, thus becoming more acceptable to local managers, employees, and the government.[8]

Overall, by the mid-1990s, although insider control still dominated in countries such as Romania, Russia, and Ukraine, more organizational diversity could be found in other transition economies. For example, in Hungary, among all the 435 companies in the first-round privatization program (Earle & Estrin, 1996), domestic outside investor-controlled firms formed the majority (226 firms, or 52%) by 1994, followed by insider-controlled firms (of which 67, or 15%, were employee controlled, and 120, or 28%, were manager controlled). There was also a small number of firms that were controlled by foreign investors (14, or 3%; see Table 5.2).

Summary

Overall, the first phase of privatization, relying primarily on insider buyouts, focused more on the speed and acceptability of the process and paid less attention to governance mechanisms aimed at performance improvement. As a result, the second phase started to concentrate on much-needed restructuring by introducing outside investors who can assert influence on insiders. In general, outsiders' shares have grown substantially (see Table 5.4). As we will explore below, while these developments are encouraging, whether the mere presence of these outsiders can be effectively translated into actual influence in corporate governance remains to be seen.

STRATEGIES OF PRIVATIZED AND REFORMED FIRMS

Given that different SOEs have become different types of privatized and reformed firms, it is not surprising that their strategic responses vary considerably. Highlighted below are three major strategies: (a) muddling through, (b) raising capital from financial markets, and (c) corporate restructuring.

Strategy I: Muddling Through

A Minimalist Strategy. "Muddling through" seems to be the predominant strategy at a large number of insider-controlled firms. They do not actively initiate strategic transformation; instead, they only react to the crisis of the day as it occurs, hoping to muddle through the process with minimal changes (McCarthy & Puffer, 1995). Three factors contribute to this minimalist strategy. First, many former SOE managers and employees became new business owners overnight. Since old habits die hard, most of them, not having any idea about the workings of a truly private firm in a market economy, simply behave as "usual." Second, the objectives of these new owners typically have little to do with restructuring for better performance. Rather, employees are mostly interested in job security. Since any major restructuring is likely to involve some layoffs, it is not surprising that employees, who may now control substantial shares, are not keen on voting themselves out of jobs. Managers are also interested in job security and are afraid of being voted out of office by employees when introducing more radical restructuring measures.

A third, and perhaps the most important, factor is that the state still maintains substantial influence. The state has been a major provider of privatization capital through subsidized loans, credits, and discounts, as well as free vouchers for insiders. It also maintains less-than-majority, but still nontrivial, amounts of shares at these firms. In Russia, for example, the state typically retains a so-called golden share in *officially privatized* firms, where it holds approximately 10% of shares (Blasi et al., 1997). The golden share gives the government a disproportionate influence: It has the right to veto (a) changes in statutory documentation; (b) decisions on reorganization and liquidation of the company; (c) decisions on acquiring equity stakes of other firms; and (d) decisions relating to spin-offs, mortgaging, and leasing out of a firm's assets (Wright et al., 1993, p. 72). Basically, the government still has to "approve" major strategic changes of privatized firms.

Can Budget Constraint Be Hardened? A fundamental purpose of privatization was to reduce subsidies to SOEs. In theory, privatized firms have to face a "hard budget constraint" with little hope of obtaining further subsidies. Compared with the socialist state, the transition state now is much weaker, internally split, and more subject to special interest pressures than before. It is often afraid of massive layoffs and social unrest as a result of large-scale enterprise failure and, therefore, is reluctant to force poor firms into bankruptcy. In contrast, capricious and contradictory government regulations and a highly unstable political situation often result in continued subsidies. In Russia, for example, shortly after the voucher privatization process started in 1992, President Yeltsin signed a controversial decree, "On Not Permitting Discrimination Against Privatized Enterprises in the Provision of State Financial Support" (Earle & Estrin, 1996, p. 50). While former SOE managers may lack competitive and managerial skills suitable for a market economy, they are usually master players in the political game. Sensing such political winds, their call for "nondiscrimination" in getting subsidies from the state is not likely to end quickly.

Basically, this muddling-through strategy is similar to the first strategy adopted by SOEs, namely, asking for more support from the government (see Chapter 4). Such a lack of change in firm behavior can be expected because the new owners of these firms do not bear the costs of capital. Most insider-led privatization involved a "giveaway" distribution of shares, with new owners having to endure little financial sacrifice. In contrast, share purchases in the West always involve financial sacrifice that makes the objective of wealth maximization for shareholders more urgent. With little to lose as shareholders, these new owners could perhaps be forgiven for trying to muddle through the process with minimal changes (Buck et al., 1998, p. 91). In addition, traditional values in favor of stability, fostered by decades of socialist rule, have further increased the inertia and strengthened the tendency not to make radical changes (Holt, Ralston, & Terpstra, 1994).

Strategy II: Raising Capital From Financial Markets

The Attraction of Financial Markets. Given the universal thirst for capital and the state's increasing unwillingness to provide subsidies, many firms have sought to raise capital from the new financial markets. To many observers, the establishment of financial markets where company shares can be freely traded indicates a major line of demarcation separating these countries from their socialist past. In Poland, for example, the new government chose to house the stock exchange in the building formerly occupied by the central committee of the Communist Party, symbolically embarking on the new road to capitalism from the bastion of the bankrupt regime (Gordon & Rittenberg, 1995). Led by China and Hungary since 1990, governments in these countries have been promoting financial markets to achieve two purposes: (a) to help firms raise more capital, and (b) to use the financial markets to discipline firms. In general, the first objective has been more successfully achieved than the second one.

To be listed, a company must conform to the specific standards outlined by the securities authorities, usually in the form of stringent accounting and disclosure requirements. Shown in Table 5.5, the number of listed companies in China, the Czech Republic, Hungary, Poland, and Russia grew from a modest start in 1990 to a sizable showing in 1995. The total amount of market capitalization in these transition economies, however, remained very low when compared with other emerging economies such as Brazil, Hong Kong, India, and South Korea, let alone developed economies. Given the general lack of domestic capital and of people's familiarity with stock markets, many firms have sought listing on foreign financial markets. For example, since the establishment of the Budapest Stock Exchange in 1990, all listed companies have been quoted parallel on the Hungarian and Austrian stock markets. Initially, approximately 70% of the trade volume in publicly traded Hungarian stocks was transacted outside Hungary, mainly in Vienna (Meszaros, 1993). In addition, other CEE and NIS firms have also sought listings on Western financial markets such as Berlin, Frankfurt, London, and New York.

Another example of overseas listing is an increasing number of Chinese firms that have been listed as red-chip companies in Hong Kong (de Trenck, 1998; Peng, Au, & Wang, 1999). Shown in Table 5.6, by the end of 1996, 24 of the top 100 largest listed firms in Hong Kong (by capitalization) were red chips. With a total capitalization of approximately HK$469 billion (US$61 billion), these 24 firms represented nearly 20% of the capitalization among the top 100 and 15% of the capitalization among all listed firms in Hong Kong. Overall, these firms have become an increasingly viable force on the Hong Kong Stock Exchange, resulting in the creation of a separate red-chip index in 1995. In addition, Chinese firms have also been listed in Frankfurt, London, Luxembourg, New York, and Tokyo (Karmel, 1994, p. 1111).

TABLE 5.5 Stock Markets in Transition, Emerging, and Developed Economies

	Capitalization ($ million)		Capitalization of GDP		Value Traded as Percentage of GDP		Shares Traded as Percentage of Capitalization		Number of Listed Companies	
	1990	1995	1990	1995	1990	1995	1990	1995	1990	1995
Transition Economies										
China	2,028	43,055	0.5	6.0	0.2	7.1	80.9	116.3	14	323
Czech Republic	—	15,664	—	35.0	—	8.1	28.0	46.9	258	213
Hungary	505	2,399	1.5	5.4	0.4	0.8	46.3	17.7	21	42
Poland	144	4,564	0.2	3.9	0.0	2.4	38.9	72.7	9	65
Russia	—	15,863	—	4.6	—	0.1	—	2.0	43	170
Other Emerging Economies										
Brazil	16,354	147,636	3.4	21.8	1.2	11.7	18.4	47.0	581	543
Hong Kong	83,397	303,705	111.5	211.4	46.3	74.4	43.1	37.3	284	518
India	38,567	127,199	12.9	39.2	7.3	4.2	66.5	10.8	6,200	7,985
South Korea	110,594	181,955	43.6	39.9	29.9	40.7	60.4	99.1	669	721
Developed Economies										
Germany	355,070	577,365	22.9	23.9	22.1	47.5	139.3	218.9	413	678
Great Britain	848,866	1,407,737	87.0	127.3	28.6	92.3	33.3	77.9	1,701	2,078
Japan	2,917,679	3,667,292	98.2	71.8	54.0	24.1	43.8	33.3	2,071	2,263
United States	3,059,434	6,857,622	55.7	98.6	31.9	73.5	53.4	85.7	6,599	7,671

SOURCE: Adapted from the World Bank (1997a, pp. 240-242).

131

TABLE 5.6 Raising Capital on the Hong Kong Stock Exchange: Red-Chip Firms From Mainland China and Other Groups of Listed Firms, End of 1996

	Hong Kong British Firms	Hong Kong Chinese Firms	Southeast Asian Firms	Mainland Chinese Red Chips
Number of firms in the top 100	13	52	11	24
Total capitalization (HK$ billion)[a]	823	1,020	87	469
Percentage of capitalization among top 100 firms	34	43	4	20
Percentage of capitalization among all listed firms	26	32	3	15

SOURCE: Adapted from Au, Peng, and Wang (in press).
NOTE: a. The Hong Kong dollar was pegged to the U.S. dollar at that time at HK$7.8 = US$1.

Initially, investors both at home and abroad responded enthusiastically (Gordon & Rittenberg, 1995; Karmel, 1994; "A Chinese Banquet," 1997). For a time, the "rush" to China, CEE, or Russia commanded strong attention from the global investment community (Curran, 1994; "The Rush to China," 1997; "The Rush to Russia," 1997). For example, during 1993, the Warsaw stock index (WIG) soared to a record increase of more than 700% (Gordon & Rittenberg, 1995). During 1996, the Russian stock market experienced 127% growth ("The Rush to Russia," 1997). In 1997, when Beijing Enterprises from China went public in Hong Kong, investors queued around the block and oversubscribed to the available shares by 1,275 times, a record. The share price went ballistic, tripling on the first day of trading (Tamlinson, 1997). Note these are sophisticated investors in Hong Kong, not inexperienced ones in Warsaw, Moscow, or Shanghai, who need basic education about, "What is a stock exchange?" Apparently many investors believe that there is value in these firms. As a result, many listed firms have successfully raised a large sum of capital.

Dissipating Investor Interest. Over time, however, the "emerging markets fever" has dissipated among investors (Schoenberger, 1996). By August 10, 1998, stock markets in Russia, China, and Eastern

Europe experienced a year-to-date *decline* of 45%, 39%, and 25%, respectively. In contrast, stock markets in Germany, the United States, and the United Kingdom witnessed a year-to-date *increase* of 45%, 22%, and 19%, respectively, during the same period ("The Equity Markets," 1998). Investors soon lose interest when many governance problems begin to surface and many firms in transition economies fail to deliver the performance that they promise. In addition to raising capital, a second objective of listing firms on financial markets, at least from the government's perspective, is to turn them into "investor-controlled" firms with effective corporate governance. It is in this area that many listed firms have utterly failed, alienating investors at home and abroad.

At least three factors have contributed to the lack of investor confidence in many listed firms after the initial period of euphoria. First, although these former SOEs may have become reformed, privatized, and even listed, they continue to be plagued by old problems and very little may have been changed. For example, "Gazprom has an aura of success about it," according to a financial analyst commenting on the largest listed company measured in capitalization ($33 billion in 1998) in Russia, which was also the largest firm in all transition economies (see Table 3.4). "But if you look close, it's a typical Russian organization. No one on the inside understands what the financial condition of the company is" (quoted by McCarthy & Puffer, 1995, p. 59). Another analyst stated that it could take 10 years to audit the enterprise. Given that Gazprom is one of the better-managed, more successful firms in Russia, we can safely assume that the financial condition at many other firms in Russia and elsewhere is even more chaotic. The inertia to continue without major changes—that is, the muddling-through strategy mentioned above—may continue to assert itself long after these firms become listed.

Second, the idea that the firm needs to maximize outside investors' wealth is alien to many managers. Historically, they operated under the old regime, which did not take any "investor interest" into consideration. After privatization, managers have become more independent because they are now owners. As a result, they have a tendency to resist outside influence (Buck et al., 1998). In China, as of May 1998, there are no legal requirements for listed companies to appoint outside directors to the board to safeguard shareholder interest. Understandably, outside influence is minimal in such a situation. In listed companies in CEE and the NIS, there may be outside board members on the board (Blasi et al., 1997; Wright et al., 1998), but their mere presence does not in itself constitute a significant voice to assert influence. In contrast, a study that my colleagues and I recently completed using data from Russia found that the presence of outside board members had *no* influence on restructuring or performance at all (Peng, Buck, & Filatotchev, 1999).

Finally, the inadequate laws and regulations governing these fledgling financial markets further worsen the situation. While some laws and regulations are "overlapping, repetitive, clumsy, ill-organized, and poorly drafted" (Lau & Johnstone, 1995, p. 130), others have major loopholes. For example, at the time of writing (October 1998), China was unique in the world in having shareholding companies and securities markets without a securities law. While various governments have tried hard to establish a legal and regulatory framework to govern these markets (Kumar, 1997), such a process takes a long time. Moreover, even after such a framework is in place, how vigorous the enforcement is remains an entirely different issue (Frye, 1997).

Controversial Practices. In this environment, many firms have taken advantage of legal and regulatory loopholes. Some of them are notorious for maintaining three sets of books, one to satisfy the taxation authorities, one for their traditional administrative superiors, and another (presumably more accurate) one for the eyes of top managers. Worse yet, none of these three sets "is compatible with generally accepted accounting principles," as I was quoted by *Newsweek* in 1997 ("A Chinese Banquet," 1997, p. 24). Which set of books is disclosed to the investing public becomes an interesting and potentially explosive issue. Although the books of these firms may have been audited by reputable, international public accounting firms before they went public, investors have found that "even the most official-looking financial information isn't always dependable" (Tamlinson, 1997, p. 64). For example, in 1993, Tsingtao, China's most famous beer maker, became the first reformed Chinese firm to list shares in Hong Kong and successfully raised $110 million in the initial public offering (IPO). However, instead of using the IPO proceeds for restructuring and expansion as promised, Tsingtao's managers loaned the money to other friendly SOEs. Many loans soured during a credit crunch in 1994, forcing Tsingtao to report losses and raising eyebrows among investors and regulators in Hong Kong ("Can China Reform Its Economy?" 1997, p. 124).

Overall, while the government may have two purposes in establishing financial markets—helping firms raise capital and disciplining them—many firms evidently have only the first objective in mind. As a result, they pay only lip service to shareholder wealth maximization. At present, the influence of outside directors on the board is weak (and in some cases nonexistent). The market for corporate control is underdeveloped because of the obstacles hostile raiders have to overcome (Peng, Luo, & Sun, 1999). By default, the only significant constraint on managers comes from product market competition, as many factories stand idle in what is increasingly a buyers' market (Buck et al., 1998). Such competition forces managers to pay attention to improving product and service quality, and not to deviate too much from profit (and by extension shareholder wealth) maximization.

Strategy III: Corporate Restructuring

While many firms resist change, even after they are publicly listed, a large number of them have realized that when product competition becomes sufficiently strong, restructuring appears to be the only way out in the long run (Krueger, 1995; Wright et al., 1998). Corporate restructuring can be conceptualized as change along one or more of three dimensions: organizational, financial, and portfolio (Bowman & Singh, 1993; Hoskisson & Hitt, 1994; Hoskisson & Turk, 1990). Organizational restructuring includes changes in governance and management structure, as well as layoffs and downsizing. Financial restructuring encompasses buyouts, buybacks, and recapitalizations. Portfolio or asset restructuring involves the sale and/or acquisition of lines of business of a firm. These three activities, in conjunction with privatization, often overlap and occur simultaneously (Buck et al., 1998; Filatotchev et al., 1996; Wright et al., 1998).

Characteristics of Restructuring Firms. One interesting question is that given so much organizational inertia and managerial entrenchment at numerous firms, what are the characteristics of the firms that have actually undertaken some restructuring? While it is difficult to generalize, restructuring firms seem to be distinguished by three criteria: (a) size, (b) ownership, and (c) managers' age. Large firms tend to have more bureaucratic, complex structures; more entrenched managers and employees; and hence more inertia against restructuring (McCarthy & Puffer, 1995). Small firms, in contrast, are more likely to initiate restructuring (Chapter 6 will discuss their strategies in more detail).

In terms of ownership, because of the reasons alluded to earlier, insider-controlled firms are least likely to be interested in restructuring. Evidence from Hungary indicated that SOEs that are in deep financial difficulties and firms controlled by foreign investors were more likely to engage in restructuring (Whitley & Czaban, 1998). For SOEs that can no longer muddle through, the scale and scope of restructuring as a last resort for survival tend to be more radical than for their privatized counterparts. Foreign investors, understandably, may tolerate less inertia and have better access to organizational, technological, and financial resources that enable restructuring. Although empirical evidence so far has been limited, substantial foreign ownership does appear to facilitate more restructuring. Using data from Slovenia, a former Yugoslavian republic, Smith, Cin, and Vodopivec (1997) found that a percentage point increase in foreign ownership is associated with about 3.9% increase in value-added. In comparison, the same level of increase in employee ownership results in only about 1.4% increase in value-added.

Another important and observable criterion that characterizes restructuring firms seems to be the age of top managers, which can be a good proxy for managers' outlook and capabilities (Finkelstein & Hambrick, 1996; Hambrick & Mason, 1984). While most managers in transition economies grew up and acquired most of their experience during the socialist era, a younger generation of managers has risen to the occasion (Chen, 1995). Compared with the old guard, they are typically more adaptive, better educated in Western ways, and less influenced by the "socialist virus" (Puffer, 1992, 1994). As a result, they may be more likely to initiate restructuring.

In Russia, for example, there is a steady decline of CEOs' age over the years (Blasi et al., 1997, p. 203). Specifically, the average age of

CEOs in office before 1992 was 52 years, and the average age of those in office since 1992 declined to 47. Among the latter group, the average age of those CEOs named in 1995 decreased further to 45. Similarly, a study conducted in 1998 by the Chinese Managers Survey System (1998, p. 136) found the average age of board chairmen and CEOs in China to be 48. During the summer of 1998, I interviewed the top managers of the investment banking subsidiary of Shanghai Industrial Holdings Limited, which is a highly successful red-chip firm listed on the Hong Kong Stock Exchange. Among a staff of 16 people at the subsidiary, the average age was 28, and more than half of them possessed master's degrees or above. These young managers successfully engineered the acquisition of United Holding by their parent company in 1997, which was the largest acquisition of a listed company in China at that time (see Strategy in Action 5.2). The five top managers whom Shanghai Industrial sent to restructure United Holding after the acquisition had an average age of 39. Among them, the CEO, two deputy CEOs, and the CFO held master's degrees (including one MBA), and the corporate counsel possessed a JD degree. Trained during the reform era, they were less constrained by the socialist legacy that plagued many other firms, and were impressively well versed in the repertoire of modern corporate practices, such as corporate strategy, mergers and acquisitions, and restructuring. Overall, it seems reasonable to suggest that the presence of younger managers trained during the postsocialist era may lead to more restructuring at privatized and reformed firms.

Strategy in Action 5.2

Shanghai Industrial Acquires and Restructures United Holding

Acquiring and Target Firms

Shanghai Industrial Holdings Limited is a "red-chip" company from China that has been listed on the Hong Kong Stock Exchange since 1996. The firm's portfolio included consumer goods and automotive parts, commercial retailing, and infrastructure development in both Shanghai and Hong Kong. During 1997, it had fixed assets of HK$711 million and revenue of HK$3.56 billion.[a] Its 1997 profits reached HK$1.02 billion, representing an increase of 311% over its profits in 1996. Despite the financial crisis that engulfed Hong Kong during the second half of 1997, its earnings per share in 1997 still reached HK$1.28, which represented an increase of 71% over those of 1996. The investing public in Hong Kong was highly impressed by this stellar performance, and the firm's shares become a constituent stock of the prestigious Hang Seng Index in January 1998.

United Holding is a textile firm that has been listed on the Shanghai Stock Exchange since 1992. Before being acquired by Shanghai Industrial, United Holding held controlling interest in 19 different textile firms in Shanghai. During 1996, it had fixed assets of 671 million yuan and revenue of 265 million yuan. Its 1996 profits were 26 million yuan and earnings per share were 0.25 yuan, both representing a modest increase of 9% over those of 1995. During the 1990s, its performance deteriorated. Its single focus on the textile industry in one region made it difficult for it to find new areas of growth, because Shanghai's textile industry as a whole was threatened by textile firms in other Chinese provinces where labor and material costs were significantly lower.

The Acquisition

Having accumulated large cash flows from retained earnings and from the Hong Kong stock market, Shanghai Industrial searched for an acquisition target. The selection criteria were (a) that the target firm was publicly listed, and (b) that it had a solid foundation. In addition, Shanghai Industrial wanted to take advantage of the local government's interest in restructuring moribund industries, hoping this might ease the approval process. As a result, Shanghai Industrial found United Holding to be an ideal target. In June 1997, Shanghai Industrial spent 118 million yuan to purchase 29% of the shares of United Holding, thus becoming its controlling shareholder. The negotiations were completed in 42 days, a relatively short period by Chinese standards. A peculiar aspect in this case, as in other M&A cases in China, is that although United Holding is publicly listed, Shanghai Industrial did not purchase its shares on the open market. United Holding had two classes of shares, namely, circulating (open market, 21%) and noncirculating (79%). The shares that Shanghai Industrial purchased were all noncirculating, and the government had to approve these transfers. At that time, the transaction was the largest one in China involving the acquisition of a listed company.

Postacquisition Restructuring

Shanghai Industrial replaced all top- and middle-level managers at United Holding; however, most of the 2,000 nonmanagerial employees were not affected. The new management team implemented a restructuring strategy by reducing the firm's dependency on textiles, which had become a "sunset" industry in Shanghai, and introducing other businesses with strong growth potential. As a result, United Holding sold off three textile subsidiaries, which generated 44 million yuan. In addition, Shanghai Industrial injected 43 million yuan to let United Holding take a controlling interest (25%) in Scientific China, which is one of the country's largest high-tech biochemical companies. On behalf of United Holding, Shanghai Industrial also invested 140 million yuan in a downtown renovation project. Profits from this project at the end of 1997 were 19 million yuan.

The aim of the restructuring strategy was to create a three-pronged source of sustainable growth, including traditional textile manufacturing, high technology, and infrastructure development. By the end of 1997, United Holding was well positioned toward its turnaround. During that critical year of transition, its profits reached 48 million yuan and earnings per share rose to 0.38 yuan, which represented increases of 84% and 52%, respectively, over 1996 levels. Managers at both United Holding and Shanghai Industrial expressed hope that United Holding had the potential to become one of the best-performing firms listed on the Shanghai Stock Exchange, which in turn may help sustain Shanghai Industrial's reputation as one of the strongest growing firms on the Hong Kong Stock Exchange.

SOURCES: Author's own interviews and annual reports of Shanghai Industrial and United Holding, 1996, 1997.
NOTE: a. The exchange rate at the time of the transaction was: US$1 = HK$7.7 = 8.3 yuan.

In sum, firms that are relatively small, in deep financial trouble, controlled by foreign investors, and/or headed by younger managers are more likely to initiate restructuring than other kinds of firms.

Processes of Restructuring. Corporate restructuring usually takes place in two steps, one for the short run and one for the long run. For the short run, it typically involves significant reduction of production and employment in order to control cash flow. In particular, activities center on the reduction of excess capacity, control of inventories, and cutback in employment. Given the difficulties outlined earlier, many painful measures are not fully carried out, and "creative" solutions have been found to avoid—or at least delay—the pain. For example, instead of laying off employees, firms induce many of them to take early retirement. Otherwise, firms may put them on call; they do not get paid unless a specific order comes in. Likewise, many suppliers continue to receive orders, but a substantial number of these orders remain unpaid. On the other hand, customer orders have often been accepted without serious consideration of the payment prospects (Wright et al., 1998, pp. 82-83). Such situations have led to a scenario of what the Chinese call the "triangular debt," whereby not paying the bill becomes a norm because "the other party" (whatever it might be) owes the focal firm too much money. Over time, however, production and employment levels do get scaled down, at least at some firms, thus leading to the second phase of restructuring.

If the company survives in the short run, it then faces the second challenge: deep restructuring aimed at improving its long-run competitive position. Deep restructuring calls for (a) organizational transformation, (b) technological upgrade, and (c) asset reconfiguration. Transforming the old organization requires massive training and retraining (Ng & Pang, 1997; Puffer, 1992, 1994). Technological upgrade is a must in an increasingly competitive landscape (Bruton & Rubanik, 1997). Asset reconfiguration, or portfolio restructuring, not only involves the sale of the unprofitable lines of business and/or social services that the firm no longer wants, but also entails the acquisition of new parts of the business that contribute value. Both the Shanghai Industrial case (Strategy in Action 5.2) and the Jenoptik case (Strategy in Action 5.3) illustrate how such a process works. In general, investors respond favorably to companies engaging in deep restructuring. For example, the share price of Jenoptik, an eastern German firm with a successful turnaround track record, jumped from $25 to $35 within 1 week after it went public on Frankfurt's *Neuer Markt* in June 1998 (Woodruff, 1998). On stock markets in Moscow, Shanghai, and Warsaw, some firms experienced a rise in their share prices by merely *announcing* that they were initiating some measure of deep restructuring. Over time, of course, investors became more sophisticated and focused more on the results, as opposed to the announcement, of restructuring.[9]

Strategy in Action 5.3

Jenoptik of Eastern Germany Restructures and Rises From the Rubble

After German unification in 1990, a sprawling eastern German SOE, Carl Zeiss Jena, was taken over by the state government. The firm turned out a bewildering array of products, from leather telescope cases to computer chips. It was overburdened with 27,000 employees, 3,000 in the canteens alone. Because Zeiss managers fled the Russian army in 1945 and set up another company, an eastern and a western German company manufactured competing precision optical equipment under the same name, Zeiss, during the Cold War. After the Berlin Wall fell in 1989, the western Carl Zeiss Group received exclusive rights to the Zeiss trademark. As a result, the eastern German firm had to change its prestigious Zeiss name to Jenoptik.

In 1991, a new top management team was installed and the federal and state governments pledged $2 billion in subsidies. During the first year, marginal businesses and services were spun off, and 17,500 employees, who had cost the firm $500 million, were laid off. Another $560 million was used to retire old debts. The obsolete downtown factories were torn down, and the firm used $175 million to construct a modern office and mall complex in their place, replacing several thousand of the jobs lost from the firm. In the end, the firm had about $645 million left for deep restructuring. Its technicians scrambled to design high-tech products that could compete in global markets. The firm had been a center for microprocessor manufacturing equipment for the entire Eastern bloc. Using that know-how, Jenoptik designed equipment to etch tiny circuits on computer chips. However, selling it proved a huge challenge. Jenoptik was completely unknown in the West, and nobody would buy crucial equipment from a company with no track record. During 1993 and 1994, another 1,200 employees were laid off.

Then the CEO realized that a drastic strategy shift would be necessary. He reasoned that the firm's only chance for survival would be to acquire other firms with solid international reputations in related fields. He persuaded Jenoptik's skeptical workers' council, which could veto takeovers, that the new strategy meant survival. With the council's blessing, the CEO acquired a number of sound high-tech companies in western Germany, such as Meissner & Wurst, a clean manufacturing specialist in Stuttgart; Krone, a telecom equipment manufacturer in Berlin; and Klimatechnik, a designer, builder, and manager of clean factories in Nuremberg. These strategic moves made Jenoptik a one-stop shop for chip manufacturers and biotechnology companies.

By the late 1990s, the shopping spree was over. The challenge was to manage the new company that had been stitched together. With a smaller workforce of 8,400, the firm has become a "mean and lean" competitor. Jenoptik is now a profitable maker of electronics, telecom gear, and clean-room equipment. It earned $38.3 million on sales of $1.4 billion in 1997. In June 1998 it went public on Frankfurt's *Neuer Markt* and sold $434 million worth of stock, the largest new issue yet by an eastern German company. Within one week, the share price jumped from $25 to $35. This remarkable turnaround is largely due to a combination of government subsidies, tough restructuring measures, and an innovative acquisition strategy. An important point of interest is whether this firm is still an "eastern German" firm, because only 1,700 of its 8,400 employees now work in eastern Germany; the rest are in western Germany and abroad.

SOURCE: Woodruff, 1998. Reprinted from the July 13, 1998 issue of *Business Week* by special permission © 1998 by McGraw-Hill Companies.

Sources of Restructuring Capital. Overall, while the short-run measures of cutting back on production and employment may save some money, long-run measures of deep restructuring call for large sums of capital. A fundamental question is where the source of such capital will be (Holmstrom, 1996). There are four potential sources: (a) state subsidies; (b) foreign companies; (c) financial markets; and (d) banks and other institutional investors. The pitfalls of direct state subsidies are well known, and they are not likely to be used on a massive scale during the transition. With the exception of the German government, whose pockets are much deeper than, say, those of the Slovakian or Romanian governments, the state in any case cannot afford subsidies on a sustainable basis. The role of foreign companies in restructuring firms in transition economies may be crucial. Yet given the large number of firms in these countries that are starving for capital, the role of foreign investment is inherently limited (more details will be discussed in Chapter 7). In terms of financial markets, nearly a decade of experience has indicated that these fledgling markets in transition economies generally suffer from a lack of transparency, regulation, and investor confidence. Global financial markets, on the other hand, have failed to show a consistent interest in firms based in these countries. As a result, these firms are left with the fourth potential source of capital: banks and other institutional investors.

Discussed earlier in this chapter, nonbank financial institutions, such as investment funds, pension funds, and venture capital funds, are novel to transition economies, and their impact is limited. On the other hand, banks, which are well established in these countries, may have to play a pivotal role to facilitate restructuring (Bonin & Leven, 1996; Van Wijnbergen, 1997). The question then becomes: Are banks capable of providing large sums of capital for restructuring as well as the necessary monitoring? Note that even by the late 1990s, many banks in these countries are still state owned. Then the nature of the question evolves into an interesting puzzle: Are state-owned banks able to facilitate corporate restructuring of privatized and reformed companies? The outlook does not appear to be very rosy: Most banks historically have been supplying subsidies to SOEs on behalf of the state, and have utterly failed to monitor these enterprises. During privatization, many banks, directed by the government, have provided preferential loans and credits to insiders. Since many insider-controlled firms are not keen on restructuring and try everything they can to muddle through the process, some banks, as a result, may have trouble getting their interest payments, let alone principal, from these firms.

Because most of the banking resources have been channeled into the remaining SOEs and change-resistant "privatized" firms, banks are chronically short of capital to support companies interested in restructuring (Johnson, 1997). In other words, the same party that failed to monitor SOEs during the previous regime and that supported insider-led privatization known for its inertia is not likely to have both the financial resources to facilitate corporate restructuring and the expertise to monitor these activities. On the contrary, the banking sector throughout transition economies is often in a state of crisis, as evidenced by the Russian crash in August 1998 ("Russia: The End of Reform?" 1998).

Overall, securing large sums of capital is crucial for restructuring (Holmstrom, 1996), as shown by the case studies of successful turnaround. The Szczecin Shipyard in Poland (Strategy in Action 4.1) sold off company-owned resorts, the entertainment center, and apartment complexes to raise cash for restructuring. Shanghai Industrial (Strategy in Action 5.3) raised capital on the Hong Kong Stock Exchange in order to carry out its acquisition and restructuring of United Holding. In this regard, Jenoptik in eastern Germany (Strategy in Action 5.4) was lucky: The federal and state governments provided much-needed cash as subsidies for the firm's restructuring. For numerous other firms that are not so lucky, the prospects of successful restructuring in the absence of significant capital appear to be bleak.

Summary and Discussion

Strategies and Rationales. Three major strategies of privatized and reformed companies have been identified in this section. Knowing what types of privatized and reformed companies the former SOEs become helps us understand which strategies these firms are likely to undertake. First, most insider-controlled firms are more likely to choose a minimalist, muddling-through strategy. Second, larger firms may want to tap into the financial markets to raise more capital, but they may not be interested in transforming themselves into investor-controlled firms. Finally, a restructuring strategy is more likely to be adopted by smaller firms; those that are in severe financial difficulties; are controlled by foreign investors; and/or are headed by younger, more aggressive managers. Taken together, these strategies are not necessarily mutually exclusive. They can be pursued together (i.e., restructuring by muddling through while trying to get listed).

It is important to recall Chapter 3, which suggests that strategic choices are the outcome of the interaction between institutions and organizations. The institutional frameworks in transition economies have been undergoing rapid and fundamental changes. *Formal* institutional frameworks are no longer in favor of state ownership and therefore call for privatization, as well as a host of new and unfamiliar legal and regulatory statutes. Changes in *informal* institutional frameworks are equally profound: Managers, employees, and other citizens have to change their dominant mind-set to adjust to the new realities (Prahalad & Bettis, 1986). For the first time, they may become real business owners, but at the same time they have to confront uncertainty, stress, and, possibly, unemployment, while trying to learn new skills that are necessary in the new economy.

Facing a bewildering institutional environment, choosing a muddling-through strategy, or its derivative, raising capital from financial markets without serious restructuring, may be a *rational* choice for many organizations. Uncertainty and ambiguity have made it difficult for many managers to operate in the short run, and nearly impossible to plan for the longer run (McCarthy & Puffer, 1995). In a setting where the state does not pursue a coherent set of policies but oscillates under different pressure groups, short-term, ad hoc adjustments to immediate pressures may be more rational than undertaking relatively large-scale and highly risky changes in pursuit of long-run strategic objectives (Whitley & Czaban, 1998). This strategic choice is consistent with the institutional perspective on business strategy in that when the rules of the game are highly uncertain, organizations will not be able to make significant investments in new capabilities and skills, and so will virtually by default continue to carry out much the same activities in similar ways as before (North, 1990; Peng & Heath, 1996; Scott, 1995). It appears that as long as privatized and reformed companies are able to survive without making substantial shifts in established routines, and no new controlling investors with the inclination and resources to implement major changes take them over, many of these firms will make only incremental, cosmetic, and limited changes.

Choosing a more proactive restructuring strategy in such an environment not only takes skill and resources, but also courage and determination. While some of these attributes, such as the possession of relatively strong products and financial capital, are more tangible, other attributes, such as the initiative, drive, and risk-taking propensity of managers, are more intangible. The combination of these tangible and intangible resources and capabilities appears to be a rare event. As a result, these resources and capabilities become valuable, unique, and hard-to-imitate drivers of firm performance that differentiate the winning companies from the large number of losing ones (Barney, 1991; Teece, Pisano, & Shuen, 1997). Evidently not every manager is capable of making tough decisions in such a dynamic and uncertain environment. Instead, some managers at privatized firms throughout CEE and the NIS have called for "renationalization" of these organizations in order to get them out of the mess (Johnson, 1997, p. 343). Such calls have been used by former communists against reformers, creating political backlash ("Russia: The End of Reform?" 1998). Overall, the challenge for governments and investors, as well as managers, throughout transition economies is to help shift the *proportions* so that more managers will choose not to backslide to old ways but to rise to the occasion.

Privatization and Corporate Governance. In terms of the three objectives of privatization, while speed and acceptability are important, ultimately it is whether firms will improve their performance that determines the success or failure of privatization. To facilitate more successful privatization, the development of corporate governance parallels with that of business strategies of privatized and reformed companies. How to control, monitor, and motivate these firms, which were full-fledged, stagnant SOEs not too long ago, is a daunting proposition. In light of the desperate need for capital, corporate governance is essential to the delivery of capital. Effective governance assures the suppliers of capital of a return on their investment. How do investors ensure that managers will return some of the profits? How can they be sure that managers will not divert the capital to other uses? Outside investors are not likely to be willing to contribute large sums of capital without satisfactory answers to these important questions.

Experience in the West has shown that sound corporate governance is typically exercised through concentrated, outside ownership, and that insider control is not conducive to restructuring[10] (Coffee, 1991; Hart, 1995). Nevertheless, many countries are stuck with a large number of insider-controlled firms due to a lack of alternatives during the first round of privatization. As a result, the challenge becomes how to motivate these firms as a second phase in the transition process (see Figure 5.1). Making sure that outside investors are represented on the board appears to be a viable first step. Possibly linking managers' pay and promotion to firm performance is a necessary second step. Experience from the West has indicated that these measures, while important, are hardly sufficient alone to induce managers to behave in a desirable fashion. Ultimately, the market for corporate control, wherein different teams of investors and managers contest for firms' control rights, will serve as a powerful disciplining mechanism of the last resort (Buck et al., 1998). However, as the experience of hostile takeover battles in China and Russia shows (Strategy in Action 5.4), the market for corporate control and exit-based corporate governance have not even reached their adolescence in transition economies (Blasi et al., 1997; Peng, Luo, & Sun, 1999). Commenting on Russia, Brada (1996) went so far as to say that "prospects of outsider control of privatized enterprises are dim in the near term and doubtful in the long term" (p. 82).

Strategy in Action 5.4

Hostile Takeover Battles in China and Russia

A Chinese Case

The first hostile takeover battle between two listed companies in China involved Baoan, listed in Shenzhen (a city bordering Hong Kong), and Yanzhong, listed in Shanghai. Baoan was a successful conglomerate and was actively seeking an acquisition target in Shanghai. Yanzhong was a manufacturer of computer and electronic accessories, stationery, and household goods. Its unsatisfactory performance resulted in low share prices, traded at 8.1 yuan[a] per share in July 1993. Baoan believed that with its generally sound manufacturing base, Yanzhong had strong potential after significant restructuring.

During September 1993, Yanzhong's share price started to rise in active trading on the Shanghai Stock Exchange, and reached 10.47 yuan on September 29. Despite rumors, no one had yet filed a disclosure report with the China Securities Regulatory Commission (CSRC), which was required when any investor accumulated 5% or more shares.[b] Few people knew that at that time Baoan already controlled 11% of Yanzhong's shares. These shares were bought by Baoan's three subsidiaries, none of whom crossed the 5% threshold. The final "attack" was launched on September 30, when Baoan pushed its control of Yanzhong's shares from 11% to 16% within a few hours. All together, Baoan spent more than one billion yuan for 4.79 million of Yanzhong's shares. The last hours of trading saw Yanzhong's share price rise to an unusually high level of more than 40 yuan per share. After securing enough control, two of Baoan's subsidiaries even sold 246,000 shares back to the public for profit. By mid-day, trading on Yanzhong's shares was stopped by the Exchange, and Baoan filed its disclosure report. Yanzhong's management had not been aware of the attempt until trading was stopped.

Having become the largest shareholder of Yanzhong, Baoan demanded board representation. Given the alleged illegality of Baoan's late reporting, Yanzhong resisted and insisted on a share buyback. In the unfolding "media war," Baoan argued that a share buyback would only result in loss to the shareholders. Baoan suggested that it was not "hostile" to Yanzhong; in fact, it planned to retain most middle managers and employees. Baoan did, however, reveal a "shadow cabinet," intending to replace the entire top management team at Yanzhong in order to carry out restructuring. CSRC announced its rulings on October 22: (a) Baoan was fined one million yuan for its late filing; (b) Baoan's profits generated by selling 264,000 shares back to the public on September 30 were to be given to Yanzhong; and (c) Baoan would not be allowed to purchase more Yanzhong shares until November 4.

In the end, the hostile takeover was not successful. Although Baoan was widely regarded as the winner by the media and investors, Yanzhong was able to resist on technical grounds. Nevertheless, management at the target firm now had stronger incentives to restructure the firm, because otherwise, the firm might become a target again and they might lose their jobs.

A Russian Case

In 1995, the Moscow-based Red October Chocolate Company was the 57th largest corporation in Russia by market value. When the takeover battle began, insiders, outside individuals, and institutional investors each owned about a third of the shares. In July, a competing food producer, Alliance-Menatep, launched the battle. Unlike the Chinese style of secret trading and buying, Alliance-Menatep put ads in newspapers offering to buy Red October shares at $7.50. Red October's management broadcast warnings over the factory's public address system that if employees sold their shares, Alliance-Menatep, once in control, would lay off most of them. To counter this warning, the acquiring firm announced its intention to make major capital investment in Red October, and made a new offer of $9.50 per share. Arguing that the company's stock was worth more than the new offer, Red October's management issued more shares and sold them to friendly investors.

Eventually, Alliance-Menatep was unable to accumulate the required 51% of the stock, and the hostile takeover technically failed. However, it taught Red October's management a strong lesson. Managers were shocked to realize that they had to be nice to investors, even those who seemed to come charging through the doors. Red October agreed to give Alliance-Menatep two seats on its board and began more seriously to restructure the firm with assistance from Alliance-Menatep.

SOURCES: Blasi, Kroumova, and Kruse, 1997; Peng, Luo, and Sun, 1999.
NOTES: a. The exchange rate at that time was US$1 = 5.76 yuan.
b. This is the same requirement as the Form 13-D requirement of the Securities and Exchange Commission of the United States.

A recent *Forbes* ranking of the *quality* of financial markets for 31 emerging economies, including such countries as Ecuador, Morocco, and Nigeria, found that most financial markets in transition economies were below average in even this group of countries (Yago & Goldman, 1998). Shown in Table 5.7, only China was found to be

TABLE 5.7 Quality of Financial Markets in Transition and Emerging Economies

Rank	Score[a]	Quantitative	Risk	Qualitative
1. Singapore	100.0	97.7	78.3	100.0
2. Taiwan	96.3	89.9	100.0	23.6
3. Hong Kong	92.9	100.0	66.3	92.7
4. South Africa	81.2	76.0	74.5	52.7
5. Chile	80.0	86.8	71.7	29.1
6. Israel	76.6	65.9	76.1	43.6
7. Greece	72.9	65.9	69.0	45.5
8. Argentina	72.0	50.3	75.0	56.4
9. **China**	**72.0**	**77.5**	**97.3**	**0.0**
10. Panama	71.4	50.4	64.1	89.1
11. Malaysia	70.8	75.2	65.8	21.8
12. Turkey	70.2	72.9	57.1	52.7
13. Peru	69.2	51.2	68.5	60.0
14. Brazil	66.5	71.3	63.0	14.5
15. Morocco	65.5	60.5	67.4	20.0
16. India	64.3	66.7	71.2	0.0
17. **Czech Republic**	**64.0**	**59.7**	**66.8**	**14.5**
18. The Philippines	62.2	57.4	56.0	45.5
19. **Hungary**	**60.6**	**43.4**	**73.9**	**9.1**
20. Ecuador	59.7	54.3	51.6	52.7
21. Mexico	56.0	66.7	44.6	25.5
22. Thailand	56.0	82.9	40.8	0.0
23. **Slovak Republic**	**50.8**	**45.0**	**54.9**	**10.9**
24. Nigeria	49.8	48.1	40.2	47.3
25. Venezuela	45.2	45.7	39.7	27.3
26. **Poland**	**44.3**	**29.5**	**69.6**	**0.0**
27. Egypt	43.1	56.6	59.2	0.0
28. Indonesia	37.8	56.6	28.3	0.0
29. South Korea	20.6	51.9	39.1	0.0
30. **Russia**	**18.2**	**42.6**	**32.1**	**0.0**
31. **Bulgaria**	**9.8**	**22.5**	**21.7**	**0.0**

SOURCE: Adapted from Yago and Goldman (1998, p. 62). **Bold** type face indicates a transition economy.

NOTE: a. The composite score is an equally weighted index of 17 variables, divided into three categories: quantitative, risk, and qualitative. Qualitative measures include (1) government spending/GDP; (2) equity market capitalization/GDP; (3) private-sector domestic credit claims/GDP; and (4) government debt/GDP. Risk measures include (5) interest-rate spread between U.S. Treasury bonds and domestic public debt; (6) stock market volatility; (7) interest rate volatility; (8) currency volatility; (9) 90-day interest rates; (10) velocity of M1 money supply; (11) equity market liquidity; and (12) IPOs in a given year as a proportion of total share issues. Qualitative measures include (13) Moody's bank ratings; (14) IMF program; (15) capital controls; (16) allowed foreign ownership; and (17) capital gains tax.

within the top 10 grouping, and Russia and Bulgaria were ranked at the bottom. Overall, the development of corporate governance in transition economies has a long way to go.

CONCLUSIONS

Compared with an organizational landscape totally dominated by SOEs, transition economies now feature a great deal of organizational diversity, including remaining SOEs, privatized and reformed firms, private and collective start-ups, as well as foreign-invested companies. Focusing on privatized and reformed companies, we can revisit the five fundamental questions in strategy posed in Chapter 1. Why firms differ (Question 1) depends on the different paths of privatization and reform they take. In contrast to the popular belief that a former SOE can be privatized into a "normal" private enterprise, the particular type of private enterprise that the ex-SOE becomes has an important bearing on the nature of the new firm. Similarly, how firms behave (Question 2) can be traced to the different constraints under which different types of private firms operate. Insider-controlled firms are more likely to exhibit inertia due to the entrenchment of managers and employees. Outside investor-controlled firms have a relatively stronger propensity to engage in some restructuring.

Question 3 asks, How are strategy outcomes affected by strategy processes? As illustrated in Chapter 3, strategic choices are the product of the interaction between institutions and organizations. To the extent that the institutional framework still allows firms to survive without serious and painful restructuring, managers are likely to be more interested in muddling through the process. Serious restructuring will occur only when the product market competition is sufficiently strong; when firm size is relatively small; when investors have less tolerance for muddling through; and/or when the firm is headed by younger, more aggressive managers.

The scope of the firm (Question 4) is determined by what a firm is capable of doing. Many privatized and reformed companies confront two challenges. The first is to reduce the burden of providing housing, schooling, medical care, and other social services they inherited from their former life. This typically involves some *shrinking* of the scope of the firm. These activities tend to be associated with the first phase of restructuring, aimed at curtailing cash flows. The other challenge is to find sustainable lines of business that are broader than the narrow product ranges in which SOEs traditionally specialize. The quest for such a competitive position typically calls for some *expansion* of the scope of the firm, through networks, mergers, acquisitions, generic expansion, or a combination of these (see Chapter 3). These activities are usually carried out during the second phase of deep restructuring. More firms have dealt with the first challenge than have dealt and/or been dealing with the second, more profound challenge. Typically, the cash raised during the first phase of restructuring is not enough. Without injection of capital from the outside, most firms have little hope of engaging in the second phase of restructuring.

The last question asks, What determines the international success or failure of firms? While we have briefly mentioned the role of foreign investors in the restructuring of privatized and reformed companies in this chapter, we will leave more detailed discussion of the strategies of foreign firms to Chapter 7.

In conclusion, there are both "diamonds and rust" among privatized and reformed companies, and their strategies vary considerably (McCarthy & Puffer, 1995). The longevity and sustainability of these strategies will depend on the shape of the evolving financial systems and on the initiative, drive, and capabilities of managers and investors. There also remains a strong need for the state to create an adequate legal and regulatory environment to ensure that the new financial institutions will compel more firms to engage in restructuring as opposed to merely muddling through. Overall, privatization has created both pitfalls and potential profits, but if the rust is scraped away, some diamonds will eventually shine through.

NOTES

1. I learned the word *equitization* from my Vietnamese students. In November 1997, I flew to Hanoi to teach a course titled "Privatization Policies and Firm Strategies" in the Hawaii-Vietnam Executive Training Program funded by the U.S. Information Agency. Upon my arrival, however, the student who came to pick me up at the airport

told me that *privatization* was a politically incorrect word in Vietnam, and suggested that I use a newly coined word, *equitization*, instead. The official party line was that equitization, derived from the word *equity*, did not necessarily lead to a complete transfer of public assets into private hands, as the word *privatization* would imply (see Riedel, 1997, p. 64). However, when I started my lecture using "equitization," all of my students, approximately 40 of them aged between 25 to 40, who were mostly managers and university faculty members, suggested that we use "privatization" anyway. One of them said: "It's just like Saigon. Although the government wants us to use the name Ho Chi Minh City, we'd still call that city its traditional name anyway. Saigon is simply easier to say."

2. Note that this chapter focuses primarily on the transformation of former SOEs, which are typically large. Strategies of newly founded private firms (start-ups), which tend to be small, will be dealt with in the next chapter.

3. Nearly 100 years after the first Model T car rolled off the assembly line, the Ford family still controls 40% of the Ford Motor Company. In January 1999, the fourth generation will take the wheel, as Bill Ford, Jr., the great grandson of the company's founder, Henry Ford, becomes chairman ("Chairman Ford," 1998). However, such long-lasting family control of the firm is an exception rather than the rule in the West. In Asia, Latin America, and some parts of Europe (e.g., Southern Italy), many owner- and family-controlled firms persist, despite their relatively large sizes (Fukuyama, 1996; Peng, 1999).

4. It is important to note that corporate governance in the "West" includes at least two major rival models: (a) the U.S./U.K.-based model, which has a high propensity to use exit-based measures, and (b) the German/Japanese-based model, which has more "patient" capital and a low propensity to use exit-based measures (see Porter, 1998, chap. 13).

5. The 51% ownership cap for insiders stipulated during the first phase of privatization in Russia (1992-1994) was routinely ignored by employees and managers. Shown in Table 5.4, four surveys conducted between 1993 and 1996 (Blasi, Kroumova, & Kruse, 1997; Blasi & Shleifer, 1996; Buck, Filatotchev, & Wright, 1998; Peng, Buck, & Filatotchev, 1999) found insider ownership to be between approximately 58% and 65%.

6. This is not a problem pertaining only to employee-controlled firms in transition economies. Experience in the West has shown that it is normal for employee ownership gradually to revert or "degenerate" to external investor control. Given the inefficiency in collective decision making, the lack of interest in such decision making among rank-and-file employees, and the retirement of the original employee-owner cohort, many owners may prefer to liquidate their shares by selling either to outside interests or to a smaller insider group, such as managers (Ben-Ner, 1988; Bonin, Jones, & Putterman, 1993; Earle & Estrin, 1996).

7. See Peng (1994, 1997a, in press-a), Peng and Heath (1996), Peng and Luo (1998, 1999), and Peng and Tan (1998) for more details.

8. This strategy will be discussed in more detail in Chapter 7.

9. Exploratory research by Chow, Fan, and Hu (1998) found that, surprisingly, investors in the fledgling Shanghai Stock Exchange seem to follow the same adaptive expectation models as more sophisticated investors in the Hong Kong and New York Stock Exchanges. These results implied that despite a very late start, Shanghai investors are rapidly learning how to play the stock market game successfully.

10. The existing empirical evidence that substantiates this statement comes mostly from research in the United Kingdom and the United States. For decades, strong insider control among Japanese corporations, especially those in the *keiretsu* networks, was noted as an "anomaly" (Gerlach, 1992). However, the recent economic crisis that engulfed Japan in the 1990s led to fundamental questions of whether the *keiretsu* facilitates or impedes restructuring (Biers, 1998; "What to Do About Asia?" 1998). Therefore, the statement that "insider control is not conducive to restructuring" seems to be increasingly valid globally.

6

Strategies of Entrepreneurial Start-Ups

The fundamental impulse which sets and keeps the capitalist engine
in motion comes from the new consumers' goods, the new methods of
production, the new markets, and the new forms of industrial
organization that capitalist enterprise creates.
—Joseph Schumpeter (1942, p. 83)

During the transition, the organizational landscape has increasingly featured a new class of smaller entrepreneurial firms that compete side by side with SOEs and privatized and reformed firms. A
common characteristic that permeates the smaller firms is their sheer
entrepreneurial energy. Focusing on these smaller firms, this chapter
attempts to shed light on three important questions: (a) How have
they risen in an environment traditionally hostile to private ownership? (b) Who are these entrepreneurs? (c) What are the strategies they
have adopted? Before proceeding, however, it will be helpful to give
some attention to understanding what entrepreneurship is.

WHAT IS ENTREPRENEURSHIP?

The Definition of Entrepreneurship

Because entrepreneurship is a multifaceted phenomenon, its definitions vary considerably. For example, Schumpeter (1942) defined entrepreneurship as carrying out "new combinations." Kirzner (1973, 1997) equated entrepreneurship with arbitration, and suggested that the best entrepreneurs are those with the ability to exploit market imperfections and imbalances. More contemporary definitions focus on the more visible and hence verifiable traits at the firm level. Specifically, entrepreneurship can be defined as the *creation of new enterprise* (Gartner, 1985; Low & MacMillan, 1988). Given our firm-level focus, we will adopt this definition, and the title of this chapter thus deliberately highlights *"entrepreneurial start-ups"* (i.e., new enterprises) as opposed to the generic labels of "company" or "firm" found in other chapters. In this sense, the term *entrepreneur* is considered equivalent to "founder of a new business" (Peng, Hill, & Wang, in press).

What Does It Take to Be Entrepreneurs?

What motivates entrepreneurs to establish new firms, while others are simply content to work for other organizations? Three perspectives have emerged, each tackling a particular aspect of this broad question.

A Psychological Perspective. Compared with non-entrepreneurs, entrepreneurs seem more likely to possess a strong desire for achievement, have a strong locus of control (i.e., the belief that they can largely control their own fate), and are more willing to take risks and tolerate ambiguity (McClelland, 1967). Overall, "entrepreneurship inevitably implies a deviation from customary behavior" (Brenner, 1987, p. 95). This perspective was supported by McGrath and MacMillan (1992), who used a sample of more than 700 entrepreneurs from nine different cultures (Australia, China, Denmark, Finland, England, Norway, Sweden, Taiwan, and the United States) and found that some entrepreneurial beliefs transcend cultural differences. What is particularly interesting is the finding that beliefs about themselves and others in their society held among entrepreneurs in China, the only Eastern bloc country in this group, are highly similar to their counterparts elsewhere.

Critics argued, however, that some of these traits, such as a strong achievement orientation, are not necessarily limited to entrepreneurs, but instead are characteristic of many successful individuals. Moreover, the wide variation among entrepreneurs makes any attempt to develop a standard psychological or personality profile futile (Low & MacMillan, 1988). The findings by McGrath and MacMillan (1992, p. 425), as conceded by the authors, are at best "exploratory" and "speculative."

A Social-Cultural Perspective. The earliest and perhaps best-known work in this tradition was Max Weber's (1930) classic, *The Protestant Ethic and the Spirit of Capitalism*, which argued that the rise of Protestantism encouraged hard work and entrepreneurship, which in turn gave rise to capitalism. Although the *causal* link between the Protestant ethic and the development of capitalism has since been hotly debated, it does seem clear that there must be some kind of connection (Fukuyama, 1996).

Sometimes called "outsider" theories in the sociological literature, one school of thought suggests that socially or culturally disadvantaged groups (e.g., minorities) may have difficulty finding employment in the mainstream corporate sector and may be driven to found their own businesses in order to support themselves. This theme has been picked up by scholars interested in immigrant entrepreneurs, such as the Chinese in Southeast Asia, Koreans in Los Angeles, Cubans in Miami, and Jews in many countries (Aldrich & Waldinger, 1990; Borjas, 1990; Busenitz & Lau, 1996; Waldinger, Aldrich, & Ward, 1990; Wilson & Martin, 1982).

However, this body of work has been challenged by studies that found that entrepreneurs tend to be *better* educated and to come from *wealthier* families where the parents owned a business (Cooper & Dunkelberg, 1987). Contrary to studies on immigrant entrepreneurs, Cooper and Dunkelberg (1987, p. 21) reported that entrepreneurs are "no more likely to be of foreign-stock" than the general population in the United States. For example, the proliferation of new ventures in Silicon Valley founded by Stanford and Berkeley graduates and on

Route 128 in Boston founded by Harvard and MIT graduates demonstrates that not all entrepreneurs come from disadvantaged, minority, and/or immigrant backgrounds.

In sum, the social and cultural diversity of entrepreneurs seems to defy aggregation. Moving away from this perspective, some researchers have recently focused increasingly on what entrepreneurs actually do, thus leading to a network perspective.

A Network Perspective. One group of scholars has argued that regardless of the psychological, social, and cultural backgrounds entrepreneurs may possess, ultimately, the creation of new ventures is the result of the interaction between entrepreneurs and their larger social context (Aldrich & Zimmer, 1986). It may therefore be helpful to focus on entrepreneurs' particular social networks. Entrepreneurs are found to be more interested in tapping into their *informal* networks (family, friends, and colleagues) than *formal* networks (banks, accountants, lawyers, and government agencies; Birley, 1985). Since all organizations need to exchange resources with other entities in order to survive (Pfeffer & Salancik, 1978), researchers suggested that, compared with non-entrepreneurs, entrepreneurs tend to be more skillful in utilizing external resources in their networks (Burt, 1992; Jarillo, 1988, 1989; Larson, 1992). Therefore, an understanding of entrepreneurship not only entails knowledge about what entrepreneurs and their firms do, but also involves an understanding of the network links connecting them to the wider world.

In sum, it takes a *combination* of factors to be entrepreneurs, including individuals' psychological and personality traits, their social and cultural backgrounds, as well as their social networks and the larger environment. An understanding of entrepreneurship has to take these three perspectives into account.

THE RISE OF ENTREPRENEURSHIP

Entrepreneurship During the Socialist Era

While it is easy to believe that there was no or little entrepreneurship during the socialist era, this impression is only partially correct.

Although socialist governments were hostile to private ownership, entrepreneurship existed in virtually all socialist countries. Over time, the entrepreneurial sector was developed to such an extent that a number of peculiar labels, such as the "gray," "second," and "underground" economy, were coined to refer to this phenomenon well *before* major transitions took place (Grossman, 1977; Rupp, 1983; Shlapentokh, 1989).

Before the transition, a small private sector had always existed. However, it was suppressed and severely limited to being small, labor intensive, and often informal. Its participants often had to confront harassment from the police, the tax bureau, as well as a host of other government agencies. Led by Hungary since 1968, virtually all socialist countries realized by the 1980s that a private sector should be at least tolerated if the economy was to be developed. While the public sector would retain its dominant position, there should be a private sector playing a secondary role in filling niches, such as small shops and restaurants, that SOEs were incapable of serving efficiently. Ideally, the two sectors would not compete but would complement each other.

Taking advantage of the loosened regulations, there was a wave of entrepreneurship during the initial stage of transitions (see Tables 6.1 and 6.2 for examples). The coexistence of a small but rapidly rising private sector and a large but declining state sector made a lot of officials uncomfortable. Former Soviet President Gorbachev wrote in 1988:

> *Perestroika* [restructuring] in economic relations is called for in order to unearth the opportunities inherent in our system, in various forms of socialist ownership. But private ownership . . . is the basis of the exploitation of man by man, and our revolution was accomplished precisely to liquidate it, in order to hand over everything to ownership of the people. (cited in Kornai, 1992, p. 445)

As a result, motivating people to work harder while making sure that the state sector remained the dominant sector required a delicate balancing act by the government. For a long time, the government imposed a limit on the size of each individual private firm. For

TABLE 6.1   The Growth of the Private Sector in Hungary, 1980-1992

Panel A: Percentage of GDP	1980	1985	1989	1990	1991	1992
1. Public sector	83	79	74	70	63	50
2. Private sector	17	21	26	29	34	42
3. Foreign-controlled sector	0	0	0	1	3	8

Panel B: Growth of Private Firms	1984	1985	1986	1987	1988	1989
1. Number of private craftsmen (%)	100%	104.8	108.4	110.8	121.1	125.8
2. Employees of private craftsmen	100%	108.1	116.1	183.1	263.3	346.3
3. Number of private retailers (%)	100%	113.7	129.3	142.1	154.2	176.9
4. Employees of private retailers	100%	121.5	141.3	169.6	188.1	208.8

SOURCES: Panel A: Adapted from Ernst, Alexeev, and Marer (1996, p. 178); Panel B: Adapted from Kornai (1992, p. 438).

instance, throughout the 1980s, the employment limit for a private firm was seven employees in Hungary and eight in China. Moreover, in many countries, due to the politically sensitive nature of the term *private ownership*, a lot of euphemisms were used, ranging from "cooperative firms" in the former Soviet Union to "individual household businesses" in China. These countries were also reluctant in the 1980s to pass legislation to protect private property.

What is remarkable is the rapid rise of entrepreneurship in such an ambiguous environment that offered little legal and institutional protection for private property. The ability to profit directly from their own hard work motivated many people, according to a Chinese term, to "plunge into the ocean" of private businesses. While the government was still extensively involved in the economy, wherever and whenever the government had relatively few restrictions on the private sector,

TABLE 6.2 The Growth of "Cooperative" (Private) Enterprises in the Former Soviet Union, 1987-1990

	January 1987	*January 1988*	*January 1989*	*January 1990*	*July 1990*
Number of firms	15,000	152,100	1,396,500	2,573,800	3,100,000
Annual increase (%)	—	914.0	818.1	84.3	—

SOURCE: Adapted from Kornai (1992, p. 440).
NOTE: — Missing data

"pockets" or "islands" of entrepreneurship, such as those in South China, started to develop (Chang & MacMillan, 1991). Private firms really started to make big "waves" and "splashes" in the 1990s, to which we now turn.

The Golden Era of Entrepreneurship During the Transition

After a period of slow but steady growth in the 1980s, private entrepreneurship blossomed in the 1990s, which can be called a "golden era" of entrepreneurship. The most fundamental driving force, of course, was the removal of the yoke of communism throughout CEE and the NIS (see Chapter 2). As a result, private firms rapidly gained momentum. The other underlying force is the continued deterioration of the SOE sector (see Chapter 4). Therefore, even for countries such as China and Vietnam, where socialism is still the official ideology, more and more people, including many in the government, realize that SOEs are not likely to be good vehicles to get these countries out of their economic backwardness and that private firms offer an attractive alternative for personal wealth, organizational growth, as well as national development. We may regard the lure of capitalism as a "pull" factor and the failure of SOEs as a "push" factor. Overall, a combination of the pull and push factors resulted in the abolishment of many restrictions on private firms. These transitions have really opened the floodgates of entrepreneurship, which rises to undermine the foundation of the socialist economy.

Since the mid-1990s, the majority of the GDP has been contributed by the private sector throughout CEE and the NIS (e.g., 75% in the Czech Republic, 70% in Hungary, and 60% in Poland and Russia by 1996). A recent study on private start-ups in Russia found that, despite the dramatic decline of the SOE sector, the private sector experienced between 15% and 150% annual growth, depending on the industry in question (Sharma & Merrell, 1997). It is the growth of the private sector that has compensated for the decline of SOEs, provided employment opportunities, and prevented many of these economies from collapsing further. However, the "private sector" in these countries not only includes private start-ups, which are the focus of this chapter, but also a substantial number of privatized, former SOEs (see Chapter 5). Given the blurring of the boundaries between these two separate types of private firms,[1] it is difficult to assess the true extent of the development of private start-ups.

Data from China, on the other hand, do offer a glimpse into the extent to which private entrepreneurship has developed (Table 6.3). Until the mid-1990s, almost all private firms in China were start-ups, because large-scale, formal privatization of SOEs had not occurred. More interestingly, official Chinese statistics distinguish two types of private firms, the smaller ones registered as "individual household businesses" (ge ti hu) with a limit of employment of eight, referred to earlier, and the larger ones, simply called "private businesses" (si yin qi ye), with no limit on the number of people they can employ.

Three interesting patterns emerge. First, between 1990 and 1995, larger private firms experienced the strongest growth in terms of their numbers and their employment, capital, and output, while smaller firms had relatively more modest growth. Although smaller firms might have experienced more rapid growth in the 1980s, larger firms were the primary driving force behind the development of the private sector in the 1990s, mostly due to the loosened regulations. Second, although the average number of employees at small firms rose gradually (from 1.59 per firm in 1990 to 1.83 in 1995), the average number of employees at larger firms actually *declined* (from 17.4 employees per firm in 1990 to 14.3 in 1995). This evidence, viewed in combination with the escalating number of "large" private firms, suggests that a substantial number of new firms, which were actually very small, were founded during the period and that their owners chose to register them openly as "private businesses" as opposed to "individual household businesses." This reflects a more entrepreneur-friendly environment in the 1990s, which contrasts sharply with the environment in the 1980s in which founding "individual household businesses" was considered a politically risky adventure. The third observation is the rising percentage of total industrial output generated by the private sector consisting of these two types of entrepreneurial firms. Although the private sector contributed a mere 0.5% of China's industrial output in 1980 (not shown in Table 6.3), it contributed nearly 6% in 1990 and 15% by 1995, whereas the share of the state sector dropped from 76% to 34% during the 1980-1995 period (Chinese Academy of Social Sciences, Institute of Industrial Economics, 1997, p. 302). Moreover, because many private business owners choose to register their firms as "collective" firms (see the section on "blurring boundaries" below), the extent to which the private sector has penetrated the Chinese economy is greatly underestimated by official statistics. In a nutshell, these data clearly suggest that the 1990s are indeed a golden era for entrepreneurial start-ups.

During the transition, the private sector has two constituent parts. The first is a traditional sector, with small-scale firms that hire very few people, invest little, and provide goods and services of modest value. The second is an expansive modern sector made possible by (a) the privatization of state property (see Chapter 5) and (b) the generic growth of entrepreneurial start-ups through accumulation of private capital (Rona-Tas, 1994, p. 49). Overall, the private sector has not only risen to challenge the dominance of the state sector, but also in many cases become the most important contributor to the economy. How private firms emerged from a complementary and secondary role to a dominant position in the economy has been one of the most fascinating aspects of the transition process.

WHO ARE THESE ENTREPRENEURS?

As alluded to earlier, what drives people to be entrepreneurs has remained an intriguing puzzle despite decades of research. Even less is known about what drives entrepreneurs in transition economies. Piecing together sketchy evidence from different countries, I focus on four types of entrepreneurs below: (a) farmers, (b) "gray" individuals, (c) former cadres, and (d) professionals.

TABLE 6.3 The Growth of Registered Private Firms in China, 1990-1995

	1990	1991	1992	1993	1994	1995
Panel A: Smaller Private Firms (Registered as "ge ti hu" or individual household businesses)						
Number of firms	—	14,170,000	15,340,000	17,770,000	21,870,000	25,280,000
Annual increase (%)	—	6.8	8.3	16.5	23.1	15.6
Employment	—	22,580,000	24,680,000	29,390,000	37,760,000	46,140,000
Annual increase (%)	—	7.9	9.7	19.1	28.5	22.2
Average employees per firm	—	1.59	1.61	1.65	1.73	1.83
Capital (billions of yuan)[a]	—	48.8	60.1	85.5	131.9	181.3
Annual increase (%)	—	22.9	23.2	42.3	54.3	37.5
Output (billions of yuan)	129.0	128.7	200.6	286.1	708.2	1,182.1
Annual increase (%)	—	-0.2	55.9	42.6	147.5	66.9
Panel B: Larger Private Firms (Registered as "si yin qi ye" or private businesses)						
Number of firms	98,000	108,000	139,000	238,000	432,000	655,000
Annual increase (%)	8.3	9.9	28.8	70.4	81.7	51.4
Employment	1,702,000	1,839,000	2,319,000	3,726,000	6,484,000	9,560,000
Annual increase (%)	3.8	8.0	26.0	60.7	74.0	47.5
Average employees per firm	17.4	17.0	16.7	15.7	15.0	14.3

Capital (billions of yuan)	9.52	12.32	22.12	68.05	144.78	262.20
Annual increase (%)	12.6	29.4	79.8	207.6	112.8	81.0
Output (billions of yuan)	11.2	13.6	18.9	42.1	107.0	229.5
Annual increase (%)	—	21.4	39.0	122.8	154.2	114.5

Panel C: Firms in Panels A and B Combined

Percentage of gross industrial output	5.9	5.4	6.3	8.8	11.51	15.14

SOURCE: Adapted from Chinese Academy of Social Sciences, Institute of Industrial Economics (1997, pp. 301-302).

NOTE: — Missing data

a. Exchange rate: US$1 = 4.78 yuan (1990), 5.76 yuan (1993), and 8.34 yuan (1995)

Farmers

According to state socialism, the socialist state, in theory at least, belonged to "workers," who usually were urban, industrial workers. Farmers in the countryside were regarded as second-class citizens who had to work in the fields, could not migrate freely to the cities, and were offered few benefits like housing, schooling, and other social welfare to which SOE employees and their families in the cities were entitled. As a result, farmers historically were not fully integrated into the orbit of state socialism, and it is precisely this "outsider" status that led them to be among the first entrepreneurs in these countries (Nee, 1989, 1991; Szelenyi, 1988).

Although private farming was eradicated and farmers were organized into communes and cooperatives in most socialist countries, Poland never nationalized its agriculture. In 1987, Polish private farmers owned more than 70% of the land and other fixed assets (Manev, Manolova, & Yan, 1998). Even in countries where private farming had not been allowed before, the loosening of government regulations spurred a great deal of private farming activities (Szelenyi, 1988). For example, communes in China, which took the government nearly 10 years in the 1950s to organize, were dismantled almost overnight, in a short span of 2 years, by the late 1970s (Nee, 1991; Zhao, 1997).

Private farming initially was taken up by families, and most of them did not bother to register their undertaking as a "business" or "company." Over time, however, some of them started to get organized along more formal lines and attempted to grow beyond the family holdings. While most of them remained small, some of the better-managed ones became more visible. The largest private company currently in China, the Hope Group, for instance, can trace its roots to private farming. Founded in 1982, it specializes in animal feed, vegetables, meat, and food processing (Au & Sun, 1998). Its 1995 sales reached approximately $20 million, 50% more than the second largest private company in China (Chinese Academy of Social Sciences, Institute of Industrial Economics, 1997, p. 313).

Some of the theories reviewed earlier can be used to explain the rise of private farming. First, farmers historically were subject to less stringent political control by the state, and, as a result, they experienced and desired far more autonomy. Second, they represented an "outside" group that could not easily migrate to the cities to find jobs. Similar to the route to entrepreneurship chosen by many immigrants, farmers thus had a stronger propensity to become entrepreneurs.[2] Finally, when government realized that collective farming, due to its inherent incentive and monitoring problems (see Chapter 2), was unable to motivate farmers to work hard, the environment became more friendly for private farmers. Private farming enabled farmers to pocket residual income directly, leading to an enormous gain in motivation and productivity that significantly alleviates the agricultural and food shortage plaguing virtually all socialist countries (Choe, 1996; Nee, 1989, 1991).

In sum, farmers tend to be among the first group of entrepreneurs who start to chip away at the foundation of state socialism. While they make a deep impact on the economy, they are not as visible as some of their entrepreneurial counterparts in urban areas, to which we now turn.

"Gray" Individuals

Because there were very few lawful possibilities for organizing entrepreneurial ventures under state socialism, unlawful ways emerged. As a result, a "gray" economy developed, with a large number of labels, including the "second," "semiprivate," "shadow," "black market," "underground," "illegal," and/or "alegal" economy (the term *gray economy* will be used for compositional simplicity here). The socialist era left a legacy of disregard for the supremacy of the law. First, there were not enough formal laws governing economic behavior; in their place were a mind-numbing number of party decrees and regulations (Peng & Heath, 1996). Second, there was little legitimacy for the laws, decrees, and regulations that did exist and that were routinely ignored (Stark, 1992). For example, a norm was widely shared that stealing from the state was not much of a crime because state-owned property was usually perceived as nobody's, or everybody's, property (Hisrich & Grachev, 1993). It is not surprising that despite its lack of legality, the gray economy was not only tolerated and accepted by the general population, but was also eagerly participated in by certain individuals

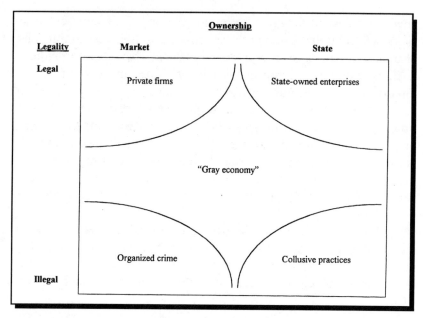

Figure 6.1. A Typology of Organizational Sectors in Transition Economies
SOURCE: Adapted from Manev, Manolova, and Yan (1998).

who might view their activities as passive resistance to the communist regime (Grossman, 1977; Rupp, 1983; Shlapentokh, 1989).

The transitions have brought "the underground entrepreneurs into the open economy" (Jones & Maskoff, 1991, p. 27). As a result, behavioral norms are in flux, and frontier-style overnight accumulation of wealth becomes possible ("The Pirates of Prague," 1996). Together with the decline of the state there has been a rise of various "gray" activities, ranging from tax evasion and bribery, which are widely practiced, to outright illegal practices found among members of mafia-like organizations (Minniti, 1995). Although organized crime in countries such as Russia has attracted significant media and public policy attention (Yavlinsky, 1998), it is probably not correct to regard all participants in gray activities as criminals. Instead, it may be useful to view all organizations in transition economies, most notably "gray" organizations, within a framework (Figure 6.1) recently proposed by Manev et al. (1998).

Three observations emerge from this framework. First, although we traditionally separate organizations in transition economies according to their ownership (i.e., SOEs vs. private firms), a second dimension, legality, also figures prominently (Manev et al., 1998). While SOEs and private firms tend to be legally registered organizations, there exist two types of illegal (and usually unregistered) entities, namely, "private" crime organizations (e.g., mafia-like organizations) and public organizations whose officials are corrupt and serve the interests of crime bosses and/or collusive interests. A second insight of this framework is the central position of the gray economy, populated by individuals who act as *intermediaries* connecting these four categories of organizations (Peng, 1998). The size of the gray economy is, of course, very difficult to estimate, and varies from one country to another. Tentative figures in the mid-1990s put the total size of the gray economy at between 20% and 30% of the GDP in Poland, more than 30% in Bulgaria, and maybe 40% in Russia (Manev et al., 1998). Sharma and Merrell (1997, p. 321) provided a more radical estimate that suggested that the unreported, gray economy in Russia may be *larger* than the official economy! A third observation is that participants in the gray economy do not necessarily belong to crime organizations, although some of them do. Most of these people are "entrepreneurs" in a classical sense: "persons who add value by brokering the connection between others" (Burt, 1997, p. 342). They blur the boundaries separating different sectors by taking advantage of the information and resource *asymmetry* across different sectors (Peng & Heath, 1996). In turn, they profit from these arbitrage opportunities (Kirzner, 1997).

The rise of gray entrepreneurs can be explained by the three perspectives on entrepreneurship noted earlier. First, these individuals tend to have a number of psychological and personality traits that distinguish them from non-entrepreneurs. They have a strong belief that they can control their own fate and are more willing to take risks and tolerate ambiguity. Second, they are typically members of outsider groups that cannot easily find regular employment in the mainstream economy. Ethnically, they include the Gypsies in Hungary and Romania, the Azerbaijanis in the former Soviet Union, and the Central Asians (people from Xinjian) in China. Socially, many of these people have a history of deviant behavior. In China, for example, a large number of urban "individual house businesses" (*ge ti hu*) in the later 1970s and early 1980s were founded by unemployed ex-convicts who had a hard time finding jobs (Tan, 1996). At a time when private firms had little legitimacy, these disadvantaged groups had little to lose by starting their own businesses. Finally, the network perspective can help explain a great deal of these activities. Operating "underground," these people shun formal transactions, preferring informal network linkages based on common ethnic, social, and experience-based backgrounds (Peng, 1994).

In sum, a large number of people have become entrepreneurs by participating in the gray economy. While some are outright criminals, not all are. Most seem to be entrepreneurs who exploit market imperfections and imbalances. While the rise of these entrepreneurs can be explained well by existing research, the reason behind the emergence of another category of entrepreneurs, former cadres, has stimulated considerable debate and will be explored next.

Former Cadres

What is especially interesting in transition economies is that a substantial number of former communist cadres have also become entrepreneurs (Rona-Tas, 1994). Usually conservative in their outlook and well treated by the government, cadres are not known for their entrepreneurial savvy. Moreover, cadres can hardly be regarded as a socially deviant group. Therefore, what motivates them to join the private sector and how they perform have attracted substantial attention leading to vigorous scholarly and public policy debates (Parish & Michelson, 1996; Szelenyi & Kostello, 1996). One part of the literature, called the market transition theory, suggested that market transitions erode the power and privileges of cadres and open new channels for traditionally disadvantaged groups (e.g., farmers, gray individuals) to emerge as entrepreneurs (Nee, 1989, 1991; Szelenyi, 1988). Possessing few entrepreneurial traits and skills, cadres would have "little or no net advantage in entering into private entrepreneurship" (Nee, 1989, p. 671).

In contrast, other scholars argued that cadres can benefit from the transitions by becoming entrepreneurs (Burawoy & Krotov, 1992; Rona-Tas, 1994). Two arguments emerge. The first, called the technocratic continuity thesis, contends that technocratic cadres can maintain their advantageous position because of their acquired expertise. Although earlier cadres tended to be revolutionary zealots with little education, by the 1980s, cadreship was strongly tied to education. Most educated people joined the Party not out of dedication to socialism, but out of opportunistic interest, to promote their careers. Given that people with more education in general are found to do better in market economies than those with less (Cooper & Dunkelberg, 1987), it follows that cadres, who as a group are more educated than the general population, are likely to be in an advantageous position during the transition (Rona-Tas, 1994, p. 45).

The second argument, the power conversion thesis, suggests that power accumulated under state socialism can be converted into assets of high value in a transition economy. During privatization, strategically located cadres can take advantage of their positions when acquiring state property (see Strategy in Action 5.1). Moreover, cadres have an advantage not just in setting up but also in operating companies, because they can tap into their personal networks to gain access to valuable information and resources from their former colleagues still in the government (Rona-Tas, 1994). Given the coexistence of multiple sectors, cadres may be especially good at brokering among different market sectors by maneuvering in the gray economy (see Figure 6.1). Although the extensiveness of personal ties and networks before the transition was amply documented (Nee & Stark, 1989), these assume special importance during the transition (Peng, 1994; Peng & Heath, 1996; Peng & Luo, 1999; Peng & Tan, 1998). From a centrally located and powerful position from which to interact with various economic players, cadres are likely to benefit from these intangible ties when they become entrepreneurs. The story of how a Chinese technocrat became a tycoon (Strategy in Action 6.1) can serve as a case in point here.

Strategy in Action 6.1

From Technocrat to Tycoon in China

For young technocrats like Weng Shanding, the brutal crackdown on the pro-democracy movement by the government in June 1989 resulted in a fundamental crisis about the legitimacy of the government as well as their own identity within such a discredited body. As a result, Weng, a rising star in the State Planning Commission of the central government in Beijing, joined the exodus of government officials into business in a process that the Chinese called "plunging into the ocean."

The return of the "ocean" has been bountiful. By 1995, Weng ran a $120 million investment company in fast-paced Shenzhen, a boomtown bordering Hong Kong and home of one of China's two cities with a stock exchange (the other is in Shanghai). Among the projects of his China New Industries Investment Company are a futures-and-commodities trading firm, a clinic to treat nearsightedness with lasers, a collection of high-tech start-ups, a major office complex, and a sports club with racquetball courts and bowling lanes.

Weng relied on his networks and contacts in the government to navigate the "waters" of the "ocean." In fact, the 17 shareholders of his company included several provincial governments from around the country and his former employer, the State Planning Commission, which provided vital protection for his (and their) interests. Over time, Weng believed, private-run companies such as his own would become a major catalyst for change in the Chinese economy. Once he had hoped that he would help change the economy while working for the government; now he realized that he and his company would have a much stronger and deeper impact on the transitions toward a market economy.

SOURCE: Engardio, 1995, p. 51.

Although the debate is still going on and the empirical evidence is sketchy, taken together, it seems that the existing findings are in favor of the technocratic continuity and power conversion arguments. For example, Rona-Tas (1994) reported that cadre-entrepreneurs in Hungary were very successful during the transition (see Table 6.4). While the average income for cadres involved in entrepreneurial

TABLE 6.4 Cadres and Entrepreneurship in Hungary, 1989-1991

Annual Income (in HUF)[a]	1989 Mean	S.D.	1991 Mean	S.D.	Mean Increase (%)
Entire population	6,790	3,710	10,770	7,170	58.6
Noncadres not involved in entrepreneurial activities	6,310	3,180	9,570	5,160	51.7
Noncadres involved in entrepreneurial activities	7,160	4,060	12,410	8,430	73.3
Cadres not involved in entrepreneurial activities	11,730	5,080	18,110	10,740	54.3
Cadres involved in entrepreneurial activities	12,050	5,080	25,330	16,680	110.2

SOURCE: Adapted from Rona-Tas (1994, p. 60).
NOTE: a. Exchange rate: US$1 = HUF59 (1989 average) and HUF64 (1991 average).
S.D. is standard deviation.

activities was already higher than that of any other group in 1989, their edge increased by 1991. Specifically, during that 2-year period, cadre-entrepreneurs more than doubled their *reported* personal income, while noncadre entrepreneurs increased their income by 73%. In comparison, the entire population experienced an income increase of 59%, and cadres not involved in entrepreneurial activities raised their income by only 54%. Given the general tendency to underreport income, the actual income of cadre-entrepreneurs may be even higher. Similar findings from China were reported by Parish and Michelson (1996). Such evidence, as well as widely reported official corruption and cadre self-enrichment, seems to have led market transition theorists to modify their position by acknowledging the importance of cadre-entrepreneurs (Nee, 1991, p. 269). However, they maintained that these findings, reflecting the nature of the "half market, half planned" economy, do not necessarily contradict the market transition theory, and that, in the long run, the importance of cadre-entrepreneurs will decline vis-à-vis other entrepreneurs (Nee & Matthews, 1996, p. 426).

While the emergence of cadre-entrepreneurs represents a new puzzle, existing research on entrepreneurship can solve at least some of it. First, despite the stereotype of their lack of dynamism, a large number of cadres are actually ambitious and achievement oriented. With the exception of a few die-hard communist fundamentalists, most of them join the cadre rank in search of better career opportunities. Despite what the government proclaims, cadres are not people of high principles. Instead, they can be better viewed as rational, opportunistic individuals driven by strong self-interest (witness the almost overnight disappearance of millions of Communist Party memberships throughout CEE and the NIS between 1989 and 1991). Therefore, it seems plausible that once they channel their considerable upwardly mobile energy into entrepreneurial activities as opposed to the dead-end political arena, their strong drive may distinguish them from non-entrepreneurs. Second, although the phenomenon of cadre-entrepreneurs is at odds with outsider theories of entrepreneurship, it is consistent with other parts of the social-cultural perspective in that entrepreneurs are likely to share certain social backgrounds and experiences. In this case, cadre-entrepreneurs have attained better educational achievement, share common experience as cadres, and possess strong network connections in and outside of the government. Finally, the social network perspective can explain very well how cadre-entrepreneurs function and prosper, which will not be repeated here.

Overall, it seems that cadres have not lost their economically advantageous position during the transition. Many cadres have quickly taken advantage of the transition process by becoming entrepreneurs. In the long run, however, the market transition theory is probably correct in that the proportion of cadre-entrepreneurs, which currently constitutes a small percentage among entrepreneurs, "will decline as the population of entrepreneurs grows and draws on new groups in society" (Nee & Matthews, 1996, p. 426). The next section focuses on a particular group of new entrepreneurs.

Professionals

As economic transitions deepen, the legitimacy of entrepreneurs and private firms rises rapidly. As a result, while many entrepreneurs in the 1980s were farmers, the unemployed, ex-convicts, and other gray individuals, in the 1990s more and more professionals, such as SOE managers, engineers, technicians, and professors, have joined the ranks of entrepreneurs. In contrast to cadre-entrepreneurs, who lead to strong public and scholarly concerns, professional-entrepreneurs have been widely supported and encouraged.

The development of the private sector can benefit from more professional-entrepreneurs in three ways. First, they help improve the professionalism of private firms, which is badly needed. Initially, private firms in transition economies were family operations with little division of labor. Lack of professionalism prevents many of them from growing to a larger scale and scope. Second, professionals improve the technological content of the products and services generated by private firms, which traditionally concentrate in low-technology, labor-intensive sectors such as farming, restaurants, and retail shops. Finally, professionals increase the legitimacy of private firms. Less-educated farmers and gray individuals with dubious backgrounds and activities do not inspire much confidence in the eyes of the public. Cadre-entrepreneurs are widely viewed with suspicion and resentment by the general public. Professionals, on the other hand, are better educated, hold prestigious positions not directly related to the party state, and have few connections with the gray economy. As a result, these individual-based reputational advantages can be translated into the trustworthiness of the firms established by professionals in the eyes of their transaction partners, the new government, as well as the general public. Professional-run private firms, in turn, are likely to attract more experienced professionals and recent college graduates, thus fueling the development of these firms (see Strategy in Action 6.2 for an example).

Strategy in Action 6.2

Beelines and Cell Phones in Russia

Beeline is the trademark of Vimpelcom, the largest cellular-telecommunications provider and one of the most successful start-ups in Russia. Vimpelcom began modestly in 1991 as the brainchild of some Soviet defense research scientists. Combining defense industry know-how, contacts in the Russian communications industry, and a management savvy still unusual for Russia, Vimpelcom offered cellular services in 40 regions of the former Soviet Union, as well as cellular roaming in parts of Europe and the United States. In the critical market of Moscow,

Vimpelcom commanded nearly 60% market share. Its revenue reached $100 million in 1996.

Most impressive, Vimpelcom beat out Russia's blue-chip giants to become the first Russian company to earn a full listing on the New York Stock Exchange. Opening its books to the scrutiny of Wall Street, it raised $66 million with a Level-3 American Depository Receipt (ADR). Priced at $20.50 when it was launched on November 15, 1996, the ADR traded for $36 in February 1997. Part of Vimpelcom's secret was having started from scratch, free of the usual Soviet-era baggage that plagues privatized enterprises. Vimpelcom built from the ground up with Western-style management and accounting principles that made it easy to present the 3 years of U.S. standard audits required to list in New York.

As demand for cellular services grew, the company planned to expand into a new, lower-cost frequency to attract more subscribers. That would give Vimpelcom the largest subscriber capacity of any cellular operator in Moscow. With its client base still 70% corporate, the aim during the late 1990s was to woo middle-class subscribers. Vimpelcom stresses customer service and is one of Moscow's most aggressive advertisers, using billboards, radio ads, and a perk called the Beeline Club, which offers customers services from airline reservations to flower deliveries.

SOURCE: Adapted from McKay, 1997.

Despite these advantages, professional-entrepreneurs are not without their share of problems. First, their professionalism leads them to be more thorough in their analysis and more cautious in decision making. As a result, their risk-taking propensity is not as strong as that of some other entrepreneurs such as, say, gray individuals. Second, development of products and services with more techno-logical content requires more capital and more long-term investment. The general environment in transition economies, characterized by policy instability and regulatory chaos, is not conducive to this kind of investment. Most firms are starving for capital, which banks have been reluctant to provide. Finally, professional-entrepreneurs' lack of connections with other sectors may be a liability rather than an asset (Dubini & Aldrich, 1991). In an environment where personal ties figure prominently, entrepreneurs without deep and strong network relations may have a lot of difficulty in getting things done (Peng, 1997a; Peng & Luo, 1998, 1999). Compared with informal wheeling and dealing, they may be more interested in formal relations through professionalization of their organizations and contractual-based transactions.

Again, some of the theories on entrepreneurship can be used to explain the emergence of professional-entrepreneurs. First, these people tend to be more achievement oriented. Once the "legitimacy barrier" for private businesses is removed, they start to join the entrepreneurial sector en masse and are likely to be highly intelligent, motivated, and hard working. Second, they tend to share certain educational background and professional experience, representing a particular mainstream social group that historically has not been particularly deviant. Finally, according to the network perspective, while professional-entrepreneurs may not be masters in mobilizing *informal* network resources, they may be more interested in tapping into *formal* networks of market-supporting institutions, such as banks, accountants, lawyers, and regulatory agencies. While they are likely to be frustrated by the lack of development of these institutions, they tend to be the underlying force lobbying for increased legislation providing better regulation to the new economy.

In sum, economic transitions have provided powerful incentives for all sorts of entrepreneurs to mushroom, ranging from farmers and gray individuals to former cadres to professionals. It is interesting to note that these different entrepreneurs tend to specialize in different fields, taking advantage of their strengths. Farmer-entrepreneurs usually focus on food and vegetable production, and then branch into distribution of farm produce and relatively low-technology manufacturing. Gray individuals are likely to specialize in various intermediary "services," such as exchanging foreign currency through black markets, obtaining quotas and approvals from people in power, and enforcing contracts (through distortion and assassination) that may be very "inefficient" to process through the court system. Cadre-entrepreneurs are known for their interest in "relationship-intensive" industries, such as trading, entertainment, and property development. Professionals-turned-entrepreneurs tend to be more interested in knowledge- and technology-based ventures, such as computer software, architectural design, engineering services, law practices, and business consulting.

While some of these fields overlap, there seem to be some discernible patterns of specialization for different types of entrepreneurs throughout different transition economies. Collectively, they create an entrepreneurial movement that helps transform these economies. Next, we move on to explore the strategies that private firms founded and operated by these entrepreneurs adopt.

STRATEGIES OF ENTREPRENEURIAL START-UPS

Being smaller and younger, entrepreneurial start-ups adopt some strategies that distinguish them from their larger and more established competitors. On the other hand, some strategies of smaller firms converge with those of other organizational forms. Highlighted below are three major entrepreneurial strategies: (a) prospecting, (b) networking, and (c) boundary blurring.

Strategy I: Prospecting

The term *Prospector* comes from an influential typology of strategy types proposed by Miles and Snow (1978).[3] Prospectors are firms with a changing market, a focus on innovation and change, and a flexible organizational structure headed by younger, more aggressive managers. In comparison, *Defenders* are firms with a narrow market, a stable customer group, and an established organizational structure managed by older, more conservative executives. The Prospector and the Defender "reside at opposite ends of [a] continuum of strategies" (Miles & Snow, 1978, p. 68). While many SOEs and recently privatized ex-SOEs may adopt a Defender strategy (see Chapters 4 and 5), entrepreneurial start-ups are more likely to adopt a Prospector strategy (Tan & Peng, 1998a). Compared with their larger counterparts, private firms are usually small, starved for capital, and weak in technological capabilities (Peng, 1997a). Yet, they are much closer to markets and, as a result, are more willing to change their product/service mix in order to serve their customers better (Tan, 1996). In general, start-ups adopt a simple organizational structure, which allows them to react quickly to opportunities or proactively outmaneuver their more established rivals such as SOEs. Moreover, start-ups have little inherited organizational baggage, low fixed costs, and the ability to attract the most capable and aggressive managers and employees. Overall, their strategic actions tend to fit well with the Prospector type in the Miles and Snow typology (Tan & Peng, 1998a).

Another way to view this strategy is to treat these entrepreneurial start-ups as "underdogs" that have very little choice but to adopt *guerrilla* warfare tactics (Tan, 1996). Underdog firms cannot compete head-on against their larger and more established rivals. Instead, smaller firms limit their activities to relatively few alternatives and conserve scarce resources for crucial battles. Such a guerrilla strategy is a successful alternative for firms with a low market share and limited resources (Harrigan, 1985). It is speed and stealth of movement that characterize entrepreneurial behavior in transition economies. Speed and stealth create disruption by preempting competitors and allow the entrepreneurial firms to be the first movers while forcing their competitors to be Defenders or Reactors. Such quick movement takes the industry to faster and more intense levels of competition, resulting in some instances in a "hypercompetitive" situation (Brown & Eisenhardt, 1998; D'Aveni, 1994). Moreover, it often gives entrepreneurial start-ups substantial *first-mover advantages* (Kerin, Varadarajan, & Peterson, 1992; Lieberman & Montgomery, 1988) by allowing them to build up a market share, increase brand name awareness, and preempt competitors in a particular niche. Shown in Strategy in Action 6.3, Poland's Optimus Computer exemplifies this entrepreneurial approach.

Strategy in Action 6.3

Optimus Computer: Enterprising in Poland

Roman Kluska, a Polish entrepreneur, could not be controlled by the government even in the old days. As deputy director of a state-owned company that repaired cars and trucks in southern Poland in the mid-1980s, he scrounged the parts to assemble and sell cars, too. Irked that the cost of energy and materials exceeded the value of the company's output, he split the plant into 20 "worker partnerships" and promised workers a share of the gains. Profits soared and salaries shot up, but the communist workers council did not like it so they voted to sack him.

With just $12 in his pocket, Kluska and his wife founded computer maker Optimus in his parents' attic in 1988. As the communist regime unraveled, Kluska leveraged family property for a $25,000 loan at 20% interest *per month*. By 1995, he held 35% of the Polish market with personal computers (PC) assembled from Intel chips, Samsung monitors, and Microsoft operating systems, sold through 1,100 outlets. After hiring top Polish engineers to add features such as portable hard drives, he could still undercut imports from Asia by 20%. Pretax profits were 9% of nearly $1 million in sales.

Other than being always unconventional, Kluska attributed the success of his start-up to a "guerrilla" strategy that sought first-mover advantages in the PC market when the PC revolution was starting to gain momentum in Poland in the early 1990s. Always moving ahead of the competitors to satisfy customers' increasing needs has been a hallmark of his entrepreneurial strategy.

SOURCE: Miller, 1995.

However, there are at least three limitations to this Prospector or guerrilla strategy. First, the industries that entrepreneurs enter need to have relatively low entry barriers, less capital intensity, and low exit costs. As a result, they tend to focus on labor-intensive farming, light manufacturing, and small-scale service industries, and to shy away from large-scale, technology- and capital-intensive industries. Second, while their larger rivals find it difficult to compete on speed and stealth, successful entrepreneurial start-ups often attract a large number of other private firms that follow these first movers. The nature of the industries the first movers enter (i.e., low entry barriers, less capital intensity) typically results in the first movers' inability to defend themselves and, consequently, to sustain a competitive advantage (Porter, 1980; Schnaars, 1994). Therefore, entrepreneurial firms, especially first movers that are unable to defend themselves, have a tendency to be footloose and to exit existing industries or niches to search for new opportunities elsewhere. Finally, while this strategy may be viable during the initial phase of the transitions when there are a large number of unfilled niches, it is questionable whether it can be pursued in the long run when the economy becomes more developed, mature, and saturated.

In sum, many private entrepreneurial start-ups exhibit a distinct and dynamic strategy that is rarely employed by other firms in transition economies. Called "guerrilla" by laymen and "Prospector" by scholars, the essence of this strategy lies in speed, stealth, and sound execution.

Strategy II: Networking

Compared with the Prospector strategy above, networking as a strategy is not an exclusive territory reserved for only entrepreneurial start-ups. The necessity for a networking strategy in transition economies was discussed extensively in Chapter 3. Basically, the lack of certain market-supporting institutions often leaves managers and entrepreneurs having to perform basic functions themselves, such as obtaining market information, interpreting regulations, and enforcing contracts (Khanna & Palepu, 1997). In an environment in which *formal* institutional constraints such as laws and regulations are weak, *informal* institutional constraints, such as those embodied in interpersonal networks, connections, and ties cultivated by managers and entrepreneurs (e.g., *blat* in Russia and *guanxi* in China), may play a more significant role in facilitating economic exchanges (North, 1990; Peng, 1994; Peng & Heath, 1996).

While every firm in a transition economy needs to pay attention to its networks, it is more important for private start-ups to have these connections. What is noteworthy about the networking efforts of these firms is their urgency, intensity, enthusiasm, and impact. Private firms initially suffer from a lack of legitimacy as new organizations due to their "liability of age" (Aldrich & Fiol, 1994), which prompts a stronger sense of *urgency* for them to establish network ties rapidly in order to compensate for this liability. Under the generic label of entrepreneurial networks are two specific types that entrepreneurs have to cultivate (Peng & Luo, 1998, 1999). The first one is with entrepreneurs and managers at other firms, such as suppliers, buyers, and competitors (Dubini & Aldrich, 1991). Good relationships with suppliers may help a start-up acquire quality materials, good services, and timely delivery.

Similar ties with buyers may spur customer loyalty, sales volume, and reliable payment. Moreover, good relations with competitors may facilitate possible interfirm collaboration and implicit collusion, while minimizing uncertainties and surprises.

While these networks and ties with other firms may be useful in most economies (Burt, 1992; Powell, 1990), a unique set of networks that entrepreneurs have to cultivate in transition economies characterized by a lack of institutional support for private firms are networks with government officials (Peng, 1997a; Xin & Pearce, 1996). Despite the new policy that on paper encourages private firms, in practice, official harassment from various government officials remains a constant danger (Nee, 1992). In Russia, for example, every private company must provide 28 *quarterly* reports to the tax authorities, of which "24 are stupid," according to an entrepreneur (Sharma & Merrell, 1997, p. 328). Taxation and regulatory policies are often self-contradictory, and even the most scrupulous entrepreneurs cannot be in consistent compliance. In China, most private firms have to pay nearly 50 different kinds of taxes and deal with more than 30 different government agencies, each of which claims to have some jurisdiction over them and collects a tax or two. One striking case occurred when a local post office could not sell all the new year's cards it printed: It forced all private firms in the area to buy the remaining inventory; otherwise, it threatened to discontinue their mail services (Chinese Academy of Social Sciences, Institute of Industrial Economics, 1997, p. 307). It is not surprising that entrepreneurs clearly understand the importance of having good relationships with government officials. Two recent studies found that the impact of network links with officials on entrepreneurial performance is *more* important than those with managers and entrepreneurs at other firms (Peng & Luo, 1998, 1999).

In addition to the urgency to develop network ties, a second characteristic that distinguishes entrepreneurial networking is its *intensity*. Basically, in addition to a "liability of age," small firms also suffer from a "liability of size" (Aldrich & Auster, 1986). Larger firms can have more organizational slack and, in the cases of some SOEs, softer budgets; smaller firms do not have these luxuries. Instead, they often face hard budget constraints and have to confront the real danger of failure and bankruptcy. For example, during an austerity program in 1989, one of every six private firms in China was declared bankrupt (Nee, 1992). As a result, smaller firms often have to intensify their networking activities with larger, more legitimate, and more powerful players in order to counterbalance such a liability, ensure survival, and, possibly, seek growth (Peng, 1997a).

Third, the nature of the businesses in which many entrepreneurial start-ups are engaged forces them to be *enthusiastic* about networking activities. Specifically, a large number of them are in service industries, which in general are more relationship-intensive than manufacturing industries. For example, in Hungary, about one third of the companies were engaged in what official statistics labeled as "real estate, rental, and services assisting business activities" by the early 1990s (Rona-Tas, 1994, p. 46). Relying more on external resources, these firms have to search constantly for clients, cultivate relations with them, and make sure that there is some possibility for repeat business after the initial contract. In addition to these "natural" sectoral differences between service and manufacturing industries, legal frameworks in transition economies are even less developed in the service sector than in the manufacturing sector. As a result, these service start-ups often have to be enthusiastic participants in the networking game.

Finally, compared with other forms of networking, entrepreneurial networking is known for its strong *impact* on firm performance (Geletkanycz & Hambrick, 1997). Three factors contribute to such a network-performance link. First, due to the small size of these start-ups, the contributions of individual entrepreneurs' networks tend to have a deeper impact on firm performance. In comparison, the impact of similar networks cultivated by managers at larger firms may be less pronounced because of larger firms' sheer size. Second, being private owners, entrepreneurs can directly pocket the residual income if their firms perform well, thus providing powerful incentives for them to engage in networking activities that may bring direct economic benefits. Managers at other firms may have less such personal incentive. Third, because entrepreneurs have more discretion in deciding how, when, and with whom to cultivate network ties, they are more capable and flexible in constructing, investing in, and improving ties compared with their counterparts in other firms. Other firms tend to have more complex, bureaucratic, and rigid structures that do not place too much freedom in the hands of their managers in terms of, say, entertainment, gift giving, bribery, or a combination of these. Taken together, these three factors lead to a more direct, positive, and visible impact of entrepreneurial networks on firm performance (Peng & Luo, 1999).

On the other hand, a networking strategy also has its share of problems. In addition to the two pitfalls discussed in Chapter 3 (i.e., lack of codification of information and lack of organizational basis for business alliances), one common and erroneous belief is to exaggerate the importance of networks. Actually, possessing effective entrepreneurial networks may be "a necessary, but not sufficient, condition for business success" (Tsang, 1998, p. 71). After all, a start-up, just like all other firms, needs to deliver value-added in the marketplace by having strengths in "traditional" areas such as product/service quality, advertising, and delivery in order to perform well in transition economies (Peng & Luo, 1999). This seems to be increasingly important in light of the drive toward more "normal," market-based competition in these countries. The implication is clear: Beyond a certain limit, an entrepreneur's time, energy, and money may be better spent building core competencies in products and services, as opposed to excessive networking activities. To borrow a term from economics, there may be *diminishing marginal returns* on networking.

In sum, while a networking strategy is more or less embraced by all types of firms in transition economies, entrepreneurial networking distinguishes itself by its urgency, intensity, enthusiasm, and impact. Some of these activities also overlap with those that we call "boundary blurring," which we turn to next.

Strategy III: Boundary Blurring

Although a boundary-blurring strategy is closely associated with networking, two specific types of boundary-blurring activities seem to stand out and to warrant separate discussions. These are the blurring of (a) boundaries separating public and private sectors, and of (b) boundaries separating legal and illegal sectors.

Blurring the Public-Private Boundary. While entrepreneurial start-ups in transition economies tend to be private firms, a surprisingly large number of them are not purely privately owned companies in a classical sense. Called "collective enterprises," these nonstate, yet nonprivate start-ups are especially visible in the Chinese economy, and they as a group have become the largest contributor (i.e., larger than the purely private sector and the SOE sector) to the GDP since the early 1990s. Their share in total industrial output increased from 22% in 1978 to more than 40% by 1996 (State Statistical Bureau, 1997, p. 411). During the same period, collective firms as a sector also exhibited the strongest growth in output, averaging 35% a year, while the overall economy and the SOE sector experienced 9% and 8% annual growth, respectively (Peng, 1997a, p. 390). The dramatic rise of these public-private *hybrid* firms during the transition has attracted significant scholarly, practical, and public policy interest.

Established to generate employment and support the local economy, many firms in this category, sometimes called "township and village enterprises," are under the jurisdiction of local township and village governments and are not regarded as "SOEs," which tend to be controlled by central and provincial governments (Byrd & Lin, 1989; Luo, Tan, & Shenkar, 1998). In contrast to CEE and the NIS, outright privatization of these firms did not occur in China until the late 1990s. However, hidden or informal privatization was widespread. Specifically, entrepreneurs can bid for long-term leases to control these firms (see Chapter 4). Although such lease agreements do not entitle leaseholders to formal property rights, in practice, these agreements are widely viewed by entrepreneurial leaseholders, as well as employees and the public, as de facto property rights (Nee & Matthews, 1996, p. 416). These hybrid firms, therefore, represent a gradual evolution from public to private ownership.

On the other hand, a large number of purely private entrepreneurial start-ups move in the opposite direction by choosing to register themselves as "collective" firms (Peng, 1997a). Given the residual antagonism against private entrepreneurs, many entrepreneurs are concerned about renewed hostility directed against them and the possible appropriation of their assets (Tan, 1996). As a result, many registered private firms have also applied to local governments to be converted to a "collective" status in an effort to "wear a red cap." Therefore, the actual contributions to the Chinese economy by real, private firms are much larger than official statistics suggest (15% of total industrial output by 1995; see Table 6.3). They may be greater than 55% of total industrial output if we add the output of the "collective" sector, a figure that is on a par with CEE and the NIS. In an environment that is still politically and institutionally unfriendly to private ownership, for many entrepreneurs it makes good sense not to advertise the private nature of their firms. As alluded to earlier, registered private firms invite greater scrutiny from the authorities in terms of taxation, safety, and environmental compliance. Even when discriminatory policies are removed, registered private firms are still at a great disadvantage in obtaining state-controlled resources such as bank credit. Frustrated by its inability to access credit, in September 1997 a highly successful private start-up in China, which was starving for bank credit, used advertisements in national newspapers to plead to the banks and to the media, stirring up a national debate on why it is so hard for private firms to raise capital (see Strategy in Action 6.4). Changing to a "collective" status allows private firms to gain better access to critical resources such as bank credit, while enabling them to be protected by local governments. Table 6.5 reveals a striking pattern of underfunding for non-SOEs in China: While their share in total industrial output and total industrial value-added rose to 67% and 81% respectively in 1994, their share of total bank loans remained at around 15%. Note that the "nonstate" firms in Table 6.5 include not only registered private firms, but also collective and foreign-invested firms. Therefore, we may safely infer from the table that the percentage of loans obtained by registered private firms is substantially smaller than the meager 15% figure obtained by all nonstate firms. It is not surprising that, facing such a harsh environment, many entrepreneurs choose to wear a "red cap" by registering their firms as collective ones.

Strategy in Action 6.4

Carpenter Tan Seeks Bank Loans

Carpenter Tan is a private company founded in 1992 in Sichuan, China, specializing in wood products. During the 1993-1997 period, it experienced a 300% annual average growth in revenue, profits, and taxes. Its sales reached $1.25 million in 1997, and its anticipated revenue in 1999 was approximately $13 million. These spectacular

TABLE 6.5 The Nonstate Sector[a] in China: Contributions and Shares of Bank Financing, 1984-1996

	(1) Percentage of Total Industrial Output	(2) Percentage of Total Industrial Value-Added	(3) Percentage of Total Bank Loans
1984	30.1	54.7	—
1985	35.2	50.5	—
1986	37.7	54.7	—
1987	40.3	51.2	17.4
1988	43.2	52.4	17.0
1989	43.9	47.5	15.7
1990	45.4	62.2	15.0
1991	47.1	56.3	14.8
1992	51.9	67.5	14.4
1993	56.9	68.7	15.8
1994	66.9	80.1	15.6
1995	69.1	94.7	—
1996	71.5	91.2	—

SOURCE: Adapted from Chen and Shi (1998, pp. 18-19).
NOTE: — missing data
a. The nonstate sector covers (a) two categories of registered private firms (see Table 6.3), (b) collective (public-private hybrid) firms, and (c) foreign-invested firms. In other words, it includes all non-SOEs, and category (1) in this table includes the figure in Panel C in Table 6.3.

achievements were not unnoticed by the media and the public, as well as the government. In fact, Carpenter Tan was named a "star enterprise" by the local government.

However, no bank was willing to provide loans to such an excellent firm. As a start-up, Carpenter Tan had a "bank" account only with a local credit union. During its first 4 years, Carpenter Tan paid interest and repaid principals on time on every loan it took out with the credit union. However, the financial resources of a credit union were limited. Carpenter Tan's size grew, but the maximum amount of loans that the credit union was able to provide was $200,000, which would cover only the firm's annual advertising expenditures in 1997.

Why did banks refuse to provide loans to a firm that would provide an outstanding return on their money, while they, on the other hand, continued supplying capital to numerous SOEs that hardly paid interest, let alone principal? Two reasons emerge. First, the vast majority of commercial banks in China are still state-owned, and the government requires that they provide so-called policy loans to support SOEs. Second, although there is no discriminatory policy banning loans to private firms, bankers practice self-imposed and unfair sanctions against private firms. One banker suggested: "If I authorize a million-yuan loan to SOEs and can't get a penny back, it's considered normal by everybody in my bank. But if I provide a loan only 10% that size to private enterprises and can't get anything back, everybody in my bank would think that there must be some embezzlement on my part. So why do I want to take any risk?"

Out of frustration, Carpenter Tan had to seek bank loans through national newspaper advertisements in September 1997, inviting interested banks to grow together with it. This event stirred up a great debate: In other countries such a stellar performance would attract competitive banks to line up to provide loans; why in China did a private firm have to take such a drastic measure to access capital?

SOURCE: Chinese Academy of Social Sciences, Institute of Industrial Economics, 1998, pp. 86-87.

Overall, while some collective firms reflect an evolution away from *public* ownership, other collective enterprises represent a movement away from *private* ownership. What is going on here? Empirical research has found that, on average, collective firms were not only more innovative, dynamic, and profitable than their SOE counterparts, but were also surprisingly superior to their registered private competitors (Dong & Putterman, 1997; Li, 1998; Luo et al., 1998). Given the general movement toward clearer specification of property rights during the transition (see Chapter 4) and the ambiguous property rights surrounding these firms, the question becomes: Can ambiguous property rights sometimes be efficient? The answer is a qualified "yes," given the particular attributes of the transition economy (Li, 1996). Two explanations emerge. First, in an environment not friendly to private start-ups, such a "collective hybrid" strategy may lead to the best of the two worlds (Nee, 1992). On paper at least, these firms still retain "public" ownership, which does not invite unwanted inquiry from higher authorities. Many local governments take these firms under their wing by providing local protectionism to shield them from harassment from other intrusive government agencies (remember, a registered private firm in China has to deal with about 30 of them separately, each collecting a tax or two). In addition, through "creeping" privatization, most of these firms operate with hard budget constraints and behave more like private firms. A second reason for these firms' better performance is that compared with central and provincial governments that have to confront many agency problems at SOEs, local governments are a lot closer to where the action is and consequently can do a better job of monitoring collective firms' performance (Walder, 1995). Given the limited coffers of the local governments, they also have a vested interest in making sure that the collective firms succeed; otherwise, the local taxation base, employment, and the general economy may be negatively affected.

The stellar performance of collective enterprises in China has led to a theory of ambiguous property rights, which suggests that "the immature market environment makes ambiguous property rights more efficient than unambiguously defined private property rights" (Li, 1996, p. 1). This theory is directly at odds with the privatization movement sweeping CEE and the NIS since the 1990s, and, consequently, results in substantial scholarly and public policy debate (Naughton, 1995). Critics suggest that collective firms were merely an intermediate organizational form reflecting a half-hearted move toward privatization, and that communist cadres and government officials, who represent a large proportion of entrepreneurs who obtain long-term leases with de facto ownership, were able to convert public assets to their own economic benefit (Sachs, 1993). Widespread corruption and nepotism associated with assigning the leases were often noted. The threat of such "power conversion," noted earlier, as well as prolonged government involvement in firm management, were precisely the reason why Sachs (1993) and other big-bang theorists saw rapid privatization as an urgent task. On the other hand, a number of authors pointed to the problem-laden process of privatization, especially during the first phase (see Chapter 5), and the miserable economic decline throughout CEE and the NIS during the early 1990s (see Chapter 2), which compared sharply with the strong growth of the Chinese economy led by the collective sector (Walder, 1995).

On balance, this firm-level debate seems to be deadlocked, similar to the outcome of a macro-level debate between "big-bang" and "evolutionary" theorists on reform policies (see Chapter 2). Given the intertwined relationship between politics and economics, a debate on what optimal organizational forms and property rights should be during the transition cannot bypass *political* factors. While privatization in CEE and the NIS is backed by their new governments' political determination, the rise of collective firms in China is equally a reflection of the political environment in which full-fledged private ownership is not favored. While the Chinese experience "does not necessarily show that privatization is not advisable elsewhere" (Walder, 1995, p. 294), it does seem to suggest that the same conditions in favor of collective ownership may hold in a similar institutional environment, such as Vietnam. For example, despite the apparent flourishing of private entrepreneurship, there was a steady *decline* of registered private sector output in Vietnam (its contributions to total industrial output dropped from 35% in 1990 to 26% in 1995; Riedel, 1997, p. 62). While the actual reason is unknown, we may infer that, similar to their Chinese counterparts, a large number of Vietnamese entrepreneurs have chosen to "wear a red cap" by registering their activities as nonprivate in order to avoid troubles and hurdles.

In sum, the public-private hybrid represents an interesting and previously unencountered phenomenon in entrepreneurship research and practice. The strategy of blurring the public-private boundary evidently has its own logic and serves many entrepreneurial start-ups well during the transition.

Blurring the Legal-Illegal Boundary. While the blurring of public-private boundaries has been extensive in China and Vietnam, the blurring of the legal-illegal boundary has reached epoch proportions in some CEE and NIS countries. Among them, Russia stands out as the most "corrupt" major economy in the world, according to a European Bank for Reconstruction and Development (EBRD) ranking (Yavlinsky, 1998). While the true extent of the gray and/or illegal economy in Russia is difficult to assess, the U.S. Department of Commerce put the figure to be as much as 40% of the GDP (USDC-ITA, 1998). Between approximately 70% and 80% of private companies may be paying extortion money to organized, mafia-type criminal gangs. Such "security" expenses may reach 15% or 20% of sales (Manev et al., 1998).

Outside Russia, rising organized crime has occurred in just about every transition economy. Taking advantage of the entrepreneurial boom, many crime organizations operate under the title of fully legal business firms with impeccable offices, letterheads, and bank accounts. Visible management is often carried out by cronies while the big boss remains behind the scenes. Colluding with corrupt officials, some of these "entrepreneurial" start-ups have privileged access to economic opportunities that are denied to legal private and public firms. Consider Multigroup, a small start-up dealing with arts and crafts, founded in Bulgaria in 1989. By 1996, it had become a giant with 8,000 employees, $1.5 billion in annual sales, and offices in a dozen countries from Russia to the Philippines. It owned or held majority interests in seven banks and more than 30 trading and manufacturing companies in Bulgaria. Despite all its successes, public opinion in Bulgaria widely suspects Multigroup of being an efficient scheme for siphoning off public money from the communist era and laundering it for the benefit of ex-communist functionaries, corrupt managers, and government officials (Manev et al., 1998).

Our purpose in addressing these gray organizations is not to indicate that they are legitimate players, but to suggest that their emergence and growth may be a *natural*, albeit undesirable, byproduct of economic transitions. The institutional perspective on business strategy discussed in Chapter 3 can be plausibly applied here. Basically, in the absence of a strong legal and regulatory regime of formal constraints, informal constraints such as "rules" and "regulations" imposed by the mafia-like organizations rise to fill the vacuum as a form of "self-government" for the purpose of facilitating economic exchanges (Peng, 1994; Peng & Heath, 1996). In many cases, the mafia has better enforcement mechanisms for contractual obligations than the weak court and regulatory systems (see Strategy in Action 6.5). In other cases, its "protection" may be more effective and equitable, since the (illegal) "security" fees that they collect may be less than the (legal!) taxes collected by the government. If companies will not be harassed by the government taxation authorities after paying "security" fees for mafia protection, then they are getting a better deal (Minniti, 1995). To the extent that crime organizations are able to provide better "services" than the predatory government, there will continue to be a demand for such services (Levi, 1988).

Strategy in Action 6.5

Cutthroat Competition

While the state-owned stores were unable to meet consumer demands in the former Soviet Union, there existed an active "free" market for a long time, from which high-quality produce and meats could be bought at higher prices. Most of the food stalls in large cities such as Moscow and St. Petersburg were dominated by hawkers from Azerbaijan, a former republic and now an independent country in the Transcaucasia region bordering Iran.

Until the late 1980s, Soviet laws prohibited individuals, such as the Azerbaijani hawkers, from forming private companies. Unable to organize legally, the hawkers formed clan-like networks based on their common ethnic and religious background to "beat" the system. Since their direct competitors, the state stores, were mostly empty (until recently), and the hawkers were usually the monopoly supplier of certain fresh produce and meats, they did not have the competitive pressures of a true market. They collectively set high prices in a cartel-like fashion and enforced the price levels with threats to those who sold below the set prices. Engaging in mutually reciprocal and supportive activities, network members collectively pursued their interests. The strong reputation effects together with the mafia-like enforcement virtually ensured that the unwritten rules of these informal networks would be adhered to in most cases, thus avoiding the need for written contracts. Opportunism would be curbed, since few Azerbaijani hawkers would dare to sell below the set prices to gain market share.

The Uzbeks from another southern republic emerged to become the Azerbaijanis' major competitors. The response of the Azerbaijanis was to attempt to incorporate the Uzbeks into the networks. The Azerbaijanis would first offer to buy the inventory from the Uzbeks. If the competitors refused to sell, they would be warned to sell at the prices set by the Azerbaijanis' networks. Otherwise, punishment, sometimes death, could come swiftly, resulting in a situation that could be literally called "cutthroat competition."

SOURCE: Peng, 1994, p. 243.

While such a boundary-blurring strategy may be viable during the initial, chaotic phase of the transition, how sustainable this strategy is in the long run, after the "dust settles," remains to be seen. As transition economies establish more and more legislation and regulations backed by gradually credible law enforcement, these gray organizations will have to confront increasing social and institutional pressures for legitimization for survival. The CEO of Bulgaria's Multi-group provided perhaps the best advice on a future strategy called "tail cutting": "The lizard survives if it cuts off its tail. It's time for our economic groups to cut off their illegal tails" (Manev et al., 1998, p. 31).

In sum, the boundaries separating different sectors in Figure 6.1 (public vs. private, legal vs. illegal) are not constant; instead, their shapes and proportions keep changing, moderated by various kinds of entrepreneurs who profit from boundary-blurring strategies.

Summary and Discussion

This section has identified three major strategies employed by entrepreneurial start-ups. Each of them shares a number of similarities with entrepreneurial strategies found elsewhere, and also differs from "traditional" strategies on a number of dimensions. A prospective or guerrilla strategy is the most classic strategy employed by many successful entrepreneurial firms elsewhere. Emphasizing speed and stealth, these firms dazzle their larger competitors. While we may wonder where to search for such first-mover opportunities in a harsh, uncertain, and resource-poor environment, we need to bear in mind that the best entrepreneurs "thrive on chaos" (Peters, 1987) and "compete on the edge" (Brown & Eisenhardt, 1998). Entrepreneurs in transition economies, even former communist cadres, share some important common psychological traits, such as a strong drive, locus of control, and risk-taking propensity, with their counterparts else-where (McGrath & MacMillan, 1992). What constitutes the en-trepreneurial process has always been "the series of discoveries gener-ated by the entrepreneurial boldness and alertness" (Kirzner, 1997, p. 73). While the fundamental dynamics underlying this process may be the same everywhere, what distinguishes entrepreneurs in transi-tion economies are their higher levels of boldness and alertness.

Similarly, a networking strategy has been the bread and butter of numerous entrepreneurial start-ups in many countries. It was also widely practiced before the transition. What is particularly interesting is the vastly increased scale and scope of networking activities during the transition. While farmers and gray individuals have been the traditional entrepreneurs in these countries, the arrival of cadre- and professional-entrepreneurs opens up many opportunities for networking that were not available previously. Running a chicken farm or a local shoe repair shop requires certain connections, but not necessarily with officials in ministries, banks, or the top echelons of state firms. Private farmers and artisans may need this type of high-level connection occasionally, and this can be found through friends of friends. On the other hand, starting and operating a trading company or a manufacturing plant requires political and professional connections, which cadres and professionals are likely to possess (Rona-Tas, 1994). While networking represents an important strategy for entrepreneurs everywhere, it often is not the only option in developed economies. In transition economies characterized by a lack of market-supporting institutions, however, such a strategy is often the only winning option for many entrepreneurs (Peng, 1994, 1997a, in press-a; Peng & Heath, 1996). As a result, the scale and scope of their networking strategy make these entrepreneurial start-ups stand out in the worldwide family of small firms.

Finally, a boundary-blurring strategy in itself is not unique to transition economies. The continuous existence of organized crime in almost every society suggests that the blurring of legal and illegal boundaries has been practiced by many "entrepreneurs" who profit from these activities. What seems striking is the degree of penetration that crime organizations have achieved in some transition economies, such as Russia, in such a short period of time. On a global scale, however, it is difficult to tell whether the overall Russian economy is more corrupt than, say, that of southern Italy or Colombia. On the other hand, the blurring of boundaries between public and private sectors, with movement from both directions, does appear to be a unique phenomenon in transition economies such as China and has been subject to intense debate. The entrepreneurial activities of such public-private hybrid firms have raised interesting questions about whether private ownership is universally optimal during the transition.

It is important to note that these three strategies are not necessarily separate, and that they are often employed concurrently by entrepreneurial start-ups. In other words, a start-up can adopt a Prospector or guerrilla strategy while engaging in intense networking activities that sometimes blur the public-private boundary and other times penetrate the legal-illegal boundary. Led by entrepreneurs constantly searching for opportunities and willing to take risks, these firms are often more active, dynamic, and flexible than their larger and more established competitors. Entrepreneurial strategies provide a dramatic comparison with the relatively more stagnant strategies employed by most SOEs and many privatized and reformed companies, thus stimulating the latter group of firms to be more entrepreneurial in order to catch up. As a result, entrepreneurial start-ups push the entire economy to a new level of competitiveness through their sheer energy and relentless strategies.

As discussed earlier, most of the existing theories in entrepreneurship bring good explanatory and predictive power to bear on these new developments. On the other hand, there are certain issues that existing research has not tackled. The first is the emergence of cadre-entrepreneurs, who may be interpreted negatively as former cadres unfairly converting their power into economic benefit. In contrast, the appearance of these entrepreneurs has been argued by others as a highly positive and encouraging development in the new economy, namely, more and more cadres are abandoning a formerly prestigious career in politics and are channeling their considerable energy into entrepreneurial (read "capitalistic") development. Another previously unencountered phenomenon in entrepreneurship research and practice is the rise of public-private hybrid firms and the movement from both directions toward the opposite ends. While some view these firms as movement toward eventual privatization, others note a large number of otherwise "private" firms voluntarily choosing to become "collective" or "cooperative" ones. Taken together, we simply do not know much about the long-term implications of these entrepreneurial developments, and need more rigorous and solid research results before informed judgments can be made.

CONCLUSIONS

The organizational landscape of transition economies has been going through dramatic changes from two directions. From the top down, a large number of SOEs have been reformed and privatized. From the bottom up, a much larger number of entrepreneurial start-ups have been established that undermine the foundation of the socialist economy and propel it into more market-driven competition. The entrepreneurial erosion of the socialist economy started to occur before the transition. More recently, the scale and scope of entrepreneurial development in these countries are unprecedented in history, leading to a direct frontal assault on the essence of state socialism. Although individual entrepreneurs are pursuing their self-interested private gains and could hardly care less about the official ideology, they collectively become participants in a great social movement whose "invisible hand" pushes a bankrupt regime aside.

Focusing on entrepreneurial start-ups, we can revisit the five fundamental questions in strategy raised in Chapter 1. Because start-ups are an embodiment of the personal characteristics and strategies of their founders, why these firms differ (Question 1) from other firms and how these firms behave (Question 2) can be found in how entrepreneurs differ from non-entrepreneurs. Given that entrepreneurs, compared with non-entrepreneurs, have a stronger achievement orientation, a deeper conviction that they can control their own fate, and are more willing to take risk and tolerate uncertainty, it is not surprising that entrepreneurial start-ups are more likely to exhibit a Prospector strategy, to engage in extensive networking activities, and to blur various organizational boundaries.

Question 3 asks: How are strategy outcomes affected by strategy processes? Since strategic choices originate in the interaction between institutions and organizations (see Chapter 3), particular entrepreneurial strategies are determined by the environmental constraints that the start-ups have to confront. In an environment where new start-ups are regarded as underdogs, these smaller firms are likely to adopt a guerrilla strategy instead of a head-on strategy. Given that these firms are typically small, flexible, and informal, they have a natural tendency to rely on informal networks, relationships, connections, and ties. Moreover, the harsh and uncertain environment further necessitates these networking activities. In addition, the spillover effects of some of these networking activities result in the penetration of public-private and/or legal-illegal boundaries by certain start-ups.

The scope of the firm (Question 4) is determined by what the firm is capable of doing. Most entrepreneurial start-ups are small and are likely to remain so. The growth of these firms is constrained by two factors: One is these firms' own capabilities, and the other is the legal and regulatory environment. From a modest start with family members and friends, most of these firms have a relatively low level of professionalism. Relying on their own resources, they can easily reach the limit of generic growth (see Chapter 3). Furthermore, the lack of adequate legal and regulatory development imposes other limits on the growth of the entrepreneurial firm. In fear of future confiscation of their assets, many entrepreneurs would rather engage in short-term profit maximization, lavish personal consumption, and/or transfer wealth overseas, as opposed to long-term reinvestment in the firm (Tan & Peng, 1999). The larger the private firm, the more likely it will invite unwanted scrutiny from higher authorities, especially when it acquires or merges with SOEs. The scope of the private firm is likely to be increased if the state is willing to make a credible commitment to create the legal institutions of a market economy.

The last question concentrates on what determines the international success and failure of firms. While examples of smaller start-ups from transition economies successfully competing overseas can be found, they are the exception rather than the rule. The next chapter will elaborate more on how foreign firms compete in these countries.

In conclusion, the emergence of entrepreneurship throughout transition economies leads to a "creative destruction" process that Joseph Schumpeter first highlighted. At the microlevel, entrepreneurial start-ups destroy the old strategy habits that emphasize conservatism by focusing on innovation, flexibility, and change. At the macrolevel, private firms create an alternative organizational form that competes with and challenges the dominance of the state sector. Taken together, these entrepreneurial challenges help move these economies to a higher level of market-based competition.

▨ NOTES

1. In Poland, for example, many individuals form private start-ups and then use the start-ups as organizational bases to bid for ownership rights for SOEs, thus blurring the boundaries between private start-ups and privatized SOEs (Wright, Filatotchev, & Buck, 1997).

2. Becoming the first entrepreneurs in a hostile environment entails extraordinary courage. In December 1978, 20 farmers in a Chinese commune decided secretly to dissolve the commune and start household-based private farming, which was illegal at that time. Every one signed an agreement that said: "We are willing to do this even if we are jailed and executed. If that happened to us, everybody else who signed this agreement would agree to raise our children until they are 18." That simple, handwritten agreement eventually led to the nationwide movement to dissolve the communes, and the rest is history. As a result, that agreement is now Collection No. GB54563 in the Chinese History Museum (Li, He, & Yau, 1998, p. 40).

3. See Chapter 8, especially Table 8.2, for a more comprehensive discussion of the Miles and Snow typology in the context of transition economies.

7

Strategies of Foreign Companies

Developing organizational capabilities has always been vital to companies' success, indeed to their very survival. . . . In the future, a company's ability to develop a transnational organizational capability will be the key factor that separates the winners from the mere survivors in the international competitive environment.

—Christopher Bartlett and Sumantra Ghoshal (1989, p. 212)

One of the most important and fascinating developments in international business in the past two decades is the opening of transition economies, which has enabled foreign companies to enter and compete in these new markets. This chapter starts with an overview of different types of international strategies, followed by a discussion of the four major strategies used in the context of competing in transition economies, namely, (a) exporting, (b) establishing strategic alliances, (c) developing option chains, and (d) acquiring local firms.

TABLE 7.1 International Strategies: Advantages and Disadvantages

	Advantages	Disadvantages
1. Exporting	• Economies of scale in production concentrated in home country	• High transportation costs • Trade barriers • Marketing distance from customers
2. Strategic alliances		
2a. Licensing and franchising	• Low development costs • Low risks in foreign market expansion	• Little control over product quality and marketing • May create competitors • Intellectual property hazards
2b. Joint ventures	• Sharing development costs and risks • Access to local partner's knowledge and assets • Politically acceptable	• Divergent goals and interests of the partners • Difficult to manage locally and coordinate globally • Limited control
3. Wholly owned subsidiaries	• Complete local control • Protection of technology and know-how • Ability to coordinate globally	• High development costs • Potential political problems

TYPES OF INTERNATIONAL STRATEGIES

Companies venture abroad in order to tap into markets potentially larger than their own, earn a greater return from their investment, and/or preempt competitors' gaining an upper hand (Caves, 1996). Consequently, three major international strategies arise (see Table 7.1).

Exporting

For most manufacturing companies, exporting is usually the first step in internationalization (Johanson & Vahlne, 1977). Exporting allows them to sell to more markets while benefiting from economies of scale associated with concentrated production in the home country. On the other hand, exporting involves high costs of transportation.

Trade barriers such as tariffs may make exporting uneconomical. In addition, an export strategy implicitly treats foreign markets as "extensions" of the home country. Such a mentality may become unwarranted when the firm exports a large proportion of its output abroad and foreign customers, in turn, demand more attention (Root, 1994). In practice, an export strategy can be implemented through (a) direct export or (b) indirect export. *Direct* export requires the company to have in-house personnel and resources to handle exporting. An *indirect* export mode employs an intermediary, such as an export trading company, to tackle foreign markets (Peng, 1998). While some companies start by direct exporting, most small manufacturers employ intermediaries first to test the waters in export markets (Peng, Hill, & Wang, in press; Peng & Ilinitch, 1998a, 1998b).

Strategic Alliances

Strategic alliances refer to a wide range of *intermediate* arrangements between two or more firms; these are neither market-based transactions (e.g., export), nor hierarchical solutions (e.g., acquisitions or wholly owned subsidiaries, discussed below). Two of the most frequently used alliance strategies are (a) licensing/franchising and (b) joint ventures.[1]

Licensing and Franchising. In a licensing arrangement, the licensor sells the rights to intellectual property such as patents and technologies to the licensee for a royalty fee. The licensor, therefore, does not have to bear the full costs and risks associated with foreign market expansion. On the other hand, the licensor does not have tight control over product quality and marketing. Licensing may create potential competitors and can lead to contractual hazards if the licensee violates the licensing agreement. Whereas licensing typically occurs in manufacturing industries, franchising is essentially the service-industry version of licensing. A primary difference is that licensing often involves technological know-how, while franchising usually focuses on management and marketing know-how.

Joint Ventures. As a "corporate child," a joint venture is a new firm that is given birth and jointly owned by two or more parent companies (Contractor & Lorange, 1988). Joint ventures can have any combination of shared ownership (e.g., 50/50, 20/80, 30/70) agreed upon by the partners. Joint ventures have three advantages. First, a foreign firm shares development costs and risks with a local partner, leading to an ideal *compromise* that offers a certain degree of control while limiting risk exposure (Hennart, 1988). Second, the foreign firm gains access to the local partner's knowledge about the host country; the local firm, in turn, benefits from the foreign firm's expertise in technology, marketing, and management (Kogut, 1988). Moreover, in many countries, political considerations may make a joint venture the only feasible entry mode (Pearson, 1991; Peng, in press-b).

In terms of disadvantages, first, joint ventures involve partners from different backgrounds and with divergent goals and capabilities. Partners may agree to collaborate for certain goals that overlap for a time, yet in the long run the relationship may become unstable when their goals diverge (Peng & Shenkar, 1997). Second, given these differences, effective operational control may be difficult to achieve since everything has to be shared and negotiated (and, in some cases, fought over; Hamel, 1991). Finally, the nature of the joint venture does not give a firm the tight control over a foreign subsidiary that it might need for global coordination (Bartlett & Ghoshal, 1989).

Wholly Owned Subsidiaries

Establishing wholly owned subsidiaries can be done by either setting up new "green-field" operations or by acquiring established local firms. There are three advantages. First, wholly owned subsidiaries give foreign firms complete equity and management control. Second, this undivided control leads to better protection of proprietary technology and know-how. Finally, wholly owned subsidiaries allow for centrally controlled global coordination of how much they will produce and how their output will be priced in a particular country. In comparison, local licensees or joint-venture partners are unlikely to accept such a subservient role. Wholly owned subsidiaries, on the other hand, tend to be the most expensive and risky method of serving foreign markets.

Making Strategic Choices

Trade-offs are inevitable when crafting international strategies (Hill, Hwang, & Kim, 1990; Tallman & Shenkar, 1994). In addition to the firm-level issues discussed above, another important strategic consideration that foreign firms, especially MNEs, have to entertain is how to maneuver against their global rivals. Sometimes MNEs choose to enter a currently immature market in order to preempt rivals (Hout, Porter, & Rudden, 1982). Other MNEs may be compelled to enter a foreign market because their rivals have already done so, and they cannot afford not to be there (Hamel & Prahalad, 1985). As a result, entry *timing* is also important, because of the potential for substantial first-mover advantages (Lieberman & Montgomery, 1988). On the other hand, firms may deliberately wait and see while first movers get "bloodied" and then enter with massive forces in search of late-mover advantages (Teece, 1986; Schnaars, 1994).

Moreover, the international strategies discussed above, strictly speaking, are only *entry* strategies. How to operate in a foreign country and coordinate these operations with global activities of the firm elsewhere once market entry has been accomplished will figure prominently in the continuous *evolution* of international strategies (Bartlett & Ghoshal, 1989). In general, the stage model of internationalization suggests that MNEs have a tendency to employ more complex strategies as they gain more experience in new markets (Johanson & Vahlne, 1977). In transition economies, many MNEs have passed the initial entry stage and are now moving aggressively to engage in "second-generation" activities, leading to a diversity of strategies, to which we now turn.

STRATEGIES OF FOREIGN COMPANIES

Except for a limited amount of East-West trade (Hisrich, Peters, & Weinstein, 1981; Hogberg & Wahlbin, 1984; Kogut, 1986; McMillan, 1981; Peng, 1992), socialist economies were by and large excluded from global economic exchanges. During the transition, the increase of foreign participation in these countries has been phenomenal, leading to a number of strategies employed by foreign companies.

Strategy I: Exporting

Scale and Scope of Export/Import Penetration. As the simplest and most basic international strategy, exporting has been used by many foreign companies. Table 7.2 provides an overview of the extent to which exports have penetrated these new markets. Note that *exports* by foreign companies are reflected as *imports* recorded by national statistics. Four observations emerge. First, with an "open door" policy dating back to 1979, China leads the pack in absorbing imports, with 10% annual growth on average during the 1980s and a more impressive 24.8% annual growth during the first half of the 1990s. Globally, China was the ninth largest importing country by 1995.[2] Second, on a smaller scale, Vietnam seems to have replicated the same pattern. Third, Visegrad countries such as Hungary and Poland also witnessed a rising wave of imports during the 1990-1995 period with annual growth of 7.9% and 26.4%, respectively. Finally, Bulgaria and Romania experienced a dramatic decline in imports in the early 1990s. These countries were still struggling in the "valley of tears" of their economic decline (see Chapter 2).

Underlying Sources of Export/Import Growth. Since the growth in the demand for imports is highly correlated with the growth of the overall economy, it is not surprising that China, whose GDP quadrupled between 1979 and 1992, has experienced strong import growth (Lardy, 1992; Overholt, 1993). Such growth has been driven by (a) the rising interest in sophisticated consumer and high-tech products, (b) the increasing demand for capital-intensive goods associated with foreign direct investment (FDI), and (c) decentralization of the foreign trade structure. After several decades of suppressed demand, Chinese consumers have begun to acquire a taste for differentiated, sophisticated consumer products such as electronics, cosmetics, and motor vehicles as their income rises. Foreign firms possess a number of advantages rarely matched by domestic competitors, namely, perceived superior quality, strong marketing savvy, and heavy advertising budgets. As a result, they are able to capture an increasing segment of the consumer market, typically centered on affluent urban areas (Schmitt,

TABLE 7.2 Merchandise Imports and Exports of Selected Transition Economies

	Imports (US$ million)		Average Annual Import Growth (%)		Exports (US$ million)		Average Annual Export Growth (%)	
	1980	1995	1980-1990	1990-1995	1980	1995	1980-1990	1990-1995
Bulgaria	9,650	5,015	4.2	-10.4	10,400	5,100	4.4	-12.6%
China	19,900	129,113	10.0	24.8	18,100	148,797	11.4	14.3
Czech Republic	—	26,523	—	—	—	21,654	—	—
Hungary	9,220	15,073	0.7	7.9	8,670	12,540	3.0	-1.8
Poland	16,700	29,050	1.5	26.4	14,200	22,892	4.8	3.9
Romania	12,800	9,424	-0.9	-5.3	11,200	7,548	-6.8	-4.7
Russia	—	58,900	—	—	—	81,500	—	—
Vietnam	1,310	7,272	8.8	24.2	339	5,026	18.8	16.9

SOURCES: Adapted from the World Bank (1997a, pp. 154-156; 1997b, pp. 242-243).
NOTE: — Missing data

1997). High-tech companies in industries such as computers, telecommunications, and aircraft have also substantially penetrated the economy. By the early 1990s, Boeing, for example, exported one out of every seven jetliners it made to China.

In addition, a large number of foreign companies also exported substantial capital-intensive goods as a part of their FDI deals. Specifically, when they set up manufacturing operations through FDI, they not only export machinery and materials for the construction of new plants, but also sell components, peripherals, and, in some cases, complete knocked-down kits, to their ventures in China (Peng, in press-b). These imports, therefore, are closely tied to the increase of FDI, which, in turn, has been a major underlying source behind the dramatic and sustained rise of Chinese *exports* in the past two decades. Because many MNEs use the country as a low labor cost manufacturing platform to produce goods for other export markets, and also because the government provides incentives and subsidies to exporting firms, China on average experienced more than 10% annual export growth between 1980 and 1995. The country, thus, rose to become the world's ninth largest exporting country by 1995 (see Table 7.2).[3]

Another driving force is the decentralization of the foreign trade regime. Before the transition, all imports and exports were monopolized by dozens of centrally controlled foreign trade corporations. Reforms have subsequently decentralized trading rights, first to provincially controlled foreign trade corporations, then to many locally controlled trading outfits, some large domestic firms, and most foreign-invested firms, resulting in thousands of firms being able to import and export goods directly. Taken together (Table 7.3), approximately 35% of foreign firms entering China between 1979 and 1993 employed an export strategy (Tse, Pan, & Au, 1997, p. 793).

These dynamics have been more or less played out in other transition economies, leading to numerous entrepreneurial opportunities for foreign exporters as well as local importers (Peng, Hill, & Wang, in press). The story of Asia Trade (Strategy in Action 7.1) serves as a case in point about how entrepreneurs as intermediaries can bridge the gap between Western exporters and Russian importers while profiting handsomely (Peng, 1998, pp. 86-87).

TABLE 7.3 Modes of Foreign Entry Strategies in Selected Transition Economies

	China	Czechoslovakia	Hungary	Poland	Russia
Sample	2,998	49	40	39	87
	(1979-1993)	(1989-1993)	(1989-1993)	(1989-1993)	(1989-1993)
Export (%)	35.0	21.3	21.2	17.6	32.5
Licensing/ franchising (%)	20.8	8.5	9.1	2.9	4.9
Joint ventures (%)	41.5	42.6	42.4	41.2	46.8
Wholly owned subsidiaries (%)	2.7	19.2	21.2	29.4	9.1

SOURCES: *China:* Adapted from Tse, Pan, and Au (1997, p. 793). *Others:* Adapted from Sharma (1995, p. 98).

Strategy in Action 7.1

Asia Trade Exports to the Russian Far East

Asia Trade is a small, Seattle-based export trading company founded by a recent Russian immigrant and his American wife in 1992. The collapse of the Soviet Union created chaos as well as opportunities. Previously, international trade was monopolized by state-run foreign trading corporations. Since the beginning of the transition, their monopoly was lost and local companies were able to import directly. The breakdown of the centrally administered trading system hit the distant Far East region especially hard. Asia Trade took advantage of the general food shortage there by bringing processed foodstuffs, such as canned foods, beverages, and flour, mostly sourced from the Pacific Northwest, to that new market.

As a huge virgin market, the Russian Far East had all the attractions for first movers. Yet, it also possessed all the dangers that would scare away many who were less than determined. The environment in the new Russia was harsh and tough in general, to say the least, and the Far East region, Russia's "wild west," was even worse. Despite the market potential, locals would not do business with strangers unless they had become friends. This cultural norm, reinforced by decades of communist rule that resulted in deep suspicion about foreigners in a region formerly guarded as a military reserve, deterred many interested foreign companies. On the other hand, export intermediaries such as Asia Trade had an advantage because one of the co-owners was born and raised there and had 7 years of previous experience in trading. Knowing whom to talk to in Russia, combined with the ability to source products in America, enabled Asia Trade to carve out a niche for itself. Its sales were half a million dollars in 1992, their first year. From a husband-and-wife team, the company grew to employ five people by 1994, and its sales climbed to $2 million that year, a quite remarkable performance given the company's age and size. More impressive, their export sales per capita reached $400,000 in 1994, which was more than twice the average among the population of small export trading companies in the United States.

During interviews, the owners attributed their success to their general knowledge of the Russian language and culture and their connections with key importers. In terms of difficulties, they complained about the hurdles of obtaining trade-related financing from U.S. banks, and they said that they often had to rely on "dubious" sources of financing from Russia in order to take title to the exports they sourced from American suppliers.

SOURCE: Peng, 1998.

Problems and Prospects. Despite these achievements, an export strategy may encounter four major obstacles. The first is the lack of demand for imports in certain CEE and NIS countries. In countries still struggling with hyperinflation, idle factories, and massive unemployment, there simply will not be a growing number of customers who can afford imports. Second, even when import demand exists, the government may impose heavy tariffs on certain consumer imports, demand that a certain proportion of imported capital goods be made at home, and require that foreign-invested firms generate enough exports to cover the foreign exchange needs for their imports. In contrast to the first problem, the third problem is too much demand for certain imported products in some countries. As export volume increases, an export strategy may become uneconomical because of the high transportation costs and trade barriers. In countries where labor costs are also low, it is usually cheaper to produce locally.

The last problem in an export strategy is that, given the strong potential of transition economies such as China, Poland, and Russia, many foreign firms have realized that these are not new markets for their old products. Instead of having an "imperialist" assumption that consumers there are just like those in the West, many foreign firms realize that they must understand the unique nature of these markets and design and market products based on the preference of local consumers (Prahalad & Lieberthal, 1998). Implicitly treating foreign markets as "extensions," an export strategy does not serve these purposes very well, thus calling for new strategies, to which we now turn.

Strategy II: Establishing Strategic Alliances

Nonequity Versus Equity Forms. Strategic alliances can entail nonequity forms such as licensing and franchising, and equity-based alliances such as joint ventures. Shown in Table 7.3, licensing and franchising were employed by approximately 21% of foreign firms in China during the 1979-1993 period (Tse et al., 1997, p. 793) and by less than 10% of foreign firms in Czechoslovakia, Hungary, Poland, and Russia between 1989 and 1993 (Sharma, 1995, p. 98). Most companies interested in entering transition economies using an entry mode beyond exporting have instead opted for equity-based joint ventures, with a broadly similar percentage (more than 40%) across these countries (Table 7.3). Even McDonald's, the "king" of global franchising, chose not to use franchising but to set up a joint venture when entering the former Soviet Union. Overall, most foreign companies seem to believe that the pitfalls of licensing and franchising far outweigh their benefits, namely, the low costs of developing new markets. Specifically, licensing and franchising provide little direct control over local firms' activities, may create potential competitors, and, in a worst case scenario, may result in unwanted exploitation of know-how by local firms. For example, John Deere, the largest U.S. agricultural equipment producer, licensed its combine technology to a Chinese firm for $7.8 million in 1981. While there is no evidence that the licensee violated the licensing agreement, it did emerge as a major competitor with a leading market share in China and $12.8 million of exports by 1990. As a result, by 1996, Deere felt compelled to establish a joint venture with its former licensee, in which Deere had a controlling interest of 60% equity with $13 million FDI (Shang, 1997; Ng & Pang, 1997).

Scale and Scope of FDI Through Joint Ventures. Having determined that exporting is not viable, licensing (or franchising) not attractive, and wholly owned subsidiaries too risky, companies naturally focus on FDI through joint ventures. Joint ventures, as opposed to outright foreign acquisitions, are also encouraged by host governments (Beamish, 1993; Pearson, 1991) and mandatory in key industries such as the Russian oil industry (McCarthy & Puffer, 1997). As a result, transition economies have witnessed a rising wave of international joint ventures, which typically constitute the bulk of FDI into these countries (Table 7.4). These joint ventures are not only set up by many experienced, large MNEs, but also by numerous small and medium-sized foreign firms that previously were not multinational (Estrin & Meyer, 1998). Smaller firms in general are more labor intensive. For a lot of smaller firms in Hong Kong, Taiwan, Austria, Germany, and Italy, the opening up of nearby transition economies, where labor costs are significantly lower and geographic and cultural distances are not great, presents a golden opportunity to improve competitiveness ("The Rush to China," 1997; "The Rush to Russia," 1997; Larner, 1998; Lau, Kwok, & Chan, 1998).

From a modest start in the late 1970s, China rose to become the second largest FDI recipient country in the 1990s (behind only the United States). It absorbed a total of $179 billion between 1979 and 1996, including nearly $42 billion in 1996 alone (Zheng, Du, & Ba, 1998). Among transition economies, no other country has seen the formation of more international joint ventures than China (Overholt, 1993). The China experience, therefore, foreshadows what could occur in other transition economies (Luo & Peng, 1998). FDI into CEE and the NIS started approximately 10 years after the launch of China's open door policy. By 1992, these countries, taken together, received $4 billion FDI, still less than, for example, Malaysia or Singapore alone in the same year (Meyer, 1995). The flow reached more than $11 billion in 1995, including receipts from major privatization projects

TABLE 7.4 Foreign Direct Investment Inflows Into Selected Transition Economies

US$ million	China	Czech Republic[a]	Hungary	Poland	Russia
1985	1,959	n/a	n/a	n/a	n/a
1986	2,244	n/a	n/a	n/a	n/a
1987	2,647	n/a	n/a	n/a	n/a
1988	3,739	n/a	n/a	n/a	n/a
1989	3,773	257	—	11	—
1990	3,755	207	—	89	—
1991	4,666	600	1,462	291	—
1992	11,291	1,103	1,479	678	—
1993	27,769	654	2,350	1,715	—
1994	34,122	878	1,144	1,875	700
1995	37,521	2,568	4,519	3,659	2,017
1996	41,726	1,500	2,000	2,682	1,600
Cumulative FDI	179,314	7,100	13,400	11,000	—
	(1979-1996)	(1989-1996)	(1989-1996)	(1989-1996)	
Annual FDI	32	130	259	63	8
per capita ($)	(1993-1995)	(1993-1995)	(1993-1995)	(1993-1995)	(1993-1995)

SOURCES: *China:* Luo (1996, p. 536) for 1985-1994 based on total *realized* investment (not total *approved* investment); Zheng, Du, and Ba (1998, p. 80) for 1995-1996; cumulative and per capita data based on the author's own calculation. *All others:* Bilsen and Lagae (1997, p. 451) for 1989-1994; World Bank (1997a, pp. 236-238) for 1995; Estrin and Meyer (1998, pp. 210-211) for 1996, cumulative, and per capita data.

NOTE: — Missing data

a. The data covered all of Czechoslovakia during 1989-1992 and only the Czech Republic during 1993-1996, including the cumulative and per capita data. The FDI inflow figure for Slovakia was $199 million for 1993, $203 million in 1994 (Bilsen & Lagae, 1997, p. 451), and $183 million in 1995 (World Bank, 1997b, p. 238). Its 1989-1996 cumulative FDI was $1 billion and 1993-1995 average annual FDI per capita was $37 (Estrin & Meyer, 1998, p. 210).

(see Chapter 5). The flow has declined since 1996, however, indicating uncertainty on the part of foreign companies. Moreover, the distribution is uneven. In the early years, Hungary attracted more than half of the FDI into CEE and the NIS. More recently, FDI into the Czech Republic and Poland also rose substantially. Russia received approximately $2 billion and $1.6 billion in 1995 and 1996, respectively, a large increase over earlier years but still minor relative to the size of the economy (Estrin & Meyer, 1998). In terms of annual FDI per capita during the 1993-1995 period (Table 7.4), Hungary led the pack ($250 per capita), followed by the Czech Republic ($130).

Although a strategic choice centered on joint ventures may be relatively easy to *formulate*, this strategy is among the most difficult to *implement*. It typically involves three phases: (a) partner selection, (b) venture negotiation, and (c) postentry operations.

Partner Selection. Similar to selecting marriage partners, choosing alliance partners is always challenging (Geringer, 1991; Harrigan, 1986). Adding to this complexity is the fact that the local partner is typically an SOE with little knowledge about the workings of market competition but considerable skills in navigating the bureaucratic waters in the host country (see Chapter 4). Foreign firms, having little experience in dealing with SOEs, encounter many problems in selecting appropriate partners. Unfortunately, many early foreign entrants did not have much freedom in choosing partners. Similar to arranged marriages, some of them ended up taking whatever local partners were recommended by host governments, and, unless they were lucky, typically got burned. The experience of Occidental Petroleum in China (Strategy in Action 7.2) can serve as a case in point here (Peng, 1995a).

Strategy in Action 7.2

Getting Burned by Coal in China

Used to meet three quarters of the demand, coal is the most important energy resource in China. Despite an abundant coal supply, the lack of effective means to exploit coal led to nationwide energy shortages that forced many factories to shut down 1 or 2 days a month in the 1980s. Therefore, seeking foreign partners to help develop energy resources became a top priority of China's open door policy. In 1980, China opened its premier coal mine, the Antaibao mine, to international bidding—the largest energy project that was ever opened to foreign firms at that time. Eight Western firms entered the bidding, and Occidental Petroleum (Oxy) beat all the competitors. Politics was instrumental in this process, and China's central leadership, led by Deng Xiaoping, was heavily involved. Politically, China preferred partnering with a major U.S. multinational as an unambiguous signal to foreign investors that the open door policy was for real. No company seemed to be a better fit than Oxy, whose chairman, Armand Hammer, was an "old hand" at doing business with the Eastern Bloc. Having met and done business with Lenin in the 1920s, Hammer had been profiting from East-West trade for decades. Since 1979, Hammer had become a frequent flyer to Beijing and a friend of Deng's. Therefore, Oxy's winning of the bid hardly surprised anybody.

In a spirit of friendship, Oxy signed a 50-50 equity joint venture contract in 1982. There was no need to select partners, because they were there waiting for Oxy. The local line-up included three Chinese state-owned enterprises and the Province of Shanxi, where the mine was located. The venture called for $700 million capital, with each side contributing $200 million and a loan of $300 million. When the feasibility study began *after* the contract was signed, the economics of the project became increasingly shaky. In the initial courtship, Oxy made a number of promises, including exporting 75% of the output. In light of falling world coal prices, American negotiators tried to make the Chinese partners take title to the coal at prevailing international prices and then try to export it, thus retreating from Oxy's earlier promise. The Chinese negotiators were surprised, and intense arguments came close to derailing the signed project. Hammer and the Chinese leadership always intervened to enforce a solution agreed upon at the top, however. Eventually, Oxy won several concessions, including relinquishing its export marketing responsibilities. The operational phase since 1986 proved to be more problematic. By 1990, it was operating at three quarters of its 12-million-ton capacity and had lost $31 million. Handled by the reluctant Chinese partners, exports were less than half of the 9 million tons Oxy originally anticipated. Dropping world prices and lower-than-expected quality all contributed to losses. Most important, Oxy managers failed to develop close working relationships with their Chinese counterparts, despite Hammer's *guanxi* (connections) at the highest possible level. Instead of working together, both sides seemed to have developed an appetite for blaming each other for whatever problems occurred.

> Elevated as a symbol of the open door policy, the venture became a flagship project that would be supported by the Chinese leadership at all costs. In a manner similar to how Deng ruled China, Hammer dismissed the idea of withdrawal from the venture and urged a "long-term" perspective. His death in 1990 made Oxy's withdrawal from the unprofitable venture inevitable.

SOURCES: Epstein, 1996; Peng, 1995a.

More successful foreign firms seem to be able to secure partners with both "strategic fit" and "organizational fit" (Geringer, 1991). *Strategic fit* refers to whether the local partner possesses complementary skills and resources that the foreign firm cannot acquire easily. For a technologically capable foreign firm, a local partner with strong marketing competencies, a leading market share, and the right connections with certain government agencies may be desirable (Shenkar, 1990). Despite the importance of networks and connections with governments, it is important to avoid a partner that can claim nothing but these dubious "intangible" resources (Luo, 1997).

While strategic fit is important, organizational fit is equally crucial (Borys & Jemison, 1989). An assessment of *organizational fit* focuses on whether the partner possesses certain organizational traits, such as goals, experience, and behaviors, that will facilitate cooperation. While the foreign partner may be interested in local market access, the local partner may be driven by the opportunity to access capital and technology in order eventually to succeed in export markets. Alternatively, a local partner may have severe financial difficulties and perceive FDI simply as a "lifeboat." Whether the local firm has had any previous experience in dealing with foreign companies may also be a good indicator of whether the proposed collaboration is likely to be successful. Finally, the behavior of the local partner is also important. A local firm that is known for secret dealings, credit problems, and legal disputes with suppliers, buyers, and partners probably will not make a good partner. The upshot is that foreign firms have to pay careful attention to the strategic and organizational fit of proposed joint venture partners. Given the lack of transparency and information in transition economies, it is often worthwhile to spend adequate time to get to know local partners before proceeding.

Venture Negotiation. Although selecting local partners is by no means easy, actual negotiations to hammer out the details can be more challenging, given the differences in negotiation styles and norms (Adler, Braham, & Graham, 1992; Peng, 1998; Pye, 1992a). In addition to dealing with local firms, foreign firms often have to negotiate with host country governments (Brewer, 1992; Jacobson, Lenway, & Ring, 1993). While host governments in developing countries have long been involved in negotiations with MNEs, the scale and scope of government involvement in transition economies tend to be more extensive. For example, the central government in China between 1979 and the mid-1980s required that the Chinese side hold at least 50% equity interest, and that foreign equity be transferred to Chinese hands virtually without compensation after a predetermined period (usually 10 years among contracts signed before 1985). Governments often possess significant power and resources that can affect the fate of joint ventures, such as rights to approve business licenses, restrict access, or grant exclusive access to certain markets. Also, in numerous cases, governments themselves came to the front of the stage and become direct partners. For example, the government of Shanxi Province was a partner of Occidental Petroleum in China, the Moscow City Council became a partner of McDonald's restaurants, and the government of the Russian Federation partnered with General Motors and Mobil Oil in different undertakings.

Adding to the complexity is that different *levels* of government (central, provincial, and local) may be involved in the negotiations. In the Chinese automobile industry, for example, three MNEs encountered officials from different levels (Figure 7.1). When AMC (and later Chrysler) was negotiating for the Beijing Jeep venture, it confronted a negotiation team composed entirely of central officials who rigidly insisted that the venture develop a brand new model for export markets outside of China (Mann, 1989).[4] Volkswagen, on the other hand, negotiated primarily with local officials from Shanghai, although there was some central involvement. While the Shanghai negotiators also

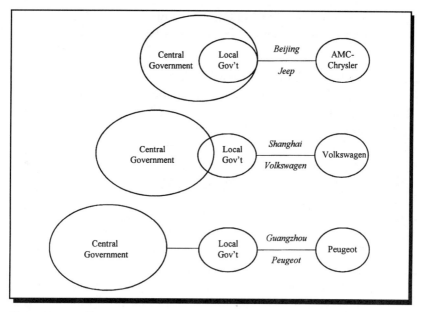

Figure 7.1. Different Government-MNE Relationships in Joint Venture Negotiations in China

wanted to develop a new model, they were persuaded by Volkswagen to focus initially on local assembly operations (Harwit, 1995). Peugeot dealt exclusively with Guangzhou city officials with virtually no central intervention. These local officials never even bothered to negotiate on the unlikely outcome of developing a new car model for export markets (Peng, in press-b).

In general, the higher the level of the government, the less risky the investment, but also the more rigid the rules. The central government tends to be more predatory and more interested in extracting the most out of any deal (Levi, 1988). Lower-level governments may be more conciliatory and sympathetic toward joint ventures, which can generate economic benefits to their jurisdictions. As a result, local governments are likely to "settle for less," and foreign companies tend to be more interested in working with local governments as opposed to the central government (Peng, in press-b). However, a very challenging and tricky part of these negotiations is that lucrative deals concluded with lower-level governments may invite scrutiny from higher authorities and, in some cases, may be revoked (Peng, 1996, p. 54). Given the rapid political changes, it may not be clear who is in charge, and those in charge today may be out of office tomorrow. Thus, practical advice for foreign companies is that they protect themselves by "getting approvals from as many authorities at as many levels as possible" (McCarthy, Puffer, & Simmonds, 1993, p. 113). These efforts, unfortunately, lengthen the negotiation time and add to its complexity.

Despite government influence, many foreign firms come to these negotiations from a position of strength. With investment alternatives and global resources, MNEs have strong bargaining power vis-à-vis the parochial SOEs and governments (Yan & Gray, 1994). As a result, it is not surprising that foreign firms can typically extract some concessions. They primarily focus on four issues. The first is equity control. They are not always successful initially since there may be upper limits on foreign ownership in some countries, especially during the early phase of the transition. Beyond equity control, the second area is management control, such as the staffing of key positions and the adoption of major organizational policies. It is in this area that foreign firms usually obtain an upper hand by exercising greater control than their equity levels would suggest (Beamish, 1993; Child, 1998). Third, foreign firms often negotiate for tax holidays, preferential tax rates, partitioning of SOEs for joint ventures (i.e., deleting non-value-adding parts such as social services), and infrastructure development paid for by the government. Finally, MNEs often bargain for relaxation of existing rules, and, over time, are usually successful. Since the mid-1980s, Chinese law no longer requires that the Chinese side hold at least 50% of the equity, and it permits wholly owned subsidiaries. The Chinese have also been flexible in renegotiating the extension of the "fade-out" provision of the original joint venture agreement (i.e., the 10-year limit in many earlier contracts), and in extending the duration of the venture to up to 50 years (Pan, 1996, 1997).

Given their complexity, joint venture negotiations can take years to complete. For example, the negotiations for Beijing Jeep, Shanghai Volkswagen, and Guangzhou Peugeot, took 4, 6, and 5 years, respectively, in the late 1970s and early 1980s (Peng, in press-b). Although more recent negotiations are faster and more efficient, they can still run between 6 months and a year (Brouthers & Bamossy, 1997, p. 293).

Postentry Operations. Managers at international joint ventures operate in a precarious world: They have to safeguard and strengthen the interests of their respective parent organizations on one hand, and to facilitate cooperation with their counterparts in the same venture on the other hand. Moreover, they often have to overcome considerable cultural and professional difference (Ring & Van de Ven, 1994). Successful joint ventures seem to have certain managerial and organizational characteristics: (a) adaptive, open-minded managers; (b) trust building; (c) joint decision making; (d) open communication; and (e) strong support from parent organizations.

Due to the complex operational environment, appointing adaptive managers with open minds cannot be emphasized too strongly. For foreign firms, it is helpful to select managers with considerable international experience and, if possible, with some facility with the local language. They should be selected not just for their technical and business skills, but also according to their tolerance, open-mindedness, and cooperative tendencies. Because of the differences of the two sides, trust building should be an ongoing activity during the operational phase (Child, 1998). This is similar to human marriages, because after the "honeymoon" is over, as the saying goes, the two sides are not likely to live "happily ever after." Given the simultaneous existence of both trust and distrust in any relationship, partners must continuously reinvigorate the relationship by demonstrating that trust outweighs distrust (Chen, Peng, & Saparito, 1999; Lewicki, McAllister, & Bies, 1998). One way to build trust is to have representatives of both parents occupy, insofar as possible, positions of equal status, in terms of such matters as titles, compensation, and office space.

In addition, joint decision making also seems necessary. To have one partner—foreign or domestic—making all major decisions increases the probability of poor performance. The environment of a transition economy, which is typically very alien to most Western managers, makes dominant foreign control risky, at least initially. Similarly, the lack of technological and managerial skills by the locals may make dominant control by them equally risky (Beamish, 1993). There is a tendency for partners to specialize in particular domains. Specifically, foreign partners may be in charge of technology and general management, whereas local marketing, human resources, and government relations may be the exclusive territory of local partners

(Lawrence & Vlachoutsicos, 1993). However, to the extent that joint ventures serve as a vehicle for organizational learning, there are powerful incentives for both partners to share decision responsibilities with each other.

Conflicts are inherent in joint ventures. Increasing the contact between opposing groups is perhaps the best way to help reduce intergroup conflict (Hambrick, Tsui, Li, & Xin, 1998). Contact leads to mutual understanding and neutralizes negative feelings. Therefore, instead of accusing each other in emotion-laden terms such as "old communist bureaucrats" or "arrogant American cowboys," open communication and constructive reconciliation are often necessary.

Joint ventures involve both frontline managers and parent company executives (as well as government officials, in some cases). Not all of them are likely to have the same commitment to the relationship (Lyles & Salk, 1996). Whenever joint ventures encounter difficulties, some executives and officials in parent organizations may increasingly argue for withdrawal (Kvint, 1994). On the other hand, joint ventures typically have senior "champions" in the headquarters who are interested in the success of these ventures. Whether these champions can successfully argue for continued commitment to these joint ventures will, to a large degree, determine the success or failure of the ventures.

In sum, few foreign companies possess all the organizational attributes for joint venture success. Many joint ventures fail because of the lack of certain attributes (e.g., open communication). Another important reason behind many failed joint ventures is the failure of foreign firms to understand their local partners, which we focus on next.

A Local Partner Perspective. Although an understanding of the dynamics of joint ventures would not be complete without knowing the local firms, many foreign firms, unfortunately, have paid inadequate attention to their partners. Such a self-centered mentality in an inherently two-way relationship is not conducive to joint venture success. Why would local firms become joint venture partners in the first place? Recall Chapter 3, in which I suggest that domestic firms are often forced to seek growth in a precarious sink-or-swim situation (Peng & Heath, 1996). As a part of their growth strategy, local companies are likely to be interested in FDI in order to acquire and

TABLE 7.5 The Performance of Foreign-Invested Versus Domestic Firms in China and Hungary

Panel A: China (Measure: Absolute performance measure)	Total Sample	Domestic Firms	Domestic-Foreign JVs	Wholly Foreign-Owned Subsidiaries
Sample	171	57	57	57
Pretax return on assets (%)	—	12.8	20.4	18.3
Operating profit margin (%)	—	16.3	21.9	23.5

Panel B: Hungary (Measure: Proportion of firms in the sample)	Total Sample	Cooper-atives	State-Owned Firms	Privately Owned Firms	State-Private JVs	State-Foreign JVs	Private-Foreign JVs
Sample	808	73	227	273	102	56	77
20% or more return on investment (%)	10.4	4.1	3.1	13.6	7.8	14.3	27.3
10% or more pretax profits (%)	19.1	12.3	12.3	21.6	15.7	30.3	32.5

SOURCES: *Panel A:* Adapted from Luo (1996, p. 540); *Panel B:* Adapted from Hooley, Cox, Shipley, and Fahy (1996, pp. 700-701).

sustain competitive advantages over their *domestic* rivals (Lyles & Salk, 1996; Shenkar & Li, in press). A number of studies (Hooley, Cox, Shipley, & Fahy, 1996; Luo, 1996) have consistently shown that local firms receiving some FDI do outperform their rivals at home by a wide margin (Table 7.5).

Given FDI's performance-enhancing effect, the question, then, boils down to *exactly* what foreign resources and capabilities local firms want. In addition to financial capital, which is sought universally, the contributions of foreign firms can be broadly categorized as (a) management, (b) marketing, and (c) technology. While many local firms may actually need *all* these capabilities, they tend to pay more attention to the acquisition of foreign technology (58% of the firms in a sample), followed by marketing (54%), according to a recent study by Shenkar and Li (in press) that found that only one third of local firms are interested in foreign management skills.

Local firms' interest in tangible, hardware technology is understandable given its relatively visible and easy-to-imitate nature (von Glinow & Teagarden, 1988). This emphasis is also a part of the output-driven legacy of the old regime. The interest in marketing can be attributed to the almost complete absence of this function in many organizations and the sudden necessity to compete that desperately demands expertise in marketing (Hooley et al., 1996). The lack of understanding of the deficiency in management is puzzling and potentially alarming. One explanation is that management involves more embedded organizational practices that are not as visible as hardware technology. As a result, management deficiency is often difficult to detect (and more difficult to acknowledge by local managers themselves!). Second, most management practices are influenced by national cultures, which may generate resistance to organizational changes introduced from abroad (Hofstede, 1980, 1991). A third explanation focuses on the old habits accumulated over decades of central planning and political upheaval, during which conservatism and defensiveness were preferred over proactive actions (Child & Markoczy, 1993; Holt, Ralston, & Terpstra, 1994). Given that a large number of managers are interested only in muddling through the reform process (see Chapters 4 and 5), they may feel the urge for some "cosmetic" changes such as more visible improvement in technology and marketing, but do not feel it necessary to make fundamental changes in management (Kanter, Stein, & Jick, 1992; Kostera, 1995).

These learning preferences of local firms, however, are at odds with what foreign firms have to offer. Influenced by the resource-based view of the firm, Western firms' quest for competitive advantage has increasingly focused on intangible, hard-to-imitate capabilities (Barney, 1991). While capital, technology, marketing, and management are important as individual resources, "it may be that not just a few resources and capabilities enable a firm to gain competitive advantages but that literally thousands of these organizational attributes, bundled together, generate these advantages" (Barney, 1997, p. 155). In the case of MNEs, it is their *managerial* capabilities that interface with different functions and link various regions that contribute to their advantages (Bartlett & Ghoshal, 1989; Dunning, 1993). Therefore, local firms' attempts to partition technology and marketing out of the overall "package" of a foreign management system is not realistic, and is likely to create management problems for joint venture operations.

In practice, local managers are found to show great enthusiasm for learning new technology and new "tricks" in marketing (Warner, 1992). On the other hand, they display less interest in improving managerial skills. For example, they may be reluctant to make decisions, take the initiative, delegate responsibilities, share information, and confront subordinates about poor performance (Child & Markoczy, 1993; Frese, Kring, Soose, & Zempel, 1996). They tend to become defensive when asked or encouraged to change, often citing that their behavior is the age-old "Chinese," "Polish," or "Russian" way that foreigners can never understand. As a result, foreign managers are often frustrated, and an often-heard complaint among them concerns the shortage of skilled local managers.

Inherent Sources of Problems. As indicated above, while foreign managers are likely to bring their own biases, problems of local managers can also derail joint ventures. Even when individual managers from both sides make genuine efforts to break out of their straightjackets, and work hard to accommodate each other, there are still a number of powerful strategic and structural forces that make joint ventures unstable. First, from a *partner selection* perspective, the seeds of failure may lie in the initial choice of an unsuitable partner, regardless of how hard partners keep trying later (Geringer, 1991). Second, from a *bargaining power* standpoint (Yan & Gray, 1994), when one partner becomes more powerful than and less dependent on the other, joint ventures may fail (Parkhe, 1993). Third, according to *organizational learning* theory, joint ventures can be conceptualized as a race to learn from each other (Hamel, 1991). Therefore, instead of engaging in open communication, participants are sometimes advised to safeguard their own know-how and to maximize their learning from the other side. Such behavior hardly inspires trust and confidence in the relationship. When one side has achieved adequate learning, the usefulness of the venture becomes questionable (Inkpen & Beamish, 1997). Fourth, from a *behavioral* point of view, while one side may be more open-minded, the other side may be unwilling or unable to reciprocate. Over time, the trusting partner may start to change its behavior, thus setting in motion the downward spiral toward eventual failure (Peng & Shenkar, 1997). Finally, according to *option theory*, joint ventures are regarded by many foreign firms from the very beginning as an intermediate step (i.e., an option) toward eventual dominant control (Kogut, 1991). These ventures, as a result, are not likely to be stable organizations with an indefinite life span. Taken together, these dynamics collectively result in high failure rates of joint ventures.

The experience of joint ventures in transition economies suggests that initially, during the honeymoon period, both sides are likely to be satisfied. For example, most studies in China prior to 1989 reported that venture performance was viewed as acceptable and satisfactory (reviewed by Beamish, 1993, p. 41). Since then, however, performance problems have accelerated, with an increasing loss of patience to wait for long-overdue profits in China ("China: Where's That Pot of Gold?" 1997; Peng, 1995a, in press-b; Shenkar, 1990). Similar experience has been reported for joint ventures in other transition economies, such as Russia, where many MNEs have been on roller-coaster rides and question the viability of the joint venture mode (Kvint, 1994; McCarthy et al., 1993).

In sum, an alliance strategy is extremely complex and taxing. Although licensing and franchising are relatively simple, their drawbacks often outweigh their benefits, thus leading to a focus on joint ventures. Joint ventures are inherently *conflict-laden* relationships. Although there are examples of successful joint ventures (see Strategy in Action 7.3), failure rates remain high in transition economies, as well as elsewhere.[5]

Strategy in Action 7.3

Shanghai Volkswagen: A Successful Joint Venture

Volkswagen started to negotiate for a joint venture with Shanghai municipal officials in 1978. The negotiation was long and difficult. While the Chinese side pressed the idea of developing a new model for export markets, the Germans resisted. Instead, the Germans suggested assembling completely knocked-down (CKD) kits for their Santana model, while increasing local content. In order to demonstrate its commitment, Volkswagen ran a trial operation before a contract was signed. It shipped CKD kits to the Shanghai Automotive Industrial Corporation (SAIC), its future partner, which used local workers to assemble them. During 1983 and 1984, about 900 vehicles were produced, and the trial proved largely successful. Eventually a contract was signed in 1984. Initially capitalized at $40 million, the joint venture was a 50-50 arrangement shared by Volkswagen and a host of Chinese partners led by SAIC. The contract specified that while Volkswagen would try to increase the local content, the responsibility for developing qualified local suppliers rested squarely on the Chinese side.

Operations began in 1985, with an initial output of 3,000 cars. Although working-level relationships between partners were good and the municipal government was supportive, serious problems developed with the central government, which demanded that a local content target of 80% be reached in one year, as opposed to 12% as of 1988; otherwise, raw material supplies were threatened to be curtailed. Such a demand was naive, considering the difficulties of localizing auto components in other countries. Honda, for example, began assembling cars in the United States in 1982, starting with 25% American components. It took Honda 10 years to approach its goal of 75% local contents. To expect the Chinese supplier industry to match or exceed this pace seemed overly ambitious. Indeed, finding qualified Chinese suppliers was difficult. After decades of isolation, many suppliers were unfamiliar with world-class standards. Further, they balked at the large investments necessary to reach Volkswagen's standards when the joint venture initially needed merely a few thousand items. When similar problems occurred at another high-profile venture, Beijing Jeep, American managers publicized the problem in the international press, and wrote a letter to the central government threatening to shut down the plant. The Germans, however, neither complained to the press, nor confronted directly with Beijing. Instead, they chose quiet persuasion and reasoned arguments, and allowed the Chinese side to find a solution to the problem. Volkswagen was fortunate in that with a pro-business, pro-reform mayor, Zhu Rongji (who more recently rose to become the new premier in 1997), the Shanghai municipal government sided with its position and lobbied Beijing on its behalf to diffuse the tension. By

1993, the Santana model eventually reached 85% local content, attaining the highest localization levels among similar ventures in China.

One of the major reasons that the municipal government showed a strong interest in the joint venture was its growing importance. Since the mid-1990s, Shanghai Volkswagen has been the largest international joint venture in China. At the venture's full capacity of 300,000 vehicles in 1997, it contributed up to 17% of municipal output and captured 52% of the sedan market in China.

SOURCE: Peng, in press-b. Used with permission of *Management International Review.*

Strategy III: Developing Option Chains

Options and Option Chains. While the formulation of an "option chain" strategy starts before the establishment of individual joint ventures, its implementation occurs *after* these ventures are in operation. Its basic ideas come from option theory, which originates in financial economics and has been recently extended to strategic management (Bowman & Hurry, 1993; Peng, 1995b; Peng & Wang, in press). Option theory suggests three basic propositions: (a) An investor makes a small, initial investment to buy an option, which leads to the right to future investment without being obligated to do so; (b) the investor holds the option until a decision point arrives, and then decides between striking the option ("call" or option to buy) or abandoning it ("put" or option to sell); and (c) investments are made incrementally, from a small amount of initial investment to a full-scale acquisition if a call is exercised (Folta, 1998).

As alluded to earlier, a joint venture can be regarded as an option (Kogut, 1991). In joint venture agreements, it is common to give first rights of refusal to the contracting parties (i.e., the right to buy the equity of the partner that decides to withdraw). When entering transition economies, many foreign companies view joint ventures as real options for future expansion and growth. Specifically, joint ventures not only reduce the total investment costs of foreign firms, but also resolve the trade-off between buying flexibility now and waiting to invest and expand later (Folta, 1998). Tying up a potential acquisition target as a joint venture partner can also preempt such a move by foreign rivals. More important, since foreign firms have limited ways to appraise the true value of the assets of local firms, which tend to be SOEs, joint ventures afford the possibility to learn the true value of these assets through "learning by working together" (Levitt & March, 1988; Luo & Peng, 1999). As information about local partners is revealed, the acquisition may be eventually completed or withdrawn. From this option perspective, an acquisition or divestment by foreign partners is often a foreseen conclusion to these ventures, even before they become operational (Kogut, 1991). For larger MNEs with multiple joint ventures in transition economies (e.g., Philips of the Netherlands and the C. P. Group of Thailand each has dozens of joint ventures in China; AT&T and Mobil Oil each has half a dozen such ventures in Russia), these ventures create *option chains* that allow for continuous assessment of opportunities for expansion or withdrawal.

While much has been written about how to set up individual joint ventures, how MNEs develop option chains consisting of multiple joint ventures has received attention only recently. Even less is known about how to coordinate operations strategically in transition economies with the global activities of MNEs elsewhere. The following section aims to shed light on such an option chain strategy, which generally entails three phases: (a) establishing a country/regional center, (b) creating proper structures, and (c) restructuring individual joint ventures.

Establishing a Country/Regional Center. Some companies active in CEE and the NIS have recently established country and regional centers, such as the Vienna-based Henkel CEE Center set up by Germany's Henkel Group (Henkel CEE, 1998) and the Moscow-based AT&T CIS Ltd. (McCarthy & Puffer, 1997). The most active development seems to be taking place in China, however, where MNEs have had a longer presence, a larger number of joint ventures, and a more urgent need to develop option chains. The following discussion, therefore, draws primarily on MNEs' experience in China (Peng, 1997b).

Initially, an MNE often sets up an initial joint venture in order to gain a foothold (or "toehold") in the country. When only one or two of an MNE's divisions operate joint ventures, the company generally does not find it difficult to achieve a unified China strategy. However, when multiple divisions of the same company seek to form their own joint ventures, any lack of coordination among them may become costly. Specifically, while some divisions may be experienced in their dealings with local counterparts, other divisions may lack such experience or fail to utilize the China expertise acquired by other units. As an MNE increases its local presence beyond the first few joint ventures, presenting a corporate-wide China strategy to the authorities may be preferable to allowing each division to initiate its own joint venture. Chinese officials dislike having to deal with multiple delegations from different divisions of the same MNE. Moreover, a united and coordinated effort can also prevent local negotiators from playing one division against another. For example, one joint venture deal may commit to a certain percentage of exports, prompting Chinese officials to push for the same export commitment in the proposal offered by another division of the same MNE, regardless of industry and market differences (Peng, 1997b).

In order to attenuate these problems, a number of large MNEs have established corporate-level China centers, often based in Hong Kong and increasingly in Shanghai.[6] The mandate of a China center is to (a) identify cross-divisional strategies and synergies, (b) coordinate overall country-level activities, and (c) provide vital support functions (Ng & Pang, 1997). Although each division formulates its own expansion plan, the center attempts to define corporate-wide policies and principles for developing joint ventures in China, including risk exposure limits, investment return thresholds, and acceptable equity and control structures. In some cases, the China center may recommend that a particular division pursue certain projects that may not be to the division's optimal benefit, but may boost the prospects of other divisions as well as the MNE's overall competitive position in the country. In terms of support functions, the China center can pool talented negotiators and employ them in different joint venture negotiations. The hope is to leverage the expertise gained in previous deals in current negotiations. Another important role that the China center plays is to coordinate government relationships. Some China centers, for example, help arrange high-level meetings between CEOs and central and provincial leaders (Peng, 1997b).

Creating Proper Structures. Despite many trials and errors, there is little consensus as to how to place the China center and how to

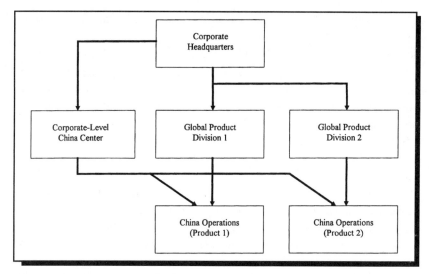

Figure 7.2. Corporate-Level China Center: The Matrix Structure

SOURCE: Adapted from Peng (1997b, p. 31). Originally published in the January/February issue of *The China Business Review*. Reprinted with the permission of the US-China Business Council, Washington, D.C., www.uschina.org/cbr.

create an appropriate overall structure conducive to the development of the option chain. Two basic approaches have emerged: a matrix structure and a country organization. The matrix structure retains the global product structure and adds a China center headed by a senior executive (Figure 7.2). General Electric, for example, adopted this structure in the mid-1990s (Ng & Pang, 1997, p. 135). This arrangement usually necessitates strong support from corporate headquarters. The most successful China centers organized along this line are characterized by close working relationships with the product divisions. By not being held responsible for short-term profitability, China centers can focus more on long-term strategic issues and country-level support activities. Common pitfalls associated with this structure, however, include lengthy decision making and potential interunit conflicts between product divisions and the China center.

First reported by Stopford and Wells (1972), the matrix structure is hardly a new organizational innovation, and its pitfalls are well known (Bartlett & Ghoshal, 1989). As a result, other MNEs attempt

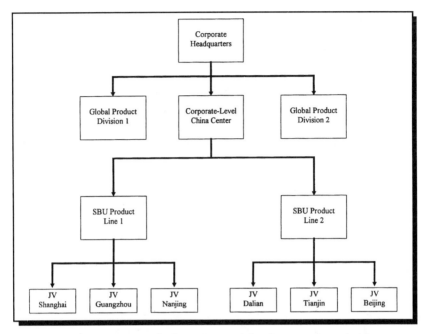

Figure 7.3. Corporate-Level China Center: The Country Organization With a Product-Based SBU Structure

to bypass the matrix structure by replacing the global product structure with a country organization, so that the China center is headed by a senior executive with country profit-and-loss responsibility (Figure 7.3). Ericsson, for instance, restructured its operations in this fashion in 1996, allowing for clearer lines of responsibility and faster decision making (Ng & Pang, 1997, pp. 163-164). However, implementing these structural changes may be difficult: First, product divisions may object to the loss of budgetary control over their China operations. Second, the complexity and diversity of various business units, especially in a diversified MNE, make it difficult for the China head to understand all units thoroughly enough to be held responsible for the bottom line (Dess, Gupta, Hennart, & Hill, 1995).

Because of China's vast size and limited market development, few products are distributed nationwide, and most local firms produce for a regional, if not local, market. As a result, multiple joint ventures in a single product line in different regions are often necessary to reach the national market. However, multiple joint ventures often make tremendous demands on the managerial resources of the corporate-level China center. As a result, large MNEs such as Motorola and Siemens create strategic business units (SBUs), which group different joint ventures according to either product line or geographic location (see Figure 7.3). In some cases, SBUs may be given significant autonomy to operate like independent entities within a large MNE. SBU executives sit on the board of directors of each joint venture in their group. In multiproduct and multibusiness companies, SBUs are important because the battle for market share is fought primarily at the SBU level (Dess et al., 1995). SBU executives are responsible for implementing overall corporate strategies for certain product lines. As a result, they are likely to have the best understanding of the competitive environment surrounding these product lines within the country, and are in the best position to formulate business-level strategies concerning certain product lines. For example, SBU executives of such electronics companies as Sony and Matsushita—rather than managers at corporate headquarters or individual joint ventures—are responsible for executing business-level strategies in the video cassette recorder, color television, and compact disc player markets in China. While most SBUs are organized according to product lines, a small number of MNEs competing in single-business markets such as hotel management or fast food services choose to implement the SBU structure on a regional basis in order to facilitate localized promotional synergies.

In companies with a large number of joint ventures, the SBU structure enables China-based executives to focus their energy on a smaller and more manageable set of joint ventures, thus helping solve the information overload problem that they typically encounter. Some SBUs even take over marketing, distribution, and accounting responsibilities to allow each joint venture to concentrate on core tasks. Given that companies have been experimenting with these structures only recently, they are likely to encounter difficulties. Based on a field study of 17 MNEs, Ng and Pang (1997, p. 153), for instance, argued that the SBU approach, emphasizing autonomy and independence, may make sense for more established markets but is not appropriate for new and frontier markets like China. Given the lack of market development, the structure may prevent mutual support and experience sharing across different SBUs, resulting in a loss of synergistic gains associated with having multiple ventures in the country. However, whether these criticisms are valid on a large sample basis remains to be seen.

In general, while China centers function more in a strategic capacity, SBUs tend to be more deeply involved with operations. It is important to note that developing option chains requires mechanisms that coordinate the activities of multiple joint ventures and generate synergies. Without more sophisticated structural solutions, these ventures will remain as isolated, individual options, but not a chain of opportunities.

Restructuring Individual Joint Ventures. Despite structural improvements, the fundamental unit of an option chain is an individual joint venture. Many MNEs realize that weak joint ventures provide a poor foundation for future growth and that restructuring is inevitable. Restructuring typically takes place first through increasing equity control.[7] Foreign firms may propose to raise their equity position incrementally. Given the inherent conflict in a shared relationship and the strong inertia on the part of some local managers, many foreign firms feel compelled to increase their equity to a dominant position. Such a position allows them to bypass the time-consuming consultation and consensus-building process associated with more-or-less equal-partner joint ventures. The financial pockets of local partners, which may be better than their domestic counterparts, are usually not as deep as those of the MNEs. Moreover, many local parent firms view joint ventures as "cash cows" to support their other money-losing operations (see Chapters 4 and 5). As a result, they are often unable to match proportionately the increase of equity according to the original ownership mix, thus effectively becoming junior partners.

Moreover, having spent enough time in the host country, some MNEs may on one hand be firmly convinced of the market potential, but on the other hand deeply frustrated by their local partners, who "sleep on the same bed but with different dreams," as the Chinese saying goes. As a result, an increasing number of them have exercised their call option to buy out the ventures by turning them into wholly owned subsidiaries (Vanhonacker, 1997). A number of foreign firms also simply buy out the troubled local partners entirely. On the other hand, other MNEs, having concluded that holding the options may be more costly than investing elsewhere, have exercised the put option by selling their equity to local partners or third parties ("China: Where's That Pot of Gold?" 1997). Occidental Petroleum's and Peugeot's withdrawals from failed ventures in China (Peng, 1995a, in press-b) serve as two cases in point here. However, selling out does not necessarily indicate a failure. A large number of overseas Chinese entrepreneurs from Hong Kong, Taiwan, and Southeast Asia have built their small-scale joint ventures in China from scratch. Since then, some of them have been able to sell their holdings to Western MNEs for a significant profit (Capener, 1996).

In sum, developing option chains requires careful structuring and incremental execution. Linking joint ventures to wholly owned subsidiaries, an option chain strategy emphasizes strategic investment flexibility (Harrigan, 1985). While this *evolutionary* strategy is clearly evident in China now, it will increasingly be played out in CEE and the NIS as well (McCarthy & Puffer, 1997). While one or two joint ventures for an MNE may suffice for smaller markets such as, say, Bulgaria, some of the larger countries such as Russia and Ukraine essentially present the same situation as in China, namely, the necessity for multiple joint ventures, the urgency to establish country-level coordination, and the need for creating proper structures to develop option chains.

Strategy IV: Acquiring Local Firms

Scale and Scope of Foreign Acquisitions. Despite the costs and risks of wholly owned subsidiaries, an increasing number of foreign firms have opted for this strategy. Initially (see Table 7.3), this strategy was employed by only a small number of firms. For example, 2.7% of entries into China between 1979 and 1993 used wholly owned subsidiaries (Tse et al., 1997). However, in 1994, one quarter of FDI entries in China were wholly owned subsidiaries (Luo, 1996, p. 536). Table 7.3 also indicates a much higher percentage (between 20% and 30%) of wholly owned subsidiaries in CEE during the first few years of transition (1989-1993), a level attained in China much later (Sharma, 1995, p. 98). In comparison, the percentage of wholly owned subsidiaries in Russia was modest (9% during 1989-1993). Although establishing wholly owned subsidiaries may be undertaken either by setting up green-field operations or acquiring local firms, the majority seem to have involved the acquisition of local companies, which will be our focus here.

Acquiring local firms may take two routes: (a) converting joint ventures into wholly owned subsidiaries and (b) acquiring local firms upon entry. Given the extensive development of joint ventures in China, the first route is used more often there. Acquiring local firms upon entry is often tied in with privatization deals, and, thus, is more likely to be found in CEE and the NIS. In the future, however, such a generalization may become inaccurate, since more foreign firms may acquire Chinese companies upon entry, and an increasing number of joint ventures in CEE and the NIS may be converted into wholly owned subsidiaries. Each of these routes will be discussed.

Buying Out Joint Venture Partners. This is essentially the "end game" of an option chain strategy (Serapio & Cascio, 1996). In addition to the deliberate option-based thinking discussed above, five reasons may prompt the initiation of such an end game. First, fundamental differences in strategic mentality and operational style make it difficult to remain in cooperation for a long time, even for successful ventures. Most local firms seek profits on a much shorter time horizon than foreign companies. Therefore, while many ventures are plagued by a lack of profits, profitable ventures often have difficulties reaching agreements on how to distribute the profits. Foreign firms are more likely to propose reinvesting the profits, while local partners may be more interested in harvesting for parent companies in need of cash.

Second, most local companies lack the drive and experience to keep up with the increasing dynamism of these economies. Although they made valuable contributions during the early phase when the market was not competitive, they may become inappropriate partners for fast-moving, aggressive foreign companies when the market matures. For example, many local firms bring to the table their connections with certain government agencies or officials. However, these connections may become useless when these agencies are dissolved and market forces take over, as in the case of the collapse of the Soviet regime during 1991 and 1992 (McCarthy et al., 1993). Since individual officials may be transferred, promoted, demoted, or jailed (in the case of corruption), personal ties with them cannot be a sustainable source of advantage (Tsang, 1998). While many joint ventures have performance problems, foreign firms in some of the more successful ventures find it hard to keep their local partners prepared and motivated for a competitive fight. Consider Krohne, a German manufacturer of electromagnetic flow meters that had had a joint venture in China since 1985. Within 5 years, the venture had a 60% market share and a comfortable operating profit. This success delighted local managers, who took it as a signal to relax and harvest. German managers, on the other hand, saw the venture's success as an invitation for competitors to enter, and they strongly urged the local partner to step up investments. Unable to reach an agreement on the strategic direction, the venture's stellar performance deteriorated, eventually causing the German firm to seek full control before it was too late (Vanhonacker, 1997).

A third common problem is associated with technology transfer. Although joint ventures enable foreign firms to protect their know-how better than licensing, local partners can still gain great access to proprietary information (Lyles & Salk, 1996). Further, typical concerns about the potential to turn local partners into competitors are magnified because of the well-known spotty enforcement of intellectual property rights in transition economies ("China: Where's That Pot of Gold?", 1997).

Interestingly, the fourth motivation is not directly related to strategic reasons as those above, but with the renegotiation *process* itself (Peng & Shenkar, 1997). When foreign firms initiate renegotiations, not all of them are prepared for a full buyout; instead, many are negotiating for increased equity control. However, local partners often react defensively and emotionally, appealing to governments, arbitration bodies, and courts in order to place the blame on foreigners. Given their lack of organizational learning, some local partners probably realize that they cannot survive without the joint venture and therefore attempt to drag on with the foreign partner, making unreasonable demands. As a consequence, the relationship deteriorates into a "same bed, different dreams, and difficult divorce" scenario. A bad "divorce" experience can only solidify the determination of certain foreign partners to dissolve the relationship as soon as possible, and some may even decide not to "marry" any local partner again. Wholly owned subsidiaries may, therefore, seem to be the only way to go.

Finally, relaxation in FDI legislation, which allows for wholly owned subsidiaries, also may have helped. Nevertheless, restrictions still exist. For example, wholly owned subsidiaries are not allowed in certain strategic industries, such as the oil industry in Russia (McCarthy & Puffer, 1997, p. 316). In China, under the current law, a wholly owned subsidiary must either use "advanced" technology or export at least 50% of its output (Capener, 1996, p. 47). It is not surprising that the highest percentage of wholly owned subsidiaries among foreign entries (see Table 7.3) occurred in Visegrad countries such as the Czech Republic, Hungary, and Poland, where legislation has been most FDI-friendly (Sharma, 1995).

In sum, a number of factors have led many firms to buy out their local partners, turn joint ventures into wholly owned subsidiaries, and, in essence, exercise the call option in option chains. Another, more aggressive, acquisition strategy will be detailed next.

Acquiring Local Firms Upon Entry. When foreign firms have other options with less capital requirements and risk exposure (e.g., joint ventures), a strategic choice of market entry through acquisitions must reflect the belief that the eventual gains will outweigh the huge costs and risks associated with wholly owned subsidiaries. Three driving forces contribute to such a determined strategic move. First, the host country environment has to meet minimum threshold requirements. To start with, legislation, such as the pieces enacted by CEE governments in the early 1990s, has to be in place. A strong commitment to privatization also seems necessary. Given the lack of domestic savings, FDI is widely regarded as a major source of privatization capital courted by governments and SOEs (see Chapter 5). The generally cheap price of SOEs also makes some of them good bargains. Yet even among countries interested in privatization, only those that use direct purchases, instead of "coupons" or "vouchers," are likely to attract foreign acquisitions. SOEs in countries such as the Czech Republic, Lithuania, and Russia can be privatized and bought with coupons and vouchers without receiving real cash. Shown in Table 7.6, countries such as Hungary, Bulgaria, Poland, and Estonia, on the other hand, required real cash to privatize SOEs, and ended up attracting a

	Hungary	Bulgaria	Poland	Estonia	Czech Republic	Russia
TABLE 7.6 Percentage of Foreign Participation in Total Transaction Value of Privatization in Selected Transition Economies, 1989-1996						
Percentage participation	58	24	22	14	5	2

SOURCE: Organization for Economic Cooperation and Development (1996, p. 25). *Trends and Policies in Privatization.* Copyright OECD, 1996.

relatively large sum of FDI to participate in their privatization (OECD, 1996). Among them, Hungary stood out as a magnet drawing FDI during the early 1990s (see also Table 7.4), not only because of the recent policies toward cash-based privatization, but also because of more than 20 years of "new economic mechanisms," which resulted in a most liberal, market-friendly environment in CEE. Such an environment, for example, led to the first major foreign acquisition in the region, General Electric's $150 million acquisition of a lighting company, Tungsram, in 1990 (see Strategy in Action 7.4). In a nutshell, according to a SWOT analysis (see Chapter 1), the environment must present enough *opportunities* and manageable *threats* if foreign acquisitions are to be undertaken.

Strategy in Action 7.4

General Electric Acquires and Restructures Tungsram of Hungary

Acquisition

This was the first large foreign acquisition in CEE and the NIS. It involved one of America's largest and best-managed MNEs and one of Hungary's oldest and most prestigious firms. Founded in 1896, Tungsram was not an average SOE. Even under the communist system, it was able to export lighting products to 100 countries, maintaining a 2% to 3% *global* market share and 5% share in Western Europe in 1985. However, by the late 1980s, Tungsram faced increasingly severe problems. Compared with its main competitors, GE, Philips, and Siemens, Tungsram had high costs, weak marketing capabilities, and insufficient R&D (only 1% to 2% of sales on R&D vs. 4% to 6% by competitors). In 1987, the government transformed Tungsram into a joint stock company, whose worth was estimated by Price Waterhouse to be approximately $100 million. In 1988, Tungsram defaulted on a loan, and bankruptcy loomed on the horizon. The GE Lighting Division (GEL) became interested when this opportunity came.

GEL competed head to head with Philips and Siemens. Each of these MNEs possessed approximately one quarter of the global market share with a total of $12 billion in sales. In Western Europe, however, GEL was very weak, with only 2% of the market share and no production base. In contrast, Philips and Siemens controlled 36% and 22%, respectively, of their home markets. Committed to being either number one or number two in *every* market in which it competed, GEL sought to improve its position in Western Europe. Acquiring Tungsram would allow it to have a low-cost production base close to Western Europe with a market share larger than GEL's own, dominance in Eastern Bloc countries, and traditionally strong R&D capabilities. In addition, Tungsram not only appeared to have strategic fit with GEL, but also certain organizational fit, because of previous collaborations, including joint ventures.

Not keen on subsidizing Tungsram, the Hungarian government could have sold Tungsram through an international tender. However, if Philips or Siemens would have acquired Tungsram, they might close it to eliminate a competitor. It is also important to note that the acquisition was negotiated *before* the final collapse of communism, when few MNEs were willing to invest in CEE. For all these reasons, the government offered GE a deal that was very attractive at that time. Negotiations progressed rapidly, and were completed in December 1989. For $150 million cash, GE acquired 50% plus one share. GE also had the right of first refusal to purchase up to 25% additional shares, should other owners (the Hungarian Credit Bank had 45%, the government 4%, and others 1%) decide to sell any of their remaining shares. In addition, GEL obtained tax exemption for the first year and 60% tax reduction for the next 5 years.

Local laws required approval by a "super majority" of 75% for major decisions. Thus, as long as there were minority shareholders, certain formalities had to be observed. As the controlling owner, GE had the right to increase its equity at its discretion. Other owners could maintain their proportion only by paying a proportionate share of the increase; otherwise their ownership would decrease correspondingly. Since Tungsram had reported losses for several years, neither the bank nor the government had any interest in putting in additional cash just to maintain their proportions. As a result, during 1990 to 1994, GE *incrementally* acquired 100% ownership, which gave it a free hand in restructuring this new wholly owned subsidiary.

Restructuring

When GEL stepped in, Tungsram was plagued by a weak financial position, overstaffing, run-down facilities, and ineffective management practices. To make matters worse, its major markets in Western Europe went into a deep recession and those in CEE and the NIS virtually disappeared in the early 1990s. Deep and costly restructuring became inevitable. By 1995, GEL had invested a total of $600 million, including $225 million for share purchases, $175 million capital expenditures, and $200 million restructuring outlays.

Restructuring efforts were multidimensional. *One-time* expenditures were spent on building upgrades, severance costs, expatriate costs, and training costs for existing staff, and write-offs of uncollectible Soviet debts. At the *business level*, Tungsram's product structure (75% lighting, 15% machinery, and 10% electronics in 1989) was reorganized. To avoid competition with GE's own products, electronics was phased out. The machinery division, formerly an exporter for markets in developing countries, became a major in-house supplier to GEL, accounting for less than 10% of total sales. Tungsram, therefore, became highly focused on its core, lighting products. At the *plant level*, GEL inherited nine plants. Initially only two were found to be worth keeping. However, it was soon realized that everywhere outside Budapest, Tungsram was the community's largest and often only employer. Intending to be a good corporate citizen, GEL closed only one plant, and all employees were guaranteed a job at a nearby Tungsram factory. Two other plants were sold to an Austrian investor and local employees through a buyout. The six other plants were kept and upgraded to a world-class level. In terms of the *labor force*, GEL painfully reduced the head count from

17,600 in 1989 to 9,300 in 1993. By 1995, however, Tungsram's employment rose to 10,200, which was rare at that time.

Slowly, the restructuring efforts were paying off. The Nagykanizsa factory became the world's largest and reportedly best quality producer of light sources, where GEL began to manufacture its most revolutionary new product, Genura, a lamp with 100 watts of light for only 23 watts of actual energy. Several other plants were designated as centers of manufacturing excellence by GEL. Tungsram was also designated as GEL's *only* global center of excellence in R&D. As a result, about half of GEL's R&D personnel resided in Hungary. This has been the only example of an MNE's large division, with $3 billion global sales, concentrating its worldwide R&D capabilities in a transition economy. While Tungsram lost a total of $243 million between 1990 and 1993, it started to turn profitable in 1994 with a $50 million profit. By 1995, GEL's market share in Western Europe was two to three times higher than the combined market share of GEL and Tungsram in 1989. In Hungary, despite some nationalistic concerns, the difficulties of Hungary's many large, unprofitable SOEs and employee- and management-buyout-based privatized firms (see Chapters 4 and 5) suggest that allowing for such a foreign acquisition was, on balance, in Hungary's long-term economic interest.

SOURCE: *Trends and Policies in Privatization.* Copyright OECD, 1996.

Second, the same SWOT analysis would suggest that foreign firms have to reach the conclusion that these acquisitions maximize their *strengths* and compensate for their *weaknesses*. Kodak's recent move in China in 1998 perhaps best illustrates this thought process ("Kodak in China," 1998). Despite Kodak's global strengths, it was relatively weak in China. Its global rival, Fuji, had always been the leader in the $800 million market, which is already the third largest in the world and which promises to be the leading market in a decade. However, no foreign company had been allowed to produce locally until Kodak's recent entry. Facing 40% import duties, Kodak and Fuji typically relied on Hong Kong-based distributors, which often smuggled the film through gray channels (see Chapter 6). This method, however, did not allow for sustained growth in this fast-growing market. By acquiring three dying filmmaking SOEs for $380 million (the first-ever large-scale foreign acquisition upon entry in China) and by committing an additional $700 million to bring their facilities to world-class standards, Kodak firmly believed that it could turn the tables and become the market leader in China. Specifically, low labor costs in China would capitalize on Kodak's strengths in efficient manufacturing, while overcoming its weaknesses associated with a lackluster market share. In addition, to prevent Fuji, or in fact any other foreign company, from imitating this acquisition strategy, Kodak managed to obtain a commitment from Beijing that no FDI in this industry would be allowed for 4 years. While not every foreign acquisition is as high profile as Kodak's or GE's, most decisions have to be justified by such a sensible SWOT analysis.

Finally, foreign acquisitions must demonstrate their benefits vis-à-vis other entry modes. The best advantage is undivided control, which allows for smoother internal operations, stronger coordination with global operations, and better protection of proprietary technology. In a more mature economy, wholly owned subsidiaries may be easier to establish. For example, Chinese regulations in the 1990s required that local officials respond to proposals for wholly owned subsidiaries within 30 days, which compares sharply with many "endless" negotiations with local firms and governments (Vanhonacker, 1997, p. 136). During the operational stage, decision making may be more efficient than in joint ventures. Finally, wholly owned subsidiaries give MNEs better incentives to transfer technology and know-how. In 1995, for instance, Tungsram was designated by GE as its only global center of excellence in R&D for the lighting division (Marer & Mabert, 1996). GE probably would not have made such a considerable investment in Tungsram's R&D capabilities had it been a joint venture (see Strategy in Action 7.4). Overall, a conducive environment, strategic needs, and operational advantages combine to suggest that acquiring local firms upon entry may be a cost-effective way of entering transition economies. However, how to make acquisitions work once the market entry is accomplished is also likely to be challenging.

Making Acquisitions Work. Acquisition decisions are typically made based on strategic fit. As a result, a lack of organizational fit between acquiring and target companies is likely to result in integration failure (Haspeslagh & Jemison, 1991). Globally, the failure rate for acquisitions is high (Ravenscraft & Scherer, 1987). Thus, making acquisitions work in transition economies where the two sides come from vastly different backgrounds is even more demanding (Welsh, Luthans, & Sommer, 1993). Given the extensive problems in most local firms, foreign acquirers are more willing to initiate radical restructuring, such as downsizing and downscoping. Chapter 5 highlighted how local firms, managers, and employees can resist these changes from their point of view. Here we focus on how foreign firms can facilitate organizational changes to make acquisitions work beyond the initially painful but often necessary measures by (a) overinvesting in expatriates, (b) strengthening training, and (c) developing capabilities.

Deploying expatriates has long been an MNE practice when developing new markets. One of the unique challenges of transition economies is that an assignment that usually requires one executive in a developed country may demand two or three managers if they can adapt well to the local environment (Peng, 1997b, p. 33). The major concern of the company is to maintain relatively strong control in the early stage when day-to-day work procedures and systems are less well developed. Given the relatively high percentage of expatriates who break their contracts and leave these countries prematurely and the continued shortage of skilled local managers, MNEs often have to *overinvest* in experienced expatriates in order to make acquisitions work. To attract high-caliber expatriates it may be necessary to employ special career development incentives, such as premium salaries and benefits, frequent promotions, and the promise of a desirable posting upon completion of a stint in transition economies. Overall, the key is to identify and attract suitable expatriate managers who are technically competent, culturally sensitive, and willing to be relocated to work in these countries.[8] The costs, however, can be staggering. For example, a British joint venture in Shanghai had just three expatriates on its payroll of 220 people; yet the salary, housing, and other benefits for these expatriates accounted for 80% of its total personnel costs (Child, 1998, p. 12).

Given the high costs of expatriates, training local managers and employees is a must. Training can take a variety of forms, such as on-the-job coaching, company-specific programs, and "back-to-school" training. Expatriate staff typically assume a heavy role when teaming up in one-on-one with local managers. A number of leading MNEs have also set up their own training centers (e.g., the Motorola University) in these countries, and sent local managers and employees overseas for training. Back-to-school training usually centers on short-term, executive courses, resulting in a cottage industry among Western and local university business schools aiming to target this clientele.

Because training is expensive, many MNEs are concerned about *retaining* high-potential local candidates. Financial incentive is often used to attract and keep capable local staff, resulting in "astronomical" wage levels by local standards. For example, a Russian investment banker's salary can be as high as $100,000 (Matlack, 1998). However, this may not be enough. Many leading companies believe that an attractive corporate culture is a major draw that can help retain high-caliber staff, in addition to a competitive salary and benefits package. As a result, companies not only need to invest in technical and business skills training, but also to provide training and socialization to facilitate employee identification with the organization.

Finally, whether subsidiaries in transition economies will blossom into stand-alone entities or will always remain as "special cases" requiring extra resources will be determined by how quickly they can develop multidimensional capabilities beyond their initial mandate (Birkinshaw & Hood, 1998). Initially, these subsidiaries are focused entities with a single purpose (e.g., manufacturing). Strategic planning, product design, and financial control typically concentrate in global or regional headquarters. Over time, local adaptation in product design, marketing, and services are likely, because of the need to serve local customers more effectively. More recently, as MNE involvement in these countries expands, there is an increasing demand to create country-or regional-level centers to coordinate multiple ventures and subsidiaries better (discussed earlier). Together with the establishment of these centers, a number of support functions such as country and regional planning may migrate to these countries. The more mature environment in these countries in the 1990s, together with more abundant local managers and professionals and the relatively low costs of employing them, have created powerful incentives to move more high-level, value-added functions from regional headquarters to these countries (e.g., from Hong Kong to Shanghai, from Helsinki to St. Petersberg, and from Vienna to Budapest and Prague).

In other words, both a pull effect and a push effect seem to drive the development of more capabilities at these subsidiaries. The pull effect is the draw of these markets, which often have been singled out as areas requiring disproportionate attention and resources. For example, at an increasing number of MNEs, the China unit has been separated from the Asia Pacific unit and reports directly to corporate headquarters. The push effect comes from the high cost of deploying a large number of expatriates and of relying on professionals in expensive cities such as Hong Kong and Vienna to provide vital support functions. Taken together, both the pull and the push effects lead to stronger development of capabilities beyond the initial mandate of these subsidiaries (e.g., GE's development of R&D capabilities at Tungsram). In the long run, whether these efforts are successful will determine, to a large degree, the performance of MNE acquisitions of local firms there.

In sum, establishing wholly owned subsidiaries is the most costly and risky international strategy. Within this particular strategic choice, converting joint ventures into wholly owned status may be relatively easy, due to foreign firms' familiarity with the local environment. Acquiring local firms upon entry has the highest degree of the "liability of foreignness" (Zaheer, 1995), which can be overcome only by superb strategic strengths, excellent implementation skills, and adequate development of subsidiary capabilities.

Summary and Discussion

This chapter has discussed a broad spectrum of strategies employed by foreign companies. These include a basic export strategy, an intermediate alliance strategy, and a more complex acquisition strategy. Connecting these discrete entry choices is an option chain strategy that focuses on the evolution from joint ventures to wholly owned subsidiaries. These connections are an important part of the stage model of internationalization (Johanson & Vahlne, 1977). While individual attributes of these strategies have been discussed at length, three common themes that cut across them are worth discussing here: (a) performance implications, (b) organizational learning, and (c) location-specific competitive advantages.

Performance Implications. Strategy is fundamentally concerned with firm performance. The evolution from relatively simple international strategies to more complex undertakings embodies a belief that more advanced strategies are likely to generate better performance. As virgin markets, transition economies provide a fascinating ground to test this basic proposition. Hard evidence, however, is difficult to find, because once a particular strategic choice is selected, what would have happened had other strategies been used is typically not known (Peng, 1998, pp. 144-146).

Given that many joint ventures have been converted into wholly owned subsidiaries and many other foreign firms have opted for direct acquisitions of local firms upon entry, the assumption seems to be that wholly owned subsidiaries are likely to perform better. However, studies by Child (1998) and Luo (1996) found that this may not necessarily be true. Shown in Table 7.5, the returns on assets and operating profit margin of wholly owned subsidiaries are not statistically different from those of joint ventures, although both groups outperform purely domestic firms in China by a wide margin. The upshot is that there is still no conclusive evidence suggesting that wholly owned subsidiaries should be the only way to go. Despite numerous joint venture failures, there may still be sound strategic reasons for some firms to pursue them. The best-performing joint ventures seem to be those in which foreign partners have sufficient influence to exercise leadership, but without being so dominant as to exclude local partners (Child, 1998).

Beyond the debate surrounding joint ventures and wholly owned subsidiaries, another commonly held belief, informed by the influential stage model, is that only by moving aggressively toward more complex strategies (or stages) can better performance be attained. MNE experience in transition economies does not fully support this view. Given the harsh environment, sometimes firms have to backtrack in order to remain competitive. The experience of IBM in Russia (McCarthy & Puffer, 1997, pp. 306-308) is indicative here. In 1993, IBM established a wholly owned facility in Russia to assemble imported components. Despite a leading market position, it had to cease production in 1996. The primary reason was that with a new 10% import tax, IBM would be consistently undersold by competitors, which were able to circumvent the tax laws (reportedly through smuggling and bribery). However, this did not mean that IBM intended to abandon the market. Instead, it reverted to exporting to Russia, and relied more heavily on local distribution alliances. In spite of some losses associated with plant closure and the reliance on more "primitive" strategies, IBM was still able to maintain its market leadership in Russia.

The experience of IBM and other similar companies enriches the traditional option chain strategy, which suggests that investments be increased incrementally and flexibly. Otherwise, options are advised to be abandoned. Recent MNE experience indicates that it may not be necessary to abandon earlier investments completely when facing performance problems; instead, *incremental withdrawal* may be more advisable. Similar to the merits of incremental increase, incremental withdrawal allows for maximum strategic flexibility. Facing these difficult but potentially lucrative markets, MNEs may have to be prepared for a bumpy ride, taking "one step back" in order eventually to take "two steps forward" (McCarthy et al., 1993).

Organizational Learning. Organization learning pertains to virtually all foreign firms. How fast and efficiently they can learn to compete in transition economies will, to a large degree, determine their success or failure there (Luo & Peng, 1998, 1999). The first decision confronting them is *when* to start learning, which boils down to an entry timing issue. Mostly focusing on product market entries, some existing studies found the existence of significant first-mover advantages (Lieberman & Montgomery, 1988), and other studies reported exactly the opposite (Teece, 1986; Schnaars, 1994). With little guidance from researchers, managers interested in entering transition economies engaged in vigorous but inconclusive debates on entry timing (Kvint, 1994). Basically, there are powerful arguments in favor of early entry, such as capturing customers and preempting rivals. There are, however, equally powerful arguments suggesting a wait-and-see strategy. The question, therefore, is an *empirical* one that has to be answered by evidence.

In a recent study, my colleague and I shed considerable light on the entry timing issue using data from China (Luo & Peng, 1998). First, there are both first-mover advantages and disadvantages during the *early* period of operations (Panel A of Table 7.7). That is, when we compared the first 3 years of performance between the first movers, which entered during 1980-1981, and the late movers, which entered during 1989-1990, first movers had better sales growth and asset turnover, while later movers had better return on assets and lower risk. Second, the longer first movers remain in operation, the more noticeable first-mover advantages will be (Panel B of Table 7.7). Specifically, early investors had superior performance in return on sales, return on equity, sales growth, and market position relative to late movers during the *late* stage of operations.

Taken together, these findings suggest that (a) there are powerful incentives to search for first-mover advantages and that (b) despite the initial difficulties for first movers during the early years, it probably pays to hang in there (e.g., the IBM approach in Russia) as opposed to withdrawing completely. Given the increasingly saturated markets in these countries in the 1990s and beyond, a practical question is: Where are new first-mover advantages? Readers raising this question need to be reminded that market "saturation" occurs only in large business centers such as Moscow, Shanghai, and Warsaw (Kvint, 1994). The vast hinterland with numerous second- and third-tier cities and regions continues to present many first-mover opportunities. Moreover, countries such as Cuba, North Korea, and Vietnam are likely to generate entirely new sets of first-mover advantages for determined and capable investors.

Having decided when to start learning, the next decision is *what* to learn. Of particular importance to MNEs is the distinction between "exploration" and "exploitation" in organizational learning (March, 1991). *Exploration* includes "things captured by terms such as search, variation, risk taking, experimentation, play, flexibility, discovery, and innovation," whereas *exploitation* entails "such things as refinement, choice, production, efficiency, selection, implementation, and execution" (March, 1991, p. 71). While both kinds of learning are important, there is a trade-off between the two, since exploitation tends to drive out exploration. In other words, because of sunk costs, some investment decisions are not easily reversible; decisions for sustained exploitary learning, once made, are likely to limit the range of exploratory learning (Levinthal & March, 1993). Few empirical studies, however,

TABLE 7.7 First-Mover Versus Late-Mover Advantages in China

Panel A: Early Operations *(Average performance during the first three years)*	First Movers *(entry during 1980-1981)*	Late Movers *(entry during 1989-1990)*	t-statistics
Sample	7	24	
First-mover advantages			
Sales growth	26.78%	15.28%	−4.27**
Asset turnover (times)	4.94	3.30	−3.31**
Late-mover advantages			
Return on assets	8%	13%	1.91*
Risk (geometric average of standard deviations of objective performance measures)	87.66	53.34	−6.23**

Panel B: Late Operations *(Standardized regression coefficients)*	Return on Sales	Return on Equity	Sales Growth	Market Share
Sample	96	96	96	96
Independent variable				
Entry timing[a] (first-mover advantages)	−0.41***	−0.43***	−0.26**	−0.24**
Control variables				
Industry	0.22**	0.28***	0.31***	0.35***
Firm size	0.01	−0.08	0.05	0.03
Equity	0.10	0.02	0.11	0.12
R&D	0.41***	0.34***	0.41***	0.47***
Model F	21.25***	21.60***	15.04***	20.66***
Adjusted R^2	0.51	0.52	0.42	0.51

* $p < 0.05$; ** $p < 0.01$; *** $p < 0.001$.
SOURCE: Adapted from Luo and Peng (1998, pp. 149, 155). Reprinted from "First Mover Advantages in Investing in Transitional Economies," by Y. Luo & M. W. Peng, in *Thunderbird International Business Review*, Copyright © 1998, John Wiley & Sons, Inc.
NOTE: a. Entry timing is measured by the time difference in months between a given foreign-invested firm's operation commencement date and January 1979, the launching date of China's "open door" policy. The larger this measure, the later the entry. The four regression models show that the later the entry, the worse the performance, as evidenced by the significantly negative coefficients for timing in all four models, after controlling for other variables.

have been able to answer how exploitation drives out exploration, and how these dynamics affect firm performance, questions that have important practical implications.

In another recent study, we addressed these important questions by using the diversity of MNEs' experience (e.g., diversity of local markets, buyers, and suppliers) to measure exploration, and the intensity of MNEs' involvement (e.g., the length of involvement) to proximate exploitation (Luo & Peng, in press). We found that both exploratory and exploitary learning contribute to MNE performance. While these results are hardly surprising, what is interesting is that, over time, the returns from exploration diminish more significantly than those from exploitation. The practical insights of these findings support the recent movement to convert joint ventures into wholly owned subsidiaries. Given that joint ventures can be regarded as "learning options" (Peng, 1995b; Peng & Wang, in press), these options tend to be good platforms for exploration. Over time, however, given the diminishing returns from exploration, it makes strategic sense to start exploitation, which may best be provided by wholly owned subsidiaries. In other words, when decision time comes, MNEs need to call the options aggressively; indecision will only diminish the value of the options the longer the firms wait. Therefore, the active transformation from "first-generation" to "second-generation" MNE activities in transition economies can be regarded as a process in which exploitation gradually drives out exploration in order to capture the best returns from organizational learning in these countries.

In sum, when to start learning, what to learn, and how to maximize the gains from learning have important strategic implications for foreign firms competing in these unfamiliar markets. These markets also possess significant location-specific advantages, to which we now turn.

Location-Specific Advantages. With no exaggeration, the history of international business is basically a quest for better locations in which to conduct business (Dunning, 1993). Recent interest in transition economies is no exception. Of particular interest is why some of these countries, such as China and Hungary, are able to attract a great deal of FDI, while others, such as Russia and Ukraine, are not doing as well. While countries are usually the unit of analysis (Porter,

1990), a more relevant unit seems to be clusters. A *cluster* is "a geographically proximate group of interconnected companies and associated institutions in a particular field linked by commonalities and complementarities" (Porter, 1998, p. 199). According to this perspective, most foreign companies are active only in several clusters in south China neighboring Hong Kong, across the straits from Taiwan, and centered on Shanghai, and in Visegrad countries (i.e., the Czech Republic, Hungary, and Poland) neighboring Western Europe. Geography has played a major part in the rise of these clusters (Naughton, 1997). Executives in Hong Kong, Munich, and Vienna, for example, can conveniently commute to plants just across the border (Stewart, Cheung, & Yeung, 1992). Beyond geographical factors, the "agglomeration" effect is also important, especially among foreign firms (Shaver, 1998). Specifically, early foreign investors are likely to attract late entrants, further strengthening these clusters. Moreover, the success of these clusters can be attributed, to a large degree, to a favorable environment in which more internationally compatible, market-supporting institutions have been established (e.g., China's Special Economic Zones; Shan, 1991).

The primary comparative advantages of transition economies are in internationally competitive low-to-intermediate technical skills for manufacturing. However, low labor costs attract FDI only in conjunction with attractive markets (Estrin & Meyer, 1998; Meyer, 1995). It is not a coincidence that the best-performing countries in attracting FDI also experienced some of the strongest growth in import demand (see Tables 7.2 and 7.3). A major concern is that within attractive clusters mentioned above, wage levels tend to rise more rapidly than productivity gains, thus eroding some of the cost advantages (Lau et al., 1998). Under these pressures, some foreign companies, especially those in labor-intensive industries, are likely to be driven to cheaper hinterland areas or alternative countries (e.g., Romania, Vietnam), thus triggering a new round of searching for the first-mover advantages discussed earlier.

In sum, the activities of foreign companies provide an interesting chapter in the long quest for location-specific advantages. What seems most fascinating is the emergence of certain regional clusters, which have been largely shaped by foreign firms. How these clusters *coevolve* with foreign companies will remain to be seen in the future.

▨ CONCLUSIONS

Following previous chapters, we will draw on the strategies of foreign firms to shed light on the five fundamental questions in strategy raised in Chapter 1. Why firms differ (Question 1) and how they behave (Question 2) can be explained simply by the foreign origin of these firms. Coming from market economies, they represent a more dynamic and capable competitive force in transition economies. It is not surprising that they are widely sought by domestic firms as venture partners.

Question 3 asks: How are strategy outcomes affected by strategy processes? The evolution of strategies of foreign firms along the option chain reflects a sophisticated approach toward strategy formulation and implementation. Large MNEs in particular engage in constant learning that, in turn, may lead to new strategic choices. While converting joint ventures into wholly owned subsidiaries may be a foregone conclusion for experienced MNEs, many local firms are totally surprised, reflecting a fundamental naïveté. Consequently they react defensively and emotionally, accusing MNEs of contemplating takeover conspiracies. Overall, compared with domestic firms, strategy outcomes and processes seem to be better integrated at most foreign firms.

Question 4 is interested in: What determines the scope of the firm? For foreign firms, increasing their scope to cover transition economies embodies a part of their *corporate-level* growth. Chapter 3 suggests that firm growth can be achieved by generic expansion, alliances, and acquisitions. An export strategy can be regarded as a part of generic expansion, using the firm's own resources to cover new markets. When the limit of an export strategy is reached, an alliance strategy represents the next step in the strategy ladder. Finally, when the pitfalls of alliances outweigh their costs, foreign companies have little choice but to start acquiring local firms in order to expand in host countries. In addition to these corporate-level strategic moves, these dynamics can also be found in their *business-level* involvement within transition economies. Basically, start-up ventures in these countries have limited tasks, such as manufacturing. Gradually, these ventures become multidimensional, with more functions. Not fully possessing some of the needed capabilities, foreign firms often collaborate with local partners. Over time, in order to ensure the growth of their operations in these countries, foreign firms engage in local acquisitions. In short, the growth of the business-level scope of foreign companies in transition economies evolves along a similar strategic path for corporate-level firm growth.

Skipped by previous chapters, the last question, What determines the international success and failure of firms? can finally be answered here. Given the complexity of international competition, any single perspective is not likely to be able to answer this broad question. Instead, we will employ an "eclectic" approach that suggests that, in a nutshell, advantages possessed by foreign firms can be categorized as ownership-, location-, and internalization-based (Dunning, 1993). *Ownership* advantages are self-evident. Without some form of ownership, many foreign firms are unable fully to leverage their strengths. *Location* advantages come from two sides: the origin of foreign companies and the location of their new activities. Given cultural and institutional influences, the country of origin is likely to influence significantly how firms do business abroad (Porter, 1990). Competitive domestic economies (e.g., Japan and the United States) may generate strong companies that can overwhelm foreign rivals. Historical expertise in dealing with transition economies (e.g., Austria and Hong Kong) may also result in a strong position in these new markets. Location advantages of transition economies, as discussed earlier, are driven by geography, factor endowments, and institutional infrastructure. Finally, *internalization* advantages refer to MNEs' abilities to preserve and strengthen the proprietary, knowledge-based assets that have been a driving force behind most of their decisions (Buckley & Casson, 1976; Hennart, 1988; Teece, 1998). Given that the raison d'être for MNEs centers on the three-pronged advantages of ownership, location, and internalization, the best foreign firms are likely to be those that have successfully acquired, deployed, and developed these advantages.

In conclusion, foreign firms have turned transition economies into a new battleground of multinational competition. The process has never been smooth. Not once, but repeatedly, foreign companies have caught "China fevers," "CEE fevers," and "Russia fevers" ("China: Where's That Pot of Gold?" 1997; Curran, 1994; "The Rush to China, 1997; "The Rush to Russia," 1997), which only cool down over time. Given the inherent fluctuation of these markets (e.g., the Russian fallout in 1998) and of the global economy in general (e.g., the Asian financial crisis since 1997), the outlook may not always be rosy, at least in the short run. In the long run, however, transition economies, taken as a whole, represent the world's largest emerging markets. Therefore, foreign companies, especially large MNEs, have to develop capabilities and secure positions in these markets if they want to remain competitive in the new millennium.

NOTES

1. There are other forms of non-equity-based strategic alliances that are neither licensing/franchising nor joint ventures. Examples include joint R&D, comarketing, coproduction, and long-term supply contracts. They are not covered because in transition economies these forms have not been used frequently.

2. The top 10 largest importing countries in 1995 were the United States ($771 billion), Germany ($446 billion), Japan ($336 billion), France ($275 billion), Great Britain ($261 billion), Hong Kong ($193 billion), the Netherlands ($175 billion), Canada ($168 billion), China ($129 billion), and Singapore ($124 billion). Given that a considerable amount of Hong Kong imports are China-bound transshipments, the actual amount of Chinese imports may be larger than the statistics for China reveal. Among other transition economies, Russia was 17th ($58 billion), Poland 28th ($28 billion), the Czech Republic 29th ($27 billion), and Hungary 32nd ($15 billion; Euromonitor, 1996, p. 38).

3. The top 10 largest exporting countries in 1995 were the United States ($584 billion), Germany ($509 billion), Japan ($443 billion), France ($286 billion), Great Britain ($237 billion), the Netherlands ($194 billion), Canada ($192 billion), Hong Kong ($174 billion), China ($145 billion), and Singapore ($118 billion). Again, a substantial amount of Hong Kong exports originate in China, which can further boost China's ranking in the list. Russia was 14th ($79 billion), Poland 25th ($22 billion), the Czech Republic 26th ($21 billion), and Hungary 37th ($13 billion; Euromonitor, 1996, p. 39).

4. Although the Beijing Jeep joint venture agreement signed in 1983 called for the development of a new car model for export (non-Chinese) markets, the joint venture never developed such a model, and has been assembling the Jeep Cherokee since then. Some interviewees suggested that AMC might have deliberately employed a "bait and switch" strategy by promising to develop such a new model though never seriously willing to do it (Harwit, 1995; Peng, in press-b).

5. There is no evidence that the joint venture failure rate in transition economies is higher than elsewhere. Globally, Harrigan (1986) and Kogut (1988) reported a 50% failure rate. More strikingly, other studies found the failure rate to be between 60% and 70% (Peng & Shenkar, 1997). Despite these high "failure" rates, scholars and practitioners have yet to come to a consensus on what exactly constitutes a joint venture "failure." Change of joint venture ownership (including one partner buying out the equity of the another) may not necessarily constitute failure, since the change may be in line with objectives of at least one of the partners.

6. These China centers have used a variety of labels, such as "holding," "investment," and "umbrella" companies, to register in China (Peng, 1997b).

7. Restructuring weak joint ventures also involves heavy investment in expatriate managers and strong efforts in training. Since these activities are extensively found in wholly owned subsidiaries, they will be discussed in more detail in the following section, "Strategy IV."

8. In contrast to conventional wisdom, expatriates who have a shorter "cultural distance" from host countries, such as overseas Chinese in China and Austrians in Hungary, do not necessarily perform better in transition economies (Selmer, 1997).

8 Retrospect and the Road Ahead

Competition for the future is competition to create and dominate
emerging opportunities—to stake out competitive space.

—*Gary Hamel and C. K. Prahalad (1994, p. 22)*

From Shanghai to St. Petersberg, from Saigon to Szczecin, competition has dramatically intensified in virtually all transition economies. It was not long ago that competition was all but absent. Markets
were closed, strategies nonexistent, and economies stagnant. In contrast, change is now *the* striking feature during the transition, thus
calling for firms to employ diverse competitive strategies to navigate
the turbulent and uncertain waters of these emerging markets. The
preceding chapters have painted a broad picture of these strategies and
explored the five fundamental questions in strategy. In this final
chapter, we will first revisit these five questions in a *comprehensive*
way. Future challenges for researchers and practitioners will then be
outlined. Overall, we will not only examine business strategies in
transition economies retrospectively, but will also suggest future competitive paths that are likely to distinguish winners from losers in these

countries, and identify future research directions that are likely to emerge in the new millennium.

▨ FIVE FUNDAMENTAL QUESTIONS REVISITED

Question I: Why Do Firms Differ?

Strategic management is not only concerned with differences in firm *attributes*, but also in firm *performance*. Why do some firms succeed while others fail? More than anything else, this performance question distinguishes strategy from other fields (Rumelt, Schendel, & Teece, 1994; Summer et al., 1990). Pick up any strategy textbook; the starting point for answering this question will almost always be an analysis of the competitive conditions of a particular industry (Porter, 1980). At a more "macro" level, the country of origin of the companies concerned is also likely to assert a significant influence on differences in firm attributes and performance (Porter, 1990). At a more "micro" level, firm-specific resources and capabilities have been widely noted as another set of fundamental drivers of firm differences (Barney, 1991). This three-pronged analysis is a powerful tool in the context of existing markets, where most of the rules of competition have already been established. Yet in transition economies, where markets are constantly changing, emerging, and disappearing, the rules are waiting to be written. This vastly complicates strategic choices, requiring a new mentality that thrives on chaos (Brown & Eisenhardt, 1998; Peters, 1987) and competes for the future (Hamel & Prahalad, 1994).

Competition in transition economies enriches the strategy literature by highlighting the importance of *institutional* frameworks in which the three-pronged analysis is embedded (Figure 8.1). Because very few firms—domestic or foreign—had much experience in competing in these countries before the transition, competitive rules—and history chapters—are being written as different firms respond to new challenges. The first source of organizational heterogeneity comes from a company's "genetic coding," which is deeply influenced by the

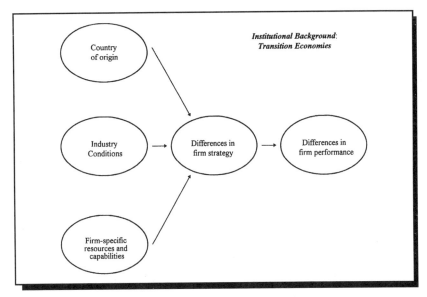

Figure 8.1. Why Do Firms Differ in Strategy and Performance?

institutional environment in which the firm is embedded. From such a "genetic" point of view, it is easy to understand why SOEs in transition economies are radically different from typical firms in the West.

A second underlying source of firm differences is adaptiveness (Meyer, 1982; Meyer, Brooks, & Goes, 1990). Under stress, some firms panic, crying out for more help and trying to muddle through the transition process. Others rise to the occasion, quickly learning to swim in the emerging ocean of competition. The history of global competition has repeatedly shown that the winners in competition are not necessarily those with the best "genetic codes"; otherwise, companies richly endowed with past success and current resources would be likely to be winners forever (Porter, 1990). What has happened in transition economies is that most of the former "pillar" enterprises, SOEs that previously occupied the "commanding heights" of the economy, increasingly become corporate dinosaurs unable to adapt to the changed environment. In their place there emerge a number of "maverick" companies that have much better foresight, set more ambitious strategic intent, and stretch their poor resource bases, doing more with less (Hamel & Prahalad, 1994).

One of the early "rules" of competition in transition economies is the necessity of having personal networks, contacts, and connections such as *guanxi* in China, *quan he* in Vietnam, and *blat* in Russia (Peng, 1997a). It seems that "who you know is more important than what you know" (Yeung & Tung, 1996, p. 54). Over time, this rule becomes a part of the self-fulfilling conventional wisdom, in that executives need constantly to build interpersonal ties, which are always helpful, with managers at other firms and with government officials. Not only local firms are eager participants in the game of building managerial networks; foreign companies, not to be outdone, also enthusiastically pursue and cultivate these ties in order to adapt to the new environment.

However, two recent studies have *empirically* disproved the conventional wisdom that suggests virtually unlimited benefits in personal networks (Peng & Luo, 1998, 1999). Shown in Table 8.1, while managerial networks with executives at other firms and with government officials account for 18% and 11% of performance differences in market share (Model 1) and return on assets (Model 4), respectively, strategy variables such as quality, payment terms, advertising, pricing, and delivery *alone* explain 38% and 20% of the variance of market share (Model 2) and return on assets (Model 5), respectively. Note that these "traditional" strategy variables, which are independent of managerial networks, are able to explain more performance differences than interpersonal networks. As shown in Models 3 and 6, it appears that managerial networks and strategy variables work hand in hand in driving firm performance, explaining 73% and 78% of the performance differences, respectively. These findings make sense because, after all, firms have to deliver value-added in a marketplace where the government no longer controls a large share of the resources. The implication is very clear: While managerial networks are important, firms also need to have core competencies in "traditional" strategy areas in order to perform well in transition economies. Thus, the old rule needs to be replaced by a new rule suggesting that managerial networks may be a necessary but not a sufficient condition for business success, in light of the increasingly market-driven nature of the competition there

TABLE 8.1 What Determines Firm Performance? Managerial Networks Versus "Traditional" Strategy Variables[a]

| | Standardized Regression Coefficients | | | | | | MANOVA Test | |
| | Market Share | | | Return on Assets | | | | |
	(1)	(2)	(3)	(4)	(5)	(6)	Wilk's λ	F
Managerial Networks								
With managers at other firms	0.31**		0.19*	0.12		0.07	0.81	13.11***
With government officials	0.38**		0.22**	0.28*		0.15†	0.75	20.66***
"Traditional" Strategy Variables								
Quality		0.35***	0.32***		0.39***	0.27***	0.44	72.03***
Payment terms		0.29***	0.14		0.14	−0.07	0.85	9.50***
Advertising		0.20*	0.13		0.12	0.05	0.89	6.26**
Pricing		0.10	0.06		−0.02	0.04	0.96	1.89
Delivery		0.06	0.04		0.07	0.03	0.98	1.10
Control Variables								
Ownership			−0.09			−0.22*	0.80	15.01***
Size (number employees)			−0.05			−0.29***	0.69	33.52***
Industry			−0.14			0.18*	0.80	15.88***
Model F	5.07	11.39	25.05	3.14	6.56	29.56		
$p <$	0.001	0.001	0.01	0.001	0.001	0.001		
Adjusted R^2	0.18	0.38	0.73	0.11	0.20	0.78		
DF (model)	2	5	11	2	5	11		

† $p < 0.10$; * $p < 0.05$; ** $p < 0.01$; *** $p < 0.001$.
SOURCE: Adapted from Peng and Luo (1999).
NOTE: a. The results are from a six-province survey of top managers at 127 firms in China. We measured these managers' networks with executives at buyer, supplier, and competitor firms, and with officials in various levels of the government. Standardized multiple regression is used to examine whether managerial networks or "traditional" strategy variables have a greater impact on two measures of firm performance. The higher the significance level (***), the more robust the results. Models 1 and 4 estimate the "net" impact of managerial networks. Models 2 and 5 assess the "net" impact of strategy variables. Finally, Models 3 and 6 focus on the joint impact of these two sets of determinants of firm performance. A MANOVA test is used to assess the relative importance of managerial networks and strategy variables on overall firm performance. The larger the F value, the more significant the impact.

(Tsang, 1998). The emergence of this new rule, again, stimulates more firms trying to adapt to this new reality to pay more attention to improving core competencies instead of engaging in excessive networking activities.

In such a rapidly changing environment, not every firm can adapt well, and many do poorly. Too often executives at SOEs and other poorly performing firms use institutional disadvantages as their excuse. They argue that privatized firms may have better incentive structures, that entrepreneurial start-ups may have more freedom in hiring and firing employees (as well as in bribing officials), and that foreign companies may enjoy preferential treatments provided by the government. Although each of these points may have some validity, it is difficult to argue that a company is systematically discriminated against by *every* aspect of its institutional environment. While SOEs are more likely to receive some form of government assistance, such as subsidies, cheap materials, and "policy" loans, privatized firms gradually have to become accountable to increasingly assertive shareholders, entrepreneurial outfits are more likely to be harassed by the tax and regulatory authorities, and foreign companies have to overcome a substantial "liability of foreignness."

In brief, firms are different not only because of their different national origins, industry conditions, and resource bases, but also due to their genetic coding and adaptive abilities. As firms increasingly have to compete on capabilities, competing on networks and connections alone is not likely to sustain a competitive advantage in these economies.

Question II: How Do Firms Behave?

Firms' strategic behavior can differ along a number of dimensions. One of the most popular ways to portray these differences is the Miles and Snow (1978) typology, which suggests four strategy types: Prospector, Defender, Analyzer, and Reactor. Defenders are firms with a narrow product market, a stable customer group, and an established organizational structure managed by older executives. In contrast, Prospectors have a changing product market, a focus on innovation and change, and a flexible organizational structure headed by younger managers. The Defender and the Prospector reside at opposite ends of a continuum of competitive strategies. The Analyzer strategy falls between Defenders and Prospectors on the continuum. Finally, Reactors have no consistent strategy and do not belong to the continuum.

TABLE 8.2 Strategic Groups Based on Ownership Differences			
	State-Owned Enterprises	*Privatized and Reformed Companies; Private-Public Hybrids; Foreign-Invested Firms*	*Privately Owned Start-Ups*
Primary Strategy	Defender	Analyzer	Prospector
Customer base	Stable	Mixed	Unstable
Product mix	Stable	Mixed	Changing
Attitude toward growth	Cautious	Mixed	Aggressive
Organizational structure	Bureaucratic, complex	Mixed	Informal, simple
Managers	Older, more conservative	Mixed	Younger, more aggressive

As alluded to in Chapters 4 and 6, most SOEs' strategies resemble those of *Defenders*, and most entrepreneurial start-ups appear to be *Prospectors* (Table 8.2). These two largely opposing strategies are mirror images of each other. On the other hand, it is more difficult to generalize about the strategic posture of privatized and reformed firms (Chapter 5), private-public hybrids (Chapter 6), and foreign-invested companies (Chapter 7). It seems plausible to suggest that, as a group, they are likely to exhibit an *Analyzer* strategy (Tan & Peng, 1998a). That is, these firms are diverse, flexible, and dynamic, willing to explore different strategies along the continuum. For privatized and reformed companies, how far away they have moved from their former life will determine their position on the strategy continuum between Defenders and Prospectors. Similarly, the actual strategy of private-public hybrids will depend on how strongly they are influenced by the two forms of ownership. Formerly collective and cooperative enterprises that have been recently leased to managers and entrepreneurs may still be under the supervision of certain government agencies and may be more Defender-like. On the other hand, private-public hybrids that are actually private firms in disguise are more likely to behave like Prospectors, despite the "red cap" they wear (Peng, 1997a). Given the diversity of foreign firms investing in transition economies, it is likely that they will adopt relatively different strategies vis-à-vis each other (but will still be viewed as a "foreign" group by local firms). For example, Japanese firms in China have been found to be more interested in establishing joint ventures with centrally controlled SOEs, indicating that Japanese firms may be more risk averse. On the other hand, American and Hong Kong firms are more likely to select partners that are controlled by lower-level governments in China, indicating a willingness to be more entrepreneurial and risk taking (Pan, 1997).

For firms within a particular industry, what we are essentially doing here is placing them in various *strategic groups* according to their ownership differences. In fact, this is the logic behind the chapter arrangements for the bulk of the book, Chapters 4 through 7. As an intermediate level of analysis between firm and industry, strategic groups have been explored by researchers for more than two decades. Yet, the field still struggles with the fundamental question: Do strategic groups really exist (Dranove, Peteraf, & Shanley, 1998)? Although no formal definition is universally accepted, a common definition for a strategic group is "a group of firms within the same industry making similar decisions in key areas" (Reger & Huff, 1993, p. 103). This loosely defined concept has resulted in a vigorous debate questioning its validity. Barney and Hoskisson (1990) and Dranove and colleagues (1998) argued that a strategic group exists *only* if the performance of a firm in the group is, at least partly, a function of group characteristics, controlling for firm and industry characteristics. Otherwise, strategic groups may be just an analytical convenience that does not add much. Given the mixed findings from studies in the West, this debate is far from resolved.

Research on firms in transition economies may contribute to the debate on strategic groups by focusing on one key variable, namely, ownership type (Tan & Peng, 1998a). One major problem with most existing studies is that they employ a host of complex and hard-to-measure variables, such as market structures and firm resources, that introduce a lot of "noise" in their results. Since practitioners are interested in intuitive simplicity, and the very purpose of strategic group studies is to understand the simplifying schemes that managers employ when conducting competitor analysis, there seems to be a need to *simplify* further the criteria used in identifying strategic groups.

Specifically, ownership type, a variable typically overlooked in existing research, may be a parsimonious yet powerful variable that can be used to predict strategic group memberships and their performance differentials in transition economies. Three underlying reasons contribute to this approach. First, practitioners in these countries usually use firm ownership to group different firms. A lot of data commonly available to practitioners in the West, especially about competitors, may not be available to executives in transition economies. As a result, a simple and easy-to-obtain variable such as ownership type is preferred. Second, many government policies, such as subsidy support, loans, and taxation, often differ based on firms' ownership types, which, in turn, are often differentiated in published government statistics. Finally, this ownership-based approach has been *empirically* supported by a number of studies using different samples, in different countries, during different time periods (Chow & Fung, 1996; Hooley, Cox, Shipley, & Fahy, 1996; Li, 1998; Luo, 1996; Tan & Li, 1996; Tan & Peng, 1998a). In general, foreign and foreign-invested firms tend to have higher performance (although there is no particular difference between joint ventures and wholly owned subsidiaries), followed by firms with private ownership (including public-private hybrids), and then by SOEs[1] (see Table 7.5). The net conclusion is that given the substantial performance differences, strategic groups based on ownership type seem to exist in transition economies.

Therefore, research on how firms behave differently in transition economies holds the promise of contributing to the development of the general literature on strategic groups (Tan & Peng, 1998a). Since most existing strategic group studies use samples of publicly traded corporations in the West, there is certainly no need to consider ownership differences. However, in an institutional environment characterized by ownership diversity, ownership differences matter a great deal. On the other hand, the identification of ownership-based strategic groups does not imply that there are permanent mobility barriers separating different groups. As previous chapters demonstrate, ownership types can be transformed by privatization, joint ventures, and hybrids, resulting in individual firms and strategic groups blurring their boundaries (Peng & Heath, 1996). Given the dynamism of these economies, these strategic groups may not be stable over the long run.

Nevertheless, it appears that strategic groups may be a useful concept, at least in the short run, to simplify competitor analysis based on a visible variable.

In sum, firms behave differently according to their strategy types and ownership types. There seems to be a link between ownership differences and strategic groups that can potentially shed light on the unresolved debate in the literature concerning whether strategic groups exist.

Question III: How Are Strategy Outcomes Affected by Strategy Processes?

This question connects strategy content with processes, and links strategy formulation with implementation. Large SOEs tend to have more rigid strategy processes, with the necessity of seeking government approval and support along the way. The impact of individual managers on strategy and performance may be limited due to these firms' sheer size. It is not surprising that they are more likely to choose a Defender strategy that has relatively infrequent changes. Private start-ups, on the other hand, are highly informal and flexible, with their owners having a greater impact on the organization and its bottom line. Therefore, a Prospector or guerrilla strategy represents a better fit for these firms, whose fast-paced maneuvers dazzle their competitors. Privatized and reformed firms are torn between their former selves and their new lease on life. They struggle to establish a new identity by being more responsive to market needs, yet at the same time continue to be plagued by inertia inherited from the old days. As a result, their link between strategy processes and outcomes may be the least consistent, sometimes fast-forwarding toward more competitive directions and other times backsliding toward the SOE way. Taken together, the strategies of various domestic firms in transition economies tend to be more *emergent* in nature. While the uncertain environment is not conducive to long-range planning, their lack of experience in formal strategic planning further leads to a flexible and opportunistic approach.

One of the best examples of *intended* strategy can be found in the option chain strategies employed by some foreign firms, which in general also exhibit close integration between strategy formulation and implementation. To be sure, not all foreign firms have such a sophisticated approach, and some of their strategies are quite emergent. What seem to be head and shoulders above the rest of the pack are a number of large, leading MNEs that engage in constant learning and assessing of opportunities through various options or "probes" such as joint ventures. These strategic probes, in turn, may incrementally lead to new strategic choices, either by converting joint ventures into wholly owned subsidiaries or by abandoning existing ventures and starting new exploration.

A gap between the emergent view of strategy, which suggests a pattern in a stream of incremental decisions, and the intended view, which portrays strategy as a grand plan, is a new view of strategy as a *stretch* focusing on strategic intent (Hamel & Prahalad, 1994). Strategic intent implies a significant stretch for the organization, which moves beyond the traditional notion of strategic fit as implied by the SWOT analysis. Since virtually no company has enough resources to pursue all the goals it wants to achieve, it is easy to be an inactive player in the strategy game and fall behind. There will always be "other" firms that seem to be better endowed. Domestic firms resent the seemingly endless sources of capital that foreign companies can tap into, while foreign companies marvel at the intractable bureaucratic maze that only domestic firms are able to navigate. SOEs envy the freedom of private firms, which, in turn, envy the protection that SOEs have. When confronting these challenges, too much attention to resource disadvantages and too much emphasis on strategic fit may prevent firms from looking forward.

However, as discussed in Question I above, resource endowments are a very poor predictor of future competitive success. It is *resourcefulness* that counts. As a result, it may be essential for top managers to set an aspiration that creates, by design, "a chasm between ambition and resources" (Hamel & Prahalad, 1994, p. 146). Such a mismatch prompts many successful firms to rise to the occasion by taking great strides to cross the chasm, as evidenced by the state-owned Szczecin Shipyard in Poland (Strategy in Action 4.1), the privatized Jenoptik in eastern Germany (Strategy in Action 5.3), the reformed Shanghai Industrial in China (Strategy in Action 5.2), the privately owned Vimpelcom in Russia (Strategy in Action 6.2), and the leading Western MNE, General Electric, which made the first large acquisition in CEE

(Strategy in Action 7.4). In each of these cases, the starting conditions were hardly encouraging, and resources almost always appeared to be inadequate. Yet top managers did have a relatively clear vision of the goal and a broad agenda of the capability-building challenges that lay ahead. Strategy outcomes at these firms are thus affected by processes that recognized the essential paradox that while strategy cannot be entirely planned, neither does it happen in the absence of a clearly articulated and widely shared aspiration. In other words, given that the future is rapidly changing, the more successful firms compete "on the edge" between today and tomorrow (Brown & Eisenhardt, 1998). Their hallmark is constant play and incremental improvements guided by broad strategic thrusts toward ambitious goals.

In brief, while there are examples of both emergent and intended strategies in transition economies, the most successful companies in these countries seem to have adopted a view of strategy as a stretch that helps bridge the gap between the two diametrically opposed ways of connecting strategy outcomes with processes.

Question IV: What Determines the Scope of the Firm?

The answer to what determines the scope of the firm boils down to the growth of the firm. What fuels the growth? What constrains it? And what are its benefits? If a firm can be viewed as a bundle of resources and capabilities, then firm growth is motivated by top managers' attempts to utilize these resources fully. Managers have three strategic choices when deciding how to grow the firm; namely, (a) generic expansion, (b) mergers and acquisitions, and (c) developing interfirm networks. Each choice is limited by a set of constraints. Research in transition economies has contributed to the literature centered on this question by highlighting the impact of *institutional* imperatives and constraints on firm growth strategies (Peng, 1994, 1997a, in press-a; Peng & Heath, 1996; Peng & Tan, 1998).

Specifically, due to a lack of organizational resources that allow for sustained generic growth and to a lack of market-supporting institutions that enable mergers and acquisitions, a strategy of developing interfirm networks is typically chosen initially. Over time, however, the benefits of this strategy—in particular, trust and mutual understanding that facilitate flexibility—tend to be outweighed by the transaction cost problems of managing and coordinating large and diverse enterprise networks on an informal basis. As a result, turning informal networks into formal holdings, parent-subsidiary relationships, and large multiproduct corporations and business groups has been on the agendas of numerous firms throughout transition economies. In the process, firms become increasingly interested in a generic expansion strategy, an acquisition strategy, or both.

The growth of the firm in transition economies, therefore, evolves from an informal stage based on interfirm networks to a more formal stage featuring generic expansion and acquisitions centered on expanding the scope of the firm. Two questions beg for explanation: (a) Does a firm benefit from its increased scope? (b) Does a business unit benefit from being part of a diversified firm? More than 20 years of research in the West have not provided satisfactory answers to these important questions (Dess, Gupta, Hennart, & Hill, 1995). Even less is known about how to answer these questions in transition economies, where corporate diversification is a more recent phenomenon.

Without much knowledge about the evidence that does exist on the pitfalls of overdiversification (Hoskisson & Hitt, 1994), many executives and government officials in transition economies such as China and Russia become highly enthusiastic about conglomerate diversification, believing that "the bigger, the better" ("The Bigger, the Better," 1998). In particular, they studied the South Korean experience of using government intervention to create large-scale business groups (*chaebol*) with considerable interest. Facing strong MNEs flexing their muscles in transition economies (Chapter 7), many local managers and officials became convinced that individual domestic firms' highly informal and entrepreneurial networking activities were not likely to result in world-class and world-scale competitors that could survive the onslaught of MNEs, and that only through Korean-style top-down, select government intervention could large business groups be created (Amsden, Kochanowicz, & Taylor, 1994). As a result, with renewed government interest the development of "financial-industrial groups" in Russia and "enterprise groups" in China has been extensive and visible since the 1990s (Freinkman, 1995; Johnson, 1997; Lan, 1998;

Peng, 1997a; Prokop, 1995). In addition to the immediate issue of foreign competition discussed above, there are powerful arguments in favor of such a strategy (Granovetter, 1994; Khanna & Palepu, 1997). Given the lack of market-supporting institutions, managers and firms in transition economies often have to perform, by themselves, basic functions normally reserved for outside organizations in the West, such as obtaining information, raising capital, interpreting regulations, and enforcing contracts. As a result, it may be more efficient to have business groups that consolidate these functions within one hierarchy and leverage their reputation to develop multiple products and industries. These arguments essentially suggest that although seen as dinosaurs in the West, conglomerates may still add value and generate synergy in transition economies.

Unfortunately, just as many firms, managers, and officials in China and Russia began to embrace the Korean *chaebol* model in earnest, the pitfalls of *chaebols'* overdiversification were exposed to the fullest extent possible in the Asian financial crisis that began in 1997. Fueled by earlier success, *chaebols'* "breakneck" growth (including some ventures as far away as Poland and Uzbekistan) indeed broke their necks and many of them were brought to the brink of bankruptcy (Biers, 1998; "What to Do About Asia?" 1998). It seems painfully obvious that conglomerates in emerging economies, such as South Korea, China, and Russia, may suffer after all from the same problems that plague conglomerates in the West: The more activities a business group engages in, the harder it is for the head office to coordinate, control, and invest in them properly. Unless a group is ready to offer concrete benefits to its affiliates, business units may be better off as independent companies. There is little reason to believe that executives of Chinese and Russian conglomerates are able to successfully tackle such a daunting challenge, at which their Western and Korean colleagues have admitted failure. Overall, there seems to be an interesting pattern of diffusion of the conglomerate diversification strategy, first in the West, then to emerging economies such as South Korea, and more recently to transition economies such as China and Russia. Given the increasing global evidence pointing to the pitfalls of conglomerates, the wisdom of moving toward a strategy of diversification in transition economies where synergy may be elusive remains highly questionable.

In sum, the scope of the firm is determined by whether the firm is interested in growth, the strategic choices it makes, and the benefits its enlarged scope offers. Although difficult to quantify, there seems to be a limit beyond which further growth may backfire. This rule holds true throughout the rest of the world, and is likely to be valid in transition economies as well.

Question V: What Determines the International Success or Failure of Firms?

Foreign firms competing abroad have to possess significant competitive advantages; otherwise, they have no hope of overcoming their inherent "liability of foreignness." Transition economies have become a new battleground of multinational competition.[2] The most successful foreign companies are those that possess and leverage three-pronged advantages based on ownership, location, and internalization (Dunning, 1993). Ownership advantages do not require full ownership of everything; however, owning a few crucial resources such as capital and technology may lead to valuable capabilities that are difficult for domestic firms to imitate.

Location advantages come from both the origin of foreign companies and the location of their new activities. Companies from highly competitive economies such as Japan and the United States are likely to overwhelm rivals in less competitive markets. Firms from countries such as Austria, Germany, Hong Kong, and Taiwan, with historical expertise in dealing with transition economies, are also likely to gain an upper hand in these new markets. Location advantages of transition economies are driven by geography, factor endowments, and institutional infrastructure. Geographic advantages are self-evident: simply witness the booming FDI activities in South China clusters neighboring Hong Kong and CEE clusters neighboring Austria, Germany, and Italy. Factor endowments such as low-cost labor are also a draw for FDI. However, beyond geographic and factor advantages, another set of advantages centers on institutional infrastructure. Most foreign companies are not keen on doing business in a location where a minimum threshold of market-supporting policies and institutions have not been put in place. Without a credible commitment to protect basic property rights, a lot of transactions simply would not have happened (North, 1990; Williamson, 1996). Otherwise, why would South Korean companies go through all the trouble to go to far away places like Poland and Uzbekistan? Why wouldn't they flock to North Korea?

Internalization advantages refer to foreign firms' abilities to preserve, strengthen, and develop their knowledge-based proprietary assets. While historically the flow of such assets as patents, processes, and technologies have been a one-way diffusion from home countries to a variety of host countries, during the more recent "innovation-driven" stage, FDI has also been increasingly used to undertake R&D abroad in order to tap into the innovation capabilities of host countries (Peng, 1995b; Peng & Wang, in press). Therefore, FDI in transition economies has not only concentrated on low-cost locations as production platforms for both domestic and export consumption, but also focused on industries that have strong innovation capabilities, such as the Russian aerospace industry (see Table 4.4) and the Hungarian lighting industry (see Strategy in Action 7.4).

It is important to note that transition economies are not easy markets and that not all foreign companies are successful there (Luo & Peng, 1999). Rather, many have failed miserably and have had to pull out. Others hang in there, hoping for the elusive "long-term" profits to materialize. The best foreign companies tend to be those that have successfully acquired, deployed, and developed competitive advantages based on ownership, location, and internalization.

Summary

These five questions represent some of the most fundamental "puzzles" about strategy and competition in transition economies. While other questions could be raised, they "all relate in one way or another to these five developed here" (Rumelt et al., 1994, p. 570). Piecing together evidence from a wide variety of sources and working with colleagues on three continents, I have attempted to address the state of the art of the answers to these five questions throughout the book. Nevertheless, these questions continue to remain intriguing puzzles for scholars and practitioners. The next two sections deal with their concerns.

RESEARCH PROGRESS
AND CHALLENGES

Up to this point, strategic management in transition economies has not played a major role in affecting the research agenda of the strategy field. While many Western MNEs have decided to concentrate disproportionately *more* resources on these markets of tomorrow, the strategy field as a whole, despite efforts by some individual scholars, seems to have paid disproportionately *less* attention to these economies in which millions of people and thousands of firms are collectively searching for competitive solutions to their problems. A complete search of all articles published by the field's premium outlet, the *Strategic Management Journal*, between its inception in 1980 and the end of 1998 found only four articles dealing with transition economies among the hundreds published.[3] In other words, the bibliography at the end of this book would have been substantially shorter had I consulted only research published in *SMJ*. This problem, however, is not confined to the strategy field. The broader field of management and organization research seems to have been plagued by a similar lack of interest, leaving important issues such as how to compete in transition economies to our colleagues in economics, sociology, political science, and area studies (Hambrick, 1994; Peng, 1994; Peng, Lu, Shenkar, & Wang, in press). In the long run, this tendency to eschew engagement with these important topics may keep the field "on the sidelines in debates about issues in which it potentially has much to contribute" (Pfeffer, 1997, p. 24).

Hoping to help correct the prevailing bias of the field, the writing of this book is motivated by a deep curiosity about, to use the language of Williamson (1996), "What is going on there?" and underpinned by a strong conviction that strategy researchers have much to gain as well as to offer by focusing on transition economies. This section attempts to take stock of our progress and offer some thoughts about fruitful directions for future research.

Testing and Developing Theories

Perhaps one of the most challenging and potentially rewarding research areas is testing and developing theories of the firm (Chapter 4).

Theories of the firm have been developed based largely on the experience of the Western firm. How relevant these theories are to the firm in transition economies thus presents a major challenge to examine their universality (Peng & Heath, 1996). It is likely that some theories may be more relevant than others. Some scholars may argue that countries such as China and Russia, given their "strange" communist past, may represent an anomaly, in that failure to support certain theories does not reduce their explanatory and predictive power (Pye, 1992b). On the other hand, it could be suggested that if some theories do not apply to a nonmarginal case (after all, more people work in Chinese companies and more Russian firms have been privatized than in any other nations), they must be judged not to be universal (Buck, Filatotchev, & Wright, 1998; Peng, Buck, & Filatotchev, 1999). Given that most social science theories are contingency- and context-based, knowing their boundaries may not be a bad thing (Cheng, 1994; Numagami, 1998; Rosenzweig, 1994; Shenkar & von Glinow, 1994).

In addition to theory testing, transition economies also present a "viable research laboratory" to develop new theories of the firm (Shenkar & von Glinow, 1994, p. 56). Massive efforts in privatization and reform can actually be conceptualized as different experiments to construct the "ideal" firm (Williamson, 1995, 1996). "Native categories" may be necessary in order to capture—and generalize from—these organizational and managerial experiments involving one third of the human race (Buckley & Chapman, 1997). Historically, far-reaching transitions have greatly stimulated intellectual development in the social sciences. More than two hundred years ago, the rise of capitalism gave birth to economics as a discipline. About one hundred years ago, sociology began as a "science of transition," studying "the epochal shifts from tradition to modernity" (Stark, 1996, p. 992). At approximately the same time, management started as a modern field of inquiry with Fredrick Taylor's writings on scientific management. It is conceivable that the unprecedented managerial and organizational challenges in transition economies will give rise to ideas, theories, and paradigms that can propel management and organization into the "field of the next millennium," to which strategic management can make important contributions through theory development. Therefore, strategy scholars stand to gain enormously both in terms of theoretical advancement and practical impact by seizing this opportunity (Peng, Lu, et al., in press).

An Institutional Perspective

As stressed throughout the book, an area in which research on transition economies has made major contributions to the literature is the institutional perspective on business strategy (Peng, in press-a). Shown in Figure 8.1, mainstream research in strategy focuses on competition in existing markets where market-supporting institutions have been well established. These broad institutions, such as property-rights-based legal and regulatory frameworks, have been taken for granted. As a result, they fade into the background, which is generally ignored by researchers. Competing in transition economies from which these institutional frameworks are largely absent reminds us how important their influence is (North, 1990). In a nutshell, "no organization can be properly understood apart from its wider social and cultural context" (Scott, 1995, p. 151). Viewed from this institutional perspective, strategic choices that Western firms make are not institution-free at all; instead, certain choices are made precisely because of the influence of the particular institutional frameworks in developed countries (Hillman & Keim, 1995). The institutional perspective, therefore, sheds considerable light on the question of why firms differ.

When trying to understand why firms differ in attributes, strategies, and performance, most scholars might start with cultural differences (Hofstede, 1980, 1991). Among the transition economies, firms in China, in particular, have been noted as embedded in the East Asian cultural tradition that places a premium on informal interpersonal ties and interfirm relations (Chen, 1995; Hwang, 1987; Hofstede & Bond, 1988; Shenkar & Ronen, 1987). At the same time, identifiable similarities between Chinese managers and their counterparts in CEE and the NIS are reported (Child & Markoczy, 1993; Peng, 1997a; Ralston, Holt, Terpstra, & Yu, 1997; Whitley, Henderson, Czaban, & Lengyel, 1996), calling for explanations beyond culture. This quest for explanations has increasingly converged on an institutional perspective, taking into account the *common* institutional background that managers and reformers in transition economies in Asia and Europe have to confront (Kornai, 1992; Peng & Heath, 1996). The institutional perspective has been particularly useful for explaining and predicting how the institutional environment during the transition has created incentives for organizations to "blur" their boundaries, through relationship building based on managers' personal trust and informal agreements, in order to achieve necessary growth and expansion. This perspective can also explain and predict how strategic choices evolve as reforms and transitions deepen and market-supporting institutions develop further. It will also shed considerable light, given the normative pressures for organizations to conform to managerial fads and fashions of the day (Abrahamson, 1996), on why and how some follower firms imitate their trend-setting counterparts (e.g., in various reform measures, in venturing to these economies from abroad) while not actually knowing the concrete benefits of doing so (Peng, in press-a).

Compared with other theoretical perspectives, the institutional perspective is still in its "adolescence" (Powell & DiMaggio, 1991; Scott, 1995). Given the preliminary stage of theoretical development and the difficulty of gaining research access (Adler, Campbell, & Laurent, 1989; Shenkar, 1994), most existing studies have been case based and qualitative in nature. While findings are encouraging and cumulative, it is often difficult to draw conclusions that have generalizability beyond the few case studies reported. After more than two decades of the development of the general literature on the "new" institutional theory and more than one decade of its application to transition economies, most scholars (including noninstitutionalists) and practitioners would agree that institutions matter, especially in these countries. In order to make further progress, future researchers, according to an influential institutionalist, Walter Powell (1996), "must tackle the harder and more interesting issues of how they [institutions] matter, under what circumstances, to what extent, and in what ways" (p. 297). In other words, instead of suggesting broad-brushed statements often heard in the literature, such as "interpersonal connections are always helpful," researchers are challenged to specify *exactly* how helpful they are (Peng & Luo, 1998, 1999). To the extent that management studies are susceptible to being caught up by fads and fashions (Abrahamson, 1996), it will be important to limit the "degree of freedom" when making sweeping statements if we as a field endeavor to be more rigorous and relevant. These tasks remain one of the greatest research challenges in future work.

A Micro-Macro Link

A natural extension of the institutional perspective is to focus on the link between executives and managers as strategists, who are microlevel individual actors, and firm strategies and performance, which are macrolevel constructs. Managers all over the world devote considerable time, resources, and energy to interacting with external entities (Mintzberg, 1973) and create and manage organizations that embody their personal backgrounds and preferences (Child, 1972; Hambrick & Mason, 1984). In transition economies, where thousands of organizations are being rebuilt or built from scratch and where market-supporting institutions are rare, the impact of individual managers on their organizations may be stronger, thus presenting a fascinating ground for exploring the micro-macro link (Peng & Luo, 1998, 1999).

When we discuss how "firms" develop their relations and blur their boundaries, what we really mean is that top managers develop interpersonal relations across organizational boundaries and translate these microlevel personal relations into macrolevel interfirm links. While most interorganizational relations have a strong social component that serves as catalyst and glue, over time, most of these successful relations are likely to be formalized in developed economies (Gulati, 1995, 1998). What is interesting in transition economies is that the process leading to eventual formalization of interfirm relations is very long, compared with what would have happened elsewhere. Sometimes, firms are not allowed to combine forces formally because of regulations, other times firms cannot legally join hands due to a lack of regulations (Peng, 1997a). Yet, these firms often have to compete, grow, and collaborate. Social capital embodied in personal relations thus becomes more important in such imperfect competition characterized by weak institutional support and distorted information. Armed with useful ties and contacts, a manager "becomes an entrepreneur in the literal sense of the word—a person who adds value by brokering the connection between others" (Burt, 1997, p. 342). Therefore, it is not surprising that the role of individual managers' boundary-spanning activities in the absence of market-supporting institutions becomes all the more important.

This social network perspective is consistent with a number of existing theories in strategy. According to the resource-based view (Barney, 1991), these ties can be regarded as valuable and unique intangible resources that are very difficult and time-consuming for competitors to replicate, thus giving firms that possess them a significant advantage. Similarly, transaction cost theory (Williamson, 1991) regards this mode of informal contracting as "relational contracting," which may help save transaction costs. In the mainstream literature, resource-based, transaction cost, and social network perspectives all suffer from a lack of concrete empirical findings unambiguously pointing to the micro-macro link due to substantial problems in measuring these highly intangible resources (Godfrey & Hill, 1995). These problems are magnified in transition economies. Therefore, research on the micro-macro link in these countries is both a significant challenge to overcome and a golden opportunity to extend the mainstream literature (Peng & Luo, 1998, 1999).

Currently we know very little about how the micro-macro link works. We know that managers in these countries engage in a lot of networking with other players. But with whom? How? And why? Two barriers prevent us from probing deeper into these dynamics. First, in a world where personal contacts are guarded as a source of competitive advantage, many managers may have the attitude that, "Who I know is exclusive information. I hardly make it known even to my friends" (quoted in Yeung & Tung, 1996, p. 6). As a result, there is little hope that researchers can obtain needed information from published sources or from a "name generator" approach typically employed in social network analysis (Burt, 1992). A second reason is that while many personal networking activities are legitimate, there are almost inevitably some dubious, secretive, and sometimes illegal activities. As a result, direct and sensitive questions, such as, "How much did you spend on gifts to government officials?" are not likely to bode well with managers. Researchers often have to ask far more general questions, such as, "How much did you spend on entertainment?" These broad questions may introduce noise into the data, let alone the difficulty of verifying such information from independent sources, something that is often demanded by top-tier journal editors and reviewers. Taken together, these two barriers require that researchers spend a lot of time establishing rapport with managers who will then feel comfortable sharing information. These requirements often necessitate a case-based, qualitative methodology that has to sacrifice generalizability due to small samples.

Despite these challenges, preliminary work on the micro-macro link has begun to shed some light on these dynamics (Peng & Luo, 1998, 1999). We know that managers cultivate extensive interpersonal ties with their counterparts at other firms such as suppliers, buyers, and sometimes competitors. They also like to be on good personal terms with government officials. What is more interesting is that compared with ties with managers at other firms, ties with government officials are found to have a more significant impact on firm performance (the standardized regression coefficients for ties with officials in Models 1, 3, 4, and 6 in Table 8.1 are larger and more significant than those for ties with other managers). Sampled managers also believe that ties with officials are more important (the larger F value from a MANOVA test in Table 8.1).

While these findings by Peng and Luo (1999) are from a 1997 survey of firms in China, where the government is still influential, it remains to be seen whether similar results hold in CEE and the NIS, where government influence has been significantly diminished. Moreover, these results were obtained from a survey by asking very general questions, such as, "How extensively have managers at your firm utilized personal ties with certain players?" Future scholars tackling the important but elusive micro-macro link can focus on more visible and less sensitive information, such as whether managers are demographically similar (e.g., age, education; Tsui & Farh, 1997), have previous experience in the same firm or government agency (Hambrick & Mason, 1984), work in the same industry (Geletkancyz & Hambrick, 1997), share interlocking director ties (Au, Peng, & Wang, in press), are employed at domestic or foreign firms (Lyles & Salk, 1996), and/or have relations with officials at different levels of government

(Walder, 1995). These efforts hold a strong potential to allow for deeper probes into the much-heralded but little-explored micro-macro link in transition economies, and to enrich the mainstream literature as well.

A Focus on Alliances

Another significant development of strategy research on transition economies occurs in the area of international strategic alliances. This area has been popular for three reasons. First, forces of globalization in the past two decades have attracted a large number of scholars paying more attention to international business issues (Boyacigiller & Adler, 1991). Second, this particular research area resonates well with the explosive growth of the mainstream literature on strategic alliances and joint ventures over the past two decades (Contractor & Lorange, 1988; Dunning, 1995). Finally, it is more appealing to foreign firms that need critical information about how to enter and operate in transition economies.

Judged by the number of publications, this area probably has received the most extensive attention and made the most visible progress. Researchers have covered a number of issues, such as investment environment (Beamish, 1993; Daniels, Krug, & Nigh, 1986; Estrin & Meyer, 1998), partner selection (Luo, 1997), venture negotiations (Davidson, 1987; Yan & Gray, 1994), entry modes (Sharma, 1995; Tse, Pan, & Au, 1997), ownership structure (Pan, 1996; Shan, 1991), investment timing (Luo & Peng, 1998), operational problems (McCarthy & Puffer, 1997; Peng, 1995a, in press-b; Shenkar, 1990), and organizational learning (Hooley et al., 1996; Luo & Peng, in press; Lyles & Salk, 1996). Nevertheless, three significant problems remain. The first is an almost exclusive focus from the foreign firm perspective at the expense of the local firm. To the extent that alliances are formed by two or more parties, the perspective of one particular party is, at best, only half of the story. While foreign firms are searching for domestic partners, local companies are also actively searching for prospective partners from abroad (Shenkar & Li, in press). Scholars may have missed a great opportunity to connect international business research from the foreign firm perspective with work on indigenous firms (Child, 1994). Since domestic firms are eager to use network-based strategies to achieve growth, the active courtship of foreign investors should be interpreted as one facet of these strategies at work (Peng & Heath, 1996, p. 519). Few studies have attempted to understand the dynamics surrounding these alliances from both sides, thus calling for more comprehensive research in the future.

A second problem is a strong emphasis on entry modes and less attention to postentry operations and evolution. This focus is not surprising, because market entry into these countries is a recent phenomenon. However, too much research on entry may result in reduced relevance to practitioners, whose more recent concerns increasingly turn to postentry operational and managerial issues (McCarthy & Puffer, 1997). In light of a large number of joint venture problems, how companies get "divorced" may be as interesting as how they get "married" (Peng & Shenkar, 1997). As more and more foreign companies exercise their call options by converting joint ventures into wholly owned subsidiaries or by abandoning unprofitable ventures, carrying out the option chain strategy successfully also becomes more important than the entry strategy (Peng, 1997b).

The last problem is too little research on other entry modes, even among entry mode studies. There are few studies that explore how companies use export strategies to penetrate these markets (Peng, 1998; Peng, Hill, & Wang, in press; Peng & Ilinitch, 1998a, 1998b). There is even less research on foreign acquisitions (Capener, 1996; Marer & Mabert, 1996; Vanhonacker, 1997). Rising interest in wholly owned subsidiaries as a mode of entry also requires more research attention. The extensive existing literature on export and acquisition strategies in the West provides a good launching pad for studying how these strategies are played out in transition economies.

In sum, research on strategic alliances in transition economies has made great progress over the past two decades, asserting its influence increasingly in mainstream journals. Future challenges lie in how to understand the local partner's perspective and connect it with research on indigenous firms, how to move beyond the initial entry, and how to understand other entry modes.

Summary

In the past, social science inquiry on socialist countries was largely relegated to the domain of area studies and set apart from mainstream, discipline-based research (Pye, 1992b). Recently, studies on transition economies have increasingly moved to the "center stage" of social science research (Nee & Matthews, 1996, p. 431). Strategy research is no exception. Significant progress has been made on the institutional perspective, the micro-macro link, and alliance strategies. In addition, there are also smaller pockets of strategy research that may emerge as substantial streams of work. They include corporate governance (Chapter 5), entrepreneurship and public-private hybrids (Chapter 6), entry timing, organizational learning, and location strategies (Chapter 7), as well as strategic groups (Chapter 8). The road ahead lies in whether scholars can develop these emerging streams of work into programmatic and cumulative bodies of findings, and, most important, test existing theories and develop new ones in these countries. These endeavors hold the potential to enrich the development of the discipline greatly while helping managerial practices, which we turn to next.

COMPETING FOR THE FUTURE— AND WINNING

From a territory unknown to strategy researchers and practitioners two decades ago, transition economies have attracted substantial scholarly and managerial attention. Still, our quest for more knowledge about these countries never seems to be satisfied. For example: "The economic system of Russia has undergone such rapid changes that it is impossible to obtain a precise and accurate account of it. . . . Almost everything one can say about the country is true and false at the same time." While this passage is certainly correct for Russia as well as all other transition economies today, it was actually written by an influential economist, John Maynard Keynes, in 1925.[4] Thus, we are confronted by several fundamental questions: Are the transitions over? What will be the future of these economies? Stark (1996) suggested that a distinctive "East European capitalism" will emerge, which will be neither the Anglo-American version nor the Asian version of capitalism. Boisot and Child (1996) believed that China would evolve into a "network capitalism" that is neither socialism nor capitalism in the classical sense. Given the intermediate nature of the transitions, I argued that "postsocialism" is perhaps a better term for capturing the essence of these economies (Peng & Tan, 1998).

However, while scholars can afford to debate the nature of the transitions and wait until breakthrough findings emerge, current and would-be managers around the world need to equip themselves with improved knowledge about the strategies of domestic and foreign firms in transition economies because they will have to compete and/or collaborate with them in the future. How, then, do they craft and implement business strategies in such an uncertain future?

The premise of this book is that transitions and changes are pervasive. Therefore, the key strategic challenges facing managers competing in transition economies are to anticipate when possible, react quickly, and lead change where appropriate. A fundamental dilemma is how to do this, not just once or every now and then, but consistently. What are the "rules" of competing in this uncertain terrain? The following summary distills the themes of this book into three broad rules that I have found to characterize firms that have succeeded in these countries—so far.[5]

Rule I: Develop Foresight

Why do some firms seem to possess over-the-horizon radar while others appear to be walking backward into the future? The most successful companies first *unlearn* some parts of their past before finding the future. While some firms, like entrepreneurial start-ups, may start from scratch, most firms in transition economies carry the baggage of the past, most of which needs to be unlearned. Even foreign firms may need to change some of their assumptions and routines when entering and operating in these new markets. Unlearning is not easy. It begins only when managers and employees are confronted with the potential disconnection between the success recipes of the past and the competitive challenges of the future (often in a "valley of tears"; see Figure 2.1). Unlearning the past enables the exploration of foresight that was previously thought impossible. Developing foresight about industries and markets requires not only deep insights into the evolution of institutions, capabilities, and technologies, but also rests as much on *imagination* as on prediction. To create the future, a company must first be capable of imagining it. Szczecin Shipyard's foresight about the global demand for mid-size container ships that it could fill while it was still in a big mess (Strategy in Action 4.1) and GE's ambition to dominate Europe through an acquisition in Hungary when no MNE was willing to invest on such a scale in CEE (Strategy in Action 7.4) can serve as powerful examples here.

Rule II: Stretch the Organization

Reality and imagination are usually separate. Strategy is about making a difference that connects reality with imagination. Because strategy is the soul of a company, it must be an integral part of the whole organization, not just the exclusive territory of a few top executives.

Strategists at successful companies start with strategic intent, which is a set of ambitious goals beyond what would normally be implied by a traditional SWOT analysis in search of strategic fit. These goals are high, but not as outrageous as such utopian goals as the attainment of global communism, which can now be dismissed as a bad joke. These goals, moreover, are communicated throughout the organization and generate excitement among employees. In the absence of clearly defined challenges, employees are more or less powerless to contribute to competitiveness. This contrasts sharply with the old days, when the goals of eventual communist victory were set high but clues for reaching them were few, leading to a widespread indifference that basically said, "It's none of my business." Stretching the organization thus entails challenging and exciting managers and employees proactively, routinely, and relentlessly. Examples of successful stretching include the communication of the company's visions between top managers and the workers' council at eastern Germany's Jenoptik during its sink-or-swim days (Strategy in Action 5.3) and the excitement generated among managers and employees at Vimpelcom about the prospects of becoming the first firm in Russia to list its stocks on the New York Stock Exchange (Strategy in Action 6.2).

Rule III: Leverage Resources

Developing foresight and stretching the organization will be meaningless if the firm does not use its resources and capabilities wisely. Most firms in transition economies start with a poor resource base, such as insufficient capital, run-down facilities, and obsolete technologies. Their only hope is to leverage whatever productive resources they do have, such as entrepreneurial drive and government connections, by concentrating resources on key strategic goals. In military terms, this strategy is one of encirclement rather than confrontation. In other words, resource-poor firms must outmaneuver rather than overpower their resource-rich competitors, leading to a guerrilla strategy typically found among smaller firms. Specifically, resource-poor firms cannot match their more affluent competitors on spending dollar for dollar, cannot afford the same entry costs, and cannot tolerate the same inefficiency and slack. In a nutshell, they cannot risk playing by their resource-rich rivals' rules; they have to do more with less. When they cannot directly compete on resources, they compete on *resourcefulness*. China's New Industries Investment Company (Strategy in Action 6.1) and Poland's Optimus Computer (Strategy in Action 6.3) typify this entrepreneurial approach. Not only do resource-poor companies need to leverage their resources, firms with abundant resources also need to do that. The ability to make bigger bets may sometimes bring bigger payoffs, but it is just as likely to bring bigger disasters. Occidental Petroleum's experience in China (Strategy in Action 7.2) serves as a case in point here. Smart resource-rich companies develop option chains, incrementally making bets and improving their odds of winning.

In conclusion, these rules, as well as the entire book, are but the entering wedges that start to probe into the workings of business strategies in transition economies; they are certainly not the final words. Companies' experiments and our learning about them are unlikely to stop anytime soon in the new millennium. One unchanging certainty is that as markets in these countries become more competitive, strategies are likely to become more important than ever. If this book could convey only one message, I would like it to be a sense of the staggering power that strategies and competition have to make things better—both for domestic and foreign companies that participate in the transitions and for economies that embrace these transitions.

NOTES

1. It is important to note that these are very broad generalizations and that exceptions certainly exist. For every strategic group, there are firms with superb performance and firms with embarrassing performance.

2. Ideally, the answer to Question V would also cover how firms from transition economies compete abroad. Such firms, so far, have been exceptions rather than the rule. Nevertheless, some of them are becoming increasingly active in overseas markets. While their activities have been reported by Au, Peng, and Wang (in press), "The China Connection" (1996), Elenkov (1995), Peng, Au, and Wang (1999), Wu (1993), and Young, Huang, and McDermott (1996), there is very little concrete empirical evidence about the scale and scope of these endeavors. Given this book's focus on business strategies *in* (not outside) transition economies, I have decided to leave this issue unexplored and look forward to seeing future work in this area.

3. The four articles published in the *Strategic Management Journal* are Adler, Braham, and Graham (1992), Tan and Litschert (1994), and Pan (1997) on China, and Elenkov (1997) on Bulgaria.

4. Quoted in Lavigne (1996, p. 92).

5. This section also draws heavily from the work of some of the best minds in strategy, such as Brown and Eisenhardt (1998), D'Aveni (1994), Hamel and Prahalad (1994), and Porter (1998).

APPENDIX

Useful Internet Resources for Further Research

Business Publications

Bloomberg Personal	http://bloomberg.com/
Business Week	http://www.businessweek.com/
CNN World News	http://www.cnn.com/world/
The Economist	http://www.economist.com/
Financial Times	http://www.ft.com/
Fortune	http://www.pathfinder.com/fortune/
Wall Street Journal	http://www.wsj.com/

Country Information

CIA World Factbook	http://www.odci.gov/cia/publications/
Country risk grading	http://www.efic.gov.au/
Political and economic risk in Asia	http://www.asiarisk.com/
Russia: State Information Services	http://www.skate.ru/
Yahoo: Regional/countries	http://www.yahoo.com/Regional/Countries/

International Organizations

Electronic Embassy	http://www.embassy.org/
International Monetary Fund	http://www.imf.org/
Organisation for Economic Co-operation and Development	http://www/oecd.org/
United Nations	http://www.un.org/
UN Information Services	http://undcp.org/unlinks.html
World Bank	http//www.worldbank.org
World Trade Organization	http://www.wto.org/

University International Business Resources

Business resources on the Web: International business
http://www.idbsu.edu/cyclops/busintl.htm

CIBER Web
http://www.ciber.centers.purdue.edu

Global Business Center
GlobalBusinessCenter/http://www.lib.csufresno.edu/

International business directory
http://international.byu.edu/ibd/directory

International business resources on the WWW
http://www.ciber.bus.msu.edu/busres.htm

International business resources page
http://sunsite.unc.edu/reference/moss/business/

Internet resources for international economics & business
http://dylee.keel.econ.ship.edu/INTNTL/int_home.htm

Ohio State CIBER
http://www.cob.ohio-state.edu/ciberweb

Resources for international business research
http://www.libraries.rutgers.edu/rulib/socsci/busi.intbus.html

Virtual international business and economic sources
http://www1.uncc.edu/lis/library/reference/intbus/

Virtual library: International affairs resources
http://www.pitt.edu/ian/ianres.html

U.S. Government Sources

Library of Congress	http://www.loc.gov/
U.S. Agency for International Development	http://www.info.usaid.gov/
U.S. Department of Commerce: International Trade Administration	http://www.ita.doc.gov/
U.S. Department of Commerce: National Trade Databank STAT-USA	http://www.itaiep.doc.gov/
U.S. Department of State	http://www.state.gov/
U.S. International Trade Commission	http://www.usitc.gov/
U.S. Trade and Development Agency	http://www.tda.gov/
U.S. Trade Representative	http://www.ustr.gov/

REFERENCES

Abrahamson, E. (1996). Management fashion. *Academy of Management Review, 21*, 254-285.

Academy of Management Journal. (1998). Special research forum call for papers: Enterprise strategies in emerging economies, *41*(1), back cover.

Adam, J. (1989). *Economic reforms in the Soviet Union and Eastern Europe since the 1960s.* New York: St. Martin's.

Adams, W., & Brock, J. (1993). *Adam Smith goes to Moscow: A dialogue on radical reform.* Princeton, NJ: Princeton University Press.

Adler, N., Braham, R., & Graham, J. (1992). Strategy implementation: A comparison of face-to-face negotiations in the People's Republic of China and the United States. *Strategic Management Journal, 13*, 449-466.

Adler, N., Campbell, N., & Laurent, A. (1989). In search of appropriate methodology: From outside the People's Republic of China looking in. *Journal of International Business Studies, 20*, 61-74.

Afanassieva, M., & Couderc, M. (1998). Restructuring of R&D organizations and the defense industry in the Russian Federation. *Journal of Applied Management Studies, 7*, 33-57.

Aharoni, Y. (1981). Performance evaluation of state-owned enterprises: A process perspective. *Management Science, 27*, 1340-1347.

Aharoni, Y. (1986). *The evolution and management of state-owned enterprises.* Cambridge, MA: Ballinger.

Alchian, A. (1965). The basis of some recent advances in the theory of management of the firm. *Journal of Industrial Economics, 14*, 30-41.

Alchian, A., & Demsetz, H. (1972). Production, information costs, and economic organization. *American Economic Review, 62*, 777-795.

Aldcroft, D., & Morewood, S. (1995). *Economic change in Eastern Europe since 1918.* Aldershot, UK: Edward Elgar.

Aldrich, H. (1979). *Organizations and environments.* Englewood Cliffs, NJ: Prentice Hall.

Aldrich, H., & Auster, E. (1986). Even dwarfs started small: Liabilities of age and size and their strategic implications. *Research in Organizational Behavior, 8*, 165-198.

Aldrich, H., & Fiol, C. M. (1994). Fools rush in? The institutional context of industry creation. *Academy of Management Review, 19,* 645-670.

Aldrich, H., & Waldinger, R. (1990). Ethnicity and entrepreneurship. *Annual Review of Sociology, 16,* 111-135.

Aldrich, H., & Zimmer, C. (1986). Entrepreneurship through social networks. In D. Sexton & R. Smilor (Eds.), *The art and science of entrepreneurship* (pp. 2-23). Cambridge, MA: Ballinger.

Allmendinger, J., & Hackman, J. R. (1996). Organizations in changing environments: The case of East German symphony orchestras. *Administrative Science Quarterly, 41,* 337-369.

Amsden, A., Kochanowicz, J., & Taylor, L. (1994). *The market meets its match: Restructuring the economies of Eastern Europe.* Cambridge, MA: Harvard University Press.

Andrews, K. (1971). *The concept of corporate strategy.* Homewood, IL: Irwin.

Ansoff, I. (1965). *Corporate strategy.* New York: McGraw-Hill.

Ash, T., & Hare, P. (1994). Privatization in the Russian Federation: Changing enterprise behavior in the transition period. *Cambridge Journal of Economics, 18,* 619-634.

Au, K., Peng, M. W., & Wang, D. (in press). Interlocking directorates, firm strategies, and performance in Hong Kong: Towards a research agenda. *Asia Pacific Journal of Management.*

Au, K., & Sun, L. (1998). Hope Group: The future of private enterprises in China. *Asian Case Research Journal, 2,* 133-148.

Aukutsionek, S. (1997). Measuring progress towards a market economy. *Communist Economies and Economic Transformation, 9,* 141-172.

Barberis, N., Boycko, M., Shleifer, A., & Tsukanova, N. (1996). How does privatization work: Evidence from the Russian shops. *Journal of Political Economy, 104,* 764-790.

Barker, V., & Mone, (1994). Retrenchment: Cause of turnaround or consequence of decline? *Strategic Management Journal, 15,* 395-405.

Barney, J. (1986). Strategic factor markets: Expectations, luck, and business strategy. *Management Science, 32,* 1231-1241.

Barney, J. (1991). Firm resources and sustained competitive advantage. *Journal of Management, 17,* 99-120.

Barney, J. (1997). *Gaining and sustaining competitive advantage.* Reading, MA: Addison-Wesley.

Barney, J., & Hoskisson, R. (1990). Strategic groups: Untested assertions and research proposals. *Managerial and Decision Economics, 11,* 187-198.

Bartlett, C., & Ghoshal, S. (1989). *Managing across borders: The transnational solution.* Boston: Harvard Business School Press.

Barzel, Y. (1989). *Economic analysis of property rights.* New York: Cambridge University Press.

Beamish, P. (1993). The characteristics of joint ventures in the People's Republic of China. *Journal of International Marketing, 1*(2), 29-48.

Beissinger, M. (1988). *Scientific management, socialist discipline, and Soviet power.* Cambridge, MA: Harvard University Press.

Bellmann, L., Estrin, S., & Lehmann, H. (1995). The eastern German labor market in transition. *Journal of Comparative Economics, 20,* 139-170.

Ben-Ner, A. (1988). Comparative empirical evidence on worker-owned and capitalist firms. *International Journal of Industrial Organization, 6,* 7-31.

Berle, A., & Means, G. (1932). *The modern corporation and private property.* New York: Harcourt.

Berliner, J. S. (1988). The informal organization of the Soviet firm. In *Soviet industry from Stalin to Gorbachev* (pp. 21-46). Ithaca, NY: Cornell University Press.

Besanko, D., Dranove, D., & Shanley, M. (1996). *The economics of strategy.* New York: John Wiley.

Biers, D. (Ed.). (1998). *Crash of '97.* Hong Kong: Far Eastern Economic Review Publishing Company.

The bigger, the better. (1998, May 21). *Far Eastern Economic Review,* pp. 10-13.

Bilsen, V., & Lagae, W. (1997). Foreign capital inflow and private enterprise development in Poland: A survey. *Communist Economies and Economic Transformation, 9,* 449-462.

Birkinshaw, J., & Hood, N. (1998). Multinational subsidiary evolution: Capability and charter change in foreign-owned subsidiary companies. *Academy of Management Review, 23,* 773-795

Birley, S. (1985). The role of networks in the entrepreneurial process. *Journal of Business Venturing, 1,* 107-117.

Blanchard, O., et al. (1991). *Reforms in Eastern Europe.* Cambridge: MIT Press.

Blasi, J., Kroumova, M., & Kruse, D. (1997). *Kremlin capitalism: The privatization of the Russian economy.* Ithaca, NY: Cornell University Press.

Blasi, J., & Shleifer, A. (1996). Corporate governance in Russia: An initial look. In R. Frydman, C. Gray, & A. Rapaczynski (Eds.), *Corporate governance in Central Europe and Russia* (pp. 78-108). Budapest and London: Central European University Press.

Boddewyn, J., & Brewer, T. (1994). International-business political behavior: New theoretical directions. *Academy of Management Review, 19,* 119-143.

Boisot, M. (1996). Institutionalizing the labor theory of value: Some obstacles to the reform of state-owned enterprises in China and Vietnam. *Organization Studies, 17,* 909-928.

Boisot, M., & Child, J. (1988). The iron law of fiefs: Bureaucratic failure and the problem of governance in the Chinese economic reforms. *Administrative Science Quarterly, 33,* 507-527.

Boisot, M., & Child, J. (1996). From fiefs to clans and network capitalism: Expanding China's emerging economic order. *Administrative Science Quarterly, 41,* 600-628.

Boisot, M., & Liang, X. (1992). The nature of managerial work in the Chinese enterprise reforms: A study of six directors. *Organization Studies, 13,* 161-184.

Bonin, J., Jones, D., & Putterman, L. (1993). Theoretical and empirical studies of producer cooperatives: Will ever the twain meet? *Journal of Economic Literature, 31,* 1290-1320.

Bonin, J., & Leven, B. (1996). Polish bank consolidation and foreign competition: Creating a market-oriented banking sector. *Journal of Comparative Economics, 23,* 52-72.

Borjas, G. (1990). *Friends or strangers: The impact of immigrants on the U.S. economy.* New York: Basic Books.

Borys, B., & Jemison, D. (1989). Hybrid arrangements as strategic alliances: Theoretical issues in organizational combinations. *Academy of Management Review, 14,* 234-249.

Bowman, E., & Hurry, D. (1993). Strategy through the option lens. *Academy of Management Review, 18,* 760-782.

Bowman, E., & Singh, H. (1993). Corporate restructuring: Reconfiguring the firm. *Strategic Management Journal, 14*(Summer), 5-14.

Boyacigiller, N., & Adler, N. (1991). The parochial dinosaur: Organizational science in a global context. *Academy of Management Review, 16,* 262-290.

Boycko, M., Shleifer, A., & Vishny, R. (1993). Privatizing Russia. *Brookings Papers on Economic Activity, 2,* 139-192.

Boycko, M., Shleifer, A., & Vishny, R. (1995). *Privatizing Russia.* Cambridge: MIT Press.

Boycko, M., Shleifer, A., & Vishny, R. (1996). A theory of privatization. *Economic Journal, 106,* 309-319.

Brada, J. (1993). The transformation from communism to capitalism: How far? How fast? *Post-Soviet Affairs, 9*(2), 87-110.

Brada, J. (1995). A critique of the evolutionary approach to the economic transition from communism to capitalism. In K. Poznanski (Ed.), *The evolutionary transition to capitalism* (pp. 183-210). Boulder, CO: Westview.

Brada, J. (1996). Privatization is transition—or is it? *Journal of Economic Perspectives, 10,* 67-86.

Brenner, R. (1987). National policy and entrepreneurship. *Journal of Business Venturing, 2,* 95-101.

Brewer, T. (1992). Government policies, market imperfections, and foreign direct investment. *Journal of International Business Studies, 24,* 101-120.

Brouthers, K., & Bamossy, G. (1997). The role of key stakeholders in international joint venture negotiations: Case studies from Eastern Europe. *Journal of International Business Studies, 28,* 285-308.

Brown, S., & Eisenhardt, K. (1998). *Competing on the edge.* Boston: Harvard Business School Press.

Bruce, A., & Buck, T. (1997). Executive reward and corporate governance. In K. Keasey, S. Thompson, & M. Wright (Eds.), *Corporate governance* (pp. 80-102). Oxford, UK: Oxford University Press.

Brus, W., & Laski, K. (1989). *From Marx to the market.* Oxford, UK: Clarendon.

Bruton, G., & Rubanik, Y. (1997). Turnaround of high technology firms in Russia: The case of Micron. *Academy of Management Executive, 11*(2), 68-79.

Brzezinski, Z. (1989). *The grand failure: The birth and death of communism in the twentieth century.* New York: Macmillan.

Buck, T., & Cole, J. (1987). *Modern Soviet economic performance.* Oxford, UK: Basil Blackwell.

Buck, T., Filatotchev, I., & Wright, M. (1998). Agents, stakeholders, and corporate governance in Russian firms. *Journal of Management Studies, 35,* 81-104.

Buckley, P., & Casson, M. (1976). *The future of the multinational enterprise.* London: Macmillan.

Buckley, P., & Chapman, M. (1997). The use of native categories in management research. *British Journal of Management, 8,* 283-299.

Buono, A., & Bowditch, J. (1989). *The human side of mergers and acquisitions: Managing collisions between people and organizations.* San Francisco: Jossey-Bass.

Burawoy, M., & Krotov, P. (1992). The Soviet transition from socialism to capitalism: Worker control and economic bargaining. *American Sociological Review, 57,* 16-38.

Burt, R. (1992). *Structural holes.* Cambridge, MA: Harvard University Press.

Burt, R. (1997). The contingent value of social capital. *Administrative Science Quarterly, 42,* 339-365.

Busenitz, L., & Lau, C.-M. (1996). A cross-cultural cognitive model of new venture creation. *Entrepreneurship Theory and Practice,* (Summer), 25-39.

Byrd, W., & Lin, Q. (Eds.). (1989). *China's rural industry.* New York: Oxford University Press.

Campbell, R. (1991). *The socialist economies in transition.* Bloomington: Indiana University Press.

Can China reform its economy? (1997, September 29). *Business Week,* pp. 116-124.

Capener, C. (1996). *A guidebook to mergers and acquisitions in China.* Hong Kong: Asia Information.

Carroll, G. (1993). A sociological view on why firms differ. *Strategic Management Journal, 14*, 237-249.

Carroll, G., Goodstein, J., & Gyenes, A. (1988). Organizations and the state: Effects of the institutional environment on cooperatives in Hungary. *Administrative Science Quarterly, 33*, 233-256.

Casson, M. (1997). *Information and organization.* Oxford, UK: Clarendon.

Caves, R. (1996). *Multinational enterprise and economic analysis* (2nd ed.). Cambridge, UK: Cambridge University Press.

Chairman Ford. (1998, September 28). *Business Week* (Asian ed.), pp. 52-56.

Chang, W., & MacMillan, I. (1991). A review of entrepreneurial development in the People's Republic of China. *Journal of Business Venturing, 6*, 375-379.

Chandler, A. (1962). *Strategy and structure.* Cambridge: MIT Press.

Chandler, A. (1990). *Scale and scope.* Cambridge, MA: Belknap.

Chen, C. C., Peng, M. W., & Saparito, P. (1999). *Specifying opportunism as human nature: A cultural perspective on transaction cost economics.* Working paper, Fisher College of Business, Ohio State University, Columbus.

Chen, D., & Faure, G. (1995). When Chinese companies negotiate with their government. *Organization Studies, 16*, 27-54.

Chen, J., & Shi, W. (1998). *An overview of private enterprise development in China.* Working paper, Faculty of Business, Hong Kong Baptist University.

Chen, M. (1995). *Asian management systems.* London: Routledge & Kegan Paul.

Chen, Y., Jefferson, G., & Singh, I. (1992). Lessons from China's economic reform. *Journal of Comparative Economics, 16*, 201-225.

Cheng, J. (1994). On the concept of universal knowledge in organizational science: Implications for cross-national research. *Management Science, 40*, 162-170.

Cheung, K., Archibald, S., & Faig, M. (1993). Impact of central planning on production efficiency. *Journal of Comparative Economics, 17*, 23-42.

Cheung, L., & Xing, L. (1994). Management myopia: A by-product of the business contract system in China? *Asia Pacific Journal of Management, 11*, 125-132.

Cheung, S. (1969). Transaction costs, risk aversion, and the choice of contractual agreements. *Journal of Law and Economics, 12*, 23-42.

Cheung, S. (1983). The contractual nature of the firm. *Journal of Law and Economics, 26*, 1-21.

Child, J. (1972). Organizational structure, environment, and performance: The role of strategic choice. *Sociology, 6*, 1-22.

Child, J. (1994). *Management in China during the age of reform.* Cambridge and New York: Cambridge University Press.

Child, J. (1997). Strategic choice in the analysis of action, structure, organizations, and environment: Retrospect and prospect. *Organization Studies, 18*, 43-76.

Child, J. (1998, August). PRC investment control: Exploring the myths. *China Direct Investor*, pp. 10-15.

Child, J., & Lu, Y. (1996a). Institutional constraints on economic reform: The case of investment decisions in China. *Organization Science, 7*, 60-77.

Child, J., & Lu, Y. (Eds.). (1996b). *Management issues in China.* London: Routledge & Kegan Paul.

Child, J., & Markoczy, L. (1993). Host-country managerial behavior and learning in Chinese and Hungarian joint ventures. *Journal of Management Studies, 30*, 611-631.

China: Where's that pot of gold? (1997, February 3). *Business Week*, pp. 54-59.

The China connection. (1996, August 5). *Business Week* (International ed.), pp. 32-37.

Chinese Academy of Social Sciences, Institute of Industrial Economics. (1997). *Zhong guo gong ye fa zhan bao gao [China's industrial development report]*. Beijing: Economics and Management Press.

Chinese Academy of Social Sciences, Institute of Industrial Economics. (1998). *Zhong guo gong ye fa zhan bao gao [China's industrial development report]*. Beijing: Economics and Management Press.

Chinese Academy of Social Sciences, Project Team. (1997). An anatomy of SOEs' severe profit problems. *Guan Li Shi Jie* [Management World], No. 1, 127-137.

A Chinese banquet of red-chip stocks. (1997, October 27). *Newsweek* (International ed.), p. 24.

Chinese Managers Survey System. (1997). A contemporary investigation of CEOs on their thoughts on the stimulation and constraints of the firm. *Guan Li Shi Jie* [Management World], No. 4, 119-132.

Chinese Management Survey System. (1998). Capabilities and training: Chinese top executives during the reform era. *Guan Li Shi Jie* [Management World], No. 4, 136-147.

Chirot, D. (Ed.). (1991). *The crisis of Leninism and the decline of the Left: The revolution of 1989*. Seattle: University of Washington Press.

Choe, C. (1996). Incentive to work versus disincentive to invest: The case of China's rural reform, 1979-1984. *Journal of Comparative Economics, 22*, 242-266.

Chow, C., & Fung, M. (1996). Firm dynamics and industrialization in the Chinese economy in transition: Implications for small business policy. *Journal of Business Venturing, 11*, 489-505.

Chow, G., Fan, Z., & Hu, J. (1998). *Testing the present value model of stock prices: Evidence from the Shanghai, Hong Kong, and New York Stock Exchanges*. Working paper, Department of Economics, Princeton University.

Clarke, D. (1991). What's law got to do with it? Legal institutions and economic reform in China. *UCLA Pacific Basin Law Journal, 10*, 1-76.

Coase, R. (1937). The nature of the firm. *Economica, 4*, 386-405.

Coffee, J. (1991). Liquidity versus control: The institutional investor as corporate monitor. *Columbia Law Review, 91*, 1277-1368.

Coleman, J. (1988). Social capital in the creation of human capital. *American Journal of Sociology, 94*, S95-S120.

Conner, K. (1991). A historical comparison of resource-based theory and five schools of thought within industrial organization economics. *Journal of Management, 17*, 121-154.

Conner, K., & Prahalad, C. K. (1996). A resource-based theory of the firm: Knowledge versus opportunism. *Organization Science, 7*, 477-501.

Contractor, F., & Lorange, P. (Eds.). (1988). *Cooperative strategies in international business*. Lexington, MA: Lexington Books.

Cook, P., & Nixson, F. (Eds.). (1995). *The move to the market? Trade and industry policy reform in transitional economies*. New York: St. Martin's.

Cooper, A., & Dunkelberg, W. (1987). Entrepreneurial research: Old questions, new answers, and methodological issues. *American Journal of Small Business, 11*, 1-20.

Culpan, R., & Kumar, B. (Eds.). (1995). *Transformation management in postcommunist countries*. Westport, CT: Quorum.

Curran, J. (1994, March 7). China's investment boom. *Fortune*, pp. 116-124.

Cyert, R., & March, J. (1963). *A behavioral theory of the firm*. Englewood Cliffs, NJ: Prentice Hall.

Czarniawska, B. (1986). The management of meaning in the Polish crisis. *Journal of Management Studies, 23*, 313-332.

D'Aveni, R. (1994). *Hypercompetition*. New York: Free Press.

Daft, R., & Lengel, R. (1986). Organizational information, media richness, and structure design. *Management Science, 32*, 554-571.

Dalton, D., Daily, C., Ellstrand, A., & Johnson, J. (1998). Meta-analytic reviews of board composition, leadership structure, and financial performance. *Strategic Management Journal, 19*, 260-290.

Daniels, J., Krug, J., & Nigh, D. (1986). U.S. joint ventures in China: Motivation and management of political risk. *California Management Review, 27*(Summer), 46-58.

Davidow, W., & Malone, M. (1992). *Virtual corporation*. New York: Harper.

Davidson, W. (1987). Creating and managing joint ventures in China. *California Management Review, 24*(4), 77-94.

Davies, H. (Ed.). (1995). *China business: Context and issues*. Hong Kong and London: Longman.

Davis, J., Patterson, J. D., & Grazin, I. (1996). The collapse and reemergence of networks within and between republics of the former Soviet Union. *International Business Review, 5*, 1-21.

Davis, J. (1996). From informal to formal markets: A case study of Bulgarian food markets during transition. *Comparative Economic Studies, 38*, 37-51.

Davis, L., & North, D. C. (1971). *Institutional change and American economic growth*. Cambridge and New York: Cambridge University Press.

DeCastro, J., & Uhlenbruck, K. (1997). Characteristics of privatization: Evidence from developed, less developed, and former communist countries. *Journal of International Business Studies, 28*, 123-143.

Demsetz, H. (1983). The structure of ownership and the theory of the firm. *Journal of Law and Economics, 26*, 375-390.

Demsetz, H., & Lehn, K. (1985). The structure of corporate ownership: Causes and consequences. *Journal of Political Economy, 93*, 1155-1177.

Dess, G., Gupta, A., Hennart, J.-F., & Hill, C. (1995). Conducting and integrating strategy research at the international, corporate, and business levels. *Journal of Management, 21*, 357-393.

de Trenck, C. (1998). *Red chips and the globalization of China's enterprises*. Hong Kong: Asia 2000 Ltd.

DeWitt, R.-L. (1998). Firm, industry, and strategic influences on choice of downsizing approach. *Strategic Management Journal, 19*, 59-79.

DiMaggio, P., & Powell, W. (1983). The iron cage revisited: Institutional isomorphism and collective rationality in organizational fields. *American Sociological Review, 48*, 147-160.

Dong, X., & Putterman, L. (1997). Productivity and organization in China's rural industries: A stochastic frontier analysis. *Journal of Comparative Economics, 24*, 181-201.

Dranove, D., Peteraf, M., & Shanley, M. (1998). Do strategic groups exist? An economic framework for analysis. *Strategic Management Journal, 19*, 1029-1244.

Dubini, P., & Aldrich, H. (1991). Personal and extended networks are central to the entrepreneurial process. *Journal of Business Venturing, 6*, 305-313.

Dunning, J. (1993). *Multinational enterprises and the global economy*. Reading, MA: Addison-Wesley.

Dunning, J. (1995). Reappraising the eclectic paradigm in an age of alliance capitalism. *Journal of International Business Studies, 26*(3), 461-492.

Earle, J., & Estrin, S. (1996). Employee ownership in transition. In R. Frydman, C. Gray, & A. Rapaczynski (Eds.), *Corporate governance in Central Europe and Russia* (pp. 1-61). Budapest and London: Central European University Press.

Earle, J., Frydman, R., & Rapaczynski, A. (Eds.). (1993). *Privatization in the transition to a market economy*. New York: St. Martin's.

Earley, P. C. (1993). East meets West meets Mideast: Further explorations of collective and individualistic work groups. *Academy of Management Journal, 36,* 319-348.

Emerging-market indicators. (1998, April 11). *The Economist,* p. 94.

Eisenhardt, K., & Schoonhoven, C. (1996). Resource-based view of strategic alliance formation: Strategic and social effects in entrepreneurial firms. *Organization Science, 7,* 136-150.

Elenkov, D. (1995). Russian aerospace MNCs in global competition. *Columbia Journal of Global Business, 30*(2), 66-78.

Elenkov, D. (1997). Strategic uncertainty and environmental scanning: The case for institutional influences on scanning behavior. *Strategic Management Journal, 18,* 287-302.

Engardio, P. (1995, June 5). China's new elite. *Business Week,* pp. 48-51.

Epstein, E. (1996). *Dossier: The secret history of Armand Hammer.* New York: Random House.

The equity markets data spotlight. (1998, August 10). *Forbes,* p. 66.

Ericson, R. (1991). The classical Soviet-type economy: Nature of the system and implications for reform. *Journal of Economic Perspectives, 5*(4), 11-27.

Ernst, M., Alexeev, M., & Marer, P. (1996). *Transforming the core: Restructuring industries in Russia and Central Europe.* Boulder, CO: Westview.

Estrin, S. (Ed.). (1994). *Privatization in Central and Eastern Europe.* London: Longman.

Estrin, S., Gelb, A., & Singh, I. (1995). Shock and adjustments by firms in transition: A comparative study. *Journal of Comparative Economics, 21,* 131-153.

Estrin, S., Brada, J., Gelb, A., & Singh, I. (Eds.). (1996). *Restructuring and privatization in Central Eastern Europe.* Armonk, NY: M. E. Sharpe.

Estrin, S., & Meyer, K. (1998). Opportunities and tripwires for foreign investors in Eastern Europe. *Thunderbird International Business Review, 40,* 209-234.

Euromonitor. (1996). *The world economic fact book* (4th ed.). London: Author.

Fama, E., & Jensen, M. (1983). Separation of ownership and control. *Journal of Law and Economics, 26,* 327-349.

Fesharaki, F., & Wu, K. (1996). *China's petroleum industry.* Honolulu: East-West Center.

Filatotchev, I., Buck, T., & Wright, M. (1992). Soviet all-union enterprises as new multinationals of the CIS. *International Executive, 35*(6), 525-539.

Filatotchev, I., Hoskisson, R. E., Buck, T., & Wright, M. (1996). Corporate restructuring in Russian privatizations. *California Management Review, 38*(2), 87-105.

Filatotchev, I., Wright, M., & Buck, T. (1992). Privatization and buy-outs in the USSR. *Soviet Studies, 44,* 265-282.

Filatotchev, I., Wright, M., & Buck, T. (1995). Corporate governance and voucher buy-outs in Russia. *Annals of Public and Cooperative Economics, 66,* 77-99.

Finkelstein, S. (1992). Power in top management teams: Dimensions, measurement, and validation. *Academy of Management Journal, 35,* 505-538.

Finkelstein, S., & Hambrick, D. (1996). *Strategic leadership.* St. Paul, MN: West.

Fischer, S., & Gelb, A. (1991). The process of socialist economic transformation. *Journal of Economic Perspectives, 5*(4), 91-105.

Fogel, D. (Ed.). (1995). *Firm behavior in emerging market economies.* Brookfield, VT: Avebury.

Folta, T. (1998). Governance and uncertainty: The tradeoff between administrative control and commitment. *Strategic Management Journal, 19,* 1007-1029.

Fombrun, C. (1996). *Reputation.* Boston: Harvard Business School Press.

Fox, I., & Marcus, A. (1992). The causes and consequences of leveraged management buyouts. *Academy of Management Review, 17,* 62-85.

Freinkman, L. (1995). Financial-industrial groups in Russia. *Communist Economies and Economic Transformation, 7,* 51-66.

Frese, M., Kring, W., Soose, A., & Zempel, J. (1996). Personal initiative at work: Differences between East and West Germany. *Academy of Management Journal, 39*, 37-63.

Friedman, M. (1990). *Friedman in China.* Hong Kong: Chinese University Press.

Frydman, R., Rapaczynski, A., & Earle, J. (Eds.). (1993). *The privatization process in Central Europe.* Budapest: Central European University Press.

Frye, T. (1997). Governing the Russian equities market. *Post-Soviet Affairs, 13*, 366-395.

Fukuyama, F. (1996). *Trust: The social virtues and the creation of prosperity.* New York: Free Press.

Furubotn, E., & Pejovich, S. (1974). *The economics of property rights.* Cambridge, MA: Ballinger.

Galbraith, J. (1973). *Designing complex organizations.* Reading, MA: Addison-Wesley.

Gartner, W. (1985). A conceptual framework for describing the phenomenon of new venture creation. *Academy of Management Review, 10*, 696-706.

Geletkancyz, M., & Hambrick, D. (1997). The external ties of top executives: Implications for strategic choice and performance. *Administrative Science Quarterly, 42*, 654-681.

Geringer, J. M. (1991). Strategic determinants of partner selection criteria in international joint ventures. *Journal of International Business Studies, 22*, 41-62.

Gerlach, M. (1992). *Alliance capitalism: The social organization of Japanese business.* Berkeley: University of California Press.

Ghoshal, S., & Moran, P. (1996). Bad for practice: A critique of the transaction cost theory. *Academy of Management Review, 21*, 13-47.

Glaeser, E., & Scheinkman, J. (1996). The transition to free markets: Where to begin privatization. *Journal of Comparative Economics, 23*, 23-42.

Global 1000 and top 200 emerging market companies. (1998, July 13). *Business Week* (Asian ed.), pp. 45-68.

Godfrey, P., & Hill, C. (1995). The problem of unobservables in strategic management research. *Strategic Management Journal, 16*, 519-533.

Gorbachev, M. (1987). *Perestroika.* New York: Harper & Row.

Gordon, R., & Li, W. (1991). Chinese enterprise behavior under the reform. *American Economic Review, 81*, 202-206.

Gordon, B., & Rittenberg, L. (1995). The Warsaw Stock Exchange: A test of market efficiency. *Comparative Economic Studies, 37*, 1-27.

Grancelli, B. (1995). Organizational change: Towards a new East-West comparison. *Organization Studies, 16*, 1-25.

Granick, D. (1962). *The red executive.* Garden City, NY: Doubleday.

Granick, D. (1975). *Enterprise guidance in Eastern Europe.* Princeton, NJ: Princeton University Press.

Granick, D. (1990). *Chinese state enterprises.* Chicago: University of Chicago Press.

Granovetter, M. (1973). The strength of weak ties. *American Journal of Sociology, 78*, 1360-1380.

Granovetter, M. (1985). Economic action and social structure: The problem of embeddedness. *American Journal of Sociology, 91*, 481-510.

Granovetter, M. (1994). Business groups. In N. Smesler & R. Swedberg (Eds.), *Handbook of economic sociology* (pp. 453-475). Princeton, NJ: Princeton University Press.

Grant, R. (1991). *Contemporary strategy analysis.* Cambridge, MA: Blackwell.

Greiner, L. (1972). Evolution and revolution as organizations grow. *Harvard Business Review, 50*, 37-46.

Grosfeld, I. (1995). Triggering evolution: The case for a breakthrough in privatization. In K. Poznanski (Ed.), *The evolutionary transition to capitalism* (pp. 211-228). Boulder, CO: Westview.

Grossman, G. (1977). The second economy of the USSR. *Problems of Communism, 26,* 26-30.

Grossman, S., & Hart, O. (1986). The costs and benefits of ownership: A theory of vertical and lateral integration. *Journal of Political Economy, 94,* 691-719.

Groves, T., Hong, Y., McMillan, J., & Naughton, B. (1995). China's evolving managerial labor market. *Journal of Political Economy, 103,* 873-892.

Gulati, R. (1995). Does familiarity breed trust? The implications of repeated ties for contractual choice in alliances. *Academy of Management Journal, 38*(1), 85-112.

Gulati, R. (1998). Alliances and networks. *Strategic Management Journal, 19,* 293-318.

Gurkov, I., & Asselbergs, G. (1995). Ownership and control in Russian privatized companies. *Communist Economies and Economic Transformation, 7,* 195-211.

Guthrie, D. (1997). Between markets and politics: Organizational response to reform in China. *American Journal of Sociology, 102,* 873-892.

Hafsi, T., Kiggundu, M., & Jorgensen, J. (1987). Strategic apex configurations in state-owned enterprises. *Academy of Management Review, 12,* 714-730.

Hafsi, T., & Koenig, C. (1988). The state-SOE relationship: Some patterns. *Journal of Management Studies, 25,* 235-249.

Hambrick, D. (1994). What if the Academy actually mattered? *Academy of Management Review, 19,* 11-16.

Hambrick, D., & Mason, P. (1984). Upper echelons: The organization as a reflection of its top managers. *Academy of Management Review, 9,* 193-206.

Hambrick, D., Tsui, A., Li, J., & Xin, K. (1998). *Composition and processes of international joint venture management groups: A new perspective on alliance effectiveness.* Working paper, Graduate School of Business, Columbia University.

Hamel, G. (1991). Competition for competence and inter-partner learning within international strategic alliances. *Strategic Management Journal, 12*(Winter), 83-103.

Hamel, G., & Prahalad, C. K. (1985). Do you really have a global strategy? *Harvard Business Review, 68*(4), 139-148.

Hamel, G., & Prahalad, C. K. (1994). *Competing for the future.* Boston: Harvard Business School Press.

Hamilton, G., & Biggart, N. W. (1988). Market, culture, and authority: A comparative analysis of management and organization in East Asia. *American Journal of Sociology, 94,* S52-S94.

Hannan, M., & Freeman, J. (1989). *Organizational ecology.* Cambridge, MA: Harvard University Press.

Hansmann, H. (1990). When does worker ownership work? *Yale Law Journal, 99,* 1751-1816.

Hanson, P. (1997). What sort of capitalism is developing in Russia? *Communist Economies and Economic Transformation, 9,* 27-42.

Harding, H. (1987). *China's second revolution: Reform after Mao.* Washington, DC: Brookings Institution.

Harrigan, K. (1985). *Strategic flexibility.* Lexington, MA: Lexington Books.

Harrigan, K. (1986). *Managing for joint venture success.* Lexington, MA: Lexington Books.

Harwit, E. (1995). *China's automobile industry.* Armonk, NY: M. E. Sharpe.

Hart, O. (1995). Corporate governance: Some theory and implications. *Economic Journal, 105,* 678-689.

Haspeslagh, P., & Jemison, D. (1991). *Managing acquisitions: Creating value through corporate renewal.* New York: Free Press.

Hayek, F. (1945). The use of knowledge in society. *American Economic Review, 35,* 519-530.

Henkel CEE. (1998). *Henkel CEE in brief.* Vienna: Henkel Central and Eastern Europe GmbH.

Henley, J., & Nyaw, M. K. (1986). Introducing market forces into managerial decision making in Chinese industrial enterprises. *Journal of Management Studies, 23,* 635-656.

Hennart, J.-F. (1988). A transaction costs theory of equity joint ventures. *Strategic Management Journal, 9,* 361-374.

Hennart, J.-F. (1993). Explaining the swollen middle: Why most transactions are a mix of "market" and "hierarchy"? *Organization Science, 4*(4), 529-547.

Hill, C. (1990). Cooperation, opportunism, and the invisible hand: Implications for transaction cost theory. *Academy of Management Review, 15,* 500-513.

Hill, C., & Hoskisson, R. (1987). Strategy and structure in the multiproduct firm. *Academy of Management Review, 12,* 331-341.

Hill, C., Hwang, P., & Kim, W. (1990). An eclectic theory of the choice of international entry mode. *Strategic Management Journal, 11*(Summer), 117-128.

Hill, C., & Jones, G. (1998). *Strategic management* (4th ed.). Boston: Houghton Mifflin.

Hill, C., & Phan, P. (1991). CEO tenure as a determinant of CEO pay. *Academy of Management Journal, 34,* 707-717.

Hillman, A., & Keim, G. (1995). International variation in the business-government interface: Institutional and organizational considerations. *Academy of Management Review, 20,* 193-214.

Hisrich, R., & Grachev, M. (1993). The Russian entrepreneur. *Journal of Business Venturing, 8,* 487-497.

Hisrich, R., Peters, M., & Weinstein, A. (1981). East-West trade: The view from the United States. *Journal of International Business Studies, 12*(3), 109-121.

Hitt, M., Ireland, R. D., & Hoskisson, R. (1997). *Strategic Management* (2nd ed.). St. Paul, MN: West.

Hoen, H. (1996). "Shock versus gradualism" in Central Europe reconsidered. *Comparative Economic Studies, 38*(1), 1-20.

Hofstede, G. (1980). *Culture's consequences.* Beverly Hills, CA: Sage.

Hofstede, G. (1991). *Cultures and organizations.* New York: McGraw-Hill.

Hofstede, G., & Bond, M. (1988). The Confucius connection: From cultural roots to economic growth. *Organizational Dynamics, 17,* 4-21.

Hogberg, B., & Wahlbin, C. (1984). East-West industrial cooperation: The Swedish case. *Journal of International Business Studies, 15,* 63-79.

Holmstrom, B. (1996). Financing of investment in Eastern Europe: A theoretical perspective. *Industrial and Corporate Change, 5,* 205-237.

Holt, D., Ralston, D., & Terpstra, R. (1994). Constraints on capitalism in Russia: The managerial psyche, social infrastructure, and ideology. *California Management Review, 36*(3), 124-141.

Holzmann, R., Gacs, J., & Winckler, G. (1995). *Output decline in Eastern Europe.* Boston: Kluwer.

Hooley, G., Cox, T., Shipley, D., & Fahy, J. (1996). Foreign direct investment in Hungary: Resource acquisition and domestic competitive advantage. *Journal of International Business Studies, 27,* 683-709.

Hoskisson, R., & Hitt, M. (1994). *Downscoping: How to tame the diversified firm.* New York: Oxford University Press.

Hoskisson, R., & Turk, T. (1990). Corporate restructuring: Governance and control limits of the internal capital market. *Academy of Management Review, 15,* 459-477.

Hout, T., Porter, M., & Rudden, E. (1982, September/October). How global companies win out? *Harvard Business Review,* pp. 98-108.

Huang, Y. (1996). *Inflation and investment control in China: The political economy of central-local relations during the reform era.* Cambridge and New York: Cambridge University Press.

Hwang, K. K. (1987). Face and favor: The Chinese power game. *American Journal of Sociology, 92,* 944-974.

Inkpen, A., & Beamish, P. (1997). Knowledge, bargaining power, and the instability of international joint ventures. *Academy of Management Review, 22,* 177-202.

Ireland, N., & Stewart, G. (1995). On the sale of property rights and firm organization. *Journal of Comparative Economics, 21,* 289-307.

Islam, S. (1993). Russia's rough road to capitalism. *Foreign Affairs, 73*(2), 57-66.

Jacobson, C., Lenway, S., & Ring, P. S. (1993). The political embeddedness of private economic transactions. *Journal of Management Studies, 30,* 452-478.

Jarillo, J. C. (1988). On strategic networks. *Strategic Management Journal, 9,* 31-41.

Jarillo, J. C. (1989). Entrepreneurship and growth: The strategic use of external resources. *Journal of Business Venturing, 4,* 133-147.

Jefferson, G., & Rawski, T. (1994). Enterprise reform in Chinese industry. *Journal of Economic Perspectives, 8*(2), 47-70.

Jensen, M. (1987). The free cash flow theory of takeovers. In L. Brown & E. Rosengren (Eds.), *The merger boom* (pp. 102-143). Boston: Federal Reserve Bank of Boston.

Jensen, M. (1993). The modern industrial revolution, exit, and failure of internal control systems. *Journal of Finance, 48,* 831-880.

Jensen, M., & Meckling, W. (1976). Theory of the firm: Managerial behavior, agency costs, and ownership structure. *Journal of Financial Economics, 3,* 305-360.

Jensen, M., & Murphy, K. (1990). Executive pay and top management performance. *Journal of Political Economy, 98,* 225-264.

Jensen, M., & Ruback, R. (1983). The market for corporate control: The scientific evidence. *Journal of Financial Economics, 11,* 5-50.

Johanson, J., & Vahlne, J. (1977). The internationalization process of the firm. *Journal of International Business Studies, 8,* 23-32.

Johnson, J. (1997). Russia's emerging financial-industrial groups. *Post-Soviet Affairs, 13,* 333-365.

Johnson, S., Kotchen, D., & Loveman, G. (1995). How one Polish shipyard became a market competitor. *Harvard Business Review, 73*(6), 53-72.

Jones, A., & Maskoff, W. (1991). *Ko-ops: The rebirth of entrepreneurship in the Soviet Union.* Bloomington: Indiana University Press.

Jones, C., Hesterly, W., & Borgatti, S. (1997). A general theory of network governance: Exchange conditions and social mechanisms. *Academy of Management Review, 22,* 911-945.

Jones, G., & Hill, C. (1988). Transaction cost analysis of strategy-structure choice. *Strategic Management Journal, 9,* 159-172.

Jowitt, K. (1991). The new world disorder. *Journal of Democracy, 2,* 11-20.

Kanter, R., Stein, B., & Jick, T. (1992). *The challenge of organizational change.* New York: Free Press.

Kao, J. (1993, March-April). The worldwide web of Chinese business. *Harvard Business Review,* pp. 24-36.

Kaplan, S. (1994). Top executive rewards and firm performance: A comparison of Japan and the United States. *Journal of Political Economy, 102,* 510-546.

Karmel, S. (1994). Emerging securities markets in China: Capitalism with Chinese characteristics. *China Quarterly,* pp. 1105-1120.

Katz, B., & Owen, J. (1995). Designing an optimal privatization plan for restructuring firms and industries in transition. *Journal of Comparative Economics, 21,* 1-28.

Keister, L. (in press). Engineering growth: Business group structure and firm performance in China's transition economy. *American Journal of Sociology.*

Kerin, R., Varadarajan, P., & Peterson, R. (1992). First-mover advantage: A synthesis, conceptual framework, and research propositions. *Journal of Marketing, 56,* 33-52.

Khandwalla, P. (1992). Gearing strategic public enterprises for internationalization: The Indian case. *Advances in Strategic Management, 8,* 317-337.

Khanna, T., & Palepu, K. (1997, July-August). Why focused strategies may be wrong for emerging markets. *Harvard Business Review,* pp. 41-51.

Kirby, W. (1995). China unincorporated: Company law and business enterprise in twentieth century China. *Journal of Asian Studies, 54,* 43-63.

Kirzner, I. (1973). *Competition and entrepreneurship.* Chicago: University of Chicago Press.

Kirzner, I. (1997). Entrepreneurial discovery and the competitive market process: An Austrian approach. *Journal of Economic Literature, 35,* 60-85.

Kodak in China: Smile, please. (1998, March 28). *The Economist,* pp. 62-63.

Kogut, B. (1986). On designing contracts to guarantee enforceability: Theory and evidence from East-West trade. *Journal of International Business Studies, 17,* 47-62.

Kogut, B. (1988). Joint ventures: Theoretical and empirical perspectives. *Strategic Management Journal, 9,* 319-332.

Kogut, B. (1991). Joint ventures and the option to expand and acquire. *Management Science, 37,* 19-33.

Kogut, B., & Zander, U. (1992). Knowledge of the firm, combinative capabilities, and the replication of technology. *Organization Science, 3,* 383-397.

Kole, S., & Mullherin, J. H. (1997). The government as a shareholder: A case from the United States. *Journal of Law and Economics, 40,* 1-22.

Kornai, J. (1980). *Economics of shortage.* Amsterdam: North-Holland.

Kornai, J. (1992). *The socialist system: The political economy of communism.* Princeton, NJ: Princeton University Press.

Kornai, J. (1995). *Highways and byways: Studies on reform and post-communism transition.* Cambridge: MIT Press.

Kostera, M. (1995). Differing managerial responses to change in Poland. *Organization Studies, 16,* 673-697.

Krueger, G. (1995). Transition strategies of former state-owned enterprises in Russia. *Comparative Economic Studies, 37*(4), 89-109.

Kumar, A. (1997). *China's emerging financial markets.* Hong Kong: Financial Times.

Kvint, V. (1994, March/April). Don't give up on Russia. *Harvard Business Review,* pp. 62-74.

Laban, R., & Wolf, H. (1993). Large-scale privatization in transition economies. *American Economic Review, 83,* 1199-1210.

Lan, H. L. (1998). *Why unrelated diversification strategy is popular in China?* Working paper, Corporate Strategy Research Center, South China University of Technology, Guangzhou.

Lange, O. (1936-1937). On the economic theory of socialism [Parts 1 & 2]. *Review of Economic Studies, 4,* 53-71, 123-142.

Lardy, N. (1992). *Foreign trade and economic reform in China, 1978-90.* New York: Cambridge University Press.

Lardy, N. (1994). *China in the world economy.* Washington, DC: Institute for International Economics.

Larner, M. (1998, May 11). Setting up shop in "Italy's Mexico." *Business Week* (Asian ed.), p. 26.

Larson, A. (1992). Network dyads in entrepreneurial settings. *Administrative Science Quarterly, 37,* 76-104.

Lau, A., & Johnstone, L. (1995). The development of China's financial markets. In H. Davies (Ed.), *China business* (pp. 117-136). Hong Kong: Longman.

Lau, H.-F., Kwok, C., & Chan, C. (1998). *Filling the gap: Extending the international product life cycle to emerging economies.* Working paper, Department of International Business, Chinese University of Hong Kong.

Lavigne, M. (1996). Russia and Eastern Europe: Is transition over? *Journal of Comparative Economics, 23,* 92-102.

Lawrence, P., & Lorsch, J. (1969). *Organization and environment.* Homewood, IL: Irwin.

Lawrence, P., & Vlachoutsicos, C. (Eds.). (1990). *Behind the factory walls: Decision making in Soviet and U.S. enterprises.* Boston: Harvard Business School Press.

Lawrence, P., & Vlachoutsicos, C. (1993, January-February). Joint ventures in Russia: Put the locals in charge. *Harvard Business Review,* pp. 44-54.

Layard, R., & Parker, J. (1996). *The coming Russian boom.* New York: Free Press.

Levi, M. (1988). *Of rule and revenue.* Berkeley: University of California Press.

Levinthal, D., & March, J. (1993). The myopia of learning. *Strategic Management Journal, 14*(Winter), 95-112.

Levitt, B., & March, J. (1988). Organizational learning. *Annual Review of Sociology, 14,* 319-340.

Lewicki, R., McAllister, D., & Bies, R. (1998). Trust and distrust: New relationships and realities. *Academy of Management Review, 23,* 438-458.

Li, D. (1996). A theory of ambiguous property rights in transition economies: The case of the Chinese non-state sector. *Journal of Comparative Economics, 23,* 1-19.

Li, S. (1998). Success in China's industrial market: An institutional and environmental approach. *Journal of International Marketing, 6,* 56-80.

Li, S., He, X., & Yau, O. (1998). *China's reform, industrial markets, and business management.* Hong Kong: City University of Hong Kong Press.

Lieberman, M., & Montgomery, D. (1988). First-mover advantages. *Strategic Management Journal, 9,* 41-55.

Lioukas, S., Bourantas, D., & Papadakis, V. (1993). Managerial autonomy of state-owned enterprises: Determining factors. *Organization Science, 4,* 645-666.

Lipton, D., & Sachs, J. (1990). Creating a market economy in Eastern Europe: The case of Poland. *Brookings Papers on Economic Activity, 1,* 75-147.

Litwack, J. (1991). Legality and market reform in Soviet-type economies. *Journal of Economic Perspectives, 5*(4), 77-89.

Long, W., & Ravenscraft, D. (1993). LBOs, debt, and R&D intensity. *Strategic Management Journal, 14,* 119-135.

Low, M., & MacMillan, I. (1988). Entrepreneurship: Past research and future challenges. *Journal of Management, 14,* 139-161.

Lu, Y. (1996). *Management decision making in Chinese enterprises.* London: Macmillan.

Lu, Y., & Heard, R. (1995). Socialized economic action: A comparison of strategic investment decisions in China and Britain. *Organization Studies, 16,* 395-424.

Luo, Y. (1996). Evaluating the performance of strategic alliances in China. *Long Range Planning, 29,* 534-542.

Luo, Y. (1997). Partner selection and venturing success: The case of joint ventures with firms in the People's Republic of China. *Organization Science, 8,* 645-660.

Luo, Y., & Peng, M. W. (1998). First-mover advantages in investing in transitional economies. *Thunderbird International Business Review* (formerly *International Executive*), *40*(2), 141-163.

Luo, Y., & Peng, M. W. (1999). Learning to compete in a transition economy: Experience, environment, and performance. *Journal of International Business Studies.* [Working paper]

Luo, Y., Tan, J., & Shenkar, O. (1998). Strategic response to competitive pressure: The case of town and village enterprises in China. *Asia Pacific Journal of Management, 15*, 33-50.

Lyles, M., & Salk, J. (1996). Knowledge acquisition from foreign partners in international joint ventures. *Journal of International Business Studies, 27*, 877-904.

Macleod, R. (1988). *China, Inc.* New York: Bantam.

Malanovic, B. (1989). *Liberalization and entrepreneurship.* Armonk, NY: M. E. Sharpe.

Maltsev, Y. (1990). Soviet economic reforms: An inside perspective. *Freeman, 40*, 88-92.

Manev, I., Manolova, T., & Yan, Y. (1998). *The governance, legality, and interdependence of firms in transforming economies.* Working paper, School of Management, Boston University.

Mann, J. (1989). *Beijing Jeep.* New York: Simon & Schuster.

March, J. (1991). Exploration and exploitation in organizational learning. *Organization Science, 2*, 71-87.

March, J., & Simon, H. (1958). *Organizations.* New York: John Wiley.

Marcus, A., Goodman, R., & Grazman, D. (1995). The diffusion of strategic management frameworks. *Advances in Strategic Management, 12B*, 115-145.

Marer, P., & Mabert, V. (1996). GE acquires and restructures Tungsram. In OECD (Organization for Economic Co-operation and Development), *Trends and policies in privatization* (pp. 149-185). Paris: OECD.

Marris, R. (1964). *The economic theory of managerial capitalism.* Glencoe, IL: Free Press.

Marshall, A. (1920). *Industry and trade.* London: Macmillan.

Marx, K. (1967). *Capital.* New York: International Publishers. (Original work published 1867)

Matlack, C. (1998, April 20). It's raining rubles on young talent. *Business Week* (Asian ed.), pp. 26-27.

Mazzolini, R. (1980). The international strategy of state-owned firms: An organizational process and politics perspective. *Strategic Management Journal, 1*, 101-118.

McAfee, R., & McMillan, J. (1987). Auctions and bidding. *Journal of Economic Literature, 25*, 699-730.

McCarthy, D., & Puffer, S. (1995, Fall). "Diamonds and rust" on Russia's road to privatization. *Columbia Journal of World Business*, pp. 56-69.

McCarthy, D., & Puffer, S. (1997). Strategic investment flexibility for MNE success in Russia: Evolving beyond entry modes. *Journal of World Business, 32*, 293-319.

McCarthy, D., Puffer, S., & Simmonds, P. (1993). Riding the Russian roller coaster: U.S. firms' recent experience and future plans in the former USSR. *California Management Review, 36*(1), 99-115.

McClelland, C. (1967). *The achieving society.* New York: Free Press.

McDonald, K. (1993). Why privatization is not enough. *Harvard Business Review, 71*(3), 49-59.

McGrath, R., & MacMillan, I. (1992). More like each other than anyone else? A cross-cultural study of entrepreneurial perceptions. *Journal of Business Venturing, 7*, 419-429.

McKay, B. (1997, February 28). Russian cell-phone company thrives by know-how and management savvy. *Wall Street Journal*, p. B5A.

McMillan, C. (1981). Trends in East-West industrial cooperation. *Journal of International Business Studies, 12*(2), 53-67.

Meszaros, K. (1993). Evolution of the Hungarian stock market. In J. Earle, R. Frydman, & A. Rapaczynski (Eds.), *Privatization in the transition to a market economy.* New York: St. Martin's.

Meyer, A. (1982). Adapting to environmental jolts. *Administrative Science Quarterly,* 27, 515-537.

Meyer, A., Brooks, G., & Goes, J. (1990). Environmental jolts and industry revolution. *Strategic Management Journal,* 11(Summer), 93-110.

Meyer, K. (1995). Foreign direct investment in Eastern Europe: The role of labor costs. *Comparative Economic Studies,* 37(4), 69-86.

Meyer, M., & Zucker, L. (1989). *Permanently failing organizations.* Newbury Park, CA: Sage.

Miles, R., & Snow, C. (1978). *Organizational strategy, structure, and process.* New York: McGraw-Hill.

Miles, R., & Snow, C. (1992). Causes of failure in network organizations. *California Management Review,* 34(4), 53-72.

Miller, K. (1995, December 4). Poland: Rising star over Europe. *Business Week,* pp. 64-70.

Milor, V. (Ed.). (1994). *Changing political economies: Privatization in post-communist and reforming communist states.* Boulder, CO, and London: Lynne Rienner.

Minniti, M. (1995). Membership has its privileges: Old and new mafia organizations. *Comparative Economic Studies,* 37(4), 31-47.

Mintzberg, H. (1973). *The nature of managerial work.* New York: Harper & Row.

Mintzberg, H. (1989). *Mintzberg on management.* New York: Free Press.

Mintzberg, H., & McHugh, A. (1985). Strategy formulation in an adhocracy. *Administrative Science Quarterly,* 30, 160-197.

Mintzberg, H., & Waters, J. (1985). Of strategies, deliberate and emergent. *Strategic Management Journal,* 6, 257-272.

Mizruchi, M. (1983). Who controls whom? An examination of the relation between management and board of directors in large American corporations. *Academy of Management Review,* 8, 426-435.

Morck, R., Shleifer, A., & Vishny, R. (1988). Management ownership and market valuation: An empirical analysis. *Journal of Financial Economics,* 20, 293-315.

Murrell, P. (1996). How far has the transition progressed? *Journal of Economic Perspectives,* 10(2), 25-44.

Murrell, P., & Wang, Y. (1993). When privatization should be delayed? *Journal of Comparative Economics,* 17, 200-213.

Murtha, T., & Lenway, S. (1994). Country capabilities and the strategic state: How national political institutions affect multinational corporations' strategies. *Strategic Management Journal,* 15(Summer), 113-129.

Naughton, B. (1994). *Growing out of the plan: China's economic reform, 1978-92.* New York: Cambridge University Press.

Naughton, B. (1995). China's economic success: Effective reform policies or unique conditions? In K. Poznanski (Ed.), *The evolutionary transition to capitalism* (pp. 135-156). Boulder, CO: Westview.

Naughton, B. (Ed.). (1997). *The China circle: Economics and electronics in the PRC, Taiwan, and Hong Kong.* Washington, DC: Brookings Institution.

Nee, V. (1989). A theory of market transition: From redistribution to markets in state socialism. *American Sociological Review,* 54, 663-681.

Nee, V. (1991). Social inequalities in reforming state socialism: Between redistribution and markets in China. *American Sociological Review,* 56, 267-282.

Nee, V. (1992). Organizational dynamics of market transition: Hybrid forms, property rights, and mixed economy in China. *Administrative Science Quarterly,* 37, 1-27.

Nee, V., & Matthews, R. (1996). Market transition and societal transformation in reforming state socialism. *Annual Review of Sociology,* 22, 401-436.

Nee, V., & Stark, D. (Eds.). (1989). *Remaking the economic institutions of socialism: China and Eastern Europe.* Stanford, CA: Stanford University Press.

Nelson, R. (1991). Why do firms differ and how does it matter? *Strategic Management Journal, 12*(Winter), 61-74.

Nelson, R., & Winter, S. (1982). *An evolutionary theory of economic change*. Cambridge, MA: Belknap.

The next hot spot for M&A: Shanghai. (1995, March 13). *Business Week*, p. 56.

Ng, S.-H., & Pang, C. (1997). *Structuring for success in China*. Hong Kong: Financial Times.

Nohria, N., & Eccles, R. (Eds.). (1992). *Networks and organizations*. Boston: Harvard Business School Press.

Nolan, P. (1995). *China's rise, Russia's fall*. New York: St. Martin's.

North, D. (1981). *Structure and change in economic history*. New York: Norton.

North, D. (1990). *Institutions, institutional change, and economic performance*. Cambridge, MA: Harvard University Press.

Numagami, T. (1998). The infeasibility of invariant laws in management studies: A reflective dialogue in defense of case studies. *Organization Science, 9*, 1-15.

OECD (Organisation for Economic Co-operation and Development). (1996). *Trends and policies in privatization*. Paris: OECD.

Oliver, C. (1991). Strategic responses to institutional processes. *Academy of Management Review, 16*, 145-179.

Oliver, C. (1997). Sustainable competitive advantage: Combining institutional and resource-based views. *Strategic Management Journal, 18*, 679-713.

Overholt, W. (1993). *The rise of China: How economic reform is creating a new superpower*. New York: Norton.

Pan, Y. (1996). Influences on foreign equity ownership level in joint ventures in China. *Journal of International Business Studies, 27*, 1-26.

Pan, Y. (1997). The formation of Japanese and U.S. joint ventures in China. *Strategic Management Journal, 18*, 247-254.

Parish, W., & Michelson, E. (1996). Politics and markets: Dual transformations. *American Journal of Sociology, 101*, 1042-1059.

Parkhe, A. (1993). A game theoretic and transaction cost examination of interfirm cooperation. *Academy of Management Journal, 36*, 794-829.

Pearce, J. (1991). From socialism to capitalism: The effects of Hungarian human resource practices. *Academy of Management Executive, 5*(4), 75-88.

Pearce, J., & Robbins, K. (1994). Retrenchment remains the foundation of business turnaround. *Strategic Management Journal, 15*, 407-417.

Pearson, M. (1991). *Joint ventures in the People's Republic of China*. Princeton, NJ: Princeton University Press.

Peck, M., & Richardson, T. (Eds.). (1992). *What is to be done? Proposals for the Soviet transition to the market*. New Haven, CT: Yale University Press.

Peng, M. W. (Ed.). (1992). *Doing business with the Chinese: Selected readings*. Seattle: University of Washington, Center for International Business Education and Research.

Peng, M. W. (1994). Organizational changes in planned economies in transition: An eclectic model. *Advances in International Comparative Management, 9*, 223-251.

Peng, M. W. (1995a). The China strategy: A tale of two firms. In C. Hill & G. Jones (Eds.), *Strategic management* (3rd ed., pp. 519-532). Boston: Houghton Mifflin.

Peng, M. W. (1995b). Foreign direct investment in the innovation-driven stage: Toward a learning option perspective. In M. Green & R. McNaughton (Eds.), *The location of foreign direct investment* (pp. 29-42). London: Avebury.

Peng, M. W. (1996). Modeling China's economic reforms through an organizational approach: The case of the M-form hypothesis. *Journal of Management Inquiry, 5*(1), 45-58.

Peng, M. W. (1997a). Firm growth in transitional economies: Three longitudinal cases from China, 1989-96. *Organization Studies, 18*(3), 385-413.

Peng, M. W. (1997b). Winning structures. *China Business Review, 24*(1), 30-33.

Peng, M. W. (1998). *Behind the success and failure of U.S. export intermediaries: Transactions, agents, and resources.* Westport, CT, and London: Quorum Books.

Peng, M. W. (1999). *A tale of four CEOs . . . in one year: Lessons for the Asian family firm.* Working paper, Fisher College of Business, Ohio State University, Columbus.

Peng, M. W. (in press-a). Cultures, institutions, and strategic choices. In M. Gannon & K. Newman (Eds.), *Handbook of cross-cultural management.* Cambridge, MA: Blackwell.

Peng, M. W. (in press-b). Controlling the foreign agent: How governments deal with multinationals in a transition economy. *Management International Review.*

Peng, M. W., Au, K., & Wang, D. (1999). *The evolution of red chips as a new organizational form: A study of interlocks and performance among firms listed abroad.* Working paper, Fisher College of Business, Ohio State University, Columbus.

Peng, M. W., Buck, T., & Filatotchev, I. (1999, August). *Post-privatization restructuring and firm performance in Russia: Theory and evidence.* Paper presented at the annual meeting of the Academy of Management, Chicago.

Peng, M. W., & Heath, P. (1996). The growth of the firm in planned economies in transition: Institutions, organizations, and strategic choice. *Academy of Management Review, 21*(2), 492-528.

Peng, M. W., Hill, C., & Wang, D. (in press). Schumpeterian dynamics versus Williamsonian considerations: A test of export intermediary performance. *Journal of Management Studies.*

Peng, M. W., & Ilinitch, A. (1998a, October). *Agent performance in export trade: A resource-based perspective.* Paper presented at annual meeting of the Academy of International Business, Vienna, Austria.

Peng, M. W., & Ilinitch, A. (1998b). Export intermediary firms: A note on export development research. *Journal of International Business Studies, 29*(3), 609-620.

Peng, M. W., Lu, Y., Shenkar, O., & Wang, D. (in press). Treasures in the China house: A review of management and organizational research on Greater China. *Journal of Business Research.*

Peng, M. W., & Luo, Y. (1998). Managerial networks and firm performance: A micro-macro link in a transitional economy. In *Best Papers Proceedings of the Academy of Management* [CD-ROM]. San Diego, CA: Academy of Management.

Peng, M. W., & Luo, Y. (1999). *Managerial ties and firm performance in a transition economy: The nature of a micro-macro link.* Working paper, Fisher College of Business, Ohio State University, Columbus.

Peng, M. W., Luo, Y., & Sun, L. (1999). Firm growth via mergers and acquisitions in China. In L. Kelley & Y. Luo (Eds.), *China 2000: Emerging business issues* (pp. 73-100). Thousand Oaks, CA: Sage.

Peng, M. W., Luo, Y., Shenkar, O., & Harwit, E. (1997). The growth of the firm in China: An information-processing perspective. In *Proceedings of the Hawaii International Conference on Systems Sciences, 3,* 428-435. Honolulu: University of Hawaii/HICSS. [Also available as CD-ROM]

Peng, M. W., & Peterson, R. (1994, November). *Multinational triangulation in management theory-building.* Paper presented at the annual meeting of the Academy of International Business, Boston.

Peng, M. W., & Shenkar, O. (1997, August). *The breakdown of trust: A process model of strategic alliance dissolution.* Paper presented at the annual meeting of the Academy of Management, Boston.

Peng, M. W., & Tan, J. J. (1998). Towards alliance postsocialism: Business strategies in a transitional economy. *Journal of Applied Management Studies, 7*(1), 145-148.

Peng, M. W., & Wang, D. (in press). Innovation capability and foreign direct investment: Toward a learning option perspective. *Management International Review.*

Penrose, E. (1959). *The theory of the growth of the firm.* New York: John Wiley.

Perkins, D. (1994). Completing China's move to the market. *Journal of Economic Perspectives, 8,* 23-46.

Peters, T. (1987). *Thriving on chaos.* New York: Knopf.

Pfeffer, J. (1997). *New directions for organization theory.* New York: Oxford University Press.

Pfeffer, J., & Salancik, G. (1978). *The external control of organizations.* New York: Harper.

Phan, P., & Hill, C. (1995). Organizational restructuring and economic performance in leveraged buyouts: An ex post study. *Academy of Management Journal, 38,* 704-739.

Pinto, B., Belka, M., & Krajewski, S. (1993). Transforming state enterprises in Poland: Evidence on adjustment by manufacturing firms. *Brookings Papers on Economic Activity, 1,* 213-270.

The pirates of Prague. (1996, December 23). *Fortune,* pp. 78-86.

Porter, M. (1980). *Competitive strategy.* New York: Free Press.

Porter, M. (1990). *The competitive advantage of nations.* New York: Free Press.

Porter, M. (1996, November-December). What is strategy? *Harvard Business Review,* pp. 61-78.

Porter, M. (1998). *On competition.* Boston: Harvard Business School Press.

Powell, W. (1990). Neither market nor hierarchy: Network forms of organization. *Research in Organizational Behavior, 12,* 295-336.

Powell, W. (1996). Commentary on the nature of institutional embeddedness. *Advances in Strategic Management, 13,* 293-300.

Powell, W., & DiMaggio, P. (Eds.). (1991). *The new institutionalism in organizational analysis.* Chicago: University of Chicago Press.

Powell, W., & Smith-Doerr, L. (1994). Networks and economic life. In N. Smesler & R. Swedberg (Eds.), *Handbook of economic sociology* (pp. 368-402). Princeton, NJ: Princeton University Press.

Poznanski, K. (Ed.). (1995). *The evolutionary transition to capitalism.* Boulder, CO: Westview.

Prahalad, C. K., & Bettis, R. (1986). The dominant logic: A new linkage between diversity and performance. *Strategic Management Journal, 7,* 485-501.

Prahalad, C. K., & Lieberthal, K. (1998). The end of corporate imperialism. *Harvard Business Review, 76*(4), 68-79.

Prokop, J. (1995). Industrial conglomerates, risk spreading, and the transition in Russia. *Communist Economies and Economic Transformation, 7,* 35-50.

Puffer, S. (Ed.). (1992). *The Russian management revolution.* Armonk, NY: M. E. Sharpe.

Puffer, S. (1994). Understanding the bear: A portrait of Russian business leaders. *Academy of Management Executive, 8*(1), 41-54.

Pye, L. (1992a). *Chinese negotiating style.* Westport, CT: Quorum.

Pye, L. (1992b). Social science theories in search of Chinese realities. *China Quarterly, 132,* 1161-1170.

Ralston, D., Holt, D., Terpstra, R., & Yu, K. C. (1997). The impact of national culture and economic ideology on managerial work values: A study of the United States, Russian, Japan, and China. *Journal of International Business Studies, 28,* 177-207.

Ramamurti, R. (1987). Performance evaluation of state-owned enterprises in theory and practice. *Management Science, 33,* 876-893.

Ramamurti, R. (1992). Why are developing countries privatizing? *Journal of International Business Studies, 23,* 225-249.

Rapacki, R. (1995). Privatization in Poland: Performance, problems, and prospects. *Comparative Economic Studies, 37*(1), 57-75.

Rapaczynski, A. (1996). The role of the state and the market in establishing property rights. *Journal of Economic Perspectives, 10*(2), 87-103.

Ravenscraft, D., & Scherer, F. (1987). *Mergers, sell-offs, and economic efficiency.* Washington, DC: Brookings Institution.

Rawski, T. (1994). Chinese industrial reform: Accomplishments, prospects, and implications. *American Economic Review, 84,* 271-275.

Redding, S. G. (1990). *The spirit of Chinese capitalism.* Berlin and New York: De Gruyter.

Reger, R., & Huff, A. (1993). Strategic groups: A cognitive perspective. *Strategic Management Journal, 14,* 103-123.

Reich, R. (1989, January 29). Leveraged buyouts: America pays the price. *New York Times Magazine,* pp. 32-40.

Richman, B. (1965). *Soviet management.* Englewood Cliffs, NJ: Prentice Hall.

Richman, B. (1969). *Industrial society in communist China.* New York: Random House.

Riedel, J. (1997). The Vietnamese economy in the 1990s. *Asian Pacific Economic Literature, 11,* 58-65.

Ring, P., & Van de Ven, A. (1994). Developmental processes of cooperative interorganizational relationships. *Academy of Management Review, 19,* 90-118.

Roll, R. (1986). The hubris hypothesis of corporate takeovers. *Journal of Business, 59,* 197-216.

Rona-Tas, A. (1994). The first shall be last? Entrepreneurship and communist cadres in the transition from socialism. *American Journal of Sociology, 100,* 40-69.

Root, F. (1994). *Entry strategies for international markets* (2nd ed.). Lexington, MA: Lexington Books.

Rosenzweig, P. (1994). When can management science research be generalized internationally? *Management Science, 40,* 28-39.

Rumelt, R. (1974). *Strategy, structure, and economic performance.* Boston: Harvard Business School Press.

Rumelt, R., Schendel, D., & Teece, D. (Eds.). (1994). *Fundamental issues in strategy: A research agenda.* Boston: Harvard Business School Press.

Rupp, K. (1983). *Entrepreneurs in red.* Albany: State University of New York Press.

The rush to China. (1997, October 13). *Business Week,* pp. 48-49.

The rush to Russia. (1997, March 24). *Business Week,* pp. 48-50.

Russia: The end of reform? (1998, September 7). *Business Week* (Asian ed.), pp. 24-27.

Russia's aircraft rivals set to become partners. (1998, February 25). *Jane's Defense Weekly,* p. 22.

Russia's state sell-off: It's sink-or-swim time. (1994, July 4). *Business Week,* pp. 46-47.

Sachs, J. (1993). *Poland's jump to the market economy.* Cambridge: MIT Press.

Sachs, J. (1994). Life in the economic emergency room. In J. Williamson (Ed.), *The political economy of policy reform* (pp. 503-523). Washington, DC: Institute for International Economics.

Schendel, D., & Hofer, C. (1979). *Strategic management: A new view of business policy and planning.* Boston: Little, Brown.

Schmitt, B. (1997). Who is the Chinese consumer? *European Management Journal, 15,* 191-194.

Schnaars, S. (1994). *Managing imitation strategies.* New York: Free Press.

Schneider, S. (1989). Strategy formulation: The impact of national culture. *Organization Studies, 10,* 149-168.

Schoenberger, K. (1996, July 22). China's boomtown is a bust for investors. *Fortune,* pp. 90-92.

Schumpeter, J. (1942). *Capitalism, socialism, and democracy.* New York: Harper.

Scott, W. R. (1995). *Institutions and organizations.* Thousand Oaks, CA: Sage.

Seagrave, S. (1995). *Lords of the rim.* London: Bantam.

Sedaitis, J. (1998). The alliances of spin-offs versus start-ups: Social ties in the genesis of post-Soviet alliances. *Organization Science, 9,* 368-387.

Selmer, J. (1997). *Birds of a feather . . . ? Overseas Chinese expatriate managers in the People's Republic of China.* Working paper, Faculty of Business, Hong Kong Baptist University.

Serapio, M., & Cascio, W. (1996). End-games in international alliances. *Academy of Management Executive, 10,* 62-73.

Sexty, R. (1980). Autonomy strategies of government owned business corporations in Canada. *Strategic Management Journal, 1,* 371-384.

Shan, W. (1991). Environmental risks and joint venture sharing agreements. *Journal of International Business Studies, 22,* 555-578.

Shang, L. (1997). SOEs' goals and values from technology transfer to joint ventures: The case of Jiamusi United Combine Factory. *Guan Li Shi Jie* [Management World], No. 4, 160-169.

Sharma, A. (1993). Management under fire: The transformation of managers in the Soviet Union and Eastern Europe. *Academy of Management Executive, 7,* 22-35.

Sharma, A. (1995). Entry strategies of U.S. firms to the newly independent states, Baltic states, and Eastern European countries. *California Management Review, 37*(3), 90-109.

Sharma, A., & Merrell, M. (1997). Russia's true business performance: Inviting international business? *Journal of World Business, 32,* 320-332.

Shaver, J. M. (1998). Do foreign-owned and U.S.-owned establishments exhibit the same location pattern in U.S. manufacturing industries? *Journal of International Business Studies, 29,* 469-492.

Shelton, J. (1989). *The coming Soviet crash.* New York: Free Press.

Shenkar, O. (1990, April). International joint ventures' problems in China. *Long Range Planning,* pp. 82-90.

Shenkar, O. (Ed.). (1991). *Organization and management in China, 1979-90.* Armonk, NY: M. E. Sharpe.

Shenkar, O. (1994). Raising the bamboo screen: International management research in the People's Republic of China. *International Studies of Management and Organization* [Special issue], 9-34.

Shenkar, O. (1996). The firm as a total institution: Reflections on the Chinese state enterprise. *Organization Studies, 17,* 885-907.

Shenkar, O., & Li, J. (in press). Skill possession and skill search among prospective partners in international cooperative ventures. *Organization Science.*

Shenkar, O., & Ronen, S. (1987). Structure and importance of work goals among managers in the People's Republic of China. *Academy of Management Journal, 30,* 564-576.

Shenkar, O., & von Glinow, M. A. (1994). Paradoxes of organizational theory and research: Using the case of China to illustrate national contingency. *Management Science, 40,* 56-71.

Shirk, S. (1993). *The political logic of economic reform in China.* Berkeley: University of California Press.

Shlapentokh, V. (1989). *Public and private life of the Soviet people.* New York: Oxford University Press.

Shleifer, A., & Vasiliev, D. (1996). Management ownership and Russian privatization. In R. Frydman, C. Gray, & A. Rapaczynski (Eds.), *Corporate governance in Central Europe and Russia* (pp. 62-77). Budapest and London: Central European University Press.

Shleifer, A., & Vishny, R. (1994). Politicians and firms. *Quarterly Journal of Economics*, (November), 995-1025.

Skocpol, T. (1976). Old regime legacies and communist revolutions in Russia and China. *Social Forces, 55*, 284-315.

Slick maneuvers. (1998, July 2). *Far Eastern Economic Review*, pp. 60-61.

Smith, S., Cin, B., & Vodopivec, M. (1997). Privatization incidence, ownership forms, and firm performance: Evidence from Slovenia. *Journal of Comparative Economics, 25*, 158-179.

Snow, C., Miles, R., & Coleman, H. (1992). Managing 21st century network organizations. *Organizational Dynamics, 20*(3), 5-20.

Soulsby, A., & Clark, E. (1996). The emergence of post-communist management in the Czech Republic. *Organization Studies, 17*, 227-247.

Spulber, N. (1991). *Restructuring the Soviet economy.* Ann Arbor: University of Michigan Press.

Starbuck, W. (1965). Organizational growth and development. In J. March (Ed.), *Handbook of organizations* (pp. 451-522). New York: Rand McNally.

Stark, D. (1992). From system identity to organizational diversity: Analyzing social change in Eastern Europe. *Contemporary Sociology, 21*, 299-304.

Stark, D. (1996). Recombinant property in East European capitalism. *American Journal of Sociology, 101*, 993-1027.

State Statistical Bureau. (Various years). *China statistics yearbook.* Beijing: State Statistical Bureau.

Stewart, S., Cheung, M., & Yeung, D. (1992). The latest Asian newly industrialized economy: The South China booming boomerang. *Columbia Journal of World Business, 27*, 30-37.

Stopford, J., & Wells, L. (1972). *Managing the multinational enterprise.* New York: Basic Books.

Stross, R. (1990). *Bulls in the china shop and other Sino-American business encounters.* Honolulu: University of Hawaii Press.

Summer, C., et al. (1990). Doctoral education in the field of business policy and strategy. *Journal of Management, 16*, 361-398.

Szelenyi, I. (1988). *Socialist entrepreneurs in rural Hungary.* Madison: University of Wisconsin Press.

Szelenyi, I., & Kostello, E. (1996). The market transition debate: Toward a synthesis. *American Journal of Sociology, 101*, 1082-1096.

Takla, L. (1994). The relationship between privatization and the reform of the banking sector: The case of the Czech Republic and Slovakia. In S. Estrin (Ed.), *Privatization in Central and Eastern Europe.* London: Longman.

Tallman, S., & Shenkar, O. (1994). A managerial decision model of international cooperative venture formation. *Journal of International Business Studies, 25*(1), 91-114.

Tamlinson, R. (1997, December 29). Betting on the red chips. *Fortune*, pp. 62-64.

Tan, J. J. (1996). Regulatory environment and strategic orientations: A study of Chinese private entrepreneurs. *Entrepreneurship Theory and Practice, 21*, 31-44.

Tan, J. J., & Li, M. (1996). Effects of ownership types in environment-strategy configuration. *Advances in International Comparative Management, 11*, 217-250.

Tan, J. J., & Litschert, R. (1994). Environment-strategy relationship and its performance implications: An empirical study of the Chinese electronics industry. *Strategic Management Journal, 15*, 1-20.

Tan, J. J., & Peng, M. W. (1998a). *Does ownership matter? A strategic group analysis in a transitional economy.* Working paper, Fisher College of Business, Ohio State University, Columbus.

Tan, J. J., & Peng, M. W. (1998b, August). *The role of organizational slack in a transitional economy: A test of organization and agency theories.* Paper presented at the Academy of Management annual meeting, San Diego, CA.

Tan, J. J., & Peng, M. W. (1999). *Culture, nation, and entrepreneurship.* Working paper, Fisher College of Business, Ohio State University, Columbus.

Teece, D. (1986). Profiting from technological innovation: Implications for integration, collaboration, licensing, and public policy. *Research Policy, 15,* 285-305.

Teece, D. (1998). Capturing value from knowledge assets. *California Management Review, 40*(3), 55-79.

Teece, D., Pisano, G., & Shuen, A. (1997). Dynamic capabilities and strategic management. *Strategic Management Journal, 18,* 509-533.

Thompson, J., & Vidmer, R. (1983). *Administrative science and politics in the USSR and the United States.* New York: Praeger.

Tsang, E. (1998). Can *guanxi* be a source of sustainable competitive advantage for doing business in China? *Academy of Management Executive, 12,* 64-73.

Tse, D., Pan, Y., & Au, K. (1997). How MNCs choose entry modes and form alliances: The China experience. *Journal of International Business Studies, 28,* 779-806.

Tsoukas, H. (1994). Socio-economic system and organizational management: An institutional perspective on the socialist firm. *Organization Studies, 15,* 21-45.

Tsui, A., & Farh, J.-L. (1997). Where *guanxi* matters: Relational demography and *guanxi* in the Chinese context. *Work and Occupations, 24,* 56-79.

Tung, R. (1981). Patterns of motivation in Chinese enterprises. *Academy of Management Review, 6,* 481-490.

Tung, R. (1982). *Chinese industrial society after Mao.* Lexington, MA: Lexington Books.

Tung, R. (1994). Strategic management thought in East Asia. *Organizational Dynamics, 22,* 55-65.

Ultimatum for the Avon Lady. (1998, May 11). *Business Week* (Asian ed.), p. 22.

USDC-ITA. (1998). Russia: Country commercial guide. Washington, DC: U.S. Department of Commerce—International Trade Administration. [Available on the Internet: *www.ita.doc.gov/uscs/ccg98/ccgoruss.html*]

van Brabant, J. (1995). Governance, evolution, and the transformation of Eastern Europe. In K. Poznanski (Ed.), *The evolutionary transition to capitalism* (pp. 157-182). Boulder, CO: Westview.

Vanhonacker, W. (1997, March-April). Entering China: An unconventional approach. *Harvard Business Review,* pp. 130-140.

Van Wijnbergen, S. (1997). On the role of banks in enterprise restructuring: The Polish example. *Journal of Comparative Economics, 24,* 44-64.

von Glinow, M., & Teagarden, M. (1988). The transfer of human resource management technology in Sino-U.S. cooperative ventures. *Human Resource Management, 27,* 201-229.

von Mises, L. (1935). Economic calculations in the socialist commonwealth. In F. Hayek (Ed.), *Collectivist economic planning* (pp. 87-130). London: Routledge & Kegan Paul.

Wake-up call for China's state sector. (1996, September 12). *Far Eastern Economic Review,* pp. 62-69.

Walder, A. (1989). Factory and worker in an era of reform. *China Quarterly,* No. 118, 242-264.

Walder, A. (1995). Local governments as industrial firms: An organizational analysis of China's transitional economy. *American Journal of Sociology, 101,* 263-301.

Waldinger, R., Aldrich, H., & Ward, R. (1990). *Ethnic entrepreneurs.* Newbury Park, CA: Sage.

Warner, M. (1992). *How Chinese managers learn.* London: Macmillan.

Weber, M. (1930). *The Protestant ethic and the spirit of capitalism.* New York: Scribner.

Weidenbaum, M., & Hughes, S. (1996). *The bamboo network: How expatriate Chinese entrepreneurs are creating a new superpower in Asia.* New York: Free Press.

Welsh, D., Luthans, F., & Sommer, S. (1993). Managing Russian factory workers: The impact of U.S.-based behavioral and participative techniques. *Academy of Management Journal, 36,* 58-79.

Wernerfelt, B. (1984). A resource-based view of the firm. *Strategic Management Journal, 5,* 171-180.

What to do about Asia? (1998, January 26). *Business Week* (Asian ed.), pp. 26-30.

White, S. (1998). *Technological systems and organizational change: China's pharmaceutical industry in transition.* Unpublished doctoral dissertation, Sloan School of Management, MIT.

Whitley, R., & Czaban, L. (1998). Institutional transformation and enterprise change in an emergent capitalist economy: The case of Hungary. *Organization Studies, 19,* 129-180.

Whitley, R., Henderson, J., Czaban, L., & Lengyel, G. (1996). Trust and contractual relations in an emerging capitalist economy. *Organization Studies, 17,* 397-420.

Williamson, O. (1975). *Markets and hierarchies.* New York: Free Press.

Williamson, O. (1985). *The economic institutions of capitalism.* New York: Free Press.

Williamson, O. (1991). Comparative economic organization: The analysis of discrete structural alternative. *Administrative Science Quarterly, 36,* 269-296.

Williamson, O. (1993). Opportunism and its critics. *Managerial and Decision Economics, 14,* 97-107.

Williamson, O. (1995). The institutions and governance of economic development and reform. *Proceedings of the World Bank Annual Conference on Development Economics 1994* (pp. 171-197). Washington, DC: World Bank.

Williamson, O. (1996). *The mechanisms of governance.* New York: Oxford University Press.

Wilson, K., & Martin, W. (1982). Ethnic enclaves: A comparison of the Cuban and black economies in Miami. *American Journal of Sociology, 88,* 138-159.

Winiecki, J. (1995). The applicability of standard reform packages to Eastern Europe. *Journal of Comparative Economics, 20,* 347-367.

Woodruff, D. (1998, July 13). Rising from the rubble. *Business Week* (Asian ed.), pp. 26-27.

World Bank. (1985). *China: Long-term development issues and options.* Washington, DC: Author.

World Bank. (1996). *World development report: From plan to market.* Washington, DC: Author.

World Bank. (1997a). *World development indicators.* Washington, DC: Author.

World Bank. (1997b). *World development report: The state in a changing world.* Washington, DC: Author.

Wright, M., Filatotchev, I., & Buck, T. (1997). Corporate governance in Central and Eastern Europe. In K. Keasey, S. Thompson, & M. Wright (Eds.), *Corporate governance* (pp. 212-232). Oxford, UK: Oxford University Press.

Wright, M., Filatotchev, I., Buck, T., & Robbie, K. (1993). *Management and employee buy-outs in Central and Eastern Europe.* London: European Bank for Reconstruction and Development/CEEPN.

Wright, M., Hoskisson, R., Filatotchev, I., & Buck, T. (1998). Revitalizing privatized Russian enterprises. *Academy of Management Executive, 12*(2), 74-85.

Wu, C. (1990). Enterprise groups in China's industry. *Asia Pacific Journal of Management, 7*(2), 123-136.

Wu, F. (1993, November-December). Stepping out the door. *China Business Review,* pp. 14-19.

Wu, J., & Reynolds, B. (1988, May). Choosing a strategy for China's economic reform. *American Economic Review,* pp. 461-466.

Xia, M., Lin, J., & Grub, P. (1992). *The re-emerging securities market in China.* Westport, CT: Quorum.

Xin, K., & Pearce, J. (1996). *Guanxi:* Good connections as substitutes for institutional support. *Academy of Management Journal, 39,* 1641-1658.

Yago, G., & Goldman, D. (1998, August 10). The democratization of capital. *Forbes,* pp. 62-65.

Yan, A., & Gray, B. (1994). Bargaining power, management control, and performance in U.S.-China joint ventures: A comparative case study. *Academy of Management Journal, 37,* 1478-1517.

Yavlinsky, G. (1998). Russia's phony capitalism. *Foreign Affairs, 77*(3), 67-79.

Yeung, H. (1997). *Transnational corporations and business networks: Hong Kong firms in the ASEAN region.* London: Routledge & Kegan Paul.

Yeung, I., & Tung, R. (1996). Achieving business success in Confucian societies: The importance of *guanxi* (connections). *Organizational Dynamics, 25*(2), 54-65.

Yin, X. (1993, November). Industrial concentration in mainland China: Changes and problems. *Issues and Studies,* pp. 1-25.

Yip, G. (1982). Diversification entry: Internal development versus acquisition. *Strategic Management Journal, 3,* 331-345.

Young, S., Huang, C., & McDermott, M. (1996). Internationalization and competitive catch-up processes: Case study evidence on Chinese multinational enterprises. *Management International Review, 36,* 295-314.

Zaheer, S. (1995). Overcoming the liability of foreignness. *Academy of Management Journal, 38,* 341-363.

Zahra, S., & Pearce, J. (1989). Boards of directors and corporate financial performance: A review and integrative model. *Journal of Management, 15,* 291-334.

Zhao, S. (Ed.). (1997). *Gong he guo jin ji feng yun lu* [An economic history of the Republic]. Beijing: Economic Management Press.

Zheng, J., Du, Y., & Ba, W. (1998). China's utilization of foreign capital: A quantitative analysis and preliminary results. *Guan Li Shi Jie* [Management World], No. 1, 80-86.

Zif, J. (1981). Managerial strategic behavior in state-owned enterprises: Business and political orientations. *Management Science, 27,* 1326-1339.

Zucker, L. (1986). Production of trust: Institutional sources of economic structure. *Research in Organizational Behavior, 8,* 53-101.

Zyuganov, G. (1996, June 17). How I'd govern Russia. *Newsweek,* p. 36.

INDEX

About the Author

Michael W. Peng is Assistant Professor of Management at the Fisher College of Business, The Ohio State University. He obtained his Ph.D. in strategic management from the University of Washington in Seattle. His dissertation was voted one of the top four best dissertations at the Barry Richman Competition, Academy of Management, and was consequently published as a book, *Behind the Success and Failure of U.S. Export Intermediaries*. He has served on the faculties of the University of Hawaii, where he received an Excellence in Research Award, and the Chinese University of Hong Kong, where he won a Best Teaching Award.

The author of more than 20 articles, chapters, and case studies, Peng has published and presented his research in Austria, Canada, China, Germany, Great Britain, Hong Kong, Singapore, South Korea, the United States, and Vietnam. His work has not only been widely read by scholarly and practitioner audiences, but has also been quoted by *Newsweek* and *The Exporter Magazine*.

In addition to teaching in regular degree programs at different universities, Peng has also taught in the Vietnam Executive Training Program funded by the U.S. Information Agency, the Japan-focused EMBA Program jointly sponsored by the Japan-America Institute of

Management Science and the University of Hawaii, and the Faculty Development in International Business Program organized by Ohio State and University of Memphis Centers for International Business Education and Research.

The author can be reached via email at peng.51@osu.edu